TAOS

TAOS

A Topical History

Taos County Historical Society

Corina A. Santistevan
Project Director

Julia Moore
Editor

MUSEUM OF NEW MEXICO PRESS, SANTA FE

CONTENTS

Taos, Catalyst for Creativity   277

Resources for Taos History   325

About the Contributors   335

The remains of one of a number of *torreones*—towers—that settlers built in the Taos Valley to defend their families in case of Indian attack. Inspecting this one in Talpa, ca. 1950, are Helen Greene Blumenschein and Antonio Vigil, the owner of the land on which the tower sat. Corina Santistevan looks on. Courtesy Corina A. Santistevan.

FOREWORD

Marc Simmons

I "DISCOVERED" TAOS in the summer of 1951 while in my early teens, and it permanently captured my affections in a way that Santa Fe and Albuquerque never could. It seemed to me then that in no place within my limited experience would a traveler find history and time-worn tradition closer to the surface of daily living than in the Taos Valley. That conviction has stayed with me over the years, even as a heavy-handed "progress" has steadily eroded the foundation of youthful idealistic and romantic observations.

It was the original members of the renowned artist and writers' colonies who initially put Taos on the cultural map. In this isolated, mountain-ringed Shangri-la, they recognized a stimulating place that could set the creative juices flowing. In fact, some philosophers and seers have even suggested that the surrounding windswept valley forms the power center of the universe, a view roughly coinciding with that held by the Taos Indians.

Corina Santistevan, an educator, preservationist, and community activist on behalf of religious and historical causes, has dreamed and worked for years toward the publication of a book that would relate the authentic story of Taos and its people. Supporting the realization of that goal has been a cadre of history-minded individuals who have rallied to the task under Corina's leadership and have contributed to the completion of the final work.

A casual glance at the table of contents reveals that a topical approach has been adopted to tell the Taos story, allowing its history to be presented from different perspectives by writers from varying backgrounds. The result is a true kaleidoscope of views, providing thoughtful readers the opportunity to comprehend yesterday's Taos in its many sundry parts.

Subjects range from the archaeology and geology of the Taos Valley, through early trails, trade fairs, buffalo hunting and agriculture, the long history of militant resistance to authority, to traditional religious and secular lifeways, the arts and literature. In sum, these pages contain a gathering of insightful, well-informed, and judicious essays, or studies, that will usefully and pleasingly serve the needs of all those with a serious interest in Taos and its past.

Taos Mountain—*Ma Who Lo* in the language of the Taos Pueblo—rises from the valley floor, its rock-ribbed elliptical bulk standing tall to form a spectacular backdrop for the town and pueblo huddled below. To the Indian people, the mountain is sacred, as is the life-supporting valley. The authors of this volume, through their contributions to its content, render their own, individual offerings to the spirit of Ma Who Lo.

ACKNOWLEDGMENTS

MIL GRACIAS, A THOUSAND THANKS, does not begin to cover the many, many individuals to whom we owe a debt of gratitude. This debt is not only to the living but also to those men and women who long ago began to preserve the journals and documents we now depend upon for knowledge of the past: the chroniclers who accompanied the explorers and settlers and who, dusty, tired, and hungry, sat in the light of a candle to record in their journals the events of the day and the Franciscan clerics who made detailed reports of their canonical visits to the mission churches of Nuevo México.

Our gratitude extends to historians who have unselfishly spent much of their lives digging into dusty manuscripts for any reliable information that might be gleaned: Adolph Bandelier, H. H. Bancroft, Ralph Emerson Twitchell, George Hammond, and Agapito Rey and all those many others who carried on the search. Speaking for myself, the debt grows as I consider the women historians such as Myra Ellen Jenkins, E. Boyd, Nina Otero Warren, Cleofas M. Jaramillo, Fabiola C. de Baca, and, for Taos specifically, Blanche C. Grant, whose three timely books preserved what has served us for nearly a century as a topical history of Taos.

Besides book friends, I acknowledge a great debt to personal friends like Helen Greene Blumenschein, who aroused my interest in the landscape as we visited prehistoric sites in the valley and who linked history-minded individuals to create a chain of everlasting friendships. Another friend was Jack K. Boyer, Bataan survivor, who returned home to spend the last years of his life preserving for Taos the Kit Carson Home, the Ernest Blumenschein Home, La Hacienda de los Martinez, the Maxwell House, the Guadalupe *morada* and who died while he was striving to save the Turley Mill.

It is the mission of the Taos County Historical Society to record and preserve the irreplaceable. The late Leonard (Andy) Lindquist heads the list of those dedicated members who embraced the idea of creating a book and saw it through to a reality. Lindquist challenged the members of the Board of Directors of the Taos County Historical Society to celebrate the millennium, the one great historical event that was on the horizon, by making some memorable contribution to history. He deserves endless gratitude for his foresight and inspiring leadership. Many, many are the thanks due to all the members of our ongoing book committees. The original members were chosen to provide skills and social contacts with the community: Jon Young, archaeologist; F. R. Bob Romero, history professor; Jenny Vincent, folklorist and musician; Mary Wheeler, social worker; Mildred Tolbert, photographer; Martha Dick, professor; Skip Keith Miller, museum curator; Anna Riddle and Sadie Knight, community liaisons; Guadalupe Tafoya, history buff and computer expert; with myself, a historian and archivist, as project director. Unforeseen circumstances dispersed some of our members; illness caused others to alter their lives. As a result, Nita Murphy, director of the Southwest Research Center, became an official member of the book team, as did Charles Hawk, authority on the roads and trails of Taos, and Ernestina Cordova, president of the Taos County Historical Society. Julia Moore, professional editor, gave countless hours over a number of years to edit and shape the entire manuscript; she wrote the headnotes and guided us into and through the unfamiliar world of publishing. These dedicated members join me in tendering our gratitude to the men and women whose contributions are the pages of this book. We thank them all for their generosity, for their willingness to give of their talent and skill to make this topical history of Taos possible, and for their everlasting patience. Their contributions have enabled us to further our mission.

At Museum of New Mexico Press, we have had the great good fortune to work with Director Anna Gallegos, Editorial Director Mary Wachs, and designers John Cole and David Skolkin. Brothers Malcolm and Robin Collier opened their own and their family's photographic archives to us, as did many other Taoseños.

Finally, there is the immeasurable debt due to the people of Taos. Time and again, as a financial need arose, the citizens of Taos responded. While agents of local financial institutions were gracious, it was the private individuals with their ten- twenty-five- fifty- or hundred-dollar gifts who made this project truly possible.

To them, we all owe our profound gratitude. *Mil gracias.*

Corina A. Santistevan
Spring 2013

INTRODUCTION

F. R. Bob Romero
Former President, Taos County
Historical Society

"Taos is not a city, Taos is not a town, Taos is not even a place. Taos is a state of mind and a power center of the universe." These words are attributed to Taos Mayor Phil Lovato in the late 1980s. He might also have said that Taos was not called a pueblo in its pre-European existence or even referred to by its now-common name, Taos.

The name Taos (rhymes with house) is not found in the historical record until the late 1500s, in the journals that document Don Juan de Oñate's colonization of New Mexico. When the Spanish first explored the area, the place we know as Taos, New Mexico, was noted as Yuraba, Uraba, Braba, and Valladolid. Contemporary historians and writers have attributed the origins of the Taos name to an Indian word meaning "Red Willow" or "people of Red Willow." Linguists verify that *Taos* is not a Spanish word, nor was it derived from Arabic or Latin, as are many of the words in the Spanish language. So, essentially, the name Taos originated from a Tiwa Indian term that perhaps began with the *T* sound and was Hispanicized as Taos. Through the centuries, however, Taos village has also been known as Don Fernando de Taos, San Fernando de Taos, and San Fernandez de Taos. The word *pueblo* is a Spanish term that means "town" or "village," and hence we have Taos Pueblo. What we can safely say is that the origin of the Taos name is part of the Taos mystique.

The founding date of Taos Pueblo is as mysterious as the origins of its name. If you ask a Native American from the Taos Pueblo about the origins of their pueblo, he or she might tell you that Taos has existed since time immemorial and that you cannot place a linear founding date on it. That same person may tell you almost nothing about how the spiritual origins of the tribe are traced to the sacred Blue Lake, high in the mountains above the pueblo, or little about the sacred Blue Lake ceremony held in late August of each year. However, Blue Lake is central to the spiritual and cultural origins of the Taos Pueblo, and the ceremonies are private and secret because they are sacred.

Nonetheless, the founding date of Taos Pueblo is still vigorously debated in academic settings. If we accept the criterion for when a community is founded from a European perspective as being the time of permanent continuous settlement of people who construct permanent institutional structures, we have at least a starting point. And if we use this definition we can reasonably state that Taos was founded either about 1,000 years ago when the Tiwa Indian people settled in the Taos Valley, or between AD 1300 and 1400, when the existing Taos Pueblo appears to have been built. From a strictly historical perspective, however, we have to consider other criteria, such as continuity and historical documentation. We need to consider Spanish colonization—when Don Juan de Oñate colonized New Mexico in 1598, visited Taos, and in that process originated the names Taos and Taos Pueblo.

The first European structure in Taos was San Gerónimo Catholic Church, which was built by the Spanish at Taos Pueblo in the early 1600s. It was during this time (about 1615) that settlement by Spanish colonists in the Taos Valley began in earnest. Since the continuity of the settlement was severed by the Pueblo Revolt of 1680, some historians have questioned the significance of the early 1600s settlement. However, after the *reconquista* was completed in 1696 by Don Diego de Vargas, Spanish colonists returned permanently to the Taos Valley.

In 1715, the Cristobal de la Serna Grant, in the Ranchos de Taos area, was ceded by the Spanish government, thus reestablishing its civil authority in the Taos Valley. This led to the establishment of the Ranchos Plaza by 1776. In 1796, sixty-three Spanish families settled the present Town of Taos on the Don Fernando de Taos Land Grant, and the Taos Plaza was established. This influx of people doubled the size of the Spanish-speaking population in the Taos Valley. In light of the sporadic course of Taos' settlement, the founding date of Taos is indefinite, adding to the mystique of Taos.

The people drawn to Taos over the centuries have been a rich mix of Indians, Spaniards, Euro-American mountain men and traders, and Anglo-Americans, all of whom have contributed their own sorts of diversity. The Indians were perhaps the most diverse, as they included the sedentary Pueblo Tiwa tribe as well as nomadic groups, including Apaches, Utes, Navajos, and Comanches. The *genízaro* groups, which became a very significant part of the Taos population, came from all of the nomadic tribes, but as detribalized Native Americans they quite often learned Spanish and embraced Christianity. As Hispanicized Indians they were adopted and acculturated into the Hispanic communities and villages in the Taos Valley. Catholicism and the Spanish language were the glue that bound the various groups.

The Spanish conquistadores and settlers were themselves the product of many diverse groups that settled on the Iberian Peninsula between 2500 BC and AD 1492. That mixture included Celts, Iberians, Greeks, Romans, Germans, Jews, and Muslim Moors and evolved into one of the most diverse melting pots found anywhere in the world. The blending of peoples continued everywhere that the Spanish settled, including in the Taos Valley. In Taos, the term "Spanish" became the label under which most people were classified by both the U.S. Census and the State of New Mexico, regardless of ethnicity. The term grew to include the influx of the French from the Louisiana Territory and mountain men and trappers of all ethnic backgrounds who came into Taos in the late 1700s and early 1800s.

The influences of the Anglo-Americans were added to the Taos mosaic in the mid-1800s during the American occupation, and the American influx and influence had its own diversity, which has included traders, artists, merchants, intellectuals, hippies, New Agers, and retirees. Somehow, Taos has found strength and vitality through its many waves of change.

People have adapted in order to survive and persevere in Taos. They have lived under five different flags, and yet they have been able to retain their cultural heritages and integrity, creating new or blended patterns. They have resisted conquest and domination by even the most recent newcomers—and have revolted at least once against every sovereign government that has been in power.

The story of Taos—and the mystery of the place—was perhaps best expressed by writer Frank Waters, who said—and I paraphrase here—that Taos has always had the curious magic of seeming to be discovered by every person who is drawn to its beauty. In essence, Taos is discovered every day.

NO PLACE
LIKE IT
ON EARTH

———————

❖

The Rio Grande flows through the Rio Grande Gorge as it crosses the Taos Valley, one of the valley's breathtaking sights. The river cut its way through upper layers of the twenty-two-mile-wide Rio Grande Rift, which for 35 million years has been opening up the North American continent. Photo Carolyn Lake.

❖ I ❖

Formative Epochs:
The Origins and Evolution
of the Taos Landscape

PAUL W. BAUER

The spectacular geography of Taos—the high altitude and clear air, the ring of abruptly rising mountains and the streams that flow from them, and the yawning chasm cutting through the high desert floor—creates a setting unlike any other. These features seem eternal, but in the context of deep time they are comparatively new. Geologist Paul Bauer introduces the geologic beginnings of Taos and the Taos Valley, explaining when and how today's landforms came to be and why the Taos Valley is one of the most dynamic landscapes on Earth. The geology of Taos has had—and continues to have—a profound influence on the peoples who have made Taos home. Bauer's long view brings the reader a special perspective on this place.

THE TAOS VALLEY RESTS in one of the most dynamic and exciting settings on the planet—if it can be said to rest. Buried beneath the plateau is an enormous fissure in the Earth's crust—the Rio Grande Rift—that is six times deeper than the Grand Canyon and thirty times wider than the Rio Grande Gorge. Still tectonically active, with chambers of molten rock deep below the surface, the rift generates minor earthquakes. Taos itself sits on the east margin of two dramatically different landscapes that form the Taos Valley. To the west of the gorge, and flat except for a few low hills, the Taos Plateau stretches as far as the Tusas Mountains. To the east rise the majestic Sangre de Cristo Mountains. Taos is situated on what geographers call the Costilla Plain, the narrow strip of land between the gorge and the mountains.

The apparent tranquillity of the Taos Plateau belies the tumultuous geologic history of the region. Evidence of past catastrophic seismic and igneous events is visible from almost anywhere in the Taos area—young fault scarps where the mountains meet the plateau and the profusion of volcanoes and lava flows that dot the valley.

During the last two billion years, the Taos Valley has seen a cycle of transformations from shallow tropical seas to vast, sand-duned deserts; from dazzling white-sand beaches to broad, meandering rivers flowing through lush fern forests; and from massive mountains to flat, dry, featureless plains. Today, the great valley of the upper Rio Grande, with its youthful volcanic cones, active earthquake faults, large landslides, and dynamic floodplains, tells us of a capricious and restless Earth whose dynamic landscapes have profoundly influenced some 10,000 years of human occupation—and whose geologic caution signs should now be heeded as we make decisions about our precious and limited land and water resources.

From the conventional human perspective of time (seconds, minutes, weeks, months, years, decades), most Earth processes—including erosion, mountain building, sedimentation, and metamorphism—occur at imperceptible rates. Rapid processes such as landslides, earthquakes, and floods, although easily perceived by humans, are not responsible for most landscapes. Only by recognizing the importance of deep time can we truly understand how geologic forces can generate a landscape as unique and spectacular as Taos.

GEOLOGIC HISTORY

Rare is the landscape that offers geologists enough information for a complete description of its geologic history; usually geologists must extrapolate from evidence found elsewhere. The Taos region is no exception; only a small fraction of the 4.5 billion years of Earth's history are preserved in the rock record. Nonetheless, after 150 years of stratigraphic sleuthing, the geologic history of the Taos region is relatively well understood, especially for the Cenozoic era, the last 65 million years of time.

The region's geologic history is best divided into two parts. The first part, comprising the Precambrian, Paleozoic, and Mesozoic eras, covers the Taos region's origin and the geologic evolution of northern New Mexico. The second, the Cenozoic era covers the development of the "modern" Taos-area landscape.

In the Beginning Was Precambrian Time
(4.5 BILLION YEARS AGO TO 542 MILLION YEARS AGO)

In New Mexico, the mountains serve as portals that reveal the oldest geologic activities. The Rocky Mountains are one of the foremost continental ranges on the planet. Extending more than 3,000 miles, from New Mexico to Canada, the range is the physiographic spinal column of North America; geologists have used the Rockies to reconstruct the early evolution of the continent. Because Precambrian rocks tend to be dense and strong, and therefore highly resistant to erosion, most of the highest peaks and steepest slopes are composed of these ancient rocks. The Sangre de Cristo Mountains near Taos expose a wide variety of Precambrian rock types and ages, including, near Wheeler Peak, the oldest known outcrop in New Mexico, gneiss that formed nearly 1.8 billion years ago.

Even though Precambrian rocks represent nearly 90 percent of the history of Earth, our knowledge of Precambrian geology is incomplete. During much of Precambrian time, the rocks exposed in the Taos area today were miles down and so tell us little of what was happening at the surface. We do know that the crust of northern New Mexico was constructed from a continental nucleus that grew southward from Canada about 1.8 to 1.4 billion years ago, mostly by accretion of fragments of crust from distant tectonic plates and intrusion of great volumes of molten granite. We also know that during the time of continental growth, immense tectonic forces caused the crust to buckle, break, and pile up in layers, resulting in what most certainly was a grand massif, or mountain range, perhaps comparable to the modern Himalaya Mountains. Those primordial peaks have long since eroded, and no direct evidence of their form remains. However, we do see the metamorphic roots of these mountains in the schist, quartzite, granite, and gneiss now exposed in many places near Taos, such as at Taos Ski Valley, the Ponce de Leon Springs near Llano Quemado, Red River Pass, the top of Wheeler Peak, and in the precipitous cliffs near Pilar. These so-called basement rocks show the effects of this turbulent history of deformation, metamorphism, and plutonism (the solidification of magma underground) and make up the foundation on which the younger Paleozoic, fossil-bearing sedimentary rocks have been deposited.

Perhaps the most intriguing Precambrian rock in the area is a colorful layered sequence of quartzite and schist that represents the metamorphosed residue of a pile many miles thick of quartz-rich sediments that formed when Taos was beachfront nearly 1.7 billion years ago. The most remarkable part of the sequence is the Ortega quartzite, a layer of nearly pure quartz sandstone that is more than 3,000 feet thick and probably represents one of the thickest sequences of pure beach sand on Earth. Although the sandstone is now a quartzite that was heated to over 900°F while deeply buried, original sedimentary forms, such as cross beds, ripple marks, and evidence of storm surges, are still preserved in the rocks of the Picurís Mountains.

No rock record exists in the Taos region for the next billion years, from about 1.4 billion to 330 million years ago.

Life and Mountains Arise in the Paleozoic Era
(542 TO 251 MILLION YEARS AGO)

Since early Paleozoic time, North America has slowly drifted over the Earth's surface, crossing the equator twice and capturing a sedimentary record of a great variety of environments, from tropical seas to glaciated continents to temperate forests. Rocks that preserve evidence of the latest tropical phase of these travels are especially well represented in the Taos area.

In late Paleozoic time, the supercontinent of Pangaea had formed, and much of what is now the western continental United States was covered by shallow equatorial seas. By about 310 million years ago, during the Pennsylvanian period (318–299 million years ago), the Ancestral Rocky Mountains of New Mexico and Colorado had emerged, leaving about 80 percent of New Mexico submerged beneath warm tropical seas. Northern New Mexico probably resembled modern-day North Carolina, with a flat coastal plain, swampy forests, and high mountains to the west. Mud, silt, sand, and gravel were eroded from nearby island highlands into a large sedimentary basin sometimes referred to as the Taos trough. A close examination of the Pennsylvanian strata near Taos reveals evidence of their original environments of deposited material: rivers, deltas, shorelines, tidal flats, and shallow seas, including features such as ripple marks, raindrop imprints, and cross beds. Over time, as the thousands of feet of sediments were buried and compacted, they converted into the sedimentary rocks that are visible today in Taos Canyon and along the Rio Grande del Rancho.

The Paleozoic seas teemed with ancient life—and death. The Taos area is acknowledged as having one of the most diverse and well-preserved fossil arrays of marine animals in North America.

Paleontologists have deduced that the Pennsylvanian sedimentary environment contained enough organic material to sustain a dense population of grazing, as well as sediment- and suspension-feeding creatures. The invertebrate fossils include mollusks (especially snails and clams), brachiopods, bryozoans, corals, fusilinids, sea lilies, sponges, crinoids, ostracods, foraminifers, and rare trilobites. The fossilized remains of vertebrate animals, such as shark teeth and an early reptile, have also been found.

Diversity of Life in the Mesozoic Era
(251–65 MILLION YEARS AGO)

Rocks of the Mesozoic era are not visible in the Taos area, although they are exposed just over the mountains near Angel Fire. During most of the Triassic and Jurassic periods, northern New Mexico was a land mass repeatedly blanketed by layers of terrestrial sand, silt, and clay. During the Cretaceous period (145–65 million years ago), the sea level rose, and much of the central U.S. was flooded by a vast western interior seaway that reached from the Arctic to the Gulf of Mexico. Until the Late Cretaceous period, northeast New Mexico was alternately land and sea, as the shoreline repeatedly advanced and retreated. Sand and gravel were deposited along streams on the flat coastal plain, and coal beds were formed in the abundant swamps. Shark teeth are common Cretaceous fossils in New Mexico. Great sequences of sandstone, shale, and limestone were deposited on the sea bottom, perhaps due to climatic cycles triggered by disturbances in Earth's solar orbit.

About 250 million years ago, following a worldwide extinction of 95 percent of sea life and three-quarters of life-forms on land, life diversified—especially the terrestrial fauna and flora. Birds, insects, flying reptiles, flowering plants, and modern mammals all appeared first in the Mesozoic era. Dinosaurs roamed the lush Mesozoic landscape of shorelines, river valleys, and swamps for 165 million years, until 65 million years ago, when a large meteorite struck off the coast of the Yucatan peninsula. The resulting ecological catastrophe probably triggered the great Cretaceous-Tertiary mass extinction that marked the disappearance of nearly half of Earth's life-forms, including the dinosaurs. The colossal impact blanketed the planet with a thin layer of chemically distinctive clay at the so-called K-T boundary layer, which has been identified in rocks just east of the Sangre de Cristo Mountains.

Mountains Come Again during the Laramide Orogeny
(80 TO 36 MILLION YEARS AGO)

The rugged form of the Sangre de Cristo Mountains is the culmination of a series of relatively recent geologic actions that reshaped western North America starting near the end of the Mesozoic era, when distant plate tectonic movements triggered the Laramide Orogeny, or mountain-building event.

The Laramide Rocky Mountains mimicked the Ancestral Rocky Mountains of the Pennsylvanian period, because Earth's crust tends to break along existing zones of weakness, such as old fault zones. This reincarnation of the Rockies began when the North American continent collided with a fast-moving plate of oceanic crust along the Pacific Ocean margin. About 70 million years ago, as the land rose, the western interior seaway was finally forced northeastward, never to return. The Laramide uplift evolved from a broad highland to a series of high-relief mountains and basins, such that, by the end of the Eocene epoch (34 million years ago) the general features of the eastern part of the Sangre de Cristo Mountains were fashioned. The rocks south of Taos contain abundant evidence of this mountain-building event, including wide fractured zones and complex contortions of sedimentary layers.

Modern Landscape Forms Take Shape in the Cenozoic Era
(65 MILLION YEARS AGO TO THE PRESENT)

The early Cenozoic era was characterized by widespread erosion of the Laramide highlands, resulting in a low-relief landscape that lasted until about 37 million years ago. At that point the San Juan volcanic field of southern Colorado began to erupt. Vast aprons of sediment that were eroded from the volcanoes blanketed south-central Colorado and north-central New Mexico for millions of years. Volcanic activity progressed southeastward through time, until the Latir volcanic field near Questa began to erupt about 25 million years ago, blanketing the region with red-hot lava and welded ash now known as the Amalia Tuff. Such a large amount of material was explosively ejected that the area collapsed along a great circular crack, called a ring fracture, forming a huge topographic depression, or caldera. (Valles Caldera in the Jemez Mountains is one of the world's finest young examples.) The Questa Caldera was about nine miles wide, although it now is extensively eroded. After the caldera collapse, molten rock continued to intrude along the ring fractures. As the magmas solidified, hot fluids percolated through the rock, and minerals such as molybdenite, quartz, and pyrite accumulated in small fractures within the granites. These fracture-fillings, or veins, are the targets of mineral exploration at the Questa molybdenum mines. This set the scene for the final major event in this geodrama, the development of the Rio Grande Rift.

THE RIO GRANDE RIFT

The geology and scenery of north-central New Mexico are as diverse as any on the planet. The reason for such diversity is simple: Taos is situated in one of Earth's few young continental rift valleys. The other great rift valley is the 4,000-mile-long East African Rift, which, in tearing eastern Africa apart, created Africa's highest peaks, deepest lakes, and some extraordinary landscapes.

The Rio Grande Rift is part of a global system of fractures in Earth's uppermost rigid layer (the lithosphere) that have formed in order to accommodate jostling of the lithospheric plates. Earth's lithosphere is broken into about a dozen major plates that move over an underlying layer of partially molten rocks (the asthenosphere). Although most of the activity associated with plate tectonics occurs at or near plate margins, in some cases, such as the Rio Grande Rift, activity occurs within a continental plate.

For the last 25 million years, plate tectonic forces have slowly torn apart the North American continent along the rift. Although the rift itself is largely hidden beneath thousands of feet of sediment, near Taos it is about twenty miles wide and as much as six miles deep. The Rio Grande did not excavate the rift. Rather, the river follows the topographically lowest path along the rift. The Rio Grande Gorge is a much smaller and younger feature and is due entirely to erosion by the Rio Grande.

The abrupt transitions from the basin to the surrounding mountains are phys-iographic and geologic boundaries that delineate the margins of the rift. Near Taos and Pilar, it is marked by steep slopes and cliffs. The eastern fault system is known as the Sangre de Cristo Fault. The southern fault, named the Embudo Fault, marks the divide between the San Luis and Española rift basins. The western margin of the rift, along the base of the Tusas Mountains, does not coincide with a major fault zone, because the rift has dropped like a trap door that is hinged along its west side.

For 15 million years, the rift extended and deepened slowly, gradually filling with sediment. By about 10 million years ago, the rift became much more active, with major development of the Sangre de Cristo Fault system and rapid sinking of the basin. The character of today's mountains developed during this time. The rift basin itself is filled with young materials (less than 30 million years old), principally sediments shed from the surrounding mountains and sediments transported south-ward by the Rio Grande and by volcanic rocks of the Taos Plateau. We can only see the youngest basin fill at the surface, although material as old as 5 million years is exposed in the bottom of the gorge and is easily visible at the John Dunn Bridge.

The Rio Grande and its three major tributaries—Rio Hondo, Red River, and Rio Pueblo de Taos—have cut deep, narrow canyons through the volcanic rocks that cap most of the southern basin. These deep river canyons provide unparalleled exposures of a diversity of tertiary volcanoes and their lava flows, and they reveal an intriguing chronicle of the birth and adolescence of the mighty Rio Grande.

ALLUVIAL FANS

The rift basin is surrounded by alluvial fans that have steadily advanced from the mountains into the basin. An alluvial fan begins to form where a rapidly moving mountain stream flows out onto a relatively flat valley floor. As the stream suddenly loses velocity, the coarsest sedimentary material is dropped by the stream. This mate-rial forms an "apron" that radiates out from the point where the mountain stream enters the valley. On the Taos Plateau, most of this clay, sand, and gravel, called the Santa Fe Group, was eroded from the mountains during the past 30 million years. Over time, alluvial fans are buried under successively younger alluvium. The youngest of these alluvial fans sustain the many sand and gravel quarries on the Taos Plateau.

Many thousands of feet of rock were shed from the mountains and transported to the valley as the mountains slowly pushed upward. Similarly, the Rio Grande has deposited mineral-rich sediment into the basin for millions of years. Much of the sedimentary material in the Santa Fe Group is porous and permeable, and where water-saturated, serves as the principal aquifer in the region. People, agriculture, and industry have tended to concentrate along the rift because of its fertile floodplain soils and prized supply of underground water.

The Volcanoes

Nearly all the isolated peaks scattered across the Taos Plateau are extinct volcanoes that erupted between 6 million and 1 million years ago. At least thirty-five discrete volcanic vents have been identified on the plateau, and there are probably many unknown buried volcanoes. The volcanoes of the Taos Plateau occur in a variety of sizes and shapes. The shape of any volcano depends on several factors: chemical composition of the magma, conditions during eruption, and the amount of erosion since eruption. Most of the volcanoes are composed of lavas of basalt, dacite, andesite, or rhyolite. Geologists divide volcanoes into four general types: cinder cones, composite volcanoes, shield volcanoes, and lava domes.

Cinder cones are the simplest form of volcano. They are small, steep-sided, circular to oval cones that are constructed from pyroclastics (scoria, cinders, ash, pumice, and lava bombs) ejected from a central vent. These volcanoes can erupt for months to years. Cinder cones can be seen in the walls of the Rio Grande Gorge. No true composite volcanoes are seen along the Rio Grande, although Mount Taylor, near Grants, is a classic composite volcano.

Shield volcanoes are gently sloping cones that are assembled entirely by successive fluid lava flows of basalt. Flows erupt from a central summit vent, or cluster of vents, and spread out in all directions, oftentimes flowing for tens of miles before solidifying. The Hawaiian Islands are a chain of immense shield volcanoes. The Taos Plateau basalts were erupted from a series of shield volcanoes located west of the river.

Lava domes (or lava cones, or volcanic domes) are formed by eruptions of thick, sticky lava that is incapable of flowing very far. The lava accumulates over and around the vent, and commonly expands from within, forming steep-sided domes with lava rubble covering their surface. Domes can be active for periods ranging from decades to centuries. Most of the large volcanoes on the Taos Plateau are domes, including topographically prominent Ute Mountain, with its pleasingly symmetrical shape.

Most of the prominent volcanic peaks on the Taos Plateau are composed of dacite, andesite, or rhyolite that erupted from 5 to 3 million years ago. San Antonio Mountain, Cerro Negro, Guadalupe Mountain, Cerro Chiflo, and Tres Orejas are all dacite domes. Cerro de la Olla, Cerro Montoso, and Cerro de los Taoses are all andesite domes. The principal rhyolite volcano, No Agua Peaks lava domes, is of special interest because of its valuable perlite deposits and the fascinating view of its internal workings as it is dissected by an active mining operation.

The most widespread volcanic rock on the Taos Plateau is a succession of dark gray basalt flows known as the Servilleta Basalt. Most of the Servilleta Basalt was erupted from a cluster of low-relief shield volcanoes near Tres Piedras, traveling miles downhill as long, thin lava flows before solidifying. Over 600 feet of basalt stacked up during about 2 million years of episodic eruptions, between 4.8 and 2.8 million years ago. By volume, the Servilleta Basalt dominates the Taos Plateau volcanic field and may encompass as much as 50 cubic miles of lava with a surface extent of more than 580 square miles. All the lavas of the Servilleta Basalt are vesicular (containing small voids), pahoehoe (ropy-type) flows that contain phenocrysts (visible crystals) of the green mineral olivine. These rocks can be seen from any location along the gorge but are especially well exposed near the Gorge Bridge. The Servilleta lavas are similar in composition to the basalts of Hawaii, both having come from deep within Earth's mantle.

THE RIO GRANDE GORGE

Where it exits the San Juan Mountains in Colorado, the Rio Grande turns southward, transects the San Luis Basin, and flows south through successive rift basins to Mexico. Beginning in southern Colorado, near Lobatos Bridge, the Rio Grande has cut the dramatic, steep-walled Rio Grande Gorge into the basalt caprock. The gorge deepens southward to a maximum of 850 feet at the Wild Rivers Recreation Area near Questa and then gradually shallows until the river exits the gorge at Pilar.

The story of the gorge begins well before the river actually began to carve into the plateau, and it is a story of two rivers and two lakes. We take up the story in the early Pleistocene era, when the San Luis Basin was divided into three distinct hydrologic (water-holding) basins separated by two topographic highs near Alamosa and Questa. The northern basin contained a huge lake—65 miles long and 150 feet deep—now named Lake Alamosa—that was fed by streams from the surrounding mountains and dammed by the San Luis Hills to the south. The central basin contained a smaller lake, now known as Sunshine Lake, fed by streams from the Sangre de Cristo Mountains and dammed by a cluster of volcanoes west of Questa. The southern basin contained a small ancestral Rio Grande, whose headwaters are today's Red River. This entirely New Mexican river system flowed southward on top of the basalt plateau over a wide, meandering floodplain, perhaps resembling the modern Rio Grande near Alamosa.

Then, about 440,000 years ago, during a wet climatic period, Lake Alamosa finally filled to capacity and overflowed its volcanic dam. During the next 100,000 years, the lake cut a canyon through the San Luis Hills, spilling over into New Mexico and eventually cutting a second canyon through the lower volcanic dam near Questa. It was only then that the Rio Grande finally became fully integrated from source to sea and began to engrave its deep gorge. Local kayakers may have indirect knowledge of this geo-drama, made conspicuous by the extreme river gradient and terrifying rapids through the Upper Taos Box of the Wild Rivers Recreation Area. Over the next tens of thousands of years, this geologic knickpoint will slowly migrate upstream toward Colorado until the entire Rio Grande has achieved a suitably modest gradient.

Glacial Sculpting of the Pleistocene Ice Ages

Periodically during the Pleistocene epoch (2.6 million years to 12,000 years ago), great ice ages—separated by warmer interglacial periods—have chilled New Mexico. Recent ice ages include the Bull Lake Glaciation, which began about 150,000 years ago, and the Pinedale Glaciation, which probably maintained full glaciation until about 15,000 years ago. This youngest great ice age covered approximately 30 percent of the planet's land surface with glaciers.

Alpine glaciers have sculpted some of the most spectacular scenery on Earth, including the Cascade Mountains, the Swiss Alps, and the Rockies. Mountains are dramatically changed by alpine valley glaciers due to the enormously erosive activities of moving ice, plus the contribution of frost wedging. In highland areas, the most obvious glacial features are those created by erosion, not deposition. Glaciated mountains tend to be angular, with jagged peaks and ridges, and oversteepened slopes. Glaciers shape the landscape through two processes, abrasion and quarrying (or plucking). Abrasion occurs when rock fragments embedded in the ice scrape along the underlying bedrock as the glacier moves. Quarrying occurs when the glacier lifts fragments of bedrock from its bed. These processes have created a diversity of distinctive landforms that are beautifully developed in the highest Sangre de Cristo Mountains.

Alpine valley glaciers widen, deepen, and straighten stream valleys into U-shaped troughs, commonly leaving tributary hanging valleys above the steep truncated spurs of the valley walls. Just below, the headwalls of high mountains are glacially carved, bowl-shaped depressions called cirques. Cirques commonly contain glacial lakes, called tarns, such as Williams Lake and Blue Lake in the mountains above Taos. When three or more cirques form around a mountain peak, they create a sharp peak called a horn. All the summits in the chain near Wheeler Peak are horned peaks. When two glaciers on opposite sides of a mountain erode upslope, they form a sharp, jagged, steep-sided ridge of rock called an arete, a common feature of the Wheeler Peak and Latir Peak Wilderness areas.

TODAY AND THE FUTURE

Long and diverse geologic histories commonly generate a wealth of natural resources that human civilization finds valuable. The Taos region is no exception and includes historic mineral extraction from the goldfields of the Elizabethtown mining district and the placer deposits of the Rio Grande; the high-grade molybdenum deposit near Questa; the metal deposits of the Twining and Red River regions; the vast Cretaceous coal beds of the Raton Basin; the coal-bed methane deposits of the Vermejo Park area; the copper veins in Copper Hill near Peñasco; the "fairy-cross" staurolites in the Picurís Mountains, the distinctive mica-rich clay used by Picurís Pueblo potters; the No Agua perlite volcano; and the world-famous Harding pegmatite mine near Dixon, which produced the strategic metals lithium, beryllium, tantalum, and columbium for twentieth-century war efforts.

In the future, as populations grow and demand for scarce resources increases, enormous pressures will be applied to exploit such resources. In the meantime, the two principal challenges facing residents of the Taos region involve aggregates (sand and gravel) and water. The Taos Plateau is blessed with abundant, easily mined sands and gravels that are essential for all construction projects. Ironically, however, the sand and gravel are located in areas that have become desirable for residential development, thus setting the stage for future conflicts. Perhaps more important, there are now concerns about maintaining an adequate supply of potable water for an expanding population in a changing climate. As a headwaters community with a splendid recharge zone in the Sangre de Cristo Mountains, Taos has a great advantage. However, surface water supplies are dependent on annual precipitation and runoff, thus leaving agriculture and in-stream flow susceptible to droughts. Groundwater pumping can have deleterious consequences to both the sustainability of aquifers and local stream and spring flows.

Because Taos is in a tectonically active setting, natural disasters will periodically occur. As rifting continues to pull the crust apart, the mountains and the basin will episodically detach through a series of small movements, each one associated with a moderate-to-large earthquake. Unreinforced adobe buildings, such as Taos Pueblo's, fare poorly in earthquakes. Earthquakes can also trigger landslides and rock falls in the foothills and canyons. Because developers and homeowners have built extensively within the floodplains of most Rio Grande tributaries, it is only a matter of time before rainstorm-triggered floodwaters lead to disaster. Although no volcanoes have erupted in the historic past, magma and ash will certainly cover the plateau again in the future. We cannot know whether the next eruption will manifest as mellow basalt flows or destructive explosions. What we do know is that as Taos continues to creep into the foothills and sprawl across the plateau, the risks associated with all these geologic processes will inflate, and the eventual costs to society will increase.

Of course, from a deep time perspective such human disasters are inconsequential. Plate tectonics will persist in its inexorably slow grind, and if rifting continues until the continent actually splits apart, Taos may someday be oceanfront property. In all probability, tens of millions of years from now, the fractured, weakened, and contorted crust of the Rocky Mountains will have again eroded to the plains, and a new cycle of orogeny will begin.

SELECTED REFERENCES

Bauer, Paul W., *The Rio Grande: A River Guide to the Geology and Landscapes of Northern New Mexico*. Socorro: New Mexico Bureau of Geology and Mineral Resources, 2011.

————. Jane C. Love, John H. Schilling, and J. E. Taggart Jr. *The Enchanted Circle-Loop Drives from Taos: Scenic Trips to the Geologic Past, No. 2.* Socorro: New Mexico Bureau of Mines and Mineral Resources, 1991.

Brister, Brian S., Paul W. Bauer, A. S. Read, and V. W. Lueth, eds. *Geology of the Taos Region.* Guidebook 55. Socorro: New Mexico Geological Society, 2004.

Julyan, Robert. *The Mountains of New Mexico.* Albuquerque: University of New Mexico Press, 2006.

Mathez, Edmond A., and James D. Webster. *The Earth Machine: The Science of a Dynamic Planet.* New York: Columbia University Press, 2007.

Price, L. Greer, ed. *The Geology of Northern New Mexico's Parks, Monuments, and Public Lands.* Socorro: New Mexico Bureau of Geology and Mineral Resources, 2010.

Wiewandt, Thomas, and Maureen Wilks. *The Southwest Inside Out: An Illustrated Guide to the Land and Its History.* Tucson, AZ: Wild Horizons Publishing, 2001.

‹ 2 ›

Archaeology
and the Pre-European History
of the Taos Valley

Jeffrey L. Boyer

Thousands of years ago the first of many waves of occupants penetrated the for-midable landscape of the Taos Valley, thus beginning the many-layered human history of the region. Archaeologist Jeffrey L. Boyer introduces the first Taos Valley residents and outlines several schools of thought about the archaeological record. He describes some of the impressive remnants of successive cultures, from earliest times to the era of the present Taos Pueblo, at the same time introducing archaeologists who have been instrumental in forming a picture of human life before Taos Pueblo was well established. The abbreviations favored by archaeologists for this time period are used here: BCE (before the common era) and CE (common era) and are equivalent to BC and AD.

Taos Valley's pre-European history is many times longer than the period since European contact.[1] The pre-European period begins with the earliest human presence in the valley more than 10,000 years ago and extends to about 1600 CE, when Spanish colonists began to settle in the valley. This long period is often referred to as prehistory, because the native people left no written records.

Archaeological Research in the Taos Valley

This chapter is a summary of current archaeological knowledge of and theories about the pre-European human presence in the Taos Valley for well over 10,000 years. Three points are important to bear in mind when reading this chapter. First, this outline of regional prehistory follows Fred Wendorf and Erik K. Reed's 1955 chronological framework for the Northern Rio Grande.[2] That framework, frequently referred to as the Rio Grande Classification, was specifically intended to differentiate the Northern Rio Grande from the San Juan Basin and Four Corners regions to the west, which had been and still are characterized using the well-known Pecos Classification.[3] Wendorf and Reed were convinced that the archaeology of the Northern Rio Grande, particularly of its Puebloan sites, was sufficiently different from that of the western regions to warrant examination and characterization within its own framework. Fifty years of subsequent research has shown that Wendorf and Reed were correct in their conviction.

Second, this chapter does not use the Navajo word *Anasazi* to refer to the pre-European Puebloan residents of the Taos Valley. Modern Pueblo people often oppose the use of an antagonistic Navajo word to refer to ancestral Puebloans. (*Anasazi* can mean "ancient enemy," "ancient stranger," "alien," "foreigner," or "outsider.") Further, differences between the archaeology of the Northern Rio Grande region and the San Juan Basin and Four Corners regions are sufficiently significant to justify thinking of them differently. *Anasazi* was used in speaking of the pre-European peoples of the San Juan Basin and Four Corners regions. Except in quotes from other references, in this chapter Northern Rio Grande peoples are called simply Puebloans or prehistoric Puebloans.

Third, the pre-European archaeology of the Taos Valley is, in reality, the archaeology of the ancestors of the historic and modern residents of the Northern Tiwa pueblos, Taos and Picurís. Metaphorically, archaeologists examining the prehistory of the Taos Valley are translating and reading pages and chapters from a book whose present and future chapters are being written right now. For the people of Taos and Picurís pueblos, archaeology confirms the continuity of their occupation of their valleys.

The Preceramic Period

Wendorf and Reed assigned archaeological remains that date before the advent of pottery to a long period of time they call the Preceramic Period. They were able to point to artifacts, now identified as Paleo-Indian, from Sandia Cave near Albuquerque and from the Estancia Basin south of Albuquerque as indicating the presence of people at the end of the Pleistocene era (ca. 10,000+ BCE).[4] Assessing late Pleistocene and post-Pleistocene remains was, however, hampered by uncertainty over the ages of those remains.

Research now allows archaeologists to subdivide Wendorf and Reed's Preceramic Period into Paleo-Indian and Archaic periods. The first is generally considered to have begun before 10,000 BCE, although there is considerable controversy over the actual age of the earliest archaeological remains in the Americas. It is also generally considered to have ended around 7000 to 6000 BCE, following the final extinction of very large mammals of the Pleistocene era.

The Paleo-Indian Period
(PRE-10,000 BCE TO CA. 6000 BCE)

The earliest occupation of the Southwest, including the Northern Rio Grande, occurred during what has become known as the Paleo-Indian Period. Within that period, archaeologists recognize three major subdivisions named for the places where the three main types of distinctive projectile points were discovered: Clovis (ca. 10,000 to 9000 BCE), Folsom (ca. 9000 to 8000 BCE), and Plano or Late Paleo-Indian (ca. 8000 to 6000 BCE). The first two, Clovis and Folsom, are towns in eastern New Mexico; Plano refers to the Great Plains.

Archaeologists have frequently characterized Paleo-Indians as big-game hunters. Some archaeologists argue, however, that Clovis people were generalized hunter-gatherers who hunted and scavenged both small and large animals, while Folsom and Plano peoples were increasingly focused on hunting large migratory game such as bison. Distinctive Paleo-Indian points may have been specialized hunting tools, giving the impression of economic dependence on big-game hunting while missing evidence of small-game hunting and plant gathering, which were probably significant components of Paleo-Indian subsistence activities.

Evidence for Paleo-Indian presence in the Taos Valley is rare and typically consists of stone projectile points and butchering tools. Fragments of fluted points (probably either Clovis or Folsom points) have been found in the Taos area and north of Tres Piedras. Younger Paleo-Indian artifacts have been found west of the Rio Grande Gorge near Tres Piedras and south of Carson; near the mouth of Taos Canyon; at Guadalupe Mountain; and east of Pot Creek. We should not assume, though, that Paleo-Indians only infrequently visited the Taos Valley. Of the hundreds (or thousands) of archaeological sites in the Taos Valley characterized by scatters of chipped stone artifacts that cannot be dated, it is quite possible that many are from the Paleo-Indian Period. This notion is supported by the many Paleo-Indian sites and artifacts found in Colorado's San Luis Valley, immediately north of the Taos Valley.[5]

The scarcity of reported Paleo-Indian remains in the Taos Valley may be attributed to the relative invisibility of these artifacts rather than to a lack of occupation. Archaeologists may not be able to recognize Paleo-Indian artifacts as temporally diagnostic, especially those associated with small-game hunting and plant gathering, nor can they be sure that these artifacts do not date to later Archaic and Puebloan occupations. Poor visibility of these remains may also be attributed to geomorphic factors. Surfaces or strata containing Paleo-Indian remains may be deeply buried and only visible in settings where these geological deposits are exposed. For all these reasons, it may not be surprising that intact Paleo-Indian sites have not been found in the Taos Valley, a region characterized by widespread sediment accumulation and soil formation and by only localized erosion. Margaret Jodry's research in the San Luis Valley, in which she combines environmental information from the Paleo-Indian Period with patterns of bison tooth eruption and wear, leads her to conclude that Folsom people visited that valley to hunt in the late summer or early fall. Later Paleo-Indians probably found fewer and smaller bison herds and apparently responded by hunting other species. There is also evidence of seed and nut processing in the area. Since late Pleistocene megafauna and the Paleo-Indians who hunted them were clearly present in the San Luis Valley, it is reasonable to presume that they were also present in the Taos Valley. If so, then it is likely that the scarcity of Paleo-Indian remains in the Taos Valley reflects geomorphic conditions that have obscured those remains.

The Archaic Period
(CA. 6000 BCE TO 1050 CE)

Archaeological evidence shows that by the early to middle sixth millennium BCE (ca. 6000 to 5500 BCE), southwestern hunter-gatherers, including those in the Northern Rio Grande, were moving toward generalized use of animal and plant resources. The time period during which this "adaptation" was common throughout the region is called the Archaic Period, and it ended as people became increasingly dependent on domesticated plants and began to live in semipermanent houses between about 600 and 1050 CE.

Between 1941 and 1946, E. B. Renaud undertook an extensive survey of the Upper Rio Grande Valley in New Mexico and Colorado.[6] His work in this area focused on nonceramic sites in the northern Taos Valley and the San Luis Valley, from which he defined a cultural tradition that he called the Upper Rio Grande Culture.

Sites of the Upper Rio Grande Culture feature a series of distinctive projectile points and the almost exclusive use of "basalt" (actually andesite and dacite) and obsidian for chipped stone tools. Renaud observed four kinds of sites: campsites, which could be divided into large, dense sites near drainages and small, sparse sites located some distance from a river or creek ("scattered finds"); workshops where "basalt" outcrops were obviously quarried and tools produced (often located near campsites); lookouts on exposed mesas, benches, or outcrops where a wide view was available; and rock shelters. A rock shelter site Renaud excavated in 1942 established clearly that the Upper Rio Grande Culture preceded Puebloan occupation or use of the area, although Renaud was unable to establish the ages of Upper Rio Grande Culture artifacts or sites.

The projectile points that Renaud used to identify Upper Rio Grande Culture sites closely resemble those later used by Cynthia Irwin-Williams to define phases within her Oshara Archaic tradition. Consequently, it has become clear that the Upper Rio Grande Culture was, indeed, Archaic in both age and economic adaptation. Irwin-Williams's research provided dates for phases with the Oshara tradition ranging from about 6000 BCE to 1 CE, while later researchers have extended the dates to about 600 CE. Those dates are generally used throughout northern New Mexico, including the Northern Rio Grande and the Taos Valley, although little attempt has been made to determine whether they are, in fact, so widely accurate.

Recently, Stephen Post has argued for what he calls the "latest Archaic," reflecting an adaptation-based rather than strictly time-based scheme to account for the fact that the shift from broad-spectrum mobile hunting and gathering to semisedentary horticulture took place at different times in different parts of the Northern Rio Grande.[7] In the Taos Valley, that shift happened after about 1050 CE, when Pueblo farmers moved into the valley from the south. Evidence for the presence of farmers should not, however, be interpreted to mean that hunter-gatherers disappeared at the same time. For centuries after the advent of farmers, hunter-gatherers pursuing an Archaic lifestyle undoubtedly continued to occupy parts of the region, particularly those areas where farming was not feasible, sharing the regional landscape with farmers who also hunted and collected wild plants. The social and economic boundaries between hunter-gatherers and farmers were probably somewhat porous, allowing hunter-gatherers to become farmers and vice versa. Such shifting of affiliations is particularly likely to occur in frontier-boundary areas, and the Taos Valley was certainly one of those beginning in the eleventh century CE.

The hundreds of Archaic sites in the Taos Valley do not reflect the development of a semisedentary, horticultural lifestyle. All are hunting and gathering sites. Their distributions across the landscape undoubtedly reflect the distributions of economic and other resources. Unfortunately, not much archaeological investigation has focused on the Archaic Period in the Taos Valley, and little can be said specifically about patterns of site location, movement of peoples within and beyond the valley, or access to and use of various resources.

The Pre-European Puebloan Period
(ca. 1050 to 1600 CE)

The Puebloan sequence in the Northern Rio Grande (regardless of names for periods or phases) began considerably later than Puebloan sequences in regions to the west and is characterized by site types, structures, and artifacts different from those found in regions to the west. In Wendorf and Reed's Rio Grande Classification, the Puebloan Period spans the years between about CE 600 and 1600 and is subdivided into the Developmental, Coalition, and Classic Periods. Those periods are known in different parts of the region by local phase names. In this discussion, we will use the phase names applied in the Taos Valley.

The Valdez Phase
(CA. 1050 TO 1225 CE)

In the Rio Grande Classification, the Developmental Period spans the years between about 600 CE and 1200 CE. By convention, this period is further subdivided into Early Developmental (600 to 900 CE) and Late Developmental (900 to 1200 CE) periods. Developmental Period sites have been identified throughout the Northern Rio Grande from the Albuquerque area to the Taos Valley. After about 900 CE, however, as Pueblo people expanded from south to north, the Developmental Period was increasingly a phenomenon of the region north of La Bajada Mesa, the steep, south-facing escarpment of the sprawling mesa about eleven miles south of Santa Fe. (La Bajada is the historic dividing point between the Rio Arriba, "upper river," and the Rio Abajo, "lower river," a distinction still in use today.)

To date, no sites in the Taos Valley that can be positively identified as Puebloan have been dated before the last half of the Developmental Period. In fact, no Puebloan sites in the Taos Valley have been dated before the mid-1000s. The earliest Puebloan occupation, which dates between about 1050 and 1225 CE, is known as the Valdez phase.[8] The Valdez phase in the Taos Valley represents the northernmost expansion of Pueblo people in the Northern Rio Grande, a process that began about 500–600 CE in the Albuquerque area. Because the Taos Valley is a marginal area for farming, the post-1050 CE occupations by Puebloan farmers were limited to the eastern side of the valley between the Rio Grande del Rancho drainage on the south and the Questa area on the north. This is the part of the valley with the most permanent or semi-permanent streams draining the Sangre de Cristo and Picurís mountains. However, Pueblo people used a much larger area for hunting, plant gathering, obtaining materials for tool manufacture, and ritual activities. Florence Ellis's research for the Taos Pueblo lands claims litigation in the 1960s identified Taos Pueblo's "traditional use area" as a roughly circular area encompassing about 700 square miles with Taos Pueblo near its center.[9] It is likely that the use area of the valley's earlier Puebloan residents, the ancestors of Taos Pueblo, was at least that large and perhaps larger. Farming and residential activities were, however, limited to the area between Pot Creek and Questa along the eastern side of the valley.

Sites from the Valdez phase of the Late Developmental Period commonly consist of deep (2.5 to 3 meters below modern ground surface) pit structures with associated surface work areas and, sometimes, with small surface structures of jacal or adobe construction.[10] Although most pit structures were probably family houses, some also probably functioned as part-time kivas, and at least three excavated sites included structures that were probably fully ritual in nature. In the Taos Valley south of Arroyo Seco, pit structures tend to be approximately circular, while those in the Arroyo Seco–Arroyo Hondo area to the north tend to be rectangular. This pattern, along with patterns in ceramic types and chipped stone and ground stone tools, points to a correlation with Taos Pueblo origin stories that identify two different groups of people occupying the two parts of the valley prior to the formation of the Taos Pueblo community.[11]

Most sites contain only one or two pit structures, although sites with several pit structures have been investigated. We do not know, however, whether any of the structures at these sites actually coexisted in time. The extent of social integration during the Developmental Period is not clear. Some archaeologists have assumed that there was little or none before the Coalition Period. Others argue that the Puebloans of the Developmental Period, including the Valdez phase in the Taos Valley, were in fact organized in communities of scattered family units not unlike communities of homesteaders on the Great Plains in the nineteenth and early twentieth centuries.

Ceramic types commonly associated with Valdez phase sites include a plain, neck-banded ware, or incised gray or brown ware known as Taos Gray, and a mineral-painted type known as Kwahe'e Black-on-White, which is often referred to in the Taos Valley as Taos Black-on-White. These types are local variants of gray and decorated types found at late Developmental Period sites throughout the Northern Rio Grande. Also present in small numbers are pottery types traded into the region from the Middle Rio Grande Valley, the Mogollon Highlands, and the San Juan Basin. They show that Northern Rio Grande Pueblo people had economic ties with regions to the south, southwest, and west while maintaining a regionally distinct trajectory of cultural development.

The Pot Creek Phase
(CA. 1225 TO 1320 CE)

The years between about 1200 and 1325 CE in the Northern Rio Grande are known as the Coalition Period and are often seen as transitional between earlier and later periods. Several researchers assert that the Coalition Period was marked by major changes that are reflected in the archaeological record. These include the use of contiguous surface rooms as domiciles more often than during the previous period and a shift from mineral-based paint to plant-based paint for decorating pottery.

The early Coalition Period in the Taos Valley is known as the Pot Creek phase[12] and dates between about 1225 and 1270 CE. This phase was apparently characterized by population consolidation from scattered pit-structure sites into small surface pueblos referred to as unit-type pueblos. Examples have been recorded in various parts of the Taos area, but only four Pot Creek phase sites have been partially excavated. Pit structures associated with Pot Creek phase sites appear to have been full-time kivas rather than houses, based on floor features that are not present in most residential pit structures. Surface room blocks were constructed of coursed adobe mud, the same technology commonly used for pit structure walls. In this technology, adobe material was formed by hand into wall segments ("courses") that were usually 0.3 to 0.5 m in height and 15 to 30 cm thick. When a course dried, another course was formed on top of it, building the walls up to the desired height. When the last wall course was dry, the wall surfaces were covered with mud plaster.

Although Kwahe'e/Taos Black-on-White is still a significant part of the ceramic assemblage from these sites, Santa Fe Black-on-White, a regionally dominant, vegetal paint type that characterizes the Coalition Period throughout the Northern Rio Grande, is also present. Incised and neck-banded Taos Gray was largely replaced by a corrugated variety.

Because so few sites from this period in the Taos Valley have been excavated, little can be said about them. Still, they are important because they became communities of aggregated family units. The processes involved in that transition and their impacts on social and economic relationships in and beyond the Taos Valley and on access to and use of natural resources are poorly understood and demand further study. They are also important because some Pot Creek phase sites are specifically identified as directly ancestral to historic and modern kiva societies at Taos and Picurís pueblos. Two excavated sites from this period, Pot Creek Pueblo (LA 260) and the Llano Quemado Pueblo (LA 1892) are ancestral to kiva societies at Taos Pueblo. Pot Creek Pueblo is also directly ancestral to a kiva society at Picurís Pueblo.

The Talpa Phase
(CA. 1270 TO 1320 CE)

The late Coalition Period in the Taos Valley is referred to as the Talpa phase and is known almost exclusively from excavations at Pot Creek Pueblo (LA 260), which suggest a beginning date of 1260 or 1270 CE. The phase is usually given an ending date of 1350 CE. However, Patricia Crown's detailed analysis of tree-ring dates from Pot Creek Pueblo suggests that the site was "abandoned" shortly after about 1320 CE.[13] Since no other sites from this phase have been excavated or dated (with the exception of parts of Picurís Pueblo),[14] we do not know whether that date can be applied to the phase as a whole.

Based on the archaeology of the Rio Grande del Rancho River Valley, where Pot Creek Pueblo is located, the Talpa phase was a period when population consolidation continued at the expense of the smaller unit-type pueblos in the area. Pot Creek Pueblo, which was first occupied during the Valdez phase, grew to perhaps 300 ground-floor rooms in eight or more room blocks, some of which were multistoried. Growth was "a process of accretion, with no clear ground plan except for the existence of separate room blocks surrounding an open plaza area. Each room block developed into a series of structures one to three rooms deep, generally enclosing a central courtyard, with an opening to the south and east."[15] Herbert Dick provided a similar description for the formation of Picurís Pueblo.

Late Pre-European History
(CA. 1320 TO 1600 CE)

No phase name has been given to the years between the end of the Talpa phase and the beginning of the historic period in the Taos Valley. Based on his excavations at Picurís Pueblo, Herbert Dick named these years the Vadito phase and dated it between about 1375 and 1500 CE. These dates are similar to those assigned to an abandoned portion of Taos Pueblo located immediately east of the occupied village, known as Red Mound or Cornfield Taos.[16]

ARCHAEOLOGISTS OF THE VALLEY

Archaeological research on the pre-European record of the Taos Valley is an interesting story of its own, one with different versions of which peoples passed through this landscape, which ones stayed, how people lived, and who remains here today. By reviewing the history of this archaeology, we begin to form a picture of what happened here before the inhabitants wrote about it.

At the end of the nineteenth century, the Swiss-American archaeologist Adolph Bandelier noted several sites south of the present town of Taos, including a small pueblo site in Llano Quemado (LA 1892) [17] that was partly excavated in 1920 by J. A. Jeançon.[18] The first to describe the large pueblo at Pot Creek (LA 260), Jeançon called that site "one of the largest adobe-walled remains the writer has seen in the Southwest." In the 1950s Taoseña Helen Greene Blumenschein, an amateur archaeologist working with the Taos Archaeological Society, inventoried several hundred archaeological sites throughout the valley and conducted excavations at sites near Pot Creek as well as near Arroyo Seco and Valdez.[19] Most scientific archaeological research in the area has occurred since the 1950s, notably by academic research conducted by the Fort Burgwin Research Center, Southern Methodist University's archaeological field school, which continues to survey and excavate in the Taos area. The University of New Mexico Archaeological Field School conducted excavations between Valdez and San Cristóbal in the mid-1960s, providing most of what little is known about early Puebloan sites in that area.

Non-academic investigations began in the late 1950s with "highway salvage" excavations near Llano Quemado and Pot Creek. Since the advent of cultural resources management (CRM) archaeology in the 1970s, the Taos Valley has seen hundreds of surveys, large and small, and excavation projects that range in scope from site testing to full-scale data recovery investigations. Most of the surveys are the ongoing work of archaeologists working for the Carson National Forest and the Bureau of Land Management as part of their resource management programs. Other surveys and most excavation projects have been performed by individuals, companies, and agencies conducting client-driven CRM investigations.

Modeling Pre-European Puebloan Life in the Taos Valley

Archaeologists working in the Taos Valley view the region from several perspectives. We can think of these perspectives as different models used to characterize their observations, models that center largely on accepting, rejecting, or ignoring the notion that the region was on the Puebloan "margin" or "periphery," an idea sometimes ascribed to Wendorf and Reed, although they were not the ones who proposed it.

The Backwoods Model

The first model characterizes the archaeology of the Taos Valley as having "provincial" qualities and argues that Puebloan development in the Taos area was behind the times because it is "at the end of the line" of Rio Grande pueblos. In this view, the early Puebloan occupants of Taos Valley were a late, peripheral branch of the Rio Grande Puebloans, which accounts for some characteristics of local, prehistoric Puebloan life. According to this model, these characteristics are visible in the presence of post-1100 CE pit structures and small pit structure clusters, supposedly in contrast to community-focused life at that time in communities to the south and west. One gets the image of people living on the margins of the Pueblo world and left behind by the cultural progress of mainstream Puebloan groups.

The Geographically Challenged Model

In the second model, which takes a middle-of-the-road view, geographical barriers created a Puebloan enclave that responded to geographic isolation by pursuing its own cultural development. This would explain local ceramic types that resemble but also differ from contemporary types to the south, a supposed time lag in the shift from subsurface to surface structures, the presence of certain distinctive architectural features (particularly a central basin-support post in pueblo rooms), and contact with Plains groups. From this model, one gets an image of a group of Puebloan people wandering into the Taos Valley only to look over their shoulders and realize that they are cut off from the rest of the world by a mountain chain, then hunkering down to create their own world.

The "Doing What Comes Naturally" Model

The third model specifically rejects the periphery notion and describes the pre-European archaeological record of the Taos Valley as bearing similarities to other Pueblo regions, while remaining significantly different and needing to be considered a region unto itself. Quite emphatically, one archaeologist asserts:

> We are not dealing with a culturally retarded group of people living on the margin of the mainstream of Anasazi development. Rather, we observe a people who successfully adapted to their own set of circumstances, a local situation distinct from that faced by other Anasazi groups.[20]

With this model, one gets an image of a group of Puebloans whose differences from other groups in the northern Southwest were not significant and only reflected adaptations to local circumstances, like the other variants of the "norm."

The "What's the Big Deal?" Model

The fourth model largely ignores the periphery concept by discussing events and processes in the Taos Valley as if they were common to the pre-European history of the Rio Grande region and the northern Southwest. Significantly, this model is the first to explicitly view the Taos Valley outside the cultural-historical paradigm that structured earlier work in the valley and the region. Some archaeologists applying this point of view use Pot Creek Pueblo to model the formation of aggregated communities in the northern Rio Grande region, with sites in the Taos Valley regarded as representative of contemporaneous sites in the entire region.

This model summons a mental image not of the Puebloan people themselves but of archaeologists shrugging their shoulders and wondering why the controversy arose at all, since the Taos Valley doesn't seem all that different from the rest of the region.

View from the west end of the pueblo plaza showing the North House of Taos Pueblo against the backdrop of Taos Mountain and the Sangre de Cristo range. Photo Howard Rainer, ca. 1980s.

The Frontier Model

Responding to these models, particularly the first three, research undertaken in the Taos Valley by the Museum of New Mexico's Office of Archaeological Studies—with which this writer is associated—has pursued an examination of the area as a Puebloan frontier, an area occupied by an expanding Puebloan population beginning in the mid- to late-eleventh century CE. This approach identifies specific attributes of frontier settlement and adaptation—attributes derived primarily from cultural geographers and cultural anthropologists who specialize in frontier studies—and compares them to the archaeological record in the Taos Valley. Benchmark frontier attributes seen in the Taos Valley include spatial and temporal population impermanence (that is, settlement mobility) as the frontier expands, distinctive community types and settlement patterns, and evidence of stretched trade and communication links with the core area(s) from which expansion took place.

The results of this research so far show that the Taos Valley was a Puebloan frontier, although there is not full agreement that frontier modeling is useful for describing all local developments. We see in this situation a melding of the local cultural-historical perspectives of the first three models with the regional and somewhat ahistorical perspective of the fourth model. This allows us to view the Taos Valley as a Puebloan frontier as well as an integrated part of the Northern Rio Grande but not as a marginal or "backwater" Puebloan development. Any apparent contradiction is resolved as we see the increasing integration of the Taos Valley into regional trends following the initial period of frontier Tiwa occupation in the eleventh century.

It appears that by the middle of the fourteenth century CE all the Puebloans of the Taos Valley were living at the villages we know as Taos and Picurís pueblos. In native oral tradition lies a deep history of the people who became Taos and Picurís, beginning with their emergences into this world from the world beneath it through a lake to the north. The people who came up through the lake brought with them group identities that are represented by archaeological sites in the Taos Valley. Over time, other people came to the valley and joined local communities. Oral history and the archaeological record agree in pointing to people entering the valley, moving around the valley while living in different kinds of houses, and eventually coalescing at the locations of the two large historic and modern pueblos. While there are differences in how the events and processes are portrayed in oral history and archaeology, those differences do not necessarily reflect inaccuracies in either record. Rather, they reflect very real differences between native and Euro-American worldviews, in how those worldviews record, maintain, and communicate historical events and processes, and in the different lessons those records hold for native peoples and for the archaeologists, anthropologists, and historians who study them.

NOTES

1. This chapter was drawn from the author's longer, fully cited paper "The Prehistory of the Taos Valley." A copy of that paper is on file at the Southwest Research Center in Taos, New Mexico.

2. Fred Wendorf and Eric K. Reed, "An Alternative Reconstruction of Northern Rio Grande Prehistory," *El Palacio* 62, nos. 5–6 (1955):131–73. Stewart Peckham, "The Anasazi Culture of the Northern Rio Grande Rift," in *New Mexico Geological Society Guidebook. 35th Field Conference: Rio Grande Rift, Northern New Mexico* (Socorro: New Mexico Bureau of Mines and Mineral Resources, 1984): 275–81.

3. Alfred V. Kidder, *An Introduction to the Study of Southwestern Archaeology* (New Haven, CT: Yale University Press, 1962).

4. "Upper Rio Grande points" and similar artifacts from the far Northern Rio Grande, "Los Encinos Culture" artifacts from the Rio Chama drainage, "Atrisco points" and other artifacts found in the Albuquerque area, and artifacts found near Manzano and Isleta all indicated to Wendorf and Reed the widespread presence of post-Pleistocene occupants of the region.

5. Margaret A. Jodry, "Paleoindian Stage," in *Colorado Prehistory: A Context for the Rio Grande Basin*, by M. A. Martorano, T. Hoefer III, M. A. Jodry, V. Spero, and M. L. Taylor (Denver: Colorado Council of Professional Archaeologists, 1999), 45–114.

6. E. B. Renaud, *Reconnaissance Work in the Upper Rio Grande Valley, Colorado, and New Mexico,* Archaeological Series, Third Paper (Denver: University of Denver, 1942); and Renaud, *Archaeology of the Upper Rio Grande Basin in Southern Colorado and Northern New Mexico,* Archaeological Series, Sixth Paper (Denver: University of Denver. 1946).

7. Stephen S. Post, "Emerging from the Shadows: The Archaic Period in the Northern Rio Grande," in *Traditions, Transitions, and Technologies: Themes in Southwestern Archaeology,* ed. S. H. Schlanger (Boulder: University Press of Colorado, 2002), 33–48.

8. Jeffrey L. Boyer, *Dating the Valdez Phase: Chronometric Re-evaluation of the Initial Anasazi Occupation of North-Central New Mexico,* Archaeology Notes 164 (Santa Fe: Office of Archaeological Studies, Museum of New Mexico, 1997). Ernestine L. Green, *Valdez Phase Occupation Near Taos, New Mexico,* Report No. 10 (Taos: Fort Burgwin Research Center, 1976).

9. Florence Hawley Ellis, "Anthropological Data Pertaining to the Taos Land Claim," in *Pueblo Indians I* (New York: Garland Publishing, 1974), 29–150.

10. Jeffrey L. Boyer, James L. Moore et al., *Studying the Taos Frontier: The Pot Creek Data Recovery Project,* Archaeology Notes 68 (Santa Fe: Office of Archaeological Studies, Museum of New Mexico, 1994).

11. Jeffrey L. Boyer, "North People and South People: Ethnohistorical and Archaeological Evidence for the Origins and Organization of Taos Pueblo," in *Chasing Chaco and the Southwest: Papers in Honor of Frances Joan Mathien,* ed. R. N. Wiseman, T. C. O'Laughlin, C. T. Snow, and C. Travis, Papers of the Archaeological Society of New Mexico 34 (Albuquerque: Archaeological Society of New Mexico, 2008), 19–35.

12. Ronald K. Wetherington, *Excavations at Pot Creek Pueblo,* Report No. 6 (Taos: Fort Burgwin Research Center, 1968); Patricia L. Crown, "The Chronology of the Taos Area Anasazi," in *Clues to the Past: Papers in Honor of William M. Sundt,* ed. Meliha S. Duran and David T. Kirkpatrick, Papers of the Archaeological Society of New Mexico 16 (Albuquerque: Archaeological Society of New Mexico, 1994); Boyer 1997.

13. Patricia L. Crown, "Evaluating the Construction Sequence and Population of Pot Creek Pueblo," *American Antiquity* 2 (1991), 291–314.

14. Michael A. Adler and Herbert W. Dick, *Picurís Pueblo through Time: Eight Centuries of Change at a Northern Rio Grande Pueblo* (Dallas: Southern Methodist University, 1999).

15. Crown 1991, 310.

16. Florence H. Ellis and J. J. Brody, "Ceramic Stratigraphy and Tribal History at Taos Pueblo," *American Antiquity* 29: 3 (1964), 316–27.

17. Archaeological sites in New Mexico are recorded in the New Mexico Cultural Resource Information System files by LA number, LA referring to the Laboratory of Anthropology, the state agency that first systematically recorded sites in New Mexico in the 1920s. LA 1892 is the Llano Quemado Pueblo.

18. J. A. Jeançon, *Archaeological Investigations in the Taos Valley, New Mexico, during 1920,* Miscellaneous Collections 81(12). (Washington, DC: Smithsonian Institution, 1929). The Pot Creek site is LA 260.

19. Helen G. Blumenschein, "Excavations in the Taos Area, 1953–1955," *El Palacio* 63: 2 (1956), 53–56; and Blumenschein, "Further Excavations and Surveys in the Taos Area," *El Palacio* 65: 3 (1958), 107–111. Blumenschein was honored in 1980 with a festschrift published by the Archaeological Society of New Mexico.

20. Anne Woosley, *Taos Archaeology* (Taos: Fort Burgwin Research Center, 1980); and Woosley, "Puebloan Prehistory of the Northern Rio Grande: Settlement, Population, and Subsistence," *The Kiva* 51: 3 (1986), 143–64.

SELECTED REFERENCES

Adler, Michael. "Why Is a Kiva? New Interpretations of Prehistoric Social Integrative Architecture in the Northern Rio Grande Region of New Mexico." *Journal of Anthropological Research* 49 (1993), 319–46.

Baker, Ruth L. "Strategies on the Frontier: Archaeobotanical Perspectives from the Edge." Paper presented at the symposium Living on the Edge: The Frontier Concept in the Prehistory of the Northern Southwest, 61st Annual Meeting of the Society for American Archaeology, New Orleans, 1996.

Blumenschein, Helen G. "Excavations in the Taos Area, 1953–1955." *El Palacio* 63: 2 (1956), 53–56.

———. "Further Excavations and Surveys in the Taos Area." *El Palacio* 65: 3 (1958), 107–11.

Boyer, Jeffrey L. "Anasazi Communities on the Taos Frontier: Introduction to Data Recovery on Blueberry Hill." In *The Blueberry Hill Road Testing Project: Results of Archaeological Test Investigations at 20 Sites and a Plan for Data Recovery Investigations at 12 Sites along Blueberry Hill Road, Taos County New Mexico,* edited by Jeffrey L. Boyer and Sonya O. Urban, Archaeology Notes 182 (manuscript), Office of Archaeological Studies, Museum of New Mexico, Santa Fe, 1995.

———. *Archaeological Investigations at the San Antonio Mountain Scoria Mine, Rio Arriba County, New Mexico.* Contract Archaeology Report No. 4. Taos: Kit Carson Memorial Foundation, 1984.

———. *Dating the Valdez Phase: Chronometric Re-evaluation of the Initial Anasazi Occupation of North-Central New Mexico.* Archaeology Notes 164. Santa Fe: Office of Archaeological Studies, Museum of New Mexico, 1997.

———. "Defining the Anasazi Frontier." Paper presented at the symposium Living on the Edge: The Frontier Concept in the Prehistory of the Northern Southwest, 61st Annual Meeting of the Society for American Archaeology, New Orleans, 1996.

———. "It Takes a Village to Dig a Kiva: Archaeological and Ethnohistorical Evidence for the Formation of Early Puebloan Communities in the Northern Rio Grande." Paper presented in the Summer Colloquium Series, Southern Methodist University's Fort Burgwin Research Center, Taos, 2000.

———. "It Takes a Village to Have a Plaza: An Argument for Early Puebloan Community Integration in the Northern Rio Grande." Paper presented at the 67th Annual Meeting of the Society for American Archaeology, Denver, 2002.

———. "Non-Sedentary Sites at San Antonio Mountain: The San Antonio Mountain Scoria Mine Mitigative Project." Contract Archaeology Report No. 5. Taos: Kit Carson Memorial Foundation, 1985.

———. "Plains Electric Cooperative's Hernandez-Taos Transmission Line: An Archaeological Inventory Survey." Contract Archaeology Report No. 8. Taos: Kit Carson Memorial Foundation, 1985.

———, James L. Moore, Daisy F. Levine, Linda Mick-O'Hara, and Mollie S. Toll. *Studying the Taos Frontier: The Pot Creek Data Recovery Project,* Archaeology Notes 68. Office of Archaeological Studies. Santa Fe: Museum of New Mexico, 1994.

Crown, Patricia L., and Timothy A. Kohler. "Community Dynamics, Site Structure, and Aggregation in the Northern Rio Grande." In *The Ancient Southwestern Community: Models and Methods for the Study of Prehistoric Social Organization,* edited by W. H. Wills and Robert D. Leonard. Albuquerque: University of New Mexico Press, 1994, 103–17.

———, Janet D. Orcutt, and Timothy A. Kohler. "Pueblo Cultures in Transition: The Northern Rio Grande."In *The Prehistoric Pueblo World, AD 1150–1350,* ed. Michael A. Adler. Tucson: University of Arizona Press, 1996, 188–204.

Green, Ernestine L. *Valdez Phase Occupation Near Taos, New Mexico.* Report No. 10. Taos:

Fort Burgwin Research Center, 1976.

Herold, Laurence C., and Ralph A. Leubben. *Papers on Taos Archaeology.* Fort Burgwin Research Center, Taos. Dallas: Southern Methodist University Press, 1968.

Hufnagle, John, Michael Adler, and Amber Johnson. "Architecture and Environment: Modeling Social Organization in the Taos Area of the American Southwest." Paper presented at the symposium "Living on the Edge: The Frontier Concept in the Prehistory of the Northern Southwest," 61st Annual Meeting of the Society for American Archaeology, New Orleans, 1996.

Lakatos, Steven A. "What Is a Rio Grande Kiva? Origin and Development of Rio Grande Pit Structures." Paper presented at the 67th Annual Meeting of the Society of American Archaeology, Denver, 2002.

Loose, Ann A. *Archeological Excavations near Arroyo Hondo, Carson National Forest. New Mexico.* Archaeological Report No. 4. Albuquerque: USDA Forest Service, Southwestern Region, 1974.

Luebben, Ralph A. "Site TA-32: A Deep Pit House and Surface Manifestation in North Central New Mexico." In *Papers on Taos Archaeology,* by L. C. Herold and R. A. Luebben, Report No. 7. Taos: Fort Burgwin Research Center, 1968.

Moore, James L. "Farming on the Northern Anasazi Frontier." Paper presented at the symposium "Living on the Edge: The Frontier Concept in the Prehistory of the Northern Southwest," 61st Annual Meeting of the Society for American Archaeology, New Orleans, 1996.

Proctor, Rebecca. "Design Sharing in Pottery from the Taos Frontier." Paper presented at the symposium "Living on the Edge: The Frontier Concept in the Prehistory of the Northern Southwest," 61st Annual Meeting of the Society for American Archaeology, New Orleans, 1996.

Seaman, Timothy J. *Archeological Investigations on Guadalupe Mountain, Taos County. New Mexico.* Laboratory of Anthropology Notes 309. Santa Fe: Museum of New Mexico, 1983.

Wendorf, Fred, and Eric K. Reed. "An Alternative Reconstruction of Northern Rio Grande Prehistory." *El Palacio* 62: 5–6 (1955), 131–73.

———, and J. P. Miller. "Artifacts from High Mountain Sites in the Sangre de Cristo Range." *El Palacio* 66: (1959).

Wetherington, Ronald K. *Excavations at Pot Creek Pueblo.* Report No. 6. Taos: Fort Burgwin Research Center, 1968.

Wolfman, Daniel, Mariann L. Wolfman, and Herbert W. Dick. *A Taos Phase Pithouse on Arroyo Seco, New Mexico.* Series in Anthropology, No. 1. Alamosa, CO: Adams State College, 1965.

Woosley, Anne. *Taos Archaeology.* Taos: Fort Burgwin Research Center, 1980.

———. "Puebloan Prehistory of the Northern Rio Grande: Settlement, Population, and Subsistence." *The Kiva* 51: 3 (1986), 143–64.

Zamora, Dorothy A. *An Archaeological Survey in Sagebrush Hills Near Taos, New Mexico.* Archaeology Notes 341. Santa Fe: Office of Archaeological Studies, Museum of New Mexico, 2004.

LA TIERRA:
STRUGGLE
FOR SURVIVAL

❖

The drive between Santa Fe and Taos circa 1915 was dusty—or muddy—rough, and hard on vehicles and passengers. This is the trip many early twentieth-century Taos notables made, including Mabel Dodge Luhan, D. H. Lawrence and wife Frieda, and tourist excursions sponsored by the Atchison, Topeka and Santa Fe Railroad. Permission of Denver Public Library, Western History Collections.

✤ 3 ✤

Caminos antiguos:
Trails into the Taos Valley

CHARLES C. HAWK

The story of settlement, cultural evolution, conflict, and development cannot be fully comprehended without some understanding of the difficulty of getting to and from the Taos Valley. Knowledge of the old trails and roads used by generations of Taoseños, both Native American and European, enhances appreciation of their resourcefulness and perseverance. All early Taos Valley residents, whether Pueblo, Spanish, Mexican, or American, used the same challenging routes, and understanding what they were up against helps us reconstruct centuries of trade and other commercial relations under different governments.

PUEBLO FAMILIES HAD LIVED and farmed in the Taos Valley for at least four centuries before the Spanish first ventured into New Mexico in 1540. And the people of Taos Pueblo were preceded by other indigenous peoples at sites in Pot Creek, Talpa, Llano Quemado, Valdez, and Arroyo Seco. In spite of the valley's abundant water and plentiful crops, however, some necessities had to be brought in from elsewhere. Likewise, reliable access to Taos remained essential for Spanish, Mexican, and, later, American settlers. Fortunately for the early Spanish colonists, the Tiwa of Taos had established many trails to facilitate trade and communication with other native peoples.

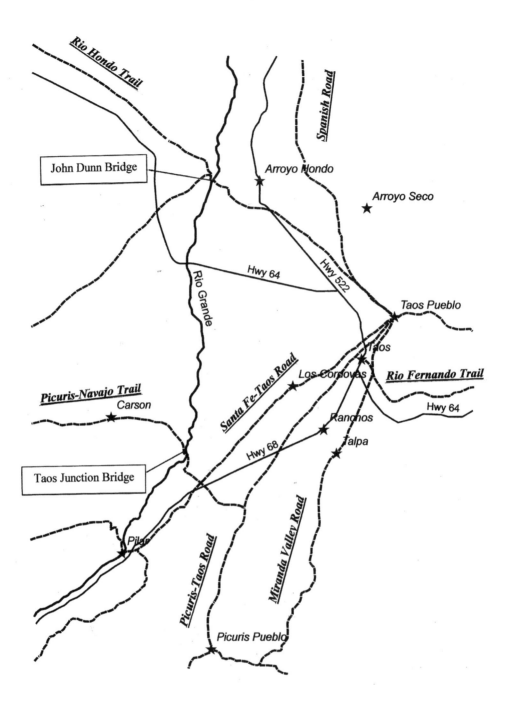

Taos Pueblo was the nexus of seven major Indian trails that connected the pueblo with Picurís and the more southern Rio Grande pueblos, the Great Plains Indians, and Navajo tribes to the west. Map: Charles C. Hawk.

Taos Valley was close enough to the plains of northeast New Mexico to enable trade with the Comanches and other nomadic Indians of that area as well as with the people of Picurís and Pecos pueblos. Well-established paths linked Picurís to San Juan and hence to other pueblos farther south.Much-used trails also connected Taos Pueblo to now-abandoned pueblos in the Chama Valley. Others allowed travel to Ute and Navajo country to the northwest.[2]

Most Indian trails were suitable only for foot traffic. Because they could not handle large numbers of horses, let alone carretas, or wagons, many native paths proved impractical for Spanish needs. Commerce between Taos and Santa Fe increased once the area was under Mexican jurisdiction after 1821 and yet again when the United States took control of the territory. By the late 1800s, four centuries of trail building and maintenance had overcome the mountain and river barriers isolating Taos. But some of the old trails were used well into the 1900s, making them among the oldest continuously used roads in the United States.

COLONIZATION AND COMMERCE: TRAILS FROM SANTA FE

The most heavily used and historically important trails into the valley were those connecting Taos with places to the south along the Rio Grande and ultimately to Santa Fe. We know of three well-traveled routes, all of them built and used by Native Americans well before Spanish colonization.

These trails witnessed some of the most important events in New Mexico history. Coronado's men traveled one of them in 1541, when the first Europeans visited Taos Valley and Taos Pueblo.[3] After Oñate's arrival in 1598, they were the caminos used by the first Franciscan missionaries and the earliest Spanish colonists to settle in Taos Valley.[4] They immediately became the commercial arteries extending from Taos Valley to Santa Fe and south into Mexico.

At the time of the Pueblo Revolt in 1680, runners from Taos Pueblo probably used these trails to convey the information needed to carry out their plan. During the Spanish reconquista of New Mexico in 1692–96, Vargas and his soldiers made at least three expeditions to Taos.[5] The northernmost Rio Grande pueblo, Taos was resistant to Spanish rule, and Vargas used these trails to get his soldiers into Taos Valley and force submission of Taos Pueblo.

The first two decades of the 1700s saw several large Spanish military and diplomatic expeditions against Indian raiders to the northwest and northeast of Taos and Santa Fe. In 1705, Captain Roque Madrid led a large force north from Santa Fe against the Navajos. Although he did not enter the Taos Valley, his troops followed the Taos-Picurís Trail and the Agua Caliente Trail to Cieneguilla (since renamed Pilar), and then traveled northwest to Navajo country.[6] In 1706 Sergeant-Major Juan de Ulibarrí led six hundred men and two thousand horses from Taos to southeast Colorado to assist in the return of the Picurís people who had fled their pueblo in 1696.

The most successful military effort against Indian raiders by the Spanish was in 1779. By this date, the Comanches had almost brought the Spanish colony in northern New Mexico to its knees. Governor Anza led a large expedition from Santa Fe and decisively defeated the Comanches near present-day Pueblo, Colorado. His expedition returned to Santa Fe through Taos.[7]

In January 1847, many residents of the Taos Valley took part in violent resistance to the newly installed American territorial authorities. The new governor of the territory, Charles Bent (1846–47), was killed in his home in Taos. Many others also died fighting, including Hispanic citizens viewed as collaborators with the Americans. The road to Santa Fe carried the news of these events; shortly after, going north on the same roads, Col. Sterling Price led a force of about four hundred troops and volunteers to Taos to suppress the resistance.[8] On the way Price's force fought two battles, one at Santa Cruz de la Cañada and the second at Embudo Pass, north of Velarde on the road between Taos and Santa Fe.

In March 1854, the U.S. Army experienced a decisive and unusual defeat at the hands of the Jicarilla Apache[9] in the Battle of Cieneguilla, fought in the mountains three miles east of Pilar. To reach the site of the battle, American dragoons from Cantonment Burgwin near Talpa followed the main Santa Fe–Taos road south to Cieneguilla, then turned east on the Agua Caliente Trail.

The Santa Fe - Taos Road

The trail closest to the Rio Grande wound over the Picurís Mountains from Velarde to the site of present-day Dixon, and then north up Pilar Mesa. The road did not follow the canyon of the Rio Grande. From the top of Pilar Mesa, it dropped into the Agua Caliente Canyon just east of Pilar, and from there proceeded northeast up Cieneguilla Creek. It then climbed over the ridge that is now the "horseshoe" of present Highway 68, angled northwest to Los Cordovas, and eventually extended to Taos Pueblo. Usable most of the year, this was the shortest and most direct trail to Taos from Santa Fe, although most of it could not support wagon travel until the mid-nineteenth century. If it was indeed used for more than 700 years, it was one of the oldest continuously traveled roads in the country—and truly a national historic treasure.

During the Spanish era this trail was one of two main branches of the Camino Real, or Royal Road, north from Santa Fe to Taos.[10] It was used by Americans continuously after 1846, and its survival was assured when the U.S. Army followed this well-known route when building a wagon-capable supply road from Santa

Fe north to Fort Garland, Colorado. The Military Road, locally known as the Camino Militar, was completed in 1876.[11]

The Picurís Pueblo - Taos Pueblo Trail

The middle trail from Santa Fe to Taos went directly north from Picurís Pueblo. It climbed Picurís Canyon, crossed upper Arroyo Hondo Creek, and climbed over a pass into Taos Valley. It was originally a major Indian communication and trading route between Taos and Picurís pueblos.[12]

Of the three main routes into Taos Valley, this trail seems to have been the least used after Spanish colonization. While it was the shortest route between the two pueblos, it was also the most difficult to negotiate. It was hard on horses and much too rocky and steep ever to be used by wagons.

On the map, a branch of the Picurís Pueblo–Taos Pueblo Trail runs northwest from the main trail after crossing the Picurís Mountains.[13] There is little documented evidence for this trail, but its presence during pre-Spanish years makes sense. It would have been the most direct and easiest trade route from the powerful Picurís Pueblo to the tribal lands in what are now northwest New Mexico and northern Arizona. After 1829 this route may also have been used by Taos Valley traders to reach the branch of the Old Spanish Trail west of the Rio Grande.

The Miranda Valley Road

The eastern and best-known trail into Taos Valley from the south was also through Picurís Pueblo. This heavily used road wound over the Picurís Mountains about ten miles east of that pueblo. It then went down Miranda Valley, crossed the Rio Rancho at Talpa, and went directly to Taos Pueblo.

This historic trail was the second branch of the Camino Real from Santa Fe to Taos.[14] It may have been the first trail followed by the Spanish to reach Taos Valley from the south. Its continuing importance was assured when at some time during the Spanish occupation it was made usable for carts and small wagons. During the Spanish, Mexican, and early American periods this road was the only continuous wagon route to Taos from the south, although after the American annexation in 1846 it deteriorated. By the early 1850s, there were many complaints that loaded wagons, particularly military ones, simply could not use it.

The Miranda Valley Road was not heavily used for as long as the road into Taos Valley from Pilar. Sometime after 1852 a trail over U.S. Hill, which roughly follows current Highway 518, was either built or improved for wagon use. Since then the Camino Real down Miranda Valley has been reclaimed by the forest. Only traces are visible today.

INDIAN AND SPANISH TRADE ROUTES TO THE WEST

From early Pueblo times to the American conquest, barter must have been an important part of the Taos Valley economy. Records of this trade are so scarce that its importance has probably been vastly underestimated. Because of the natural barrier of the Rio Grande Gorge, communication to and from Taos Valley to the west was extremely difficult. We know of only two trails that allowed people and horses to cross the Rio Grande from either direction.

The first two fords of the Rio Grande probably originated and saw considerable use as Indian trails. Both may have been heavily used by Spanish and Mexican traders for private commerce with the Utes and Navajos to the west and northwest. During the late Mexican period, both may have been part of the "Taos connection" to the Old Spanish Trail west of the Rio Grande.

Taos Junction Crossing: The Picurís-Navajo Trail

Usable only on foot or horseback, the old trail on the east wall of the Rio Grande Gorge above Taos Junction Bridge is still visible and can be followed. In places it is very steep but as a whole is a surprisingly easy grade. The trail crossed the river either at the location of the present Taos Junction Bridge or at the site of the original 1914 bridge two hundred yards upstream. Its route up the west side of the gorge has largely been destroyed by the current highway to Carson.

This trail was the most direct pre-Spanish trade route from Picurís Pueblo to Native American trading partners across the Rio Grande to the northwest. Pre-Spanish petroglyphs, and even primitive structures, are located on or close to the trail on both sides of the river. The extent of trade between Picurís and the northwest, as with other intertribal trade, has probably been underestimated. The Picurís-Navajo Trail connects places occupied by Indian tribes but not by later settlements separated. For Spanish, Mexican, and American purposes, other routes across the Rio Grande would have been more useful.

John Dunn Bridge Crossing: The Rio Hondo Trail

Like the crossing of the Rio Grande at Taos Junction Bridge, the river crossing at the present John Dunn Bridge was determined by topography. On the east side of the river, the Rio Hondo cuts its way through the village of Arroyo Hondo to empty into the Rio Grande. Its grade is steady, and its canyon provides a natural, though rugged, avenue from the upper mesas of Taos Valley to the river in the gorge below.

In April 1854, a major U.S. military expedition against the Jicarilla Apaches crossed the river at this point. Commanded by Lieutenant Colonel Philip St. George Cooke from Fort Union, near Watrous, New Mexico, and accompanied by Kit Carson, the troops started from Taos, crossed the river at the mouth of the Rio Hondo, and turned southwest to Servilleta Plaza and Ojo Caliente. The easy part, down the Rio Hondo Canyon, was still a "difficult canyon for the passage of troops."[15] The steep ascent out of the gorge on the west side of the river was much more perilous.

Carson described it vividly:

> The Del Norte River [Rio Grande] was high but it had to be crossed. The bed of the river is full of large rocks and, in crossing, the horses would be sometimes only to their knees in the water and then have to step off of a rock. They would be over their backs and would necessarily have some trouble in ascending the next rock . . . . We had now to ascend from the river. The canyon is at the lowest calculation 600 feet high, but, by leading the animals cautiously through the different windings of the trail, we ascended.[16]

Until the 1830s, this route was likely used almost exclusively for commerce with Indian tribes to the northwest. Small groups of Taos traders—whether Spanish or Indian—traveled by foot or horseback, perhaps accompanied by pack animals. The trail described by Carson in 1854 would have been perfectly adequate for their needs. The lure of profit probably drew small trading parties northwest (even if illegally) much more than surviving documents show. This river crossing was the only direct way to get there.

Shortly after the Denver and Rio Grande Railroad built its narrow-gauge line on the west side of the river in 1880, a bridge was built and the trail was improved to allow wagons to go safely up and down the west side of the gorge. The railroad stations closest to the bridge were at Servilleta and Tres Piedras, about eight to ten miles away. They were the primary links between Taos and the railroad from 1880 until the first Taos Junction Bridge was built in 1914.

To the North: Artery of the Fur Trade

Before 1876, there was only one primary road north out of Taos Valley, known sometimes as the Spanish Road and sometimes as the Taos Road. Well into the twentieth century this route was also known by locals as the Trappers Trail and at times the Kiowa Trail. However, these later names do not appear in the historical record.

The Spanish Road was an Indian trail connecting Taos Pueblo with Indians to the north. At different times various side trails branched off and braided back into the main route. The road continued to be used for trading with native tribes throughout the Spanish occupation. Neither before nor after Spanish colonization was commerce with the north as heavy as that with the south, and the area north of Taos, at least before 1800, was probably dangerous for small groups of traders. The Utes and Navajos could not always be counted on for a friendly welcome.

Most traces of this trail disappeared long ago. Its route south must have been easy from the vicinity of San Luis, Colorado, to Questa. From Questa to Taos travel was much more difficult. Steep mountain ridges run east to west and extend all the way to the Rio Grande Gorge. To find the easiest way, both Indians and Spaniards had to take a route that ran well east of the river. Because of that, the Spanish Road entered Taos Valley near the site of Turley Mill, rather than closer to the Rio Grande at Arroyo Hondo. Near Turley Mill the Spanish Road crossed the Rio Hondo and went directly to Taos Pueblo.

American fur trappers began to use the Spanish Road after Mexico gained its independence from Spain in 1821. Until that date, Spanish colonial policy prohibited any trade with the French, English, or Americans based in St. Louis. Newly independent Mexico, in need of the benefits of trade, welcomed traders. As a result of this change of trade policy, the Santa Fe Trail from Missouri to Santa Fe became a major commercial route. This is the colorful period when Taos became the fur trade center of the southern Rockies.[17]

As early as 1824—and likely before that—both fur companies and independent trappers used Taos as a base for trapping expeditions to the north. Taos was much closer than St. Louis to the central Rockies. Supplies could be brought more cheaply by wagon from Missouri over the Santa Fe Trail than by pack trains up the Platte River. Many trapping expeditions went north to the best fur country and returned to Taos with their catches, and some traders from Taos attended the Rocky Mountain Rendezvous, an annual trade fare in southern Wyoming, to sell their pelts at cheaper prices than their St. Louis competitors. Fur companies opened stores in Taos to buy furs and equip trappers. In addition, the lure of Taos as a comparatively comfortable and permanent base in the Rockies caused many trappers and traders to settle permanently in Taos. Thus the Spanish Road became the "trappers trail" north from Taos in the years after 1821 when Taos was an important Western fur trading center. It continued to be used primarily for that purpose until the late 1830s. After the beginning of immigrant traffic on the Oregon Trail in 1841, Taos traders also used the Spanish Road to bring supplies to needy pioneers. From Taos they took horses, mules, food, wagon parts, and many other items to sell or trade at Fort Laramie on the North Platte River. They made good profits and often stopped to trap on the way back to Taos.

The fur trade was also responsible for one of the most interesting business operations in Taos Valley, Turley Mill, built about 1830. The mill was the residence and business location of Simeon Turley, one of Taos Valley's best-known fur trade suppliers and distillers. It was certainly no accident that Turley built his establishment where the Spanish Trail crossed the Rio Hondo. Turley's most celebrated product, an extremely potent liquor or *aguardiente* later named Taos Lightning, was in great demand as a trade item throughout the mountains.

TRAILS TO THE EAST: LOCAL ENTERPRISE AND TRADE

The Sangre de Cristo Mountains east of Taos Valley were an almost impassable barrier to the eastern plains of New Mexico. But as in the north and south, Taos Pueblo and Spanish interests required contact with this remote area. Routes of travel—extremely difficult ones—were created to answer economic imperatives.

Before Spanish colonization, Taos Pueblo traded with tribes on the Eastern Plains. This trade benefited both groups. The Plains dwellers needed agricultural products from Taos Pueblo, and in return they offered tanned hides, tallow, and other items desired at the pueblo.

The routes used for this commerce are uncertain. The map shows two such trails east. One trail ran up the Rio Pueblo from Taos Pueblo. It crossed the divide to Moreno Valley over Apache Pass. Of course, foot traffic probably took many routes, depending on the season and other factors. The second trail followed the Rio Fernando from Taos Valley to what is now Valle Escondido. It is labeled the Rio Fernando Trail on the map. At Valle Escondido, this trail divided. One branch went northeast and crossed into Moreno Valley over Apache Pass. From there its route is uncertain. It probably followed the general course of the present power line east over the high mesas to Rayado. From there, traders went wherever they thought their customers might be. As agricultural production increased after Spanish occupation, trade using these trails undoubtedly increased. Unregulated and often illegal, particularly the lucrative trade in slaves or captives, trade was undertaken by individual entrepreneurs, farmers, and craftsmen, with a few animals carrying relatively small amounts of grain or other goods. It must have been more profitable to go east to the customers than to wait for the possibility that the customers would come to Taos.

This commerce is another example of the enterprise and courage of Taos Valley residents. The distances were sometimes immense, often extending into Oklahoma and Texas. Especially after Comanches began raiding the colony in the early 1700s the danger to private traders with small amounts of goods would hardly seem worth the risk. We have no documents to reveal the economic impact of trade between Taos Valley and the Eastern Plains, but many Pueblo and Spanish Taoseños saw trade with the Comanches as more profitable than that in markets closer to home, and this commerce continued in various forms until the mid-1800s.

After 1821, these trails served a different but very important purpose. St. Louis merchants used them as a smuggling route to Taos from the Santa Fe Trail. Wagons could not be used, but pack trains could. When wagons on the Santa Fe Trail reached either the Rock Crossing of the Canadian River or the Rayado River, goods were transferred from wagons to mules. The now-lighter wagons proceeded to Santa Fe, paying lower import duties. The mules were taken over Apache Pass to Taos, the goods they carried hidden from local officials. This smuggling practice made Taos the "unofficial" terminus for some of the Santa Fe Trail trade. It also made Taos the favorite location for American merchants. Unfortunately, the open and blatant violation of Mexican law by both American and local traders planted seeds of discontent and envy. It undoubtedly contributed to the intensity of the 1847 revolt against American authority in Taos.

For enthusiasts of history there is another, special dimension to the study of these historic trails. Because of Taos geography, parts of the old trails still exist. Standing on these traces today, we can experience some of what the historic figures may have felt when they entered the Taos Valley. We see the same vistas today as Don Diego de Vargas did when he was descending Miranda Canyon in the 1690s, as Fray Alonso de Benavides did when he came into the valley from Picurís in 1776, and as Spanish colonists beheld upon entering the valley on the Camino Real. We can literally walk in the footsteps of those who came to Taos before us.

NOTES

1. Herbert E. Bolton, *Coronado on the Turquoise Trail* (Albuquerque: University of New Mexico Press, 1949), 309–10.

2. Rick Hendricks and John P. Wilson, *The Navajos in 1705* (Albuquerque: University of New Mexico Press, 1996), 10–11.

3. George P. Hammond and Agapito Rey, eds. *Narratives of the Coronado Expedition 1540–1542* (Albuquerque: University of New Mexico Press, 1940), 244–45.

4. George P. Hammond and Agapito Rey, eds. *Don Juan de Oñate: Colonizer of New Mexico, 1595–1628.* (Albuquerque: University of New Mexico Press, 1953), 320–21.

5. Ruth Marie Colville, *La Vereda: A Trail Through Time* (Alamosa, CO: San Luis Valley Historical Society, 1996), xiii–xxvii.

6. Hendricks and Wilson, *Navajos,* 13–15.

7. Alfred Barnaby Thomas, *Forgotten Frontiers* (Norman: University of Oklahoma Press, 1935), 139.

8. Michael McNierney, *Taos 1847* (Boulder, CO: Johnson Publishing Company, 1980), 45–53.

9. James A. Bennett, *Forts and Forays: A Dragoon in New Mexico*, Clinton E. Brooks and Frank D. Reeve, eds. (1948. Reprint: Albuquerque: University of New Mexico Press, 1995), 53–54.

10. Helen G. Blumenshein, "Historic Roads and Trails to Taos," *El Palacio* 75: 1 (Spring 1968), 9–19.

11. Francis T. Cheetham, "El Camino Militar," *New Mexico Historical Review* 15:1 (January 1940), 10.

12. Surveys of the Gijosa and Cristobal de la Serna Land Grants (microfiche of original documents). Bureau of Land Management Regional Office, Taos, NM.

13. Blumenschein, "Historic Trails," 12–13; U.S. Geological Survey "Taos and Vicinity" quad, 1936.

14. Blumenschein, "Historic Roads," 17.

15. Harvey L. Carter, *Dear Old Kit: The Historical Christopher Carson* (Norman: University of Oklahoma Press, 1968), 136.

16. Ibid.

17. David J. Weber, *The Taos Trappers* (Norman: University of Oklahoma Press, 1968), 192–210.

SELECTED REFERENCES

Bannon, John Francis. *The Spanish Borderlands Frontier, 1531–1821.* 1970. Reprint, Albuquerque: University of New Mexico Press, 1974.

Benavides, Alonso de. *Fray Alonso de Benavides' Revised Memorial of 1634.* Ed. Frederick Webb Hodge, George P. Hammond, and Agapito Rey. Albuquerque: University of New Mexico Press, 1945.

Bennett, James A. *Forts and Forays: A Dragoon in New Mexico, 1850–1856.* Ed. Clinton E. Brooks and Frank D. Reeve. 1948. Reprint, Albuquerque: University of New Mexico Press, 1995.

Blumenschein, Helen G. "Historic Roads and Trails to Taos." *El Palacio* 75: 1 (Spring 1968).

Bolton, Herbert E. *Spanish Exploration in the Southwest, 1542–1706.* New York: Charles Scribner's Sons, 1916.

———. *Coronado on the Turquoise Trail: Knight of Pueblos and Plains.* Albuquerque: University of New Mexico Press, 1949.

Carter, Harvey L. *Dear Old Kit: The Historical Christopher Carson.* Norman: University of Oklahoma Press, 1968.

Cheetham, Francis T. "El Camino Militar." *New Mexico Historical Review* 15:1 (January 1940).

Colville, Ruth Marie. *La Vareda: A Trail Through Time.* Alamosa, CO: San Luis Valley Historical Society, 1996.

Garrard, Lewis H. [Hector Lewis Garrard]. *Wah-to-yah and the Taos Trail.* 1850. Reprint Norman: University of Oklahoma Press, 1955.

Goetzmann, William H. *Exploration and Empire.* New York: Alfred A. Knopf, 1966.

Gregg, Kate L. *The Road to Santa Fe.* Albuquerque: University of New Mexico Press, 1952.

Hafen, LeRoy R. *The Mountain Men and Fur Trade of the Far West.* 10 vols. Glendale, CA: Arthur H. Clark, 1965–72.

———, ed. *Ruxton of the Rockies.* Norman: University of Oklahoma Press, 1950.

Hammond, George P., and Agapito Rey. *Don Juan de Oñate, Colonizer of New Mexico, 1595–1628.* 2 vols. Albuquerque: University of New Mexico Press, 1953.

———, eds. *Narratives of the Coronado Expedition, 1540–1542.* Albuquerque: University of New Mexico Press, 1940.

Hendricks, Rick, and John P. Wilson. *The Navajos in 1705.* Albuquerque: University of New Mexico Press, 1996.

Jackson, Donald, ed. *The Journals of Zebulon Montgomery Pike.* Norman: University of Oklahoma Press, 1966.

Kenner, Charles L. *A History of New Mexican-Plains Indian Relations.* Norman: University of Oklahoma Press, 1969.

Kessell, John, and Rick Hendricks, eds. *By Force of Arms: The Journals of Don Diego de Vargas, 1691–1693.* Albuquerque: University of New Mexico Press, 1992.

Martinez, Wilfred. *Anza and Cuerno Verde: Decisive Battle.* 2nd ed. Pueblo, CO: El Escritorio, 2004.

McNierney, Michael. *Taos 1847.* Boulder, CO: Johnson Publishing Co., 1980.

Oliva, Leo E. *Soldiers on the Santa Fe Trail.* Norman: University of Oklahoma Press, 1967.

Perkins, James E. *Tom Tobin, Frontiersman.* Pueblo West, CO: Herodotus Press, 1999.

Simmons, Marc. *The Last Conquistador.* Norman: University of Oklahoma Press, 1991.

Thomas, Alfred Barnaby. *After Coronado: Spanish Exploration Northeast of New Mexico, 1696–1727.* Norman: University of Oklahoma Press, 1935.

———. *Forgotten Frontiers: A Study of the Spanish Indian Policy of Don Juan Bautista de Anza, Governor of New Mexico, 1751–1778.* Norman: University of Oklahoma Press, 1932.

Twitchell, Ralph E. *Leading Facts of New Mexican History.* 5 vols. Cedar Rapids, IA: Torch Press, 1911–17.

Weber, David J. *The Taos Trappers: The Fur Trade in the Southwest, 1540–1846.* Norman: University of Oklahoma Press, 1968.

❖ 4 ❖

Taos' Early Trade Economy

Elizabeth Cunningham and Skip Keith Miller

The Taos Valley has always been a commerce and trade nexus. The network of trails so skillfully plotted by Indians in the Taos Valley were conduits of commerce long before Europeans reached the valley and were essential to establishing and maintaining Taos' reputation as an important trading center for hundreds of years. The story of Taos' trade economy is an exciting account of imagination, ingenuity, energy, courage, and, above all, change. Pueblo Indians, Plains Indians, Spanish settlers, Mexican government officials and Mexican traders, French and American trappers, traders, and military men—all were involved. Comanche Indians, always ready to jump on an opportunity, played a largely destabilizing role that added to the dynamic nature of the trade fairs.

CONNECTED TO THE OUTSIDE WORLD by trails that fanned out in all directions, the native inhabitants of the Taos Valley had established a center for trade perhaps 300 years before the Spanish *entrada* in 1540.[1] In fact, from prehistoric times the isolated valley at the base of the Sangre de Cristo Mountains had been the site of contact and exchange among many diverse peoples. Early reports, substantiated by archaeological finds, offer evidence that commerce between Plains tribes and the Rio Grande pueblos—including

Fiesta de San Gerónimo, Pueblo de Taos, 30° de Setiembre 1885.

Taos Pueblo on September 30, 1885, the feast of San Gerónimo, patron saint of the pueblo's Catholic mission church. The celebration coincided with the annual autumn Taos trade fair, which had always drawn great numbers of Plains Indians and Navajos before the onset of winter. Photo Southwest Research Center, Taos.

Taos—was constant for centuries. Items available at the pueblos differed, and so did the Plains "customers" for various pueblos' products. In economic terms, Taos Pueblo Indians were the primary source of trade items and were the major customers of the nomadic tribes of the area that is now northern New Mexico, southern Colorado, and probably even Oklahoma. Rivaling Taos Pueblo as a trade center for this vibrant Indian commerce was Pecos Pueblo, sited at the southern end of the Sangre de Cristos just east of the dividing ridge. In the early 1600s the tribes living in northeast New Mexico and southern Colorado likely favored trading at Taos. More southerly tribes would likely have looked to Pecos, which was larger than Taos.

Bison (buffalo) hunting probably first brought the Plains Indians into contact with Taos Pueblo, and this led to the pueblo's becoming a leading trade center for bison products—tanned hides and robes, jerked (dried) meat, and tallow. The exact mix of trade in Taos at this time is still not known. Agricultural staples that were cultivated in northern New Mexico—corn, beans, and piñon nuts—were prized by the semi-nomadic Plains Indians. In the fall of 1599, while exploring eastward from the first Spanish base in Nuevo México, San Juan de los Caballeros, Oñate's nephew, Vicente de Zaldívar, encountered Indians from Taos and Picurís returning from the Plains with bison hides, meat, tallow, suet, and salt. Zaldívar noted that they had traded cotton blankets, or *mantas,* pottery, corn, and small green stones.[2] The blankets and turquoise ("green stones") must have come from the southern Rio Grande pueblos; these items were never produced at Taos or Picurís. Another account by Zaldívar describes Plains traders, probably Apaches, as they followed roaming bison with their pack dogs dragging hides, meat, and tents on *travois.*[3] These Plains traders set up camp and traded their wares for corn, blankets, and probably other items.

Of all the Rio Grande pueblos, Taos had the closest ties with the Plains Indians, whose bows, arrows, lances, moccasins, and buckskin clothing Taos adopted. It also adapted Plains ceremonies, such as the Buffalo Dance and the War Dance, and in certain rhythms and song lines one can hear Plains qualities in songs still sung at Taos Pueblo. Yet, although the Pueblos and Plains tribes had a long history of interaction and contact, cultural influences were considerably short of acculturation.

Because of population movements and intertribal conflicts on the Eastern Plains, Taos' Plains trading partners changed many times. Some of the changes, as we will see later, taxed the strength and ingenuity of both Taos Pueblo Indians and their Spanish neighbors. But Taos survived, and its importance grew. Pecos, by contrast, did neither.

The Spanish settlers of the early 1600s were subsistence farmers not traders, but their domestic items would have been attractive to Taos Pueblo's people. Likewise, the Pueblo Indians had items the settlers needed. Spanish presence also expanded the types of goods available for trade to Plains Indians. It is reasonable to assume that the volume of trade at Taos increased from the early 1600s to the Pueblo Revolt of 1680. For much of the seventeenth century, trade at Taos was probably "local" in the sense that items obtained by trade from Plains tribes were primarily used in the Taos Valley by Pueblo and Spanish farmers. Correspondingly, items traded to the Plains Indians were likely produced at the pueblo and by settlers of the valley.

While the Taos Indian trade was important for the survival of the Spanish farming families in the Taos Valley, the economic potential of trade caught the eye of the colony's officials in Santa Fe. In the 1600s the Spanish governors and other officials tried as much as possible to use the Plains trade to their own advantage. In fact, some of the only items for profitable export to Mexico or even Spain were obtained through trade with the Plains peoples. In this early period, Spanish officials focused primarily on Pecos. We do not know the extent of Santa Fe's impact in altering the structure or content of commerce in Taos. It is highly likely that Spanish interest in hides and the slave trade would have increased such traffic in Taos, as it did farther south.

Before 1680, four or five *estancias* were established by Spanish farmers away from the pueblo.[4] We do not know if the Spanish settlers in the Taos Valley economically exploited the Taos Indians to the extent done farther south along the Rio Grande. There, certain Spanish officials—both secular and religious—forced Indians to work for them and appropriated significant percentages of Indians' agricultural yield under the practice of *encomienda*. Much of that was used for trade. Economic exploitation at Taos was probably limited for three reasons: the small size of the Spanish population in the valley, Taos Pueblo's protection of Spanish settlers from hostile Indian raiders, and Taos' distance from Santa Fe's military garrison.

Taos as Nuevo México's Strategic Trade Center

Both before and after reconquest in the 1690s, major changes began which would vastly increase the economic and strategic importance of the Taos trade. First, there was gradually increasing commerce along the Camino Real, the main artery between La Nueva España and its provincial northern territory. Opened in 1598 by New Mexico's founder and first governor, Don Juan de Oñate, the Camino Real originated in Mexico City, coursed northward in Mexico through Chihuahua, passed the sites of present-day El Paso, Las Cruces, Albuquerque, Santo Domingo Pueblo, to San Juan Pueblo (later to nearby Santa Fe), with a northern extension to Taos. At first, in the early seventeenth century, mission and merchant caravans left Mexico not oftener than every three years, bringing settlers, newly appointed Franciscan friars, livestock, agricultural products, tools, and furnishings for settlers and the Catholic missions of northern New Mexico. In time, their frequency increased. More Spanish goods came, primarily for an expanding population of colonists but also useful for trade. New Mexico was not well endowed with export products, however. By the early 1700s, dreams of vast mineral wealth had largely faded, and there were few local industries.

But the demand in Mexico for hides, tanned leather skins, live sheep, piñon nuts, and slaves—already an established part of the Taos trade—could still yield substantial profit. Slaves were Indians who had been kidnapped and sold by Indians. Caravans, called *conductas,* were organized on an annual basis, usually leaving Taos in late October or early November in order to reach Mexico by mid-December. Merchants took their families with them, which was safer than leaving them at unprotected homes and which swelled the number of travelers to a safe mass of hundreds as they passed through Apache country on their way to Mexico. The return trips afforded new settlers comparatively safe passage to the upper Rio Grande.

A second factor in the growth of Taos trade in the early 1700s was a revolutionary change in Taos Pueblo's Plains trading partners. Before 1700, Taos attracted various tribes of Apaches. Although mounted, these Apaches were not particularly warlike; some were semi-agricultural. Within two decades after 1700, these Apaches had either been killed or displaced by Comanche migrating south along the Front Range of the Rockies. The Comanche had emerged as a distinctive tribe of about a dozen separate groups in the late 1600s when they broke away from the Shoshone Indians of the Northern Plains and intermountain West. They acquired Spanish horses at Taos Pueblo and quickly integrated a mounted way of life. Horses allowed them to migrate, augmented their skills as hunters, and made them formidable warriors. Their numbers increased dramatically, in part through the taking of women and children prisoners. By 1730, Comanches dominated in northeastern New Mexico and what is today the Texas Panhandle. Also present at this time were Navajos from the north and northwest. Their hunters were highly skilled and could produce many more hides for trade than had ever been available. But managing trade with these more aggressive tribes, most of whom would rather raid than barter, was a major challenge.

Third, the new nomadic Indian arrivals posed a military threat not just to the Spanish but to the Pueblo peoples as well. Before the Pueblo Revolt, Pecos had been the main port of entry for Plains products into the Rio Grande Valley. But after 1700 Pecos was vulnerable. Comanches raided Pecos relentlessly, stealing, killing, and taking captives rather than trading. By 1730, Pecos could no longer function as a trade center. Taos was not as physically susceptible to attack as Pecos. The valley's Spanish settlers also added substantially to its defense, and although Comanche and other nomadic tribes raided Taos when they could, they also traded. Perhaps they learned that Taos was too strong to destroy. And they must also have realized that the Pueblo-Spanish population of the valley made good customers for their hides, skins, and slaves.

After reconquest by Vargas, finally completed in 1696 in Taos, threats from hostile Indians forced the Spanish and the Taos Pueblo people to recognize that their economic and physical survival depended on cooperation. Taos was the strongest and closest pueblo to the hunting grounds of these newer Indian populations. Comanches and others, having begun to trade at Taos, could be persuaded to trade even more. Ensuring regular trade fairs at Taos was a critical protective tool for the Taos Pueblo people, and Spanish officials could use the fairs to give these dangerous tribes incentives to trade, not attack, for what they needed. It could also increase the Plains products available to the Spanish for domestic use or—more important to officials—for export to Mexico.

The first report of Comanche trading at Taos was in 1705. These fierce Plains warriors became Taos' most important Plains trading partners until the end of Spanish rule in 1821. By the 1720s the governor in Santa Fe and the Taos Indians had negotiated with the Comanche specific times of the year for peaceful trade fairs at Taos, although at times the Comanche would return to the Taos Valley after the fairs were over to raid.[5] For the most part, however, the closely run Taos trade fairs successfully increased commerce and lessened the Comanche threat to the colony. Without the Taos trade fairs, the Comanche onslaught in the rest of New Mexico might have come many years before it did.

The fair was a yearly event (and later, several times a year) which originally took place in July or August. Its dates varied from year to year, according to moon phases. The site, it is believed, was the many-acre grasslands known later as Los Estiércoles, now El Prado. Apache, Ute, and Comanche lodges and tipis filled the field—as many as two hundred at the height of the fairs—along with Spanish friars, colonists, soldiers, captive Indians, and even on occasion the colony's governor or lieutenant governor. In a letter to Mexico City in 1750, Governor Tomás Vélez Cachupín (1749–54 and 1762–67) explained the nature and price of trade with the Comanches:

> Although the Comanche nation carries on a trade relation with us, coming to the pueblo of Taos, where they hold their fairs and trade in skins and Indians of various nations, whom they enslave in their wars, for horses, mares, mules, hunting knives, and other trifles, always, whenever the occasion offers for stealing horses or attacking the Pueblos of Pecos or Galisteo they do not pass it up.[6]

In 1754 Vélez Cachupín wrote instructions to Spanish officials in Don Fernando de Taos advising them to maintain friendship with the Indians because of the trade benefits to the people of the province. He emphasized the settlers' dependence on trading for hides, which in turn they used to purchase goods for their families. The economic interdependence between the Plains Indians, Taos Valley settlers, and Taos Pueblo had become a fact of life. When there was war, trade suffered. And without trade the Spanish in northern Nuevo México could not survive.

Vélez Cachupín also outlined the peace policy he had carefully crafted between the Spanish and Taos Pueblo on one side and the Comanches and Utes on the other. In order to have successful trade fairs at Taos, peacefully attended by the Plains tribes, all participants needed guarantees of safety as well as the prospect of good trading. He urged the Spanish officials in Taos to protect the Comanches at the fairs and to administer fair justice whenever settlers took advantage of the Indians. He emphasized the importance of the governor's attendance at the fairs, knowing that his presence would quickly settle any altercations that arose. Lack of protection at the Taos trade fairs by the previous governor had created resentment among the Comanches, who had resumed attacks on both Spanish settlers and the Pueblo people in the valley.[7]

Vélez Cachupín also set trade standards that lasted, with minor changes, through the remainder of the 1700s. He fixed values for both Comanche and Spanish trade items. For example, a Comanche tanned bison hide was worth one Spanish broad knife. Two bison robes could be exchanged for a lower quality bridle decorated with red trade cloth. A Comanche-owned, French-made pistol brought a better quality Spanish bridle.[8] High values were placed on slaves; an Indian girl captive was worth a she-mule and scarlet trade cloth, or two good horses with such trifles as a short cloak or riding cloth thrown in.

Thus Spanish diplomacy kept the vital trade pattern at Taos fairly stable during the first half of the 1700s. Taos, not Pecos, was now the port of entry for most Plains Indian goods. It appears that all parties—settlers, Taos Pueblo Indians, Spanish officials, and the Plains tribes—benefited. During this period, however, Spanish officials not only had to manage peace with their Indian trading partners, but they encountered a new political threat from the northeast, the French.

THE TAOS TRADE AND SPANISH GEOPOLITICS

The Taos trade in northern Nuevo México may appear quite remote from Spanish interests in international politics in the early eighteenth century. Not so; they were closely linked. In the first half of the 1700s, Spain, France, and Great Britain all were competing to expand and protect their empires in North America. One of the most important reasons Spain recolonized Nuevo México after the 1680 Pueblo Revolt was to place a Spanish barrier between other powers and the rich silver mines in northern México. Nuevo México, in fact, had many more Spanish colonists than did the areas comprising Arizona, California, or Texas—all part of the La Nueva España. Until 1763, when the French ceded the Louisiana territory to Spain, maintaining its Nuevo México colony was as important to Spain for geopolitical as for economic reasons.

Viewed in political terms, Taos was the northern tip of the Spanish Empire in the New World. Its protection was therefore always of great political importance in Mexico City, and the French particularly were viewed as a threat by Spanish officials. In the early 1700s French trade goods began to appear at the Taos fairs through Plains Apaches, who had taken or traded for them from the Pawnee in present-day central Nebraska. (The Pawnees obtained goods from French traders in the Platte or Missouri River valleys.) The trade items of special concern were French guns, gunpowder, and other weapons. Ironically, the shortage of firearms in the colony made Spanish settlers dependent on trade with Apaches and Comanche for the very weapons they needed to defend themselves against those same tribes.

Rumors began to reach Santa Fe about French traders establishing permanent trading or military posts along the Platte River and, while never substantiated, these stories raised great alarm. The Spanish reacted in four ways. First, as described above, they intensified efforts to solidify trade with the Plains tribes. Keeping those groups more dependent on trade with Nuevo México than with the French or Pawnees, the Spanish reasoned, would help keep the peace. The Taos trade fairs were the primary tool of Mexico City's economic policy to keep French trade influence at bay.

Second, Spanish officials used the Taos trade fairs as a diplomatic opportunity to forge more structured alliances with the Plains tribes. If this could be done, the Indian groups would have less incentive to shift trade to the French or join the French in an assault on the colony. This appears to have been fairly successful and is a great credit to the diplomatic skills of some Spanish officials. The Plains tribes continued to depend on the Nuevo México trade, of which the Taos fairs were the primary instrument. The feared French threat never materialized.

Third, the Spanish took military steps to gain intelligence about French intentions. The first such Spanish military effort took place in 1706, when Juan de Ulibarrí led a large force of Spanish soldiers and Indian auxiliaries from Taos into eastern New Mexico, then north into southeastern Colorado. Ulibarrí found no French, but the Plains Apaches he met added to the rumors of French traders farther north on the Platte River. While having no military impact, Ulibarrí probably impressed the Apaches he met with the power of Spain. Politically, his expedition had a positive result.

Spain's most ambitious military expedition to the northeast was the biggest military disaster in the colony's history. In 1720, a Spanish force looking for the French got as far north as the Platte River. There they were ambushed by Pawnees and Frenchmen and almost wiped out. This led to panic in Santa Fe, renewed requests for additional troops, and the establishment of a fort on the eastern side of the Sangre de Cristos. Spain's refusal of these requests helped ensure that the Taos fairs remained one of the colony's most important economic and political buttresses in protecting its northern frontier and is one of the reasons Pecos's trade fairs withered.

Finally, Spanish authorities simply arrested French traders and confiscated their goods. After serving their sentences they usually were returned to the Mississippi Valley. Although the once-feared French military threat to the colony never materialized, French traders did enter Nuevo México. The first recorded appearance in Taos was in 1739. Two French brothers, Pierre and Paul Mallet, traveled to Taos from Illinois to trade. They and many others were arrested and returned home. Certainly some did succeed in bringing valuable goods to Taos and returning with handsome profits. The inventory of merchandise seized from two French traders by Governor Vélez Cachupín in 1752 lists goods used in the North American interior in the mid-eighteenth century. Among the more unusual or expensive items were fabrics of flowered silk, muslin, laces, and black silk lace. More common fabrics included various kinds of woolen material, linen cloth, and "spotted" and bordered white or brown cotton fabric, along with various colors of ribbon. Articles of clothing included beaver hats, woolen and cotton caps, shoes, gloves, and handkerchiefs of cotton and silk.[9]

After 1763, the year France had to cede Louisiana to Spain at the end of the French and Indian War, any possible French political threat vanished. The role of the Taos fairs in eighteenth-century geopolitics ended successfully. French, English, or American traders penetrating the colony thereafter posed economic, not political, challenges.

Nuevo México at Bay: The Comanche Onslaught

By 1760 the balance of economic and military interests so skillfully maintained by the Spanish between the Comanche and Rio Grande Valley residents began to unravel. This did not happen because of an alliance between the French and the Comanche against the colony, as the Spanish had feared for years. It appears to have happened because of the growing power, including French guns, of the Comanche themselves.

During these years, efforts throughout northern Nuevo México to maintain Comanche dependence on the Taos trade continued, but raiding increased dramatically. It is not clear why Comanche behavior changed. Because there were a good number of different Comanche groups, it was impossible to communicate or negotiate for peace with them as an entire tribal nation. Perhaps there were trade grievances on the part of some of the Comanche groups. Possibly leadership changes among the raiders produced more warlike leaders. Or maybe Comanche numbers increased to the point where they felt strong enough to simply take what they needed. But whatever the reasons, the years between 1760 and 1781 were essentially two decades of war with this very formidable foe.

On August 4, 1760, a very large Comanche war party attacked in the Taos Valley. Settlers took refuge in a large *estancia* "which stood in the middle of the plain" belonging to a family named Villalpando.[10] The raiders killed many settlers, stole livestock, and kidnapped numerous women and children who had taken refuge there. An account of 1776 kept alive the memory of Villalpando's wife's bravery: "Seeing that they were breaking down the outside door, [she] went to defend it with a lance, and they killed her fighting."[11] With the consent of the Taos Indians, some thirty-six families of settlers were living at the pueblo for protection, according to the 1760 account of visiting Bishop Pedro Tamarón of

Durango, Mexico.[12] In 1772 Governor Pedro Fermin de Mendinueta (1767–77) reported another major attack on Taos. In addition to large organized attacks like these, both Taos and other settlements were hit with frequent small raids. By the end of the 1760s, losses of livestock, agricultural products, and Pueblo and settler lives began to offset the benefits of any peaceful trade with the Plains tribes, and the advantages of the Comanche trade were gone.

These two decades were the most critical time in the post-*reconquista* history of the Spanish in northern Nuevo México. Much reduced trade, along with mounting losses to the Plains raiders, created an economic and military crisis. Because of the small numbers of Spanish soldiers and Pueblo warriors, settlers could not be protected. Small remote settlements, like the *ranchos*, were abandoned, and settlers moved to larger centers such as Santa Fe, Taos, and the lower Rio Grande pueblos. Agricultural production dropped. In more populated areas, including those in the Taos Valley, settlers were ordered to leave their small *ranchitos* and build fortified plazas where they could be defended. Two such plazas built under this policy—Las Trampas de Taos (Ranchos de Taos) and Plaza del Cerro in Chimayó—are still partly extant.

GOVERNOR DE ANZA, THE COMANCHE PEACE, AND THE TRADE FAIRS

In 1778 Juan Bautista de Anza became governor. He carried out a brilliant three-part strategy to restore security and the Indian trade. A year after his arrival in Nuevo México, Anza (1778–88) launched a mounted expedition of 600 troops against the fierce Comanche leader Cuerno Verde (Green Horn). In the Front Range of the Rockies in present-day southern Colorado, they killed the Comanche chief, his son, and many of his warriors. In 1781 Anza's troops repulsed Comanche attacks in Nuevo México with such force that the Indians solicited for peace at Taos Pueblo. Finally, in 1786, Anza negotiated a lasting truce with the Comanche in Nuevo México, the Comanche Peace.

Anza's second strategy was to restart peaceful and regular commerce. He granted a Comanche request to reestablish the trade fairs at Taos and Pecos. To ensure peace at the trade fairs, close supervision by government officials was required. One summary describes the new rules:

> Then on the ground designated for the fair he marked out two lines so that the contracting parties, each positioned on the outside of one, could exhibit and hand over to each other in the space between whatever goods they had to exchange. With this arrangement, the presence of that chief [Governor Anza], the opportune positioning of troops, official overseers,

and the abolition of the abusive contributions that the latter used to charge the heathens as a fee for permission to trade, this fair took place in ideal calm and good order.[13]

Anza agreed to allow the Comanches to move closer to Nuevo México, but in return they were required to remain at peace with Spain and all of Spain's Indian allies. The governor also instituted two new policies. One granted the Comanches the right to air their grievances with the governor in Santa Fe. The second promised the Indians annual gifts. The latter strategy, as officials in Mexico City realized, cost less than what they were spending on sending more troops north.

Anza's successor, Governor Fernando de la Concha (1789–94), guarded the Comanche peace with the same fervor. Each spring when the caravans came up the Camino Real from Mexico to Santa Fe, the Indians would receive such items as brightly colored cloth, hats, shoes and other articles of clothing, bars of soap, mirrors, strings of beads, coral, cigarettes, and *piloncillos* (hard cones of raw brown sugar). Indeed the money spent on keeping the peace was a bargain compared to the cost of having to be at war with them.

Following the establishment of peace with the Comanches, a period of prosperity and growth took hold in which Nuevo México's barter system evolved toward a cash economy. The frequency and numbers of trade fairs increased, as noted by Governor Concha in 1789. Three months after taking office he wrote, "In the short time since my arrival, seven fairs have been held at the pueblo of Taos, a very considerable one at that of Pecos, and another at Picurís."[14]

This increase in trade warranted the establishment of a second annual caravan to Chihuahua. That same year Concha estimated that trade goods amounting to 30,000 pesos worth of livestock, fruit, and cotton and woolen textiles were sent south. A decade later, sheep and wool had become important trade items. *Churro* breed sheep, raised in Nuevo México, yielded three times the amount of wool compared to those in Mexico. The demand for them and their wool grew so much that in August of 1800 an unscheduled caravan was sent south, delivering over 200 cattle and nearly 19,000 *churro* sheep along with pelts and wool. On August 28, 1803, Governor Fernando de Chacón reported that 25,000 or 26,000 sheep were being exported each year to Chihuahua.[15]

Trade items of earlier years, such as hides and skins from the traditional Plains Indian fairs and piñon nuts and woolen textiles from the Pueblos, still appeared on manifests, but lists at the turn of the nineteenth century show the addition of domestic livestock such as oxen and sheep. The biggest difference was the variety of cloth goods that were woven by the Spanish settlers, such as cotton and wool blankets, *colchas* (embroidered cloth), *sayales* (sackcloth), and *medias* (woolen stockings). The *colchas*, known for their beautiful color and variety of design, were in high demand and were considered to be better than those made in Mexico.

The Comanche Peace, population growth among the settlers, and the increase in surplus products for trade brought growing prosperity to northern Nuevo México. The Taos trade fairs resumed their role, for a time at least, as a critical institution in the northern Nuevo México economy.

MEXICAN INDEPENDENCE AND THE END OF THE TRADE FAIRS

Mexican independence from Spain in 1821 accelerated the decline of the Taos trade fairs from their peak around 1800. Mexican officials, contrary to Spanish policy, welcomed American traders who crossed the plains from St. Louis. The Americans who ventured to the New Mexican capital from Missouri eventually were welcomed for two reasons: they brought items previously unavailable to northern Nuevo México, and they undercut by as much as two-thirds the prices merchants in Mexico were charging. With the opening of Santa Fe Trail in 1821, trade caravans from St. Louis mostly went to Santa Fe, and thus Santa Fe quickly replaced Taos, Picurís, and Pecos as the major trading center for goods from the East.

Manufactured goods from the Americans replaced animal skins for many purposes, so hides and other items the Comanches offered were no longer as desired as in the past. The Indians found it increasingly difficult to produce trade goods that could compete with the great variety of manufactured products suddenly arriving by the Santa Fe Trail. Their traditional role as middlemen was quickly disappearing.

Other historical forces were at work, including demographic change. Coincident with the rapid increase in Spanish population at the beginning of the nineteenth century was a dramatic population decline in the Plains tribes. Reoccurring waves of diseases, such as smallpox, took a huge toll on native populations. Furthermore, the growth of New Mexican villages in the early 1800s allowed the development of numerous small, locally established trade operations. The rise of a regional mercantile class within the scattered communities of northern Nuevo México began. The impact of this on the Taos trade fairs was profound. For example, around 1810, Severino Martínez opened the first trading post in Taos at his small hacienda in Ranchitos, a settlement about four miles distant from the village of Don Fernando de Taos. Built shortly after 1804, the Hacienda de los Martínez was a fortified dwelling with sufficient storage facilities to provide for year-round trading with Pueblos and settlers. By offering a continuous market for all manner of goods, Martínez exemplified the new style of trader who was to swiftly render the trade fairs obsolete.

In 1805 the Comanches left Nuevo México for the Canadian River area of Texas, taking their substantial business with them. The Indian gift fund, which had contributed to friendly trade with the allied tribes, was nearly exhausted by 1821. Without gifts, the tribes were not attracted to Santa Fe or Taos and sought trade opportunities elsewhere.

Although the Taos trade fair era died out, the relationships and trade patterns between the Indians and the settlers remained intact in the Taos Valley. Up until World War II descendants of the Spanish settlers and the Pueblo people still traded goods for services. The Feast Day of San Gerónimo, celebrated every September 30, is an audible echo of the Taos trade fairs, which were first mentioned in Spanish documents in 1723. Each fall, when Native Americans from all over the West come to Taos with their wares, the San Gerónimo Fiesta at Taos Pueblo rekindles some of the character and excitement of Taos' trade fairs past.

NOTES

1. This chapter is adapted from "Trade Fairs in Taos," by Elizabeth Cunningham and Skip Keith Miller, in *El Camino Real de Tierra Adentro,* Vol. 2, Cultural Resources Series, no. 13 (Santa Fe: New Mexico Bureau of Land Management), 1999. Early Spanish reports confirm that these trade patterns were well established when the first Spanish settlers entered the Taos Valley in the early 1600s.

2. Alfred Barnaby Thomas, *After Coronado: Spanish Exploration Northeast of New Mexico, 1696–1727,* 2nd ed. (Norman: University of Oklahoma Press, 1966), 7.

3. Ibid. Before the Spanish introduced horses, dogs were pack animals. They would be harnessed with a *travois*—a frame made of wood poles that splayed out where it touched the ground.

4. The names associated with these holdings are Lucero de Godoy, Domingo de Herrera, Francisco Gomez Robledo, Bartolome Romero, and Pablo Francisco Villalpando. See F. R. Bob Romero's chapter, "Land Grants: *Tierras de la gente,*" in this volume.

5. In 1723, by royal decree, the Spanish officially established annual trade fairs at both Taos and Pecos.

6. John L. Kessell, *Kiva, Cross and Crown: The Pecos Indians and New Mexico, 1540–1840,* 2nd ed. (Albuquerque: University of New Mexico Press, 1990), 357.

7. Elizabeth A. H. John, in her *Storms Brewed in Other Men's Worlds: The Confrontation of Indians, Spanish, and French in the Southwest, 1540–1796,* 2nd ed. (Norman: University of Oklahoma Press, 1996), 315–35, presents a balanced summary of Governor Vélez Cachupín's enlightened governance of the Comanches.

8. Eleanor B. Adams, ed. *Bishop Tamarón's Visitation of New Mexico, 1760* (Albuquerque: Historical Society of New Mexico, 1954), 56.

9. Cordelia Thomas Snow, "A Headdress of Pearls: Luxury Goods Imported over the Camino Real during the Seventeenth Century," in *El Camino Real de Tierra Adentro* (Santa Fe: New Mexico: Bureau of Land Management 1993), 69–76.

10. Francisco Atanasio Domínguez, *The Missions of New Mexico, 1776: A Description, with Other Contemporary Documents,* trans. and ann. by Eleanor B. Adams and Angélico Chávez (Albuquerque: University of New Mexico Press, 1951), 251. Estancias were large

holdings of land with irrigated farmlands and adjacent pastures found in the Rio Grande Valley in the seventeenth century. Later, as smaller holdings became more common, the terms *hacienda* and *rancho* came into use.

11. Adams, *Bishop Tamarón's Visitation,* 58.

12. Ibid., 57.

13. Kessell, *Kiva, Cross,* and Crown, 406.

14. Ibid., 408.

15. Ralph Emerson Twitchell, *The Spanish Archives of New Mexico.* vol. 2. Cedar Rapids (IA: Torch Press, 1914).

SELECTED REFERENCES

Adams, Eleanor B., ed. *Bishop Tamarón's Visitation of New Mexico, 1760.* Albuquerque: Historical Society of New Mexico, 1954.

Bailey, Jessie Bromilow. *Diego de Vargas and the Reconquest of New Mexico.* Albuquerque: University of New Mexico Press, 1940.

Bailey, L. R. *Indian Slave Trade in the Southwest.* Los Angeles, CA: Westernlore Press, 1966.

Baxter, John O. *Las Carneradas: Sheep Trade in New Mexico 1700–1860.* Albuquerque: University of New Mexico Press, 1987.

Domínguez, Francisco Atanasio. *Missions of New Mexico, 1776: A Description, With Other Contemporary Documents,* trans. and ann. by Eleanor B. Adams and Angélico Chávez. Albuquerque: University of New Mexico Press, 1951.

Frank, Ross Harold. "From Settler to Citizen: Economic Development and Cultural Change in Late Colonial New Mexico, 1750–1820." PhD diss., Berkeley: University of California, 1992.

Grant, Blanche C. *When Old Trails Were New: The Story of Taos.* New York: Press of the Pioneers, 1934. Reprint, Santa Fe: Sunstone Press, 2007.

Hammond, George P., ed. *The Plains Indians and New Mexico.* Albuquerque: University of New Mexico Press, 1940.

Ivey, James E. "Seventeenth-Century Mission Trade on the Camino Real." In *El Camino Real de Tierra Adentro.* Santa Fe: New Mexico Bureau of Land Management, 1993.

John, Elizabeth A. H. *Storms Brewed in Other Men's Worlds: The Confrontation of Indians, Spanish, and French in the Southwest, 1540–1795.* Norman: University of Oklahoma Press, 1996.

Kenner, Charles L. *A History of New Mexican-Plains Indian Relations.* Norman: University of Oklahoma Press, 1969.

Kessell, John L. *Kiva, Cross and Crown: The Pecos Indians and New Mexico, 1540–1840.* 2nd ed. Albuquerque: University of New Mexico Press, 1990.

Moorhead, Max L. *New Mexico's Royal Road: Trade and Travel on the Chihuahua Trail.* Norman: University of Oklahoma Press, 1958.

Scholes, France V. "Civil Government and Society in New Mexico in the Seventeenth Century." In *New Mexico Historical Review* X: 2 (April 1935).

Simmons, Marc. *Coronado's Land: Essays on Daily Life in Colonial New Mexico.* Albuquerque: University of New Mexico Press, 1991.

———. *New Mexico: A Bicentennial History.* The States and the Nation series. New York: W. W. Norton, 1977.

———. *Spanish Pathways: Readings in the History of Hispanic New Mexico.* Albuquerque: University of New Mexico Press, 2001.

Snow, Cordelia Thomas. "A Headdress of Pearls: Luxury Goods Imported over the Camino Real during the Seventeenth Century." In *El Camino Real de Tierra Adentro.* Santa Fe, NM: Bureau of Land Management, 1993.

Snow, David H. "Purchased in Chihuahua for Feasts." In *El Camino Real de Tierra Adentro.* Santa Fe, NM: Bureau of Land Management, 1993.

Sturtevant, William C., gen. ed. *Handbook of North American Indians.* Vol. 9, *The Southwest.* Alfonso Ortiz, ed. Washington, DC: Smithsonian Institution Press, 1979.

Thomas, Alfred Barnaby. *After Coronado: Spanish Exploration Northeast of New Mexico, 1696–1727.* 2nd ed. Norman: University of Oklahoma Press, 1966.

———. *The Plains Indians and New Mexico, 1751–1755.* Albuquerque: University of New Mexico Press, 1940.

Twitchell, Ralph Emerson. *The Spanish Archives of New Mexico.* 2 vols. Cedar Rapids, IA: Torch Press, 1914.

Woosley, Anne L. *Taos Archeology.* Fort Burgwin Research Center. Dallas, TX: Southern Methodist University, 1980.

❖ 5 ❖

Land Grants: *Tierras de la gente*

F. R. Bob Romero

From the earliest years of Spanish rule to the present day, perhaps no single subject has generated more passion and conflict in Taos than Spanish and Mexican land grants. Originally parceled out by Spanish colonial officials to encourage settlement, land grants later became a focus of those who were intent on acquiring title to vast holdings of Taos Valley land. The following chapter is an introduction to the history of these land grants. It also shows how differing interpretations of the language of the grants planted seeds of mistrust among many Taoseños, which, when disagreements arise, still threaten the stability of the community.

ALMOST EVERYONE WHO LIVES EAST of the Rio Grande in the Taos Valley resides on land that is or once was part of a grant of land made by the Spanish or Mexican governments. The awarding of land grants was the Spanish royal government's way of encouraging its subjects to settle and maintain lands claimed in the king's name in this remote margin of the empire. Grants also provided tangible yet nearly cost-free rewards for service to the royal government. After 1821, the Mexican government continued to award land grants. In all, the Spanish and Mexican governments made several hundred grants in the territory encompassed by the State of New Mexico.

The brief Mexican-American War ended Mexico's control of the area, with the formal peace Treaty of Guadalupe Hidalgo ratified by Congress on March 10, 1848. By 1850 New Mexico was an organized territory of the United States, and U.S. laws were applied to land ownership. To be recognized as legally valid, a land grant had to be patented by the U.S. government. Taos County has sixteen patented grants, including the eight Spanish grants in the Taos Valley.

Except for the pre-1680 grant to Taos Pueblo, all eight were issued between 1715 and 1815. Their legacy has deeply imprinted the history of Taos and still has a pervasive and complicating effect on land ownership, land tenure, land use, and water rights. Some land grant issues and disputes remain unresolved and continue to affect socioeconomic relationships among the various ethnic groups in the Taos Valley.[1]

LAND GRANTS

The Spanish government made land grants to pueblos, to individuals, and to groups of people. The earliest land grant in Taos Valley, to the Pueblo Indians of Taos, was made well before 1680 and is known as the Taos Pueblo League Grant. It is significant that the king of Spain made a land grant to each village (pueblo) of Indians "in order that it be conserved for the maintenance of its [people]; so that they have the use and can not give or sell without permission of the King." A particularly illustrative Spanish defense of Indian lands occurred as late as 1815, when Governor Alberto Maynez resisted three successive appeals from farmers residing and farming within the original Taos Pueblo League Grant. "Based upon the principle that their rights to the league which His Majesty granted them are incontestable," he wrote, "it is my opinion that the right is on their [the Indians'] side."[2] Every settled community of Pueblo Indians in the province was thus recognized by the Spanish, who from the establishment of pueblo land Grants and throughout their governance generally tried to defend the rights of the Indians against encroachment by Spanish settlers.

The Taos Pueblo League Grant measured 5,000 varas (a vara is a unit of measure equal to 33.33 inches, or 3 geometric feet) in each direction from "the cross in the [pueblo] cemetery" for a total of about 17,360.55 acres, or 27.125 square miles (see Table 1).[3] This grant of land around the pueblo village, guaranteed by the Spanish Crown, has been instrumental in upholding land claims by the Native Americans under all three governments.

Private land grants, known as *sitios*, were made to individuals—usually to reward service to the government, especially military service. With continuous occupation for a specified period of time, this land could become the private property of the grantee and could be sold. The third type is a community grant. Community grants were a very important and ingenious part of the Spanish and Mexican governments' strategy for settling and defending Nuevo México's mostly unpopulated frontier. Such a grant gave individual families a parcel of land they could irrigate and plant and on which they could build a house. The bulk of the grant, however, was reserved for shared community use: grazing stock, gathering wood, harvesting timber, hunting, and watering. While an individual parcel holder could acquire the parcel as private property by residing on it for a specified number of years, the community lands were to remain common property and were not supposed to be sold. Such is still the case with Indian reservation lands.

TABLE 1

Land Grants in the Taos Valley Confirmed
by Congress for Which Patents Were Issued

Name	Grantees	Date	Acres	Patented
Rancho del Rio Grande	10 families	1795	91,813.15	1909
Arroyo Hondo	44 families	1815	20,000.38	1908
Cristóbal de la Serna	C. de la Serna	1710/1715	22,232.57	1903
Francisca Antonia de Gijosa	F. A. de Gijosa	1715	16,240.64	1908
Antonio Martínez	Antonio Martínez	1716	61,605.48	1896
Don Fernando de Taos	63 families	1796	1,817.24	1909
Taos Pueblo League	Taos Pueblo Indians	pre-1680	17,360.00	1864
Antoine Leroux	Juan Bautista Pedro Vigil Vigil Y Santillano Cristóbal Vigil	1742	56,437.00	1911

Compiled from Rowena Martinez, Land Grants in Taos Valley, *Publication No. 2, Taos County Historical Society, Taos, New Mexico, 1968.*

Community grants were acquired through a formal process that began with a petition to the king's representative in Nuevo México, the governor in Santa Fe, for a specific type of grant, either private or community.[4] Typically an application declared that the petitioner had no land, or had insufficient land, to support a family.

The petitioner described the parcel desired, asserting that it was vacant land, and promised to settle and farm it according to the laws.

Actual possession of a grant of land had to be certified by an alcalde (a local governmental official with judicial, executive, and police authority) but only after it was ascertained that Indians' rights were not being infringed upon and that they did not object. The final act of possession took place in the presence of the alcalde on the land itself. The grantee pulled up grass from the land, threw stones, and shouted a version of "Long live the king and may God guard him!" As recorded in Taos on June 15, 1715, at the granting of the Cristóbal de la Serna Grant, "Having performed the prescribed ceremonies and conducting said Captain Cristobal Serna over the tract, he pulled up grass and threw stones, and in witness thereof I signed it with the attending and eye witnesses aforesaid, on said day, month and year."[5]

The land that later became the Cristóbal de la Serna Grant once belonged to Don Fernando Durán y Chávez. A second tract of land that in the 1700s would become the Antonio Martínez Grant was owned by Don Diego Lucero de Godoy (sometimes Godoi); Bartolomé Romero originally owned the land that became the Gijosa Grant. Other names found in historical documents are Domingo de Herrera and Francisco Gómez Robledo. The river that flows from Taos Canyon is called Río de Fernando, and originally the town of Taos was known as Don Fernando de Taos. Diego Lucero de Godoy and Domingo de Herrera were soldiers for the Crown and were in Guadalupe del Paso at the time of the 1680 attack by the Pueblos. Lucero de Godoy's thirty-two-member extended family of sons and servants lived in what has been called a *casa-corral* (house with corral) or *plazuela*. Río Lucero bears his name. Herrera's entire family—wife, mother-in-law, and seven children—were killed in the Pueblo Revolt. Although nothing has yet been unearthed about the family of Francisco Gómez Robledo, he may have been an *encomendero,* as his father was. Bartolomé Romero has many descendants in New Mexico and southern Colorado.

Durán y Chávez and Godoy survived the 1680 revolt, but none of the family returned to the Taos Valley to reclaim the land after the 1696 reconquest, which was marked by the return of some church missals and vessels and a very large oil painting of Our Lady of Aránzazu that the people of Taos Pueblo had kept safe for sixteen years.[6]

The sort of Spaniard who arrived in the Taos Valley after reconquest was very different from the early conquistadores who had come in 1540 with Francisco Vásquez de Coronado and in 1598 with Juan de Oñate—men driven by hopes of glory and quick riches. Settlers, by contrast, were subsistence farmers. While the missionary Franciscan friars remained active throughout the 1700s, the main objective of the Spanish colonists in the eighteenth century was to work the land in order to provide for their families and survive.

Sources of water largely account for the patterns of settlement in Taos, with grants along the Rio Grande and Taos Valley's six tributaries being highly desirable.

Acequias were constructed to irrigate crops in the narrow river valleys.[7] Throughout the 1700s the resilient Taoseño settlers built ranchos and little villages called *placitas*. The census of 1796 lists six placitas in the area: Plaza de San Francisco (Ranchos de Taos); Plaza de Santa Gertrudis [location unknown and possibly an error in recording the census]; Plaza de Nuestra Señora de Guadalupe (Don Fernando de Taos); Plaza de la Purísima [Concepción] (Upper Ranchitos); Plaza de San Francisco de Paula (Lower Ranchitos); and Nuestra Señora de los Dolores (Cañon).[8]

To gain a context for the practice of granting land, it helps to understand that Europeans and Native Americans viewed land differently. The Europeans saw land chiefly as a private commodity, while Native Americans generally viewed land as something that could not be individually possessed or owned.[9] Even so, the Spanish treated land, especially communal land, as a resource for the benefit of the entire community and not just one individual.

In Spanish colonies such as Nuevo México, community land grants or hybrid land grants with communal lands were the norm. This difference became a problem in New Mexico once the area came under American jurisdiction because English law, social customs, and mores were applied to Spanish and Mexican land grants without provision for the ownership of communal lands. Consequently, many of these communal properties became public lands and were then designated as national forests or were claimed by the U.S. government to be managed by the Bureau of Land Management (BLM). As a result, the Hispanic settlers who had worked and lived on communal lands for centuries considered themselves dispossessed.

The scrupulous care that the Spanish had exercised dissipated under Mexican rule, with the result that large grants of land were issued with uncertain and vague boundaries, such as the huge Maxwell Grant in northeast New Mexico (formerly the Beaubien-Miranda Grant). Land grabs followed, causing tension and turmoil around Taos in the mid-1800s. In fact, one of the underlying reasons for the Taos Revolt of 1847 was the conflict between Taoseños and "newcomers" such as Governor Charles Bent and Charles (Carlos) Beaubien over Mexican-issued land grants. According to land grant researcher Rowena Martinez, "Of the six persons murdered in Taos on January 19, 1847, four were grantees of large land grants issued by New Mexico governor Manuel Armijo under the auspices of the Mexican government."[10]

American sovereignty in New Mexico commenced after the Treaty of Guadalupe Hidalgo was ratified. Even though the treaty states that the common lands of the Spanish communities would be protected, they were not. Rather, says land grant scholar Malcolm Ebright, "The evidence strongly suggests that U.S. courts and Congress did not meet the obligations assumed by the United States under the Treaty of Guadalupe Hidalgo. The main reason for this was [that] the land grants were issued under one legal system and adjudicated by another."[11] As a result, much of the land that had been included in the original land grants in the Taos Valley, especially the common lands, is no longer part of the original grants. "A number of

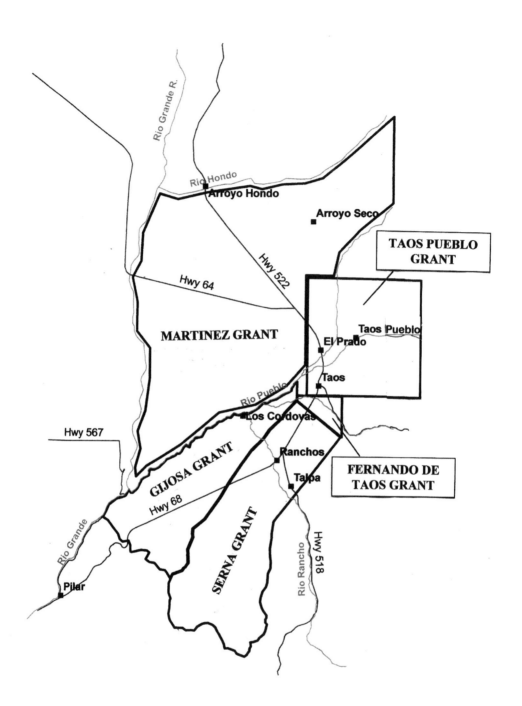

Schematic map of the first five Spanish land grants in the Taos Valley. The earliest was Taos Pueblo League Grant, followed by the Serna, Gijosa, Martínez, and Fernando de Taos grants. Map: Charles C. Hawk.

land grant heirs, legal scholars, and other experts," Ebright asserts, "have charged that activities under the two federal statutory New Mexico community land grant procedures did not fulfill the United States' legal obligations under the treaty's property protection provisions."[12]

Different studies have come to different conclusions, but several facts are indisputable. In California, a Board of Land Commissioners was established in 1849 to adjudicate land grants there. Land grant claims were confirmed fairly promptly and conclusively at the rate of 73 percent in California. In New Mexico the first surveyor general was not appointed until 1854, and ultimately the percentage of confirmed land-grant claims in New Mexico varies from 24 to 55 percent, depending on who made the calculations. The duty of the surveyor general was to report his recommendations to Congress as to whether claims should be confirmed or rejected. Understaffed and severely hampered in their investigations, the surveyors general worked for almost four decades in a "woefully inadequate" system.[13] By 1889 there was a complete breakdown of the surveyor general system, with a backlog of 116 land grants awaiting congressional action. On March 3, 1891, a law establishing a five-judge Court of Private Land Claims was signed by President Benjamin Harrison.[14] This began a twenty-year process whereby most of the land grants in the Taos Valley were confirmed and patented, though fifteen land-grant claims elsewhere in the county were not confirmed or patented. Much precious time had been lost, giving unscrupulous speculators ample opportunity to enrich themselves, usually at the expense of the settlers living on the grants.[15] While the surveyor-general system was inefficient and incompetent, the Court of Private Land Claims procedure was too little too late to protect the land grants of New Mexico's Hispano settlers.

In contrast, the U.S. government did ensure the protection of Indian lands by assuming the role of trustee. "The United States does have a fiduciary relationship with the Indian Pueblos in New Mexico and it protects community lands that the Pueblos obtained under Spanish sovereignty."[16] So although the Indian reservation lands are held in common by the Native Americans, they are protected by the U.S. government and cannot be sold. In the twentieth century some of the land that Taos Indians had lost to the U.S. government was returned to Taos Pueblo, such as Blue Lake and surrounding lands in 1970 and the Bottle Neck tract in 1993.[17]

Synopses of the history and status of four of the Taos Valley's eight patented land grants follow, offering a glimpse into the complexity of land ownership in the Taos Valley.

Cristóbal de la Serna Grant

The oldest non-Pueblo land grant in the Taos Valley is the Cristóbal de la Serna Grant ceded in 1710 and revalidated in 1715. The land had been claimed and worked by Don Fernando Durán y Chávez until just before the Pueblo Revolt of 1680. The Serna Grant, as it has become known, includes present-day settlements of Ranchos de Taos, Cañon, Lllano Quemado, and Talpa. The southern boundary is *"la sima de Picurís"* (the top of Picurís Peak), and the western boundary is the Camino del Medio—the Middle Road—to Picurís. The eastern boundary is marked by a mound that today is on the border of the Rancho del Rio Grande Grant. The northern boundary originally was La Cruz Alta (High Cross), a large wooden cross that stood until the late nineteenth century at the southeast corner of Cruz Alta Plaza. Cristóbal de la Serna was a captain in the Spanish army and commanded the Santa Fe presidio from 1712 to 1715, and thus the Serna Grant was a large parcel of land given to a prominent private individual for military service:

> In 1710, Spanish army captain Cristobal de la Serna petitioned Governor Joseph Chacon Medina Salazar y Villasenor, Marques de Penuela, for a grant of land in the Taos Valley. The Marques was the provincial governor under authority of Juan Fernandez de la Cueva, Duque de Albuquerque, Viceroy of Mexico, whose authority came straight from, and only from Philip V. Duke of Anjou, King of Spain. Governor Penuela granted Serna's petition in April of that year, but Serna could not take possession of the grant because of his military duties. He therefore requested revalidation of the grant on May 31, 1715 to then Governor Flores Mogollon, who approved the grant the same day.[18]

Serna's possession of the grant marks the reestablishment of Spanish civil authority and resettlement in the Taos Valley and is a milestone in the history of Taos.[19]

In 1724 the Serna Grant changed hands when two of Serna's children, Juan and Sebastiana, signed a deed to Diego Romero, also known as El Coyote. *Visitador* Juan Paez certified the title to the land grant in a document dated November 24, 1724. Diego Romero died in 1742, and in 1743 the Serna Grant was partitioned to Barbara Montoya, his widow, and to Romero's three children from a previous marriage.[20]

In the late eighteenth century, settlers who had the few rancherias on the Serna Grant lived in the pueblo for protection from raiding Comanches. By the end of the century, they apparently had moved out, some of them to Las Trampas de Taos, as Ranchos de Taos was known for a long time.[21] The Ranchos Plaza vicinity became the core, and the pastures, woods, and watering places were used as common lands, as the land-grant document stipulated. By 1796, the population of Las Trampas de Taos numbered about 200 Spanish-speaking people.[22] In 1815, the Ranchos church, San Francisco de las Trampas, was documented as being in use, after being licensed by the diocese of Durango, Mexico, in 1813.[23] Throughout the 1800s Las Trampas de Taos continued to grow; by 1837 the Serna Grant had a population of 1,290 inhabitants, and by 1876, with approximately 3,000 people, was more populous than the area around the town of Don Fernando de Taos.[24]

A petition for confirmation of the Serna Grant was filed on behalf of all heirs, and on August 30, 1892, a decree confirmed the grant. When the Serna Grant was surveyed in April 1894 it was found to contain 22,232 acres. The U.S. Congress issued a patent for the grant on January 19, 1903. In 1924 an association was formed to protect the rights of members and owners of the Serna Grant. In the 1941 New Mexico Reassessment Survey, the system and existence of *linias,* strips of property, which can be traced to at least 1876, was formalized, and linias were given legal descriptions with metes and bounds. Due to an error in the survey or perhaps for some other reason the legal descriptions did not correspond to the ancestral claims of the land-grant heirs. This snag has led to a confusing situation: the Serna Grant now has different land claimants to the same land according to either the 1941 survey or ancestral claims. Consequently, the lands have multiple assessments for taxes. In addition, some people have built homes and developed land and now claim it by "adverse possession." Since the Eighth District Court decision in 1983 determined that the Serna Grant is a private, not a community, grant, some of the heirs and claimants have begun to quiet title their claims through the adjudication process. However, claimants with linias too narrow to survey or who have deeds without a legal description are losing their property rights in spite of the U.S. government's commitment to protect them under the Treaty of Guadalupe Hidalgo.[25] Currently much of the communal land in the Serna Grant remains in dispute or cannot be put to beneficial use by most claimants, and the future and legal status of the title is clouded.

Francisca Antonia de Gijosa Grant

Another Taos Valley land grant ceded in the early 1700s was the Gijosa (also Quijosa) Grant, the only grant of land in Taos Valley made to a woman. Francisca Antonia de Gijosa was living with her husband in Santa Fe after the reconquest. When she was widowed she began raising sheep to support herself and her children.

> By 1715 she had accumulated a herd of sufficient size to warrant the petition-ing of Governor Juan Ignacio Flores Mogollón for a grant. She requested that the grant cover the tract of land located in the Taos Valley which formerly had been owned by Bartolomé Romero, but had been abandoned since the Pueblo Revolt. In cognizance of his duty to protect widows, Mogollón, on September 20, 1715, made the requested grant and directed the alcalde of Taos to place the grantee in possession of the premises. Upon receiving notice of the grant and the governor's order, alcalde Juan de la Mora Pineda assembled the leading officials of Taos Pueblo at the Royal House [a building bordering the pueblo that housed Spanish officials] and in the presence of his witnesses

and the grantee, explained the terms of the grant to the Indians. Since they
did not dispute the concession, the alcalde proceeded to the grant where he
pointed out the . . . boundaries of the concession and placed the grantee in
royal possession of the lands embraced therein.[26]

On May 25, 1725, because Francisca Antonia de Gijosa had moved back to Santa
Fe, she conveyed the property to Baltazar Trujillo, who claimed an adjoining tract
of land which had been granted to him in 1702. On June 22, 1725, Trujillo asked
Alcalde Enrique Jirón y Cabrera to place him in possession of the Francisca Antonia
de Gijosa Grant and the tract granted to him in 1702. The alcalde encountered no
opposition and placed Trujillo in possession of both tracts as a single body of land.
Trujillo in turn sold the consolidated grant to Baltazar Romero on July 12, 1732, and
the consolidated grant was subsequently referred to as the Gijosa Grant. Baltazar
Romero then sold the Gijosa Grant to five individuals on August 14, 1752, and the
cotenants partitioned the cultivable portion of the grant amongst themselves. The
balance of the grant was then held in common by its owners as pasture for livestock.
According to the records of the surveyor general, "During the next century and a
quarter the grant was continuously occupied and claimed by the descendants of the
five parties among whom it had been partitioned."[27]

Surveyor General Henry M. Atkinson on April 28, 1878, proclaimed the Gijosa
Grant as valid, but the recommendation was not acted on by Congress. The records of
the Office of the Surveyor General show that "on June 18, 1892, Felix Romero for himself and on behalf of the other owners of the Gijosa Grant, filed suit against the United
States for confirmation."[28] The Court of Private Land Claims in its opinion dated March
1, 1893, held that it was satisfied that the plaintiff had established a valid and complete
claim and therefore confirmed title thereto in the heirs and legal representative of the
original grantees. The diamond-shaped grant, which was patented in 1903, was found
to have 16,240.64 acres in its official survey completed in September 1901.

The Gijosa Grant today is predominantly private property, although the Taos
Valley Overlook tract was recently acquired by the Bureau of Land Management
(BLM) for preservation purposes. The southern part of the old grant includes the
National Guard Armory site, the UNM-Taos Klauer Campus, the Taos Country
Club, Los Córdovas, Cordillera, and Upper Ranchitos areas.

Antonio Martínez Grant

In 1716 Antonio Martínez from Sonora, Mexico, appeared before Governor Felix
Martínez to advise him that he wished to settle in the Taos Valley and wished to
register the tract of vacant land that formerly belonged to Diego Lucero de Godoy
in the 1600s. Pursuant to the king's policy to encourage settlement of the frontier

area, Governor Martínez granted him the tract on December 20, 1716, according to the boundaries originally held by Diego de Godoy. The usual precautions were taken to advise Taos Pueblo representatives, and Miguel Tenorio de Alba delivered royal possession to Martínez.[29]

Although there is no evidence that Antonio Martínez actually occupied the land,[30] the heirs of Antonio Martínez petitioned Surveyor General James K. Proudfit on January 17, 1876, asking that the grant be confirmed. Proudfit docketed the claim as the Lucero de Godoy Grant but took no action on it. The next surveyor general, Henry M. Atkinson, recommended on October 4, 1878, that the grant be confirmed, but his successor, George W. Julian, recommended the rejection of the claim. The conflicting claims coming out of the Surveyor General Office caused Congress not to act.[31]

Once again it fell to the Court of Private Land Claims to take action on a New Mexico land grant. And on February 9, 1893, the court confirmed the entire grant, which, according to the survey, contained 61,605.46 acres. The survey was subsequently approved by the court, and a patent was issued on May 8, 1896.[32]

The Antonio Martínez Grant is located west of the town of Taos and extends to the western bank of the Rio Grande in the vicinity of the Rio Grande Gorge Bridge. Generations of Martínezes have lived and worked on the land. The Martínez Grant was the subject of a book by Frank Waters entitled *To Possess the Land,* which documents how early-twentieth-century developer Arthur Manby attempted to acquire the entire grant through "hook or crook" after it was patented in 1896.

Don Fernando de Taos Grant

On May 1, 1796, sixty-three families were placed in possession of the Don Fernando de Taos Grant, a community grant ceded by Governor Don Fernando de Chacón. The Don Fernando de Taos Grant was the smallest land grant in the Taos Valley and was approved by alcalde Antonio José Ortiz.

Patented in 1909, the Don Fernando de Taos Grant is located in today's downtown Taos and was the beginning of the Taos Plaza and La Loma Plaza in the present Historic District. This grant encroached on the Taos Pueblo League Grant as well as the Serna and Gijosa grants. The encroachment into the Taos Pueblo League Grant created issues of easement and ownership of streets in the northern part of the Town of Taos that were not resolved until the 1990s.

LEGACY OF THE LAND GRANTS

One of the community grants in the Taos Valley awarded in the late 1700s and early 1800s was the enormous Rancho del Rio Grande Grant, east of the Serna Grant, made in 1795. The Arroyo Hondo Grant was made to forty-four families in 1815. The eighth grant, the Antoine Leroux Grant, had been made earlier, in 1742, to Juan Bautista Vigil, Pedro Vigil y Santillano. In 1860 Leroux claimed that the grantees had not occupied the land, and the land was awarded to him. In two sections, the Antoine Leroux Grant straddles a long east-pointing finger of the Antonio Martínez Grant. The result of this burst of grant-making was a dramatic increase of citizens in the Taos Valley.

Unlike the ownership of water rights in the Taos Valley, the ownership of most of the lands that were once part of Spanish land grants in Taos Valley has now been adjudicated. Even though historically Hispanic communities suffered injustice in losing ancestral communal lands and many Hispanos today have the sense that "our lands were stolen," the issue of whether the land is communal or private land of the historic land grants of the Taos Valley has been largely settled. The only unresolved issues on some of these land grants are who will have possession of the land and who can prove legal title on certain portions of these lands.

NOTES

1. Documents suggest that other land grants were made but were abandoned or relinquished early on.

2. Myra Ellen Jenkins, "The Taos Pueblo and Its Neighbors," New Mexico Historical Review 16, no. 2 (April 1966): 103.

3. Today Taos Pueblo reservation lands total approximately 150,000 acres.

4. The authority to issue a land grant belonged to the king, but the process was in fact delegated to the viceroy in Mexico or to the territorial governor in Santa Fe.

5. *Land Grants in Taos Valley,* Rowena Martinez, ed. Publication No. 2, Taos County Historical Society (1968), 5.

6. Our Lady of Aránzazu was highly venerated in northern Spain in the rugged and mountainous Basque province of Guipùzcoa. The large modern Sanctuary of Aránzazu is located in the municipality of Oñate. There has been speculation that the original mission to Taos Pueblo was dedicated to Nuestra Señora de Aránzazu.

7. F. R. Bob Romero and Neil Poese, *A Brief History of Taos* (Taos: Kit Carson Historic Museums, 1992).

8. John O. Baxter, *Spanish Irrigation in Taos Valley* (Santa Fe: New Mexico State Engineer Office, 1990), 18.

9. *Treaty of Guadalupe Hidalgo, Findings and Possible Options Regarding Longstanding Community Land Grant Claims in New Mexico* (Washington, DC: United States General Accounting Office 2004).

10. Ibid.

11. Malcolm Ebright, *Land Grants and Lawsuits In Northern New Mexico* (Albuquerque: University of New Mexico Press, 1994, 3.

12. Ibid., 7.

13. Ibid.,40.

14. Ibid., 45.

15. Ibid., 40.

16. *Treaty of Guadalupe Hidalgo, Findings and Possible Options.*

17. R. C. Gordon-McCutchen, *The Taos Indians and the Battle for Blue Lake* (Santa Fe: Red Crane Books, 1991).

18. "Defendant Serna Grant Association Trial Brief: History of the Serna Grant" (March 7, 1983), 1.

19. "Vision 2020 Master Plan" (Town of Taos, February 1999).

20. "Serna Grant Association Trial Brief," 4.

21. Jenkins, "The Taos Pueblo and Its Neighbors," 98.

22. "Serna Grant Association Trial Brief," 6–7.

23. John L. Kessell *Spirit Vision: Images of Ranchos de Taos Church* (Santa Fe: Museum of New Mexico Press, 1988), 117.

24. "Serna Grant Association Trial Brief," 9–10.

25. Malcolm Ebright, *The Tierra Amarilla Grant: A History of Chicanery* (Santa Fe: Center for Land Grant Studies, 1980).

26. Archive No. 309 (Mss., Records of the Spanish Archives of New Mexico).

27. Archive No. 957 (Mss., Records of the Spanish Archives of New Mexico).

28. The Gijosa Grant, No. 109 (Mss., Records of the Surveyor General of New Mexico (SGNM).

29. Fray Angélico Chávez, *Origins of New Mexico Families in the Spanish Colonial Period* (Santa Fe: Historical Society of New Mexico, 1954), 60.

30. Jenkins, "The Taos Pueblo and Its Neighbors," 95.

31. The Lucero de Godoy Grant, No. 115 (Mss., Records of the SGNM).

32. The Antonio Martínez Grant, No. 116 (Mss., Records of the SGNM).

SELECTED REFERENCES

Baxter, John O. *Spanish Irrigation in Taos Valley.* Santa Fe: New Mexico State Engineers Office, September 1990.

Chávez, Fray Angélico. *Origins of New Mexico Families: A Genealogy of the Spanish Colonial Period.* Rev. ed. Santa Fe: Museum of New Mexico Press, 1992.

Ebright, Malcolm. *Land Grants and Lawsuits in Northern New Mexico.* Albuquerque: University of New Mexico Press, 1994.

———. *The Tierra Amarilla Grant: A History of Chicanery.* Santa Fe: Center for Land Grant Studies, 1980.

Gordon-McCutchen, R. C. *The Taos Indians and the Battle for Blue Lake.* Santa Fe: Red Crane Books, 1991.

Jenkins, Myra Ellen. "The Taos Pueblo and Its Neighbors." *New Mexico Historical Review* 16: 2 (April 1966).

Kessell, John L. *Spirit Vision: Images of Ranchos de Taos Church.* Santa Fe: Museum of New Mexico Press, 1988.

Land Grants in Taos Valley. Martinez, Rowena, ed. Publication No. 2, Taos County Historical Society, 1968.

Mss. Records of the Surveyor General of New Mexico (SGNM). State Records Center and Archives, Santa Fe.

The New Mexico State Planning Office and White, Koch, Kelley, and McCarthy, Attorneys at Law. Land Title Study. Santa Fe: State Planning Office, 1971.

Romero, F. R. Bob, and Neil Poese. *A Brief History of Taos.* Taos: Kit Carson Historic Museums, 1992.

Spanish Archives of New Mexico (SANM). State Records Center and Archives, Santa Fe.

Treaty of Guadalupe Hidalgo, Findings and Possible Options Regarding Longstanding Community Land Grant Claims in New Mexico. Washington, DC: United States General Accounting Office (GAO), June 2004.

Van Ness, John R., and Christine M. Van Ness, eds. "Spanish and Mexican Land Grants in New Mexico and Colorado." *Journal of the West* (1980).

"Vision 2020 Master Plan." Town of Taos, February 1999.

❖ *6* ❖

Borregos y trigo:
A Culture of Sheep and Wheat

John O. Baxter

Until very recent times, the economic and cultural life of the Taos Valley—one of the most fertile and well-watered valleys in New Mexico—was dominated by agriculture. The success of all the peoples who have lived here for centuries in coaxing a living out of a very harsh environment has been remarkable. Some aspects of this story are explored in this chapter.

———————————————

FROM PREHISTORIC TIMES TO THE PRESENT, agriculture has been crucial to life in the Taos Valley.[1] The Spanish explorers who came to the valley in 1540 found that farmers at Taos Pueblo had been cultivating corn, beans, and squash for hundreds of years. During the colonization of Nuevo México, a few Hispano frontiersmen established ranchos or rancherias near the pueblo and introduced new crops, such as wheat. The newcomers soon discovered that with irrigation wheat thrived in the valley's cool climate, in spite of its short growing season.

Fray Juan Augustín de Morfi, writing toward the end of the eighteenth century, described the land around the pueblo:

> In a valley pleasant and good-looking, watered by four
> small streams or creeks, one of which passes through the

center of the pueblo . . . . It enjoys many and very fertile fields. To the north of the pueblo and at a little more than a musket shot is a large pond where are estimated more than three hundred springs of good water which, irrigating the lands nearby, produce the best pastures of the kingdom. The timber for construction and fuel is close to the pueblo and in abundance. . . . At three leagues [south] from the pueblo is a ranch with abundance of arable lands even more fertile than those of the pueblo.[2]

The imported domestic animals—horses, mules, cattle, pigs, and sheep—added a new dimension to life in this remote area, although during the colonial era livestock production was limited. After 1800 sheep became the most favored species for their meat and wool. Eventually, wheat farming and sheep ranching were the predominant bases for Taos' agropastoral economy, and they remained so for many years. For a long time, Taos was referred to as the Breadbasket of New Mexico. Since World War II, however, the valley's economy has changed very significantly. Few residents now earn a living from farming or ranching alone, though many families continue these pursuits part time and are able to maintain a rural lifestyle.

Early Spanish Farmers

With the Pueblo Revolt of 1680, the Hispano families who had settled in the Taos area were forced to leave their homes and join the general retreat from Nuevo México. After thirteen years in exile at El Paso, a good many of them came back up the Rio Grande with the leader of the *reconquista*, General Don Diego de Vargas. Subsequently the Taos area was reoccupied by several pioneer families who received land grants from provincial governors acting in the name of the Spanish Crown. To support themselves, the grantees constructed *acequias* and planted crops. Undaunted by harassment from nomadic Indian tribes, they persevered, and, with support from their neighbors at the Taos Pueblo, they managed to establish small communities in the Ranchos de Taos and El Prado areas. In 1776, when the Franciscan friar Francisco Atanasio Domínguez inspected Nuevo México's missions for his superiors in Mexico City, he marveled at the bountiful agricultural production in the "very beautiful valley."[3] In addition to gardens, both Pueblo Indians and Spanish settlers raised ample crops of wheat and corn. During normal years, the combined output satisfied local needs and also supplied a surplus that could be traded or shared with less fortunate communities that were suffering from drought.

Toward 1800, Nuevo México's population began to increase significantly. As growth continued, some families at the older settlements—Santa Cruz de la Cañada (southeast of Española), Chimayó, and Chamita (northwest of Española)—had difficulty finding sufficient farmland and sought new locations toward the northern frontier. Recognizing their needs, officials in Santa Fe authorized additional grants in unsettled areas. At Taos, Governor Fernando Chacón approved the Rio Grande del Rancho and Cieneguilla grants in 1795 (in the areas of Ranchos de Taos and Pilar, respectively) and the Don Fernando de Taos Grant one year later. In 1796, the local alcalde conducted a census in which he enumerated 510 Pueblo Indians and 779 Hispano *vecinos,* clearly indicating substantial growth in his jurisdiction. After the turn of the century, expansion continued as other settlements were founded at Arroyo Seco and Arroyo Hondo.

THE NINETEENTH CENTURY

In the early 1800s, many newcomers arrived in Taos hoping to find improved opportunities for their dependents. Notable among them was Severino Martínez of Abiquiú. Attracted by the region's fertile soil and usually reliable water supplies, in October 1803 Martínez purchased a sixty-vara tract of land from Antonio Archuleta at the small plaza of San Francisco de Paula in today's Lower Ranchitos. Described enigmatically as "*tierra de pan de llevar*" (land suitable for growing wheat), the tract adjoined the Rio del Pueblo, which provided water for irrigation. In the spring of 1804 the Martínez family loaded their possessions on carts and pack animals, gathered their livestock, and set forth on the circuitous trail leading from the lower Chama Valley to their new home.

Once established at Taos, the family prospered and soon was active in local commercial, political, and religious affairs. Their original residence, a modest four-room adobe house, was expanded in every direction to become the imposing structure known today as Hacienda de los Martínez. Don Severino accumulated additional lands along the Rio del Pueblo, where he regularly harvested good crops of grain and other commodities. Nearby, his sheep grazed on verdant pastures, providing wool that was spun and woven into various textiles by servants at the hacienda. Surplus crops were traded with Plains tribes, who offered horses, buffalo meat, and all kinds of hides in return. Martínez then swapped these products and woolen textiles to merchants plying the Camino Real to cities in Mexico's interior. From the traders, Don Severino Martínez and his neighbors obtained clothing, firearms, tools, special foods, and other manufactured goods that were otherwise unavailable on the frontier. These practices of farming and ranching formed the basis of the local economy. Although very few Taoseños became as wealthy as Martínez, many of them depended on agriculture and trade to support their families.

In 1827, six years after Mexico gained independence from Spain, Severino Martínez died. Subsequently, Nuevo México experienced another change in sovereignty, officially becoming part of the United States under terms of the Treaty of Guadalupe Hidalgo on February 2, 1848. In January 1847, between the time the us declared war on Mexico (May 13, 1846) and the treaty-signing, Indians from Taos Pueblo and some Hispano allies revolted against the new government, the so-called 1847 Revolt, which was soon suppressed. Weeks later, a party of non-Hispano mountain men crossed the Sangre de Cristo Mountains via Palo Flechado Pass—through Cimarrón Canyon, roughly paralleling present-day Route 64)—on their way to the village of Don Fernando de Taos. As they rode out of the canyon, a youthful Lewis H. Garrard recorded his impressions of Taos' agriculture as follows:

> The valley, in every direction, was cultivated and, in the total absence of fences, presented the unusual sight of one large field stretching away for miles, intersected by numerous ditches.
>
> The melting snow from the mountain flows to the valley, where it is turned into large acequias; from there into branches, and again into each man's possession. . . . Wheat and corn form the principal products. . . . The former is used extensively in the manufacture of "Taos whiskey," with which everyone becomes well acquainted, if he forms one of a mountaineer party.[4]

Because Garrard came to Taos in the spring, he was unable to observe the harvest, which took place after the grain ripened. According to other observers, crops were first cut with a primitive sickle. When fully ripe, the wheat was threshed by driving a flock of goats around and over a stack of sheaves, while the wind carried off most of the straw and chaff. Photographs from a later period show that farmers continued to use the same threshing methods for a very long time.

Within a few years of Garrard's visit, a new market developed for the wheat raised on the irrigated fields he had described so vividly. After the Mexican-American War, responsibility for controlling the nomadic Indians who had been troubling the region's frontier settlements fell to the U.S. Army, which proceeded to establish a number of forts at various points across New Mexico. Feeding the troops stationed at these far-flung outposts required large quantities of flour and other commodities. Since transportation costs from Midwestern quartermaster depots were prohibitive, whenever possible the military encouraged local production. Although New Mexicans harvested plenty of wheat, their facilities for manufacturing flour were much too small for commercial purposes; grain had been processed by simple, water-powered mills that turned out quantities of flour sufficient only for local consumption.

Sensing opportunity, Cerán St. Vrain, a merchant with extensive landholdings in the Taos area, established the valley's first large-scale flour mill on the Rio Grande del Rancho near the *placita* of Talpa. A former business partner of Charles Bent, New Mexico's first governor under U.S. administration (1846–47), St. Vrain came to Taos as a trader in 1825 and became a Mexican citizen six years later. In Westport, Missouri, he purchased equipment for the Talpa site and several other locations where he had an interest in milling. On December 3, 1849, he signed a contract to furnish the U.S. Army annually for three years with one million pounds of "good, merchantable superfine flour." St. Vrain's flour was in fact somewhat coarse and gritty. Nevertheless, army procurement officers liked the big savings in freight charges, and as New Mexico's largest purveyor of flour St. Vrain supplied military posts from the Talpa mill until it burned to the ground in 1864.

Evidently, the destruction of St. Vrain's mill had little effect on wheat production in the Taos Valley. U.S. Census records show that the valley's output increased from about 40,000 bushels in 1860 to more than 90,000 bushels ten years later. The county's corn crop also rose from 24,000 to 52,000 bushels during the same period. New processing plants replaced the one destroyed in the blaze. By 1870, Frederick Müller, a German-born merchant, had erected a large mill at Los Ranchos that turned out 8,000 pounds of flour per day, powered by a sixteen-foot water wheel valued at $18,000. Subsequently another German immigrant, Alexander Gusdorf, established a large gristmill on the Rio Grande del Rancho with capital provided by the Staab family, prominent businessmen from Santa Fe. Like St. Vrain, Gusdorf produced much of his flour for delivery to the U.S. Army. In 1879, he caused a stir throughout the valley by building a three-story, steam-powered mill that manufactured 10,000 barrels of flour annually. A visionary, Gusdorf has been credited with introducing a number of technological advances to Taos, including the first horse-drawn binder for harvesting grain and the first mechanical threshing machine.

Although Gusdorf's mill bought large quantities of local wheat, many Taos farmers continued to patronize smaller enterprises that served only the proprietor plus friends and neighbors. In the years when wheat was one of the valley's main crops, each village had several mills. In 1880, there were eleven of these traditional mills operating on the Rio Grande del Rancho, in addition to those located on other streams. Slow and noisy, their design had hardly changed since the colonial period. Many remained in place as local landmarks for years after Gusdorf's gigantic plant went up in flames in 1895. Talpa still had seven mills in the 1930s, and Llano Quemado had at least two. The only extant mill structure today is the Inocencio Durán Mill. Durán's grandson, Guillermo Santistevan, added reinforcements to the small building in the 1950s; the ditch that drew water from the *acequia madre* of the Rio Grande to turn the grinding mechanism is still visible. On the register of New Mexico's Historic Sites, the Durán Mill is on Camino de Abajo la Loma, about one mile west of SR 68.

Crop farming had dominated agricultural production at Taos during the eighteenth century, but sheep ranching became more significant after about 1800. Since the colonial era, New Mexicans had raised all kinds of livestock for food, fiber, and transport. But as time passed sheep became the most important species. When Fray Atanasio Domínguez stopped at Taos in 1776, he found that neither the Taos Pueblo people nor their Hispanic neighbors owned many sheep. Flocks subsequently increased, however, possibly because of a respite in hostilities with Plains tribes. After Severino Martínez died in 1827, an inventory of his estate included

For many generations, sheep farming was a way of life and the principal livelihood of many Hispanic families. The annual spring sheep drive from the valley floor to the high, stream-watered mountain meadows above Taos lasted until the end of World War II, before Taos' economic base shifted. Photo John Collier Jr., ca. 1940s–1950s, courtesy of Mary E. T. Collier and the Collier Family Collection.

approximately 1,200 sheep, along with smaller numbers of cattle, horses, and mules. Like other New Mexicans, Martínez raised *churro,* hardy little double-coated animals descended from the common sheep of Spain that came with the earliest settlers in the sixteenth century and which adapted readily to the semiarid ranges of the New World. Although churro fleeces are somewhat skimpy, the long-staple wool is ideal for hand-processing, allowing woolen textiles produced by the Martínez household to play an important part in Don Severino's trading ventures.

As their flocks multiplied, the Martínez family probably made use of an institution known as *partido* to manage them. Under terms of the usual partido contract, a sheep owner loaned a certain number of ewes to a *partidario,* a reliable person who assumed responsibility for them during a given time period. Each year, the partidario paid interest to the owner in wool and lambs, generally about 20 percent of the increase. When the contract ended, he was obligated to return the same number of ewes of the same age as those originally received. With good fortune, the partidario accumulated a flock of his own from his share, but he also risked falling deeply in debt to his *patrón* in case of adversity.

As sheep numbers increased, Taos ranchers began to trail their flocks across the Sangre de Cristo Mountains to new pastures on the east side. Once settled on fresh grass, ewes and lambs grew fat; but the remote location made them vulnerable to Indian raiders. Early in 1846 a band of Utes suddenly appeared at a place called Cerro de Gallina and carried off 8,000 sheep and 400 cattle. Hoping to recover its stock, the Martínez family and other ranchers unsuccessfully attempted to overtake the thieves. Despite this bitter experience, sheep owners continued to run large herds over the mountains during the 1840s and 1850s. After the discovery of gold in California in 1849, their courage was rewarded when a new market for sheep suddenly developed on the West Coast. A huge population increase in gold country caused a corresponding demand for food supplies of all kinds, including mutton from far-off New Mexico.

Recognizing a chance for profit, a number of New Mexicans began speculating in sheep. Undaunted by the risks resulting from the long trail drive, several entrepreneurs set forth in the spring of 1852, including "Uncle Dick" Wootton of Taos, a former mountain man and fur trapper. Early in the year, Wootton assembled 9,000 churros that he had purchased from local herders near Watrous, north of Las Vegas. Although he failed to name the sellers in his account of the expedition, Taos ranchers were probably well represented among them. After driving his flock to Taos to secure supplies and additional *pastores,* Wootton departed on June 25, headed toward the San Luis Valley. From there, he proceeded along the Old Spanish Trail across Colorado into Utah. At Salt Lake City, Uncle Dick was entertained by Brigham Young, the Mormon patriarch. In October, he topped the Sierra Madre and descended to Sacramento, where he peddled the sheep to various buyers during the winter. Most of his stock brought $8.75 per head, which netted a handsome profit for the old mountain man.

While Uncle Dick was winding up his affairs in Sacramento, another colorful frontiersman left Taos, hoping for financial gain from a similar venture. Early in 1853, Kit Carson bought 6,500 churros in the Rio Abajo to sell at western markets. Other investors included Lucien B. Maxwell, John W. Hatcher, and some of their mountain-man friends. From a jumping-off point across the Sangre de Cristo Mountains at Rayado, Carson's party, like Wootton's, followed a northern route, traveling along the Front Range of the Rocky Mountains as far as Fort Laramie in present Wyoming. There they joined the well-worn Emigrant Trail to California. In August, the sheep traders reached Sacramento, where they sold the trail-weary stock for $5.50 per head. Although the market had slipped badly since Wootton had made his sale, Carson called the venture a big success.

After Carson's return, the demand for sheep in California continued to soften. Early in 1855 a leading San Francisco bank was forced to close its doors, plunging the region into a deep depression. Trade in livestock and other commodities ground to a halt as conditions deteriorated further. Because of poor communications, sheep ranchers back in New Mexico remained unaware of the catastrophe and continued to organize big drives to the West Coast. With the outbreak of the Civil War in 1861, the sheep trade between New Mexico and California ended abruptly. As federal troops withdrew from western garrisons, travel became risky along the usual trails. Bands of sheep presented inviting targets for southern sympathizers and restless Indians seeking food supplies. When peace returned, New Mexico's sheep industry underwent a fundamental reorientation. Previously, the region's churros had been valued primarily as producers of mutton; demand for their wool was limited to local hand-processors. During the war, this relationship changed suddenly, as the nation's need for vast amounts of woolen goods drove commodity prices ever higher. Hoping to increase production, ranchers brought in well-bred Merino rams to crossbreed with their churro ewes, which doubled fleece weights almost immediately.

In 1860, just before the Civil War began, a government census enumerated some 75,000 sheep in Taos County, suggesting that ranges there were moderately stocked. During the next several years, numbers declined somewhat as new markets opened to the north. Impressed by the churros' hardiness, ranchers sought breeding stock with bloodlines able to withstand extremes of heat and cold in a harsh climate. Another lucrative market developed to the east near the end of the 1870s, as large numbers of sheep left the territory to be fattened on irrigated fields in Kansas and Nebraska. After consuming a ration of corn and alfalfa, they were sent on to Midwestern packing plants for slaughter. Responding to increased demand and foreseeing a bright future for their industry, sheep ranchers enlarged their herds by retaining more of their ewe lambs. By 1880, approximately 186,000 head grazed on Taos County ranges.

As sheep numbers exploded, business procedures began to change in the ranch country of New Mexico. With the arrival of the railroad, powerful mercantile establishments took control of almost every aspect of wholesale and retail trade in rural areas. Based in Las Vegas, Chama, Española, and other business centers, the mercantile firms were headed by Anglos, some of them German Jews who had recently emigrated from Europe. Recognizing the vital role of the sheep industry in the territorial economy, the merchants were soon deeply involved, extending credit to carry ranchers through the year with the understanding that the lenders would receive their wool and lambs when they were marketed. During the 1890s, the Charles Ilfeld Company of Las Vegas, New Mexico, competed for business at Taos by enlisting Alexander Gusdorf as its agent in buying sheep and wool. Organized in 1904, the Bond McCarthy Company maintained a large general store at Taos and, with Justin McCarthy in charge, controlled much of the local commodity trade. Eventually, the merchants became sheep owners, making use of the traditional partido system to manage their flocks.

Inevitably, the huge buildup in sheep numbers led to extensive overgrazing throughout the Taos region. As pastures deteriorated, ranchers also lost the use of some of the common lands of the land grants that their ancestors had received under Spanish rule. When the U.S. Court of Private Land Claims approved the Don Fernando de Taos Grant in 1899, for example, the official survey placed the east boundary of the grant at the mouth of Fernando Canyon. In past years, the original settlers had always insisted that their lands extended at least twenty miles further east to the crest of the mountains at Palo Flechado Pass. Thus, the justices' ruling deprived their descendants of thousands of acres of grass. During the administration of President Theodore Roosevelt, when large portions of the public domain were segregated for conservation purposes, the federal government included Fernando Canyon in the Taos Forest Reserve, which two years later became Carson National Forest. Under Forest Service regulations, Taoseños had some limited access to traditional grazing lands, but only after obtaining permits and paying fees, a bitter pill to swallow.

THE TWENTIETH CENTURY

As the new century began, water allocation and restricted grazing land were not the only problems facing Taos farmers and ranchers. In past years, valley farmlands had been divided and subdivided through inheritance among succeeding generations, which resulted in ever-decreasing shares for each heir. In many cases, landholdings became too small to sustain a family, a condition that was aggravated by an increased need for cash to supplement farm income.

After the arrival in New Mexico of the Atchison, Topeka and Santa Fe Railroad in 1878, the territory became integrated into the national economy—although that line bypassed Santa Fe by eighteen miles. Rail transport brought an enticing array of manufactured goods previously unknown in the territory: modern farm equipment, new clothing and shoes, cast-iron stoves for heating and cooking, kitchen utensils, and many other items that made life easier for the settlers. Because of additional spending, rural families found that surplus grain and livestock no longer provided the means to cover debts at the local store, and this forced them to consider new ways to make up the shortfalls. At the same time, the newly available items provided a means for the local farmers to earn the money they now needed in order to pay with cash rather than trading goods, as had been the custom.

The Denver and Rio Grande Railroad's 125-mile-long narrow-gauge line between Santa Fe and Antonito in southern Colorado operated from 1880 to 1941. Unofficially, it was called the Chili Line. The D&RG had spent about $30,000 in 1880 attempting to grade the line north of Española in the direction of Taos but abandoned the project when surveys showed that construction of such a line was not feasible. The D&RG did, however, establish and maintain stations at Taos Junction and Tres Piedras on the west side of the Rio Grande. With the cooperation of the D&RG and the merchants of Taos, a bridge over the wild Rio Grande was constructed about 150 yards upriver from today's Taos Junction Bridge on SR 570. This made it possible for wagons to carry merchandise to and from the Taos Junction station and Taos itself for delivery to such Taos merchants as Gerson Gusdorf, Alvin Burch, the Bond McCarthy company, Charles Ilfeld, and others.

The wagon drivers were called *fleteros*, derived from a Spanish word for freight, *flete*. Fleteros were farmers who owned carts and a strong, well-trained team of horses. From Taos, the wagons transported bags of wool from sheep farms, sacks of wheat and other grains, sacks of piñon nuts gathered in the fall, and fruits and vegetables, according to the season. From the railroad stations they brought back dry goods, furniture, farm equipment, and barrels of oil. Theirs was difficult and dangerous work. The gorge, with its huge lava rocks and isolated trees lining the sides, was an awesome challenge, and the steep, narrow road they traveled was fraught with dangers. In the winter when the roads were ice-covered, the horses had to be shod frequently in order to have traction. Only here and there was there room to get past other fleteros or vehicles. Once across the narrow wooden bridge, the grade on the west side was a little less difficult, but the pitch on the return trip was steep enough that blocks of wood were used to slow the backward thrust of the wagon load. But such difficult and dangerous work enabled men to keep bread on the table and to stay in Taos with their families.

Always eager traders, some Taoseños began to travel to other communities, acting as middlemen in commodity deals. After the harvest, some valley farmers loaded their wagons with wheat, which they hauled to Chimayó to barter for the apples, apricots, and chili peppers grown there. Next, they proceeded to Colorado, where they exchanged fruit and peppers in San Luis Valley towns, receiving potatoes and pinto beans in return.

During the 1920s, men from Taos often left their farmlands in charge of their wives and children and traveled to other states in search of employment. Experienced in every aspect of the sheep industry, many of them went to Colorado, Wyoming, or Utah, where they hired on as shearers, herders, or camp tenders at one of the big ranching operations. Usually they were away for six or seven months, from early spring until the owners sold their lambs in the fall. Colorado also offered opportunities for work at the mines near Leadville, in the sugar beet fields around Greeley, and in the potato patches up and down the San Luis Valley. Some New Mexicans found work on section crews that maintained railroad right-of-ways at various locations throughout the West. None of these jobs paid high wages, but living expenses were minimal, so that workers could save much of what they earned. In the 1930s, as the Great Depression gripped the national economy, employment became hard to find, and many New Mexicans were forced to rely on government programs for their survival.

As adequate range became scarcer, sheep numbers dwindled at Taos, and the industry began to decline, a trend that accelerated when prices for lambs and wool collapsed during the Great Depression. Of those who remained in the livestock business, many shifted from sheep to cattle, a process encouraged by Forest Service personnel, who believed the "woolies" were more damaging to range lands than cattle. Also, because cattle require less daily supervision than sheep, ranchers with town jobs found that by working on weekends they could responsibly manage their herds.

Taos Valley agriculture has continued to change through the years in many ways. Wheat farming and sheep ranching are no longer important to local residents in the ways they once were. More recently Taoseños have continued to farm the same lands planted long ago by their ancestors but have integrated important changes. Most landowners now have jobs in town, and the irrigated fields that once produced thousands of bushels of wheat and corn have been seeded to alfalfa and other types of hay. Nonetheless, traditional Taoseños still irrigate their gardens and hay fields and care for the animals that have always been part of their lives. By so doing, they maintain their long agricultural heritage and contribute significantly to the ageless character of the Taos Valley.

NOTES

1. The information in this chapter may be found in much expanded form in two of the author's books, both cited in Selected References at the end of the chapter. *Borregos* is "sheep"; *trigo* is "wheat."

2. Alfred Barnaby Thomas, *Forgotten Frontiers* (Norman: University of Oklahoma Press, 1932), 96–97.

3. Eleanor B. Adams and Fray Angélico Chávez, eds. *The Missions of New Mexico, 1776: A Description by Fray Francisco Atanasio Domínguez with Other Contemporary Documents* (Albuquerque: University of New Mexico Press, 1956), 110.

4. Lewis H. Garrard [Hector Lewis Garrard], *Wah-to-yah and the Taos Trail* (Cincinnati, OH: W. H. Derby & Co., 1850. Reprint, Norman: University of Oklahoma Press, 1955), 178–79.

SELECTED REFERENCES

Adams, Eleanor B., and Fray Angélico Chávez. *The Missions of New Mexico, 1776: A Description by Fray Francisco Atanasio Domínguez with Other Contemporary Documents.* Albuquerque: University of New Mexico Press, 1956.

Baxter, John O. *Las Carneradas: Sheep Trade in New Mexico, 1700–1860.* Albuquerque: University of New Mexico Press, 1987.

———. *Spanish Irrigation in Taos Valley.* Santa Fe, NM: State Engineer Office, 1990.

Carlson, Alvar Ward. "New Mexico's Sheep Industry, 1850–1900: Its Role in the History of the Territory." *New Mexico Historical Review* 44 (1969): 25–49.

DeBuys, William. *Enchantment and Exploitation: The Life and Hard Times of a New Mexico Mountain Range.* Albuquerque: University of New Mexico Press, 1985.

Dorman, Richard L. *The Chili Line and Santa Fe the City Different.* Santa Fe, NM: R.D. Publications, 1996.

Frazer, Robert W. "Purveyors of Flour to the Army: Department of New Mexico, 1849–1861." *New Mexico Historical Review* 47 (1972): 213–38.

Garrard, Lewis H. [Hector Lewis Garrard]. *Wah-to-yah and the Taos Trail.* Cincinnati, OH: W. H. Derby & Co., 1850; reprint, Norman: University of Oklahoma Press, 1955.

Grubbs, Frank H. "Frank Bond: Gentleman Sheepherder of Northern New Mexico, 1883–1915." *New Mexico Historical Review* 36 (1961): 274–345.

Parish, William Jr. *The Charles Ilfeld Company: A Study of the Rise and Decline of Merchant Capitalism in New Mexico.* Cambridge, MA: Harvard University Press, 1961.

Sherman, John. *Taos: A Pictorial History.* Santa Fe, NM: William Gannon, 1990.

Thomas, Alfred Barnaby. *Forgotten Frontiers.* Norman: University of Oklahoma Press, 1932.

Twitchell, Ralph Emerson. *The Leading Facts of New Mexico History.* 5 vols. Cedar Rapids, IA: Torch Press, 1911–1917.

Weber, David J. *On the Edge of Empire: The Taos Hacienda of los Martínez.* Santa Fe: Museum of New Mexico Press, 1996.

Wentworth, Edward Norris. *America's Sheep Trails.* Ames: Iowa State College Press, 1948.

✤ 7 ✤

Taos *Ciboleros:* Hispanic Bison Hunters

Jerry A. Padilla

*New Mexico's bison hunters—*ciboleros*—represent one particularly colorful profession which arose to fill several needs created by Taos Valley's cold climate, protein-needy population, and economic role as a trading center. (Other such adaptations were* Comancheros *and* fleteros.*) The late journalist and historian Jerry A. Padilla's story of Taos'* ciboleros *offers a vivid picture of early* norteños *lifeways.*

Some of the Hispanic Southwest's most colorful and specialized citizens were *ciboleros,* mounted bison hunters. In the heyday of bison hunting—the mid-eighteenth to late-nineteenth century—small communities of Hispanic settlers in Nuevo México, including in Taos, relied on ciboleros for the protein in their diet and for hides to keep them warm.

Twice a year for nearly two hundred years, ciboleros from northern New Mexico and west Texas would make organized hunting trips through the mountains and grassland valleys of eastern New Mexico and east-central Texas, following herds of wild oxen—bison, or buffalo—to secure meat and hides for consumption back home.[1] Trader and author Josiah Gregg described what he saw when he came across a party of ciboleros on July 1, 1844:

> These hardy devotees of the chase usually wear leathern trousers and jackets, and flat straw hats; while, swung

Dense herds of bison (buffalo) roamed the eastern plains, offering pelts, hides, and meat for Native Americans and Spanish settlers. Bison hunters, ciboleros, thinned these herds, and the coming of the western railroads brought about their near extinction. Photo Bill Siether, ca. 1985, courtesy of Nita Murphy.

upon the shoulder of each hangs his *carcage* or quiver of bow and arrows. The long handle of their lance being set in a case, and suspended by the side with a strap from the pommel of the saddle, leaves the point waving high over the head, with a tassel of gay parti-colored stuffs dangling at the tip of the scabbard. Their fusil [short musket], if they happen to have one, is suspended in like manner at the other side, with a stopper in the muzzle fantastically tasselled [*sic*].[2]

Centuries of Hispano equestrian expertise had followed the hardy pioneers from Old World Spain. Perfected in Mexico and the northern reaches of La Nueva España, Nuevo Méxicano cibolero horses were from the same ancestral stock as wild *mesteños*, or mustangs, adapted by nomadic indigenous peoples and descended from the original Spanish barbs brought to North America in the sixteenth century. Ciboleros' horses were guided with knee or foot pressure, leaving the hunters' hands free for throwing a lance or fitting arrows on their powerful bow strings. Hoofbeat thunder, prairie dust, and the smell of animal blood and sweat accompanied these mounted lancers and archers as they rode into the herd of these horned giants—which could run as fast as 30 miles an hour—seeking the choice cow or bull. A fat cow, which might weigh as much as 1,110 pounds, was preferred for its meat, while a ton-weight bull was the most sought-after hide.

With a rope tied around his waist and attached to the horse's neck, a rider would pick a target, charge, and maneuver into position. Clouds of dust could block out the sight of all but the closest of their fellow hunters. It demanded great skill and strength to bring down a full-grown bison with a couple of arrows or a lance thrust at exactly the right spot between certain ribs.

Ciboleros lucky enough to have a working firearm could hope to be rewarded with an easier kill, and there was always a chance that a cibolero, toppled by an enraged bison, might not be able to remount and thus escape death. While most survived the *corrida*, every year a few were returned home to their Rio Grande and Sangre de Cristo villages for proper burial. The others came home as heroes, because they brought meat to see villagers through another season and, if it was an autumn hunt, buffalo robes to help keep the people warm during the coming winter.

Every Hispanic New Mexican village, town, *rancho,* or hacienda had its cibolero. His profession, as it were, was to make twice-yearly hunts for bison meat, skins, wool, and implements made from bones and horns. They were from all parts of New Mexico and southern Colorado, and a good number made their homes in the Taos area. Ciboleros traveled in large groups, which would elect a leader, a *mayordomo.* They took *agregados,* or added workers, as skinners, wranglers, and butchers to help slice up the meat into strips to be dried and packed before returning. On a corrida, once the allotted number of needed bison had been killed, every able-bodied person accompanying the hunt would begin slicing a set amount of meat to hang and dry.

Nobody could go to sleep until the portion assigned by the hunt's mayordomo had been prepared for curing. Sometimes families came along to help with the butchering, curing, and packing. Some ciboleros were sent in the employ of their patron or boss to procure meat for his herders and other workers and their families.

These New Mexican hunters and their ancestors, using lances and bows and arrows, had learned to hunt bison from Pueblo and nomadic Plains Indians. They would make the six-week round-trip journey to the plains in early October after the harvest, and again in June after spring planting. In the fall, ciboleros collected dried meat and bison skins, then with winter coats, for robes. In June they hunted mainly for meat, when bison coats were slipping wool and not as good for making winter coats or robes. The Hispanic men and women who interacted with bison respected them just as did Native Americans, taking only what was needed to get through a season and never wasting. The leather and every bit of the bison were utilized. Securing hides to tan for local use and for trade on the Chihuahua Trail (as the Camino Real was known in New Mexico) was an added bonus. A real demand in Mexico was smoked buffalo tongue, considered a delicacy by Mexicans too far from the herds to hunt their own. Many a cibolero would make ends meet by sending a load of smoked bison tongues south with the periodic Chihuahua trade caravans.

While the upper class could butcher beef, sheep, pigs, or poultry whenever they wanted it, usually poorer farmers could only count on a kid goat or a lamb from the *patrón* to celebrate a baptism, *prendorio* (engagement party), wedding, or some other family-oriented life event. Protein for ordinary Spanish and Mexican colonials in New Mexico came largely from sources that could be hunted, which made the role of the cibolero very important. Even the *haciendados*, owners of haciendas, sent employees with the caravans to procure dried meat and smoked tongues for families and *peones* in their employ.

In order to enter the lands of the Comanche and Kiowa, the hunters carried trade goods, which they bartered for permission to hunt the herds that the Plains Indians and other nomadic peoples considered their source of survival. To get ready for the trips, hunters prepared supplies for the journey and for barter. Those who actually rode into the bison herds, the *cazadores*, would practice with their horses. These special mounts were only ridden by the ciboleros and were used just for hunting bison.[3]

The South Plains were dominated by the Numunuh, or Comanche, and the Caigua, or Kiowa. Relations between these peoples and the Pueblo peoples and Hispanics were generally good after 1786, when Governor Juan Bautista de Anza (1778–88) secured peace with the Comanche chieftain Ecueracapa (Leather Cloak), after having defeated the nemesis of Hispano New Mexico, the fierce Comanche warrior chieftain Cuerno Verde (Green Horn) in 1779. Barter of New Mexican agricultural products with the Lords of the South Plains helped create and maintain goodwill between the Comanche, Kiowa, and Nuevo Méxicano, both Hispanic and

Pueblo. By the late 1790s, through efforts of interpreter, scout, and hunter Juan Lucero, the Kiowa also joined Anza's Comanche peace.

While hunting bison east of the New Mexico settlements was the norm, until the mid-nineteenth century there was a herd that ranged in the immense intermountain valley on the western side of the Rio Grande west of Taos and into Colorado's San Luís Valley. (Before 1861, when Colorado became a U.S. Territory, a sizable area of southern Colorado was also administered as part of Taos County.) Juan de Dios Gonzales, a cibolero from Ranchos de Taos—and possibly earlier from Abiquiú—preferred hunting this particular herd. Such surnames as García, Romero, Cortés, Gonzales, Martínes, Rodarte, Olonia, Suaso, and Medina are representative of family names of ciboleros from Taos County.

The late Cleofes Vigil, troubadour, historian, and folklorist from San Cristóbal, used to perform a ballad about Juan de Dios Maés, who was killed by accidentally impaling himself on his lance when his horse tripped in a prairie dog hole on the north Texas prairies. Although Maés was from Las Vegas, the son of an alcalde, this ballad came to be known throughout New Mexico and southern Colorado. And the late Pedro José Lucero of Des Montes often repeated a tale told by his father, José Refugio Lucero, about cibolero adventures. A favorite story of his was about a woman from Culebra, as the area of San Luís, Colorado, was known at that time, whom he named only as María Dolores. Instead of waiting for ciboleros to return, she would join them and hunt her own winter meat.[4]

CIBOLEROS AND THE TAOS VALLEY

There are a few local oral traditions about individual ciboleros from Taos County. Some of these are verified by Mexican Census Records for Taos researched and compiled by Dr. Josue Julián Vigil, retired professor at New Mexico Highlands University. Francisco Olonia of Fernando de Taos is reputed to have learned his hunting skills while living among Plains Indians apparently after having been taken captive as a young child. Coming home as an adult, he put his skills to work hunting bison. Most of the following information was collected during this author's interviews with descendants between 1966 and 2005.

Tomás García was a cibolero from Arroyo Seco, and he was sometimes accompanied by fellow hunter Taoseño Felipe Martínez. José Angel Gonzales, of 1837 Revolt fame, was described by Rafael Chacón in his memoirs as a "nimrod engaged in the honorable profession of *cibocibollero* [*sic*]."[5] Bison hunting was one of the lifeways this Taos-area native pursued before becoming the ill-fated governor of New Mexico for a few months during the so-called Chimayó Revolt against the administration of Mexican Governor Albino Pérez (1835–37).[6]

José Maria Rodarte was a native of the Llano de San Juan area near Peñasco. According to Alberto Vidaurre, Taos genealogist, Alvino Ortega and Jesús María Ortega were ciboleros and were also from Llano de San Juan; Manuel de Jesús Vasques from Peñasco hunted bison. Benjamin Cortés, Blas Griego, José Portelanse, ciboleros and cazadores, and the aforementioned José Angel Gonzales often led *caravanas de ciboleros* from Ranchos de Taos.

Cipriano Solano, who lived most of his life in the Springer-Miami, New Mexico, area and whose grandmother, Serafina Leal Solano, was from Ranchos de Taos, used to explain that when the ciboleros left from Taos they would gather with other hunters at El Lucero, near present Buena Vista, and elect a mayordomo before proceeding into the prairies. Solano's father, Rafael Antonio Solano, hunted bison from Tecolote and Loma Parda. Cipriano Solano, believed to have been born about 1870, used to tell of the remnant bison herds near Loma Parda when he was a youngster. "We'd take a burro to haul the meat back after hunting. One cíbolo would provide meat for several families almost a year in those days."

There are tales told in the San Luís Valley about ciboleros who lived close enough to herds of bison on the eastern side of the Sangre de Cristo Mountains that they regularly practiced their skills roping bison calves. A humorous story told by the late Elena Bustos Lucero of San Francisco, Colorado, was about cibolero mayordomo Abundo Martínes, her neighbor, who was born when that area was still part of New Mexico. She would happily tell about a hunt during which a hunter was yelling to the others, "a las gordas, a las gordas, atinen a las gordas" (at the fat, at the fat, aim at the fat [ones]). Martínes intervened telling him, "a las que se pueda, hijo de la chingada" (whichever ones you can get, sonofabitch), admonishing those under his command to take whichever bison were easiest, considering the danger involved.

José Guadalupe Lovato, of Taoseño origins, eventually settled in northeastern New Mexico, by way of Mora. He is remembered as having often led cibolero *caravanas* and was elected several times as mayordomo by fellow hunters. According to the 1860 United States Census, other ciboleros and cazadores were identified as professional hunters from the Conejos precinct of Taos County. Among these was Antonio Trujillo, aged thirty-nine. Also from this area were Jesús María Suaso, twenty-nine years old, José de la Luz Olguin, age twenty-nine, and José Doroteo Palilla [Padilla?], age fotry. Ciboleros include Hermenegildo Gallegos, fifty-six, from Arroyo Seco, and Bernabé Tafoya, forty-three, from Taos. Miguel García, twenty-eight, was from Arroyo Hondo. According to Bonifacio Fernández, retired educator of Taos, his grandfather, Pedro Luís Fernández, participated in bison hunting.

Most area families have kept alive tales and traditions about ancestors and relatives who participated in the pursuit of the American bison. It is a tradition that lives on in folk tales, songs, and stories that grandparents and elders still recall.

NOTES

1. The bison is the North American species of the bovidae family, which in Africa and Asia is represented by species of buffalo. In North America, common usage has made the word *buffalo* the common synonym for bison, in New Mexican Spanish, *cibolo*. The word *cibolo* is thought to derive from a Zuni word for bison. After the coming of the railroad in the 1870s and 1880s, bison herds were slaughtered nearly to extinction.

2. Josiah Gregg, *The Commerce of the Prairies* (Norman: University of Oklahoma Press, 1954), 90.

3. The difference between a *cibolero* and a *cazador* was not great, except that a cibolero hunted bison primarily and might engage in other agricultural pursuits the rest of the time. A cazador made his living by hunting year-round. When not out on the plains as part of an expedition for his village, he hunted for skins, furs, and meat in mountainous areas. Elena Bustos Lucero, of San Luís, Colorado, and Pedro José Lucero, of Des Montes, Taos County, New Mexico, concurred in this distinction when the author interviewed then in the 1980s.

4. Some of Lucero's relatives moved into the Taos area, and at least one of them, Pedro Lucero, was listed as a cazador in nineteenth-century documents brought to light by retired state historian Robert J. Torrez. See his "Voices from the Past: Finding *Cautivos, Ciboleros, Anantes,* and Patriots in the Archives," *Nuestras Raíces* 16: 4 (Winter 2001): 126.

5. Jacqueline Dorgan Meketa, *Legacy of Honor: The Life of Rafael Chacón, A Nineteenth Century New Mexican* (Las Cruces, NM: Yucca Tree Press, 2000), 35.

6. Janet Lecompte, *Rebellion in Rio Arriba 1837* (Albuquerque: University of New Mexico Press, 1985), 37.

SELECTED REFERENCES

Interviews and oral history
Bonifacio Fernández, Taos, New Mexico. Interview by Jerry A. Padilla, August 2005.

Elena Bustos Lucero, San Luís, Colorado. Interview by Jerry A. Padilla, October 1985.

Pedro José Lucero, Des Montes, Taos County, New Mexico. Interviews, various times between 1980 and 1990.

Maximiliano Maximo Padilla, Springer, New Mexico. Unpublished family history, as told to Jerry A. Padilla, before Max Padilla's death December 6, 1968.

Cipriano Solano, Springer, New Mexico. Various interviews 1966 and 1967 by Jerry A. Padilla before Solano's death and as related by his daughter-in-law, Bernice Solano, Springer, New Mexico, Winter 1974.

Alberto Vidaurre, genealogist, Taos, New Mexico. Interview by Jerry A. Padilla, July 2002.

Publications

Arellano, Dr. Anselmo F. Unpublished monograph: testimony of Don Albino Chacón on New Mexico land grants, n.d.

Gregg, Josiah. *Commerce of the Prairies.* Norman: University of Oklahoma Press, 1954.

Kavanagh, Thomas W. *The Comanches: A History, 1706–1875.* Bloomington: American Indian Studies Research Institute, Indiana University, 1996.

Kenner, Charles L. "The Ciboleros." In *A History of New Mexican Plains Indian Relations.* Norman: University of Oklahoma Press, 1969.

Meketa, Jaqueline Dorgan. *Legacy of Honor: The Life of Rafael Chacón, A Nineteenth Century New Mexican.* Las Cruces, NM: Yucca Tree Press, 2000.

Vigil, Cleofes. "Los Ciboleros, Hispanic New Mexican Folk Music and Alabados." Presentation at The Rio Grande Institute, Fall Forum, Ghost Ranch, Abiquiú, New Mexico, Autumn 1985 (audiotaped by Vicente Martínez).

Vigil, Josue Julián. "Early Taos Censuses and Historical Sources." Compiled by the author. Copyright 1983. Editorial Telarana, P.O. Box 914, Las Vegas, New Mexico.

United States Federal Census 1860, Taos County, New Mexico State Records and Archives Center, Santa Fe, New Mexico.

CONFLICT: WARRIORS, CITIZENS, AND SOLDIERS

❖

Today the ruin of an earlier Church of San Gerónimo at Taos Pueblo is a haunting memorial to the resisters and their families who died within its walls when the U.S. Army destroyed and burned the church and convent to crush the Rebellion of 1847. The single tower was partially rebuilt and stabilized. The view is through the camposanto gates. Courtesy Taos County Historical Society.

＊ 8 ＊

Defiant Taos

Robert J. Torrez

The seventy tortuous miles between Taos and Santa Fe put Taos beyond the periphery of effective government control during the Spanish, Mexican, and early U.S. Territorial periods. For more than three centuries, Taos' independent and often-defiant population was quick to resist authority and prone to armed action. The bloody Taos Revolt of 1847, introduced here, is given closer scrutiny in the chapter that follows this one by former State Historian Robert J. Torrez. Together the five chapters in this section make clear that Taos was not a peaceful place.

From the beginning, the people of *el norte*, as Nuevo México was often called, were independent in their ways, and on several occasions the *norteños* of Taos were instigators of defiant resistance to real or perceived oppression by ruling governments. Taos' remoteness and its location at the extreme northern reaches of both the Spanish Empire and the Mexican Republic may account for the insistent self-determination shown by the indigenous peoples of the Taos Valley and the Spanish settlers from the early seventeenth century on. As early as 1613 the Taos Indians refused to pay tribute until the Spanish threatened force, and they resisted the Franciscan friars' efforts to Christianize them until the 1620s, when the first mission church was built at the pueblo. In 1640, the people of Taos Pueblo rose up again, killed the resident friar and several Spanish soldiers, and burned the mission church. They torched it again about 1660.

The Pueblo Revolt of 1680

The region's relative freedom from close scrutiny undoubtedly enabled Popé (Po'pay), the Ohkay Owingeh (Santa Clara Pueblo) revolutionary, to spend the years after 1675 in relative anonymity and safety at Taos Pueblo while he contemplated and organized the Pueblo Revolt of 1680. With Popé in residencce, Taos Pueblo became the epicenter of this transformative event of New Mexico history. It was at Taos that Popé—now thought by many historians to have been a shaman—received his purported spiritual guidance, sent messages and instructions to the other seventy or so pueblos and the Hopi villages, and built the needed credibility for his cause, which was to vanquish the vanquishers. By 1680, the Spanish settlers in the Taos Valley—about seventy in all—were alarmed. Indeed, two settlers from Taos sent one of three warnings to the governor in Santa Fe that rebellion was imminent.

It was also from Taos that Popé sent runners to each pueblo with a knotted yucca-fiber cord that signaled the day for the revolt to begin. The effectiveness of the planning at Taos, and the fervor Popé instilled in the Taos Pueblo people, guaranteed the success of the uprising in the Taos Valley, which took place in August of 1680. In Taos, all but two Spanish males were killed, including the priest. Days later, it was largely Taos Pueblo warriors who reinforced the rebels laying siege to Santa Fe, and they may well have provided the margin for victory there. After twelve days of siege, Governor Don Antonio de Otermín abandoned Santa Fe. Spanish officials and military, churchmen, and settlers who were not killed fled south to El Paso. The Pueblo Revolt effectively eliminated Spanish presence in Nuevo México for twelve years, although Otermín led a failed effort to retake the territory in 1681–82. Taos was the last pueblo to submit to Don Diego de Vargas. On the fourth attempt to secure it, beginning in 1692, Vargas took Taos Pueblo for good on October 9, 1696.

In late 1681, a captive rebel from San Felipe Pueblo gave his account of Popé's post-revolt plans to the authorities in El Paso:

> As soon as the Spaniards had left the kingdom an order came from the said Indian, Popé, in which he commanded all the Indians to break the lands and enlarge their cultivated fields, saying that now they were as they had been in ancient times, free from the labor they had performed for the religious and the Spaniards who could not now be alive. He said that this is the legitimate cause and the reason they had for rebelling, because they had always desired to live as they had when they came out of the lake of Copala [in southern Colorado].

TAOS TAX REVOLT OF 1816

Following the return of the Spanish under Vargas in 1692–96 and through the eighteenth century, the population along the Taos frontier grew slowly. During the nineteenth century, however, the population increased significantly. It is within the context of this expansion that in March 1816 Governor Alberto Maynez (1814–16) responded to a series of unusual and troubling reports from Taos, indicating that more than two hundred citizens had been placed under arrest for protesting a new and onerous tax on real property. This episode is known as the Taos Tax Revolt of 1816. The governor had distributed the order to the various alcaldes throughout New Mexico, instructing them to proceed with collection of the tax, but cautioned them not to do so in a heavy-handed manner.

After some preliminary inquiries, Governor Maynez received a petition signed by "those jailed at Taos." The letter complained of the administration of their alcalde mayor, Pedro Martín, and emphatically stated that they no longer wanted to recognize don Pedro as their alcalde. The petitioners concluded their letter by reiterating their loyalty to the king and asked that they be allowed to travel to Santa Fe and speak to the governor. Only Taos appeared on the verge of rebellion, so Governor Maynez appointed the retired military officer Juan de Dios Peña to proceed to the region and investigate.

Peña's inquiry revealed that in compliance with the governor's orders Pedro Martín, the alcalde mayor, had held a number of community meetings to read the proclamation. At each place, there had been murmurs of protest, but he apparently did not encounter major problems until he gathered the residents of San Geronimo de Taos (Taos Pueblo), where fifty-eight citizens gathered to hear what the alcalde had to say. Martín apparently was fed up with hearing complaints, and when several individuals expressed their concerns he lost his temper. Against the governor's order not to be heavy-handed, Martín threatened to arrest anyone who protested. This further inflamed the crowd, and in response Martín arrested and jailed three of the most vociferous protesters. But the crowd did not disperse. Instead, the resisters asserted that they all deserved to be arrested because every person present felt the same as those who had been jailed. Martín apparently agreed, arrested the entire group, and marched them to the jail, which soon overflowed into the plaza.

It appears that the protest spread quickly. By the time Peña arrived at Taos, he found 280 persons under arrest. On June 26, after collecting hundreds of pages of testimony, Peña submitted his report to Governor Maynez. Although everything seemed relatively quiet at this point, Maynez decided he wanted to speak directly to those involved and ordered five *apoderados*, or authorized representatives, be elected to come to Santa Fe and speak on behalf of all the Taos residents.

Those elected—Felipe Sandoval, Francisco Sandoval, Vicente Trujillo, Pedro Antonio Martín, and José Antonio Archuleta—along with alcalde mayor Pedro Martín, proceeded to Santa Fe and presented their case to Governor Maynez. The citizens of Taos had gotten themselves into a situation that could be interpreted as treasonous, a charge that under Spanish law carried the most serious consequences possible. After due consideration, Maynez concluded it was in the best interest of all involved if charges against the Taos residents were dropped. For their part, the Taoseños acknowledged they had been wrong to defy don Martín, who was the governor's legally appointed representative. They confessed to their "thoughtless and involuntary actions," publicly acknowledged the governor's authority as a representative of the Spanish king, and agreed that the tax had been imposed by legitimate authority. Although alcalde Martín believed he had acted with the best of intentions, he admitted his flawed approach and submitted his resignation. Taxes still had to be paid, but the citizens of Taos had made their point. Through their defiance, they forced the replacement of an unpopular public official, yet they maintained their status as loyal subjects of a distant but respected royal authority.

THE REVOLT OF 1837

Taos was indirectly involved in the *norteño* uprising known both as the Revolt of 1837 and the Chimayó Rebellion, the bloody year that began as an uprising against an unpopular Mexican governor, Albino Pérez (1835–37), and was centered at Santa Cruz de la Cañada, east of Española near Chimayó. Taos *cibolero* José Gonzales was recruited by the Santa Cruz rebels to be governor after Pérez and many of the top officials in his administration were murdered by Santo Domingo Indians. Gonzales's *junta popular,* disorganized and lawless, could not control the large rebel force based at Santa Cruz and was successfully opposed by a counter-revolutionary force under former governor Manuel Armjio that had been organized by a priest in the southern New Mexico town of Tomé. Gonzales was arrested just a month after being in office.

Another Taoseño, Pablo Montoya, a former alcalde, was the leader of about 3,000 rebels who marched on Santa Fe in September only to be defeated by Armijo's troops. Released from jail in Santa Fe, Gonzales rejoined rebel forces in Santa Cruz and prepared to march again to Santa Fe. The two armies joined battle between Santa Cruz and Pojoaque, with Armijo's army routing the rebels. Gonzales fled to Santa Cruz, where he was executed on orders from Armijo. The third Taoseño affected by the general unrest was Padre Antonio José Martínez, who as the local leader of the Catholic Church in Taos, experienced both the anger—including death threats—of his parishioners when he vigorously opposed the revolt and the suspicion by many in Santa Fe that he was behind the entire affair.

While there were other smaller and minor battles fought between the Spanish and the Indians over water rights and land encroachment, the next major act of defiance saw the Spanish and Indians united in their resistance. The Revolt of 1837 was followed ten years later by the Revolt of 1847.

The Taos Rebellion

Taos was at the center of an insurrection against the U.S. Army known as the Revolt of 1847, also as the Taos Rebellion. On January 19, 1847, a group of citizens from Don Fernando de Taos and Taos Pueblo, led by the same José Pablo Montoya who had been active in the Revolt of 1837, and Tomás (Tomasito) Romero, from the pueblo, converged on the home of Charles Bent, the first civil governor under U.S. administration (1846–47). Before the day was over, Bent and several other officials and individuals who were considered sympathetic to the new American government lay dead. Within days, the insurrection spread throughout northern New Mexico.

These events had their origins in the August 1846 occupation of New Mexico by the American army during the early stages of the Mexican-American War (1846–48). Brigadier General Stephen Watts Kearny had been sent by the U.S. War Department to subdue New Mexico and California shortly after the United States declared war on Mexico. As the Americans marched south on the Santa Fe Trail from Fort Leavenworth, Kansas, toward Santa Fe in mid-August, Mexican Governor Manuel Armijo (1827–29 and 1838–46) decided to abandon the territory, enabling Kearny and his 1,657-man Missouri Volunteers of frontiersmen, farmers, mechanics, artisans, lawyers, doctors, teachers, and students—the Army of the West—to occupy the capital without firing a shot. By the end of that summer, General Kearny had instituted a set of laws by which New Mexico was to be governed and had appointed American trader Charles Bent as territorial governor under military law.

Although Hispanic New Mexicans had offered no military resistance to the American army, most were frustrated, resentful, and unhappy with the self-proclaimed new government. For despite General Kearny's declaration to the contrary, until the Treaty of Guadalupe Hidalgo was ratified in 1848 New Mexicans were still citizens of the Republic of Mexico, and their country was still at war with the United States. By the middle of December 1846, rumors of increased resistance were serious enough to prompt Governor Bent to order the arrest of several influential individuals he suspected of being leaders and prime movers of this opposition.

In spite of the arrests, planning for an uprising apparently continued, culminating in the January 19, 1847, murders of Governor Bent, his brother-in-law, four U.S. appointed local officials, and others in Taos, at Turley's Mill in Arroyo Hondo, and Rio Colorado (Questa). Over the next few days, violence spread to Mora and at some other areas to the northeast. More than a thousand insurrectionists rallied and armed themselves with the intention of marching on Santa Fe and taking New Mexico back from the Americans. The revolt appears to have been badly organized, its enthusiastic participants poorly led, under-armed, and inadequately equipped.

On January 23, Colonel Sterling Price and a force consisting of more than 350 troops and several pieces of heavy artillery moved north through deep snow to meet the New Mexican forces. Between January 24 and 28, Colonel Price's troops defeated the resisters in a series of battles at Santa Cruz de la Cañada and Embudo Pass—between present-day Velarde and Dixon. By February 1, the New Mexicans had retreated to the Pueblo of Taos, where they fortified their positions and waited to meet the advancing American army. The assault on the pueblo began on February 3. After a fierce two-day battle, the Americans succeeded in breaching the walls of the old church there and routing the New Mexicans. In every encounter, the Americans' artillery proved a decisive difference. When the smoke cleared from the battlefields, an estimated 250–300 Indians and Spanish were dead, dozens were prisoners, and the church, San Geronimo, was in ruins.

The crushing defeat of the norteños officially ended this brief and violent episode of New Mexico history. Back in Taos, the day after the battle ended, a series of events unfolded which have become known as the Treason Trials. They began when the military convened a court to try Pablo Montoya, Tomás Romero, and several dozen men captured following the desperate battle at the pueblo. Montoya and Romero were to be tried together. Romero, though, was shot and killed by a guard who claimed the prisoner had tried to escape from Taos jail. Consequently, on February 6, Montoya stood alone to hear the guilty verdict and his sentence: to hang for his "rebellious conduct" against the United States, along with other charges related to his leadership in the insurrection.

Montoya was hanged on the plaza of Don Fernando de Taos the next day. Before court adjourned, at least fifteen other men suffered by hanging. Later that summer, on August 3, 1847, six more executions were carried out in Santa Fe. A report of these final executions records the sad tolling of all the church bells in Santa Fe as the men were hanged. It was a harrowing final act of one of the most tragic periods in New Mexico history.

For a century and a half, published sources described the men involved in these events in terms that range from "band of murderers" to "miserable, ignorant, deluded wretches." One popular early twentieth-century textbook prepared for use in New Mexico's schools dismissed the Taoseños who participated in these events as having come from a population "whose chief means of livelihood was to stir up trouble." Published histories have tended to treat these men anonymously, possibly in the hope that if they remained nameless they would remain undeserving of any recognition or honor. This author is not alone in suggesting that instead of dishonorable near-anonymity, the resisters deserve to have the circumstances of their crimes and their trials reevaluated. A second, more detailed look is the subject of the chapter "1847: Revolt or Resistance?"

SELECTED REFERENCES

"Estado que manifesta el numero de basallos. . . ." Spanish Archives of New Mexico, 1621–1821 (no number), microfilm reel 21, frame 545.

Insurrection against the Military Government in New Mexico and California in 1847 and 1848, Senate Document 442 (56th Congress, Session 1), Serial #3878.

Garrard, Lewis H. [Hector Lewis Garrard]. *Wah-To-Yah and the Taos Trail.* Cincinnati, OH: W. H. Derby & Co., 1850. Reprint, Norman: University of Oklahoma Press, 1955.

Lecompte, Janet. *Rebellion in Rio Arriba 1837.* Albuquerque: University of New Mexico Press, 1985.

McNierney, Michael, ed. *Taos 1847: The Revolt of Contemporary Accounts.* Boulder, CO: Johnson Publishing Co., 1980.

New Mexico and California, Message of the President of the United States, House of Representatives Executive Document 70 (30th Congress, Session 1), Serial #521.

Spanish Archives of New Mexico, 1621–1821 (#2655), microfilm reel 18, frames 391–577.

Twitchell, Ralph Emerson. *The History of the Military Occupation of the Territory of New Mexico from 1846 to 1851* (Glorieta, NM: The Rio Grande Press, 1963).

REFERENCE SOURCES

Except for the section on the Pueblo Revolt of 1680, this chapter is based almost entirely on the primary records found in New Mexico's microfilm editions of the archival collections of the New Mexico State Records Center and Archives. The abstract of the 1796 Taos jurisdiction census is taken from "Estado que manifesta el numero de basallos. . . ," Spanish Archives of New Mexico, 1621–1821 (no number), microfilm reel 21, frame 545. Persons wishing to consult the manuscript record of the Taos Tax Revolt of 1816 can find these in the Spanish Archives of New Mexico, 1621–1821 (#2655), microfilm reel 18, frames 391–577.

Janet Lecompte, *Rebellion in Rio Arriba 1837* (Albuquerque: University of New Mexico Press, 1985) cites Taoseños' participation in the Revolt of 1837. Much of the material from the Revolt of 1847 can be found in records of the United States Congress. Primary among these is New Mexico and California, Message of the President of the United States, House of Representatives Executive Document 70 (30th Congress, Session 1), Serial #521, and Insurrection against the Military Government in New Mexico and California in 1847 and 1848, Senate Document 442 (56th Congress, Session 1), Serial #3878. No secondary sources on the revolt were utilized for this article, but readers may be interested in consulting Ralph Emerson Twitchell, *The History of the Military Occupation of the Territory of New Mexico from 1846 to 1851* (Glorieta, NM: The Rio Grande Press, 1963) and Michael McNierney, ed., *Taos 1847: The Revolt of Contemporary Accounts* (Boulder, CO: Johnson Publishing Co., 1980). A first-hand account of these events can be found in Lewis H. Garrard [Hector Lewis Garrard], *Wah-To-Yah and the Taos Trail* (Cincinnati, OH: W. H. Derby & Co., 1850; reprinted Norman: University of Oklahoma Press, 1955).

9

1847: Revolt or Resistance?

Alberto Vidaurre

Of the many episodes of violence in Taos' history, none is more written about or more bitterly remembered than the "Taos Revolt of 1847," in which New Mexico's Governor Charles Bent and several prominent American citizens were murdered. Only recently has this tragedy been reevaluated in the context of its time. What emerges is a classic instance of the need to revise the traditional account—one largely shaped and dominated by the "victors'" point of view—and look again at whether the 1847 Revolt has been judged fairly. There were many victims of this violent uprising, and the pain it caused is still felt in Taos. In genealogist Alberto Viduarre's account, the martyred resisters come alive again.

ON FEBRUARY 12, 2002, both houses of the New Mexico State Legislature unanimously approved a Joint Memorial requesting the president of the United States and the governor of New Mexico to posthumously pardon the hundreds of New Mexican landowners and residents who, by rebelling against the United States Army's claim on and occupation of New Mexico in 1847, had died ingloriously and under a cloud of shame.[1] Some died fighting; others perished at the hands of hopelessly biased juries. Hector Louis Garrard, a seventeen-year-old trapper from Cincinnati who headed for Taos when he heard about the murders of Governor Charles Bent and the others, recorded his indignation at the way the resisters were being tried: "Justice! Out upon the word, when its distorted meaning is the warrant for murdering those who defend to the last their country and their homes."[2]

Garrard showed exceptional clarity in recognizing that the "poor wretches," whose sentencing he witnessed in the Taos courtroom and whose executions he described in his now-classic *Wah-to-yah and the Taos Trail,* had not committed acts of treason against the U.S. government. But until recently his contrarian estimation was a minority opinion, at least in conventional literature. Once the U.S. Army took control of Nuevo México in August 1846, both the contemporaneous and historical accounts of the so-called Taos Revolt have focused on the American victory and have downplayed Hispanics' and Indians' motives for the uprising. Only quite recently has the standard account been challenged by questions like: who were the resisters, and what impelled them to act with such vehemence and violence?

To answer these questions one must look at Mexican-American relations in the quarter century before 1846 and, of course, at the effects of the American takeover of Nuevo México. When Mexico broke free of Spain's deteriorating colonial grasp in 1821, Nuevo México's remote northern frontier passed from Spain's reasonably orderly and predictable—if very distant—governance to spotty attention from Mexico, which as a new nation was roiled by internal discord and occasionally even anarchy.

Under Spanish colonial policy, trade by locals with anyone outside the colony had been illegal. Therefore the only manufactured goods lawfully available to Taoseños were from Mexico or Spain. These products were scarce and expensive. By the early 1800s, local Spanish traders and French and American suppliers had begun meeting the demand for cheaper, more abundant goods by smuggling them into Taos.

When Mexico gained independence from Spain in 1821, the new government in Mexico City saw the benefits of revoking the old Spanish prohibitions. Mexico quickly and successfully allowed trade on the Santa Fe Trail between northern New Hispanic and the Missouri Valley. Along with cheaper goods, more available markets, and import duties for Santa Fe, the policy produced a new merchant class, both Mexican and American. By the 1840s, the new trade pattern had brought prosperity to those who took advantage of it. Most of Taos' farm families could not.

Charles Bent was one of these American merchants. He first came to New Mexico in 1829, and beginning in 1832 maintained a home in Taos with Taoseña Maria Ignacia Jaramillo, who bore their children. His company's operations were very successful, and he prospered. But there is evidence that Bent had little respect for his Hispanic neighbors and that he was probably not as well liked in his home town of Taos as he believed himself to be.

What made Bent an enemy of many Taoseños was his success, along with other Americans and Mexican citizens, in obtaining grants of enormous tracts of land around Taos. The lands involved had been used in common by Taoseños for generations, and there was genuine fear that the Americans and their Mexican partners were stealing the land. This generated even more mistrust between Bent and many locals.

Along with material goods, many *americanos* brought their long-established prejudices against non-European peoples and their biased preconceptions of both Indians and Hispanos of the Southwest. Eastern traders and visitors to Nuevo México under Mexican sovereignty were for the most part contemptuous and condescending toward local politics and justice, soldiers, local women, and priests. They viewed the settlers of Nuevo México, most of whom were darker skinned than many Euro-Americans, as inferior. In fact, the vast majority of Hispano settlers who moved north out of Mexico were of mixed blood through intermarriage with Indians in Mexico and Nuevo México and with blacks who had lived as slaves and servants in Mexico throughout the Spanish Colonial period.[3] Many Americans also dismissed the colonial Spanish Catholic Church as regressive when comparing it to Protestantism and were scornful of what they regarded as a lack of culture in this remote outpost of Mexico. On the eve of the Mexican-American War, Rufus B. Sage, who visited Taos in September of 1843 or 1844, wrote his impressions of Nuevo México:

> There are no people on the continent of America, whether civilized or uncivilized, with one or two exceptions, more miserable in condition or despicable in morals than the mongrel race inhabiting New Mexico. . . . Next to the squalid appearance of its inhabitants, the first thing that arrests the attention of the traveler on entering an [*sic*] Mexican settlement, is the uninviting mud walls that form the rude hovels which constitute its dwellings.[4]

In their arrogance, the Americans utterly failed to appreciate the strong folk culture and lifeways that had made survival possible in the face of isolation, hostile Indians, and a harsh physical environment. Perhaps most significantly they did not comprehend that both the Indian and Hispano landholders had developed cooperative, not competitive, relationships in order to sustain themselves and their respective cultures. For their part, the Hispano settlers and the Indians perceived the Americans as "arrogant, aggressive, unscrupulous racists who endangered the very existence of Mexico as a nation."[5]

By the time Brigadier General Stephen W. Kearny and his 1,657-man Army of the West rode into Las Vegas, New Mexico, on August 15, 1846, under orders to take Nuevo México for the United States before moving on to secure California, serious conflict was inevitable. The Mexican-American War was in full gallop. The Taos Revolt was one tragic expression of this collision of cultures and values.

UPRISING

Kearny's first official action was in Las Vegas, an important commercial town on the Santa Fe Trail but not the provincial capital. He climbed to the top of a building that faced the town plaza and, through a translator, delivered the following proclamation:

Mr. Alcalde and people of New Mexico, I have come amongst you by the orders of my government, to take possession of your country, and extend over it the laws of the United States. We consider it, and have done so for some time, a part of the territory of the United States. We come amongst you as friends—not as enemies; as protectors—not as conquerors. We come among you for your benefit—not for your injury.

Henceforth I absolve you from all allegiance to the Mexican government and from all obedience to General Armijo. He is no longer your governor. I am your governor.[6]

Three days later, on Tuesday, August 18, 1846, Kearny and his army took the Mexican provincial capital, Santa Fe, after Mexican Governor Manuel Armijo surrendered without resistance, disbanded his military forces, and fled south to Chihuahua, Mexico, with a bodyguard of ninety dragoons.

American military proclamations notwithstanding, Nuevo Méxicanos were citizens of Mexico until the signing of the Treaty of Guadalupe Hidalgo two years later, on February 2, 1848, and they smarted and smoldered at being ordered around by Americans. In an undated letter written about the time of the Taos Revolt and mentioning San Juan de los Caballeros, the writer says: "We have declared war with the American[s] and it is now time that we all take our arms in our hands in defence [defense] of our abandoned Country that we may try if possible to regain the liberty of our unhappy Country[.]"[7]

By December 1846, restive anger over new and unfamiliar laws imposed by Kearny and widespread dissatisfaction with American governance, including the imposition of license fees for businesses, had provoked plans for revolt. The first plan was to murder Colonel Sterling Price, whom Kearny had put in charge of the Santa Fe garrison, and the recently appointed territorial governor, Charles Bent, on Christmas Eve 1846 in Santa Fe.[8] When the plot was betrayed to the new American officials, some fourteen suspects were arrested, and two others fled south and escaped. Some of those arrested were released for lack of evidence, and the others were acquitted in a military court in early January 1847.

To Indians at Taos Pueblo, the new government was decidedly a threat to their well-being. They clearly felt their way of life was threatened by the cocky, self-proclaimed new "owners." Always before, governors had listened to Indian grievances and had tended to protect the Indians' civil and property rights. With the Americans, things were different. In the winter of 1846–47, at least two men from the pueblo were in jail on charges of larceny. When confronted by a party from the pueblo shortly before his murder, Governor Bent refused to release the Indians, saying that their situation had to be handled through the legal processes of the United States.[9] This early test of how the Americans would treat Indians frayed nerves.

In Don Fernando de Taos (Taos) and at Taos Pueblo, rage and frustration boiled over. In the early morning hours of Tuesday, January 19, a group of New Mexican and Indian resisters attacked, killed, and scalped Governor Bent and brother-in-law Pablo Jaramillo and slaughtered five other men: Narcisco Beaubien, son of the circuit judge, and his unnamed Indian slave; Circuit Attorney James White Leal; Sheriff Stephen Luis Lee; and Prefect José Cornelio Vigil.

Hector Lewis Garrard gives a quiet account of Bent's demise.[10]

> I visited the house in which Governor Bent was murdered, who, with district attorney, J. W. Liel [James White Leal], came from Santa Fé to issue a proclamation. While here in Fernández with his family, he was, one morning early, roused from sleep by the populace; who, with the aid of the Pueblos de Taos, were collected in front of his dwelling, striving to gain admittance. While they were effecting an entrance, he, with an ax, cut through an adobe wall into another house. The wife of the occupant[11] a clever though thriftless Canadian, heard him; and, with all her strength, rendered him assistance, though she was a Mexican. He retreated to a room, but seeing no way of escaping from the infuriated assailants, who fired upon him through a window, he spoke to his weeping wife and trembling children, clinging to him with all the tenacity of love and despair; and taking paper from his pocket, endeavored to write, but fast losing strength, he commended them to God and his brothers, and fell pierced by a Pueblo's [Taos Indian's] ball. Rushing in and tearing off the gray-haired scalp, the Indians bore it away in triumph.[12]

After their rampage in Don Fernando de Taos, the resisters moved on to Turley's Mill in Arroyo Hondo, about nine miles to the north. After a two-day assault on the mill, they killed occupants Albert Turbush, William Hatfield, Louis Tolque, Peter Roberts, Joseph Marshall, and William Austin.[13] Not all accounts agree where mill owner and "Taos Lightning" distiller Simeon Turley died. More than one account says that he escaped, was discovered hiding in the mountains, was turned in, and was shot in the head after the second day of fighting.[14] Other sources count Turley among those murdered at the mill. There is no mention of what became of Turley's common law wife, Maria Rosita Vigil y Romero, and their seven young children. Violence spread north to Rio Colorado (Questa), where two American trappers, Mark Head and William Harwood, were killed. Before it ended, the uprising continued in Mora and San Miguel counties, where there were significant additional casualties.

Recent excavation of the Turley Mill site shows that the two-storey stone-and-adobe main building may have been the largest non-Pueblo structure in all of New Mexico (larger even than the Palace of the Governors in Santa Fe). It was a famous distillery, a major fur-trading site, and it sold basic supplies to the frontier population.

There are a number of possible reasons why Indians and local Hispanos may have
targeted the mill, the most obvious of them being that the American-owned mill
was perceived as an example of brash American attitudes toward the local population
and its slim resources. Although Turley was well spoken of, he had been harvesting
large amounts of timber from what was community property of the Arroyo Hondo
Grant of 1815. The mill had a very large pit kiln for making charcoal, some of it used
at the mill to distill Taos Lightning, some apparently for blacksmithing, and some
probably for export. Turley's whiskey reached tribes on the Great Plains.[15]

When word of the murders reached Santa Fe, Colonel Price[16] quickly put together
a force of Missouri Volunteers, infantrymen, and dragoons, which, together with a
company of local mountain men enlisted by Bent's trading partner, Cerán St. Vrain,
totaled just over 350 men. In late January of that snowy winter the U.S. troops started
north, encountering the large but untrained and disorganized force at points along
the road from Santa Fe to Taos. Estimated variously at several hundred to more than
1,000 resisters, they dug in first at Santa Cruz de la Cañada, just east of Española
(January 24), and in the mountains at Embudo Pass (January 29). Equipped with
howitzers and much superior munitions, at each of these engagements the U.S.
prevailed, driving the resisters back north toward Taos and the defensible pueblo.
Colonel Price's report to the adjutant general lists thirty-six enemy killed and an
unknown number wounded at Santa Cruz; at Embudo Pass, twenty were killed and
an unknown number wounded.

Price's and St. Vrain's soldiers and artillery reached Fernando de Taos on February
3 and, toward evening, were in position 250 yards outside the thick walls of the Pueblo.
After two and a half hours of shelling and attempts to breach the adobe barrier, the
troops retired for the night. The next day the resisters and other Pueblo families—altogether several hundred people—took refuge in the pueblo church, San Geronimo de
Taos. St. Vrain's company was posted to a field east of the church to capture any who
might try to flee the church and make a run for the mountains. Price's troops charged
and crossed the walls, attacking the mission church from the west and north. Garrard
reconstructs the scene:

> A fire was opened by the howitzers [short- to medium-range cannons]
> at four hundred yards, and, after some skirmishing by the infantry and
> Burgwin's command of dragoons, the enemy retreated to the church, from
> the numerous loopholes of which they poured out a galling fire. The battery
> was now ordered up within a hundred yards, which had some effect, but
> the balls striking the tough mud walls did not always penetrate. Burgwin's
> dismounted men then stormed the front door of the church. After a spirited
> attack of several minutes, they were ordered to the west side, where, with
> axes, a breach was cut, through which they entered, several losing their
> lives. The cannons were run up to the breach—the bursting of the bombs

in the small space, in which so many were crowded, caused great destruction of life. "The mingled noise of bursting shells, firearms, the yells of the Americans, and the shrieks of the wounded," says my narrator, an eyewitness, "was most appalling."[17]

Captain Burgwin suffered a mortal wound as he led his unsuccessful assault on the front door of the church.[18]

From the American standpoint, the Taos Revolt of 1847 was under control. The pueblo church was in ruins, and altogether in the January engagements and at Taos Pueblo the Americans had killed many of the resisters—perhaps more than two hundred fifty.[19] Of the many resisters who were killed in battles with the U.S. Army, only two are listed in local church burial records. *Murio En La Guerra* (killed in war) were José Francisco Trujillo (February 6) and Pedro Antonio Trujillo (February 13). One Taoseño was listed *Murio En Un Movimiento Publico* on January 20 (killed in a public disturbance). His name was Antonio Ascencio Gallegos, whose allegiance is not known. The Americans reported losing fourteen men, with fifty-one wounded in the battles at Santa Cruz, Embudo Pass, Taos Pueblo, and Mora.[20] A good number of them were buried in the American Cemetery, now Kit Carson Cemetery, in Taos.

"Treason" Trials and Executions

Price's response to the "insurrection" was to call for a court in Taos to try the accused. Five Taos men were identified as the suspected leaders of the uprising: José Pablo Montoya, who had been active in the Revolt of 1837; Pablo Chávez and Jesus Tafoya, both of whom were killed during the uprising; Tomás (Tomasito) Romero, from the pueblo, who was shot and killed by an army private while in custody in the Taos jail.[21] The fifth man, Manuel Cortez, was never apprehended and is thought to have fled to Mexico. Within three weeks of the attacks and two months before the first term of the U.S. Circuit and District Courts for the Northern District of New Mexico were convened in Taos on April 5, Pablo Montoya was tried by a drumhead military court in Taos. (The term *drumhead court* came into use about 1825 to mean a court convened on or near the field of battle to deal rapidly and summarily with charged offenses committed during military operations. It refers to the use of a drumhead as a table.) Montoya was summarily sentenced and, with women and children looking on from rooftops, was hanged in Taos Plaza on February 7, leaving his wife, María Teresa Esquivel, and six children: Juan José, Jesús Maria, José Quirana, Antonio José, María Manuela, and María Teodora. Neither baptism nor burial records survive. Some of Montoya's descendants still live in the Taos Valley.

Impartiality and other principles of American justice were cast aside in the makeup and conduct of the first term of the U.S. District Court. The judges

were two of Bent's close friends: Joab Houghton, a civil engineer, was chief jus-
tice. Charles (Carlos) Beaubien, who was born Charles Hipolyte Trotier but took
Beaubien as his surname, was the presiding judge. (His son, Narcisco, had been
one of those murdered.) Beaubien was "assisted" by a soldier named Wharton.
Associate justice was Antonio J. Otero from Valencia County. The names of the
jurors recorded for the several trials include Narcisco's brother-in-law, Lucien
Maxwell, and some men known to be sympathetic to Bent. The rolls list: Juan
Miguel Baca, Edmond Chadwick, Bautiste Charleyfoe, C. L. Corrier, Benjamin
Day [also recorded as Davy], Rafael de Luna, Antonio Dewitt [also recorded as
Duet, Duett, Deitt, and Dutt], Asa Estes, Robert Fisher, John Hatcher, Peter
Joseph, Henry Katz, William Le Blanc, Manuel Lafore, Antonio Leroux, Basal [also
given as Basil and Berall] LeRew, George Long, Horace Long, Julian Lucero, Elijah
Ness, Charles Ortibus, Joseph Paulding, Joseph Play, Charles Roubidoux, Rafael
de Serna, Lewis Simmons, Charles Town, Vidal Trujillo, José Ignacio Valdez, José
Manuel Valdez, Pedro Valdez, and Thomas Whitlo.[22]

George Bent, one of the governor's three brothers, was foreman of the grand
jury, and Elliott Lee, a member of the grand jury, was the brother of the slain sheriff,
Stephen Louis Lee.[23] Also listed on the venire—or pool—from which the grand jury
could be drawn were James S. Barry, Joseph M. Graham, Antonio Ortiz, José Gregory
Martínez, Miguel Sanchez, Mariano Martin, Matias Vigil, Gabriel Vigil, Santiago
Martínez, Ventura Martínez, José Cordoval, Felipe Romero, Ramonde Cordoval,
Antonio Medina, José Angel Vigil, Antonio José Bingo, and Juan Bennette Valdez.[24]
Ceran St. Vrain, the governor's business partner, was court interpreter. A young Frank
(Francis) P. Blair Jr. was prosecuting U.S. attorney; he had just been admitted to
the bar in Kentucky, his native state. Trapper and Indian trader Archibald Charles
Metcalf, at the time of the trial, was sheriff in charge of the executions—boarding
the prisoners, erecting the gallows, and hanging those sentenced. Young Garrard, who
was an eyewitness to the trials, described the counsel for the defense as a volunteer
army private on furlough.

Garrard observed:

> It certainly did appear to be a great assumption on the part of the Americans
> to conquer a country and then arraign the revolting inhabitants for treason.
> American judges sat on the bench, New Mexicans and Americans filled the
> jury box, and an American soldiery guarded the halls. Verily, a strange mix-
> ture of violence and justice—a strange middle ground between the martial
> and common law.[25]

Court records of April 1847 give the names of sixteen men tried and sentenced
for their part in the resistance over a period of eight days, April 6 through April 13.
Except for one man charged with high treason, all were charged with and found

guilty of murder and were sentenced to death by hanging. Listed here in the order of their dates of execution are the men condemned in those trials: Hipolito (Polo) Salazar sentenced for high treason, José Manuel Garcia, Manuel Antonio Romero and his brother Ysidro Antonio Romero, Pedro Lucero, Juan Ramon Trujillo (April 9); Indians Francisco Naranjo, José Gabriel Romero, Juan Domingo Martin, Juan Antonio Lucero, and El Cuervo (April 30); Manuel Miera, Juan Pacheco, Manuel Sandoval, Rafael Tafoya (April 30); and Juan Antonio Ávila (May 7). Not one of the accused resisters entered a plea of guilty. "Appeals were not much in favor in this court, for each homicide the convict was hanged before a transcript could have been written."[26]

The sixteen were sentenced and hanged in groups, the first six condemned on Wednesday April 7. Garrard supplies details:

> [They] were sentenced to be hung on the following Friday [April 9]—hang-man's day. When the concluding words "*muerto, muerto, muerto*"—"dead, dead, dead"—were pronounced by Judge Beaubien in his solemn and impressive manner, the painful stillness that reigned in the courtroom and the subdued grief manifested by a few bystanders were noticed not without an inward sympathy. The poor wretches sat with immovable features; but I fancied that under the assumed looks of apathetic indifference could be read the deepest anguish. When remanded to jail till the day of execution, they drew their *sarapes* [sic] more closely around them.[27]

Two days later, on April 9, Garrard witnessed the hanging of Hipolito Salazar, José Manuel Garcia, the brothers Manuel Antonio Romero and Isidoro Antonio Romero, Pedro Lucero, and Juan Ramon Trujillo:[28]

> Bidding each other "*adios,*" with a hope of meeting in Heaven, at word from the sheriff the mules were started and the wagon [on which they stood] drawn from under the tree. . . . The bodies swayed back and forth, and, coming in contact with each other, convulsive shudders shook their frames . . . the bodies writhed most horribly.
>
> While thus swinging, the hands of two came together, which they held with a firm grip till the muscles loosened in death.[29]

A careful study of church records of Our Lady of Guadalupe in Taos has brought to light humanizing details about a number of the men executed or killed in the uprising. Padre Antonio José Martínez, who was then parish priest, noted each man's full name and the names of his father, mother, and wife. Children living at the time of their father's death are listed in order of their births, with dates of baptism given. In a brief paragraph in his own hand, Padre Martínez notes whether he was able to administer the holy sacraments of the dying or whether the victim died without that privilege. Each man was assigned to the same plot in the church cemetery, as was the custom then.[30]

Of the six who died on April 9, José Manuel Garcia was the first to be sentenced by the U.S. District Court. He was married to Maria Francisca Archuleta in October 1837. They had three boys and three girls, and only one daughter survived him. Padre Martínez recorded the burial, noting that Garcia did not have a will (*no tuvo que testat*) and that he was to be buried in plot #6.

Hipolito Salazar was the second man to be sentenced, on April 7, 1847, by the U.S. District Court and the only one condemned for high treason. Padre Martínez wrote:

En este curato de Taos a los nueve dias del mes de Abril de mil ochocientos curenta y siete (1847), yo el Parroco Don Antonio Jose Martinez en el cemeterio de Nuestra Señora de Guadalupe di sepulcro al cadaver de Hipolito Salazar, esposo que fue de Maria Polonia Serre, vecinos de esta Plaza de Nuestra Señora de Guadalupe. Dicho difunto murio por sentencia judicial y le administre los Santos Sacramentos de Penitencia y Comunion. Testo lo___que tenia___testameto lo agarro Metcafe. Le quedaron tres hijos vivos dicho sepul ___fue en el tramo 6°, y pa que con esta firme Antonio Jose Martinez (Rubrica).

In this parish of Taos on the ninth day of the month of April eighteen hundred and forty-seven, I, the parish priest Don Antonio José Martínez, on the cemetery grounds of Our Lady of Guadalupe, buried the dead body of Hipolito Salazar, who was the husband of María Polonia Serre, citizens of this Plaza of Our Lady of Guadalupe. Said deceased died by judicial sentencing. I administered the holy sacraments of penitence and communion to him. I testify that what he had in testament be taken by Metcafe [Charles Archibald Metcalfe, acting sheriff]. He is survived by three sons. Said burial took place in plot #6, and therefore I sign Antonio José Martínez. [rubric]

The other four who were hanged on April 9 were sentenced on April 7. They included the Romero brothers, Ysidro Antonio and Manuel Antonio, whose parents were Ysidro Romero and Matiana Paez from Le Joya (now Velarde). The brothers were from Plaza de los Dolores (Our Lady of Sorrows village, now Cañon). Ysidro was married to Margareta Durán. Their two children were Andres Avelino and Juana de la Cruz. Sixteen-year-old Manuel Antonio received the holy sacraments and was buried with his brother and the others in plot #6 at Our Lady of Guadalupe cemetery.

The fifth man to die on April 9 was Juan Ramon Trujillo, born in La Plaza de los Dolores (Arroyo Hondo) on May 9, 1823. He was married to María Antonia Coca on February 19, 1844. Their one child was José Guadalupe Trujillo, born in Guadalupe Plaza on November 18, 1846. Juan Trujillo's death record confirms that he and his family lived in Guadalupe Plaza at the time of his death. He too was buried in the

Guadalupe church cemetery. No records have come to light for the sixth person to die on April 9, Pedro Lucero.

On April 10, 1847, Manuel Sandoval, Manuel Miera, Juan Pacheco, and Rafael Tafoya were tried and sentenced to hang from the neck until dead. Manuel Sandoval was seventeen years old, the legitimate son of Manuel Sandoval and Maria Benita Martínez. On April 30, Padre Martínez administered the holy sacraments to him; he was also buried in plot #6. Rafael Tafoya was married to Maria Rafael Gonzales, both from Our Lady of Guadalupe parish. Again Padre Martínez states that Tafoya died as the consequence of a judicial sentence and received the holy sacraments before dying. He had no surviving children and was buried in plot #6 with the others. No family or other information has been found for Manuel Miera or Juan Pacheco.

Francisco Naranjo, José Gabriel Somoro [Samora], Juan Domingo Martin, Juan Antonio Lucero, and El Cuerroe [El Cuervo] are identified as Indians in the court records. Court hearings for them were held on April 8, 1847. They were charged with murder and sentenced to hang. The hangings took place on April 30, 1847. No family or burial records have been found for any of them.

The last of the resisters to be executed was Juan Antonio Ávila. His court hearing was on April 13, 1847. Charged with murder, he was sentenced to hang and died on May 7, 1847. Records are unfortunately silent about Ávila.

Padre Martínez also buried four of the attack victims: Pablo Jaramillo, Governor Bent's brother-in-law; José Narciso Beaubien, Carlos Beaubien's unmarried nineteen-year-old son; sheriff, trader, and trapper Stephen Luis Lee; and José Cornelio Vigil, a prefect and probate judge who was fifty-nine when he was murdered. The padre noted that he had not been able to administer the holy sacrament of dying to any of them. Beaubien was buried in plot "sisto" (#6); the others were interred in plot #4. Beaubien was not married. The other three were married to women of local Hispanic familes: Pablo Jaramillo to Maria Manuela Martínez, Stephen Lee to Maria de la Luz Tafoya, and José Cornelio Vigil to Maria de los Reyes Baca.

The other victims, presumed not to be of the Catholic faith, were buried in the newly created El Cemeterio Militar,[31] on land donated by Theodora Martínez Romero, Padre Martínez's housekeeper.

The 2002 Joint Memorial Resolution, offered in recognition of the resisters' Mexican citizenship at the time of the 1847 Revolt, was an important acknowledgment. Yet more remains to be done to identify other, including living, descendants of these men, whose stories are as tragic as those of the better-known victims of the Taos Rebellion.

NOTES

1. This chapter is an adaptation of an article, "1847 Revolt —Taos and Surrounding Areas," in *Raíces y Ramas*, a publication of the National Society of Hispanic Genealogy

3: 4 (Winter 2001). This article should be consulted for more detailed genealogical and biographical information on the victims of the revolt, especially the seventeen resisters who were convicted of murder or treason shortly after the revolt. I have consulted church baptism and marriage records of Taos, Santa Fe, and Abiquiú. These are listed in the Selected References.

Julie Montoya-Martinez, sixth-generation descendant of resistance leader José Pablo Montoya, has written "Taos Revolt 1847: A Fight for a Way of Life," an unpublished research paper which concentrates on Montoya. A copy is on file at the Southwest Research Center in Taos.

Julia Moore, editor of this book, consolidated source material as a narrative. Corina A. Santistevan provided translations of Padre Martínez's burial records.

2. Lewis H. Garrard [Hector Lewis Garrard], *Wah-to-yah and the Taos Trail* (Cincinnati, OH: W. H. Derby & Co., 1850; reprinted, Norman: University of Oklahoma Press, 1955), 173.

3. David J. Weber, in *Foreigners in Their Native Land: Historical Roots of the Mexican Americans*, David J. Weber, ed. 30th Anniversary Edition (Albuquerque: University of New Mexico Press, 2003), 17.

4. Rufus B. Sage, quoted in Ibid., 72.

5. Weber, *Foreigners in Their Native Land*, 61.

6. Howard Bryan, *Wildest of the Wild West* (Santa Fe, NM: Clear Light Publishers, 1991), 18.

7. New Mexico Primary Sources from the National Archives Rocky Mountain Region. www.archives.gov/rocky-mountain/education/materials/primary-source-lessons-new-mexico: 5. San Juan de los Cabelleros was the name Oñate gave the site of the first Spanish settlement, occupied for less than a year, at Okay Owingeh, long known as San Juan Pueblo.

8. Michael McNierney, ed., *Taos 1847: The Revolt in Contemporary Accounts* (Boulder, CO: Johnson Publishing Co., 1980), 4. James W. Goodrich, "Revolt at Mora, 1847," *New Mexico Historical Review* (January 1972), 50.

9. It is unlikely that the Indians actually stole as charged. As they lived communally, Indians generally borrowed and loaned material goods rather than possessing them.

10. Probably because of his youth and his lack of scholarly training, certain scholars have questioned the veracity of Garrard's account of events in Taos. His secondhand account of Bent's death may not be as credible as his eyewitness accounts of the trials and hangings, which are certainly worth studying.

11. The house referred to belonged to Bent's good friend Thomas Boggs, whose wife, Rumalda Luna Boggs, was Maria Ignacia Jaramillo Bent's sister and thus Bent's sister-in-law. The third Jaramillo sister, Josefa, was married to Kit Carson. At one of the trials, the three married Jaramillo sisters sat together in the courtroom. "The dress and manners of the three ladies bespoke a greater degree of refinement than usual" (Garrard, 181).

12. Garrard, *Wah-to-yah*, 176.

13. Oral tradition of at least one Taos Pueblo family, that of John Suazo, as recorded by

Anne L. MacNaughton, relates that Arroyo Hondo was the first target of the resisters, with Fernando de Taos following. See Anne L. MacNaughton, "When the Soldiers Came: One Taos Pueblo Family's Story of the Revolt of 1847," on file at the Southwest Research Center in Taos. This interesting unpublished research paper, written about 2005, offers variant accounts and interpretations of what happened. Suazo also published an account that cites Turley Mill as the first target: *Horsefly* [Taos], May 15, 2005.

14. Blanche C. Grant, *When Old Trails Were New: The Story of Taos* (New York: Press of the Pioneers, 1934), 94. Janet Lecompte, *Pueblo, Hardscrabble, Greenhorn: The Upper Arkansas, 1832–1856* (Norman: University of Oklahoma Press, 1978), 194. Ernest Lyckman, in an undated and unpublished paper titled "A Review of the Ranch, Trading Post, Mill and Distillery of Simeon Turley, Cañoncito, Arroyo Hondo, Taos County, New Mexico 1930–1847," sides with Lecompte in saying that Turley escaped and was shot the next day.

15. Excavations are under the direction of Albert Gonzales in fulfillment of requirements for the PhD degree in the Department of Anthropology at Southern Methodist University. His as-yet-unpublished and incomplete findings were presented in a talk, "Burning Discontent: Indigenous Anxiety and the Destruction of Turley Mill," June 21, 2011, at the Fort Burgwin campus of SMU.

16. Within two years of leaving New Mexico, Stephen Watts Kearny (1794–1848) died of malaria—but after he had helped take California for the U.S. and had been made military governor of the territory and major general. Colonel Price (1809–1867) was military governor of New Mexico after Kearny left for California. Price returned to civilian life as a slave-owning tobacco farmer after the Mexican-American War ended. At the outbreak of the Civil War, he sided with the Confederate cause and led a number of losing battles. When the war ended, Price left for Mexico without surrendering. He died in 1867 after his colony of Confederate exiles in Veracruz, Mexico, failed.

17. Garrard, *Wah-to-yah*, 186.

18. Captain John Henry King Burgwin, a graduate of West Point serving with the 1st Dragoons, had led the battle at Embudo Pass on January 29, 1847. The U.S. Army's Taos cantonment, now Fort Burgwin, was named in Burgwin's honor at its founding in 1852. It closed in 1860, when troops were consolidated at Fort Union, about fifty miles southeast of Taos. In the 1950s, under the direction of archaeologist Fred Wendorf, the old wooden fort buildings were excavated. In 1964, Southern Methodist University began to acquire and develop the former fort as a center for liberal arts, archaeology, and anthropology with its SMU-in-Taos program.

19. The number of resisters killed in the pueblo battle ranges from 150 up to several hundred.

20. *Niles' National Register* (Baltimore, MD: April 17, 1847), 112.

21. An army private noted as Fitzgerald (also Fitzpatrick) went into the Taos jail and shot Romero in the head at close range before the trial. In February 1847, he escaped Taos and was not seen again.

22. Francis T. Cheetham, "The First Term of the American Court in Taos, New Mexico," *New Mexico Historical Review* 1: 1 (January 1926), 23–35.

23. During the attack on January 19–20, Elliott Lee was sheltered by Padre Martínez and thus likely escaped death.

24. The venire for the grand jury appears on page 209 of "Pioneer Freemasons in the Winning of the Southwest," an unpublished, undated manuscript by historian Francis T. Cheetham, a copy of which was presented to Bent Masonic Lodge #42, A.F. and A.M. in Taos, New Mexico, by Wallace, Everett, and Lowell Cheetham in June 1955 and is in the Lodge's possession. It was probably written between 1926 and 1930.

25. Garrard, *Wah-to-yah*, 172.

26. Cheetham, "The First Term," 26.

27. Garrard, *Wah-to-yah,* 172–73.

28. The prison where the condemned were housed and the execution grounds beyond it is described as being at the edge of town, with only fields to the north of it. Ibid., 195.

29. Ibid., 197–98.

30. These church records are presented in full in the author's article "1847 Revolt—Taos and Surrounding Areas," in *Raíces y Ramas Journal* 3: 4 (Winter 2001), 2–16.

31. The name was changed to American Cemetery in 1852 and to Kit Carson Cemetery in 1869, when Carson was buried there. The cemetery is just north of Kit Carson Park in downtown Taos.

SELECTED REFERENCES

Archives of the Archdiocese of Santa Fe. Microfilm, Reel 42, Taos Burials.

Bryan, Howard. *Wildest of the Wild West.* Santa Fe, NM: Clear Light Publishers, 1991.

Cheetham, Francis T. "The First Term of the American Court in Taos, New Mexico." *New Mexico Historical Review* 1: 1 (January 1926), 23–25.

Garrard, Lewis H. [Hector Lewis Garrard]. *Wah-to-yah and the Taos Trail.* Cincinnati, OH: W. H. Derby & Co., 1850; reprint, Norman: University of Oklahoma Press, 1955.

McNierney, Michael, ed. *Taos 1847: The Revolt in Contemporary Accounts.* Boulder, CO: Johnson Publishing Co., 1980.

Twitchell, Ralph Emerson. *The History of the Military Occupation of the Territory of New Mexico from 1846 to 1851.* Denver: The Smith-Brooks Company, 1909. Reissued Denver: Rio Grande Press, 1963.

Vidaurre, Alberto. "1847 Revolt—Taos and Surrounding Areas." In *Raíces y Ramas*, a publication of the National Society of Hispanic Genealogy 3:4 (Winter 2001), 2–15.

Weber, David J., ed. *Foreigners in Their Native Land: Historical Roots of the Mexican Americans.* 30th anniversary edition. Albuquerque: University of New Mexico Press, 2003.

10

Taos, the Jicarilla Apache, and the Battle of Cieneguilla

DAVID M. JOHNSON, CHRIS ADAMS, LARRY LUDWIG, AND CHARLES C. HAWK

In 1846, when the United States first gained sovereignty over what had been Nuevo México, the U.S. Army was sent into northern New Mexico, in part to protect the settled populations from attacks by nomadic Indians. Some tribes were hostile, and some were peaceful. Mistakes of judgment by the American military were not uncommon. The 1854 Battle of Cieneguilla, the result of a misjudgment, was the first and the bloodiest U.S. military setback up to that time. Recent field research by the authors of this chapter has given us a true picture of an unnecessary and bloody encounter. This chapter is an excellent window on the complex relationships between all three wary populations who shared the Taos Valley in the 1840s.

IN THE HISTORY OF INDIAN WARFARE in the West, the U.S. Army suffered only a handful of decisive defeats. The Battle of Cieneguilla remains the third worst defeat for the U.S. Army in the West, surpassed only by the Fetterman Fight[1] in 1866 and the Battle of the Little Bighorn in 1876.

Despite the significance of this battle, it is not familiar to students of western or of Taos history. This is partly because until

2002 the location of the battle was not known. The discovery of the battle site by archaeologists from the Carson National Forest, the Bureau of Land Management, and the National Park Service has made accurate interpretation of the battle possible—thus allowing it to take its proper place in history.

On March 30, 1854, six years after New Mexico had become a U.S. territory, troops of the U.S. 2nd Dragoons found themselves at a campsite in the small Hispanic village of Cieneguilla (now Pilar). They had arrived there at 1:00 a.m. after a night march from their post at Cantonment Burgwin, southeast of Taos. Lieutenant John W. Davidson, commander of Companies F and I of the 2nd Dragoons, had been ordered there to observe and control the movements of Jicarilla Apache but not to attack them.

Lt. Davidson seems to have had some knowledge of where to find the Jicarilla in the mountains east of Cieneguilla. About two hours after beginning his march east, Lt. Davidson found them. Someone fired a shot, and the Battle of Cieneguilla began. By nightfall, one-third of the dragoons lay dead in the mountains. A good number of the rest were wounded and spent the night at Ranchos de Taos before being transported to Cantonment Burgwin the next day;[2] some of those men died within days. Most of the horses and equipment were lost.

Taos and the Jicarilla Apache

The Jicarilla Apache lived, hunted, and farmed near Taos throughout the eighteenth and first half of the nineteenth centuries. In 1719 the Spanish described several Jicarilla settlements near Cimarrón as composed of small adobe houses with irrigated agriculture.[3] Unfortunately, these settlements were vulnerable to devastating raids by the newly arrived Comanche. By the early 1730s, in order to get the Jicarilla into an alliance against the Comanche, the Spanish moved a band of Comanche-displaced Jicarilla to the Taos area.

While this "resettlement" did not last long, it had some important consequences. It increased interdependence between Hispanics and the Jicarilla. Apache assistance against the Comanche assured peaceful relations with Hispanic settlers throughout the 1700s. The alliance also allowed the Jicarilla to continue much of their traditional way of life. They continued to hunt on New Mexico's eastern plains and farm near the Rio Grande. But eventually the Jicarilla and Hispano farmers began to compete for the same land. This was a competition the Jicarilla could not hope to win. From 1730 to about 1800 it was not too important; both groups were still dependent on each other. But after the Comanche peace in the late 1700s, and the resulting increase in the Hispanic population, the Jicarilla began to be seen as a threat, not an ally.

THE JICARILLA AND THE CIENEGUILLA SETTLEMENT

By the end of the 1700s, the Jicarilla were farming and hunting on both sides of the Sangre de Cristos. The mountain valleys south of Taos were also part of their territory, and for a part of every year they lived and hunted along well-known trails to Taos.

In 1795 the Spanish governor agreed to a request by Hispanic settlers for the Town of Cieneguilla Land Grant.[4] The grant included land along the Rio Grande at present-day Pilar as well as much of the mountains to the east. But the Jicarilla had also been seasonally farming at Cieneguilla well before the 1795 grant. In 1822 they petitioned for a grant of land at Cieneguilla. Hispanics at Cieneguilla and Taos vigorously opposed the petition:

> That the Jicarilla nation has always been at peace with us cannot be denied and has rendered us some service, when as auxiliary forces they have joined us in campaign against our enemies, but it is not violent to affirm, that in the first, they acted from necessity, in consequence of being a persecuted tribe, timid, despicable and limited in force on account of their small numbers of warriors.[5]

Taos officials accused the Jicarilla of thefts and murders in the vicinity. These, they claimed, supported "the just repugnance the people have, to having at this place such malicious and perverse residents."[6] The Jicarilla's request was denied.

The reaction to the 1822 petition shows that the era of dependence on the Jicarilla was over. Hispanic settlers were taking land they had traditionally farmed. Their hunting grounds on the eastern plains were getting crowded with both other tribes and with Hispanic hunters and traders. The Jicarilla were slowly being squeezed out of their economic base.

THE JICARILLA AND THE AMERICANS

When New Mexico became part of the United States in 1848, the Jicarilla Tribe was small, only about 400 persons and 150 fighting men.[7] American policy toward them was inconsistent, mostly because of the dual authority over Indian affairs in the territory. The superintendent of Indian affairs and local Indian agents had civil authority and were responsible for the management and care of the tribes. The military was responsible for ensuring the safety of civilians and keeping the peace, by force if necessary. The actions of territorial political officials added to the mix; many wanted simply to open Indian lands for settlement as quickly as possible.

Another problem was money. Often the Indian agents did not have enough funds to feed the tribes and thus avoid raiding. An example is an 1851 treaty made with one band of Jicarilla. The Indians agreed to live peacefully and farm well west of the Rio Grande in exchange for provisions, education, and annuities. But Congress did not ratify the treaty. The funds to provide what had been promised were never appropriated. After crop failures, the effort collapsed. Although most Jicarilla remained peaceful, some raiding on the east side of the Sangre de Cristos resumed. The same thing happened in 1853 when a similar treaty effort failed for lack of federal support.

For the Jicarilla, most Americans' low opinion of them was yet another problem. Charles Bent, for example, reported to Washington, DC, that the Jicarilla numbered only about 400 persons and were a lazy and cowardly people who roamed the region without any permanent settlements and lived habitually by theft and barter of pottery.[8] His was not the opinion of a newcomer to northern New Mexico. He had made his living trading with Indians since 1829.

THE BATTLE OF CIENEGUILLA

At the start of 1854, the garrison at Cantonment Burgwin was commanded by Major George Blake and consisted of two companies of the 2nd Dragoons. Each company had two officers and about forty-five mounted troopers. The senior company commander, Lt. John W. Davidson, was a West Point graduate of the class of 1846. He had fought in California during the Mexican War and was in several battles with Indians. By all accounts he was a capable and popular officer, with unquestioned courage under fire.

Fort Union was commanded by Lt. Col. Philip St. George Cooke, the most respected officer in the mounted service, if not in the entire U.S. Army. He had experience in the Southwest, and with Indians, dating from 1829.[9] Cantonment Burgwin at Taos was in his area of command.

In January 1854, military concern with the Jicarilla began to increase. On January 14, Territorial Governor David Meriwether sent a letter to the army listing numerous complaints of Apache depredations against civilians near Las Vegas. The senior military officer in the territory, General John Garland, had become skeptical of such complaints, and replied to the governor:

> Whilst on the subject of Indian depredations, I beg to call your Excellency's attention to the fact, generally known in New Mexico, that large armed parties of New Mexicans are in the habit of going into the Indian Country, or perhaps more properly speaking, their hunting grounds, where they kill off the very game upon which the Indians depend for subsistence. This will have the effect, of course, of forcing upon the Indians the necessity of either breaking up these hunting parties or of depredating upon the settlements, or worse than either, of starving to death.[10]

Nevertheless Garland ordered Lt. Col. Cooke at Fort Union to investigate the reported depredations. On January 29 Cooke reported to Gen. Garland these results:

> It appears as a result of this investigation, that the complaints made to the Governor, had but little colour of truth.—That the priest [at San Miguel] had lost no sheep—that a very few animals of an abandoned herd were eaten by the Indians, probably half starved; that the [New Mexican] hunting party were not at "Red River" but intruders near the Arkansas beyond the territory:—That the white men were murdered by New Mexicans who were not punished.
>
> It would seem that white men and Indians are at present most in need of our protection.[11]

Thus Garland and Cooke were quite aware of the locals' eagerness to blame any losses on Indians. Neither officer was about to start a war based on such complaints. But a month later Cooke received credible reports of Jicarilla stock raiding north of Fort Union. He ordered Lt. David Bell to respond. Bell left Fort Union with about thirty dragoons on March 2. On March 5 he encountered a party of thirty Jicarilla Apache. After a tense standoff and some discussion, the Apache ran for cover. Firing broke out. Five Jicarilla and two dragoons were killed. The Jicarilla escaped and promptly ran off a large herd of Fort Union's cattle pastured a few miles away.

Shortly after Lt. Bell's fight, Cooke received a letter from the alcalde of Mora reporting that forty-five lodges of Apache had arrived there "in great alarm" and claiming to be peaceful. In response Cooke made his first request for help from Major Blake at Taos, directing him as follows:

> As empowered by Dept. Order No. 15—of which you have been furnished a copy, I have to call upon you for a company, strengthened, if necessary, to 45 or 50 mounted men, to march as soon as practicable to the village of Mora. There are believed, to be forty five [sic] lodges of Apaches camped three miles from there: they came in five or six days ago, in real or pretended alarm, professing innocence & a desire for peace:—there are at least ten men among them—there maybe 70 or 80.[12]

Maj. Blake responded by sending one of his companies of dragoons to Mora. Lt. Davidson left Taos for Mora on March 21. Somewhere between Picurís and Mora, Davidson's troops met the Jicarilla, who were heading west towards Picurís. Apparently most of the tribe was present: women, children, and 107 warriors.[13] They showed no hostility toward Davidson's Dragoons. That evening Davidson left his troops at Mora and rode to Fort Union to report directly to Cooke. Lt. Bell was with Cooke at Fort Union and describes Davidson's visit as follows:

On the evening of the 21st of March Lt. D. arrived at Ft. Union from Mora where he had left his company and reported to Col Cooke for instructions. . . . He stated that on his way from Cantonment Burgwin to Ft. Union where he had been ordered by Col. Cooke he met the Apaches in a canon [*sic*] between the former place and Mora, that he had halted his command and, with Col. Brooks, had a talk with them; he described them as being overwhelmed with fear and protesting that they desired peace. . . . He also commented on the miserable quality of their arms, and their mean shrinking deportment, at the same time averring that he was sorry that they did not show some signs of hostility, for that if the(y) had he would have "wiped them out."[14]

Cooke's next orders to Major Blake were probably carried back to Taos the next day by Davidson:

I have instructed Lt. Davidson to march his company back to his post, the Apaches in larger numbers, than was supposed, having been met by him on their way to Taos (Having started before receiving any message from me). The only cooperation I have to ask of you at present is to watch or control these Indians until there is a settlement with the rest of the tribe. Their warm professions of friendship are founded on their present fears, & poverty of their horses.[15]

These orders reflect both Cooke's patience and his experience with Indians. He wisely chose to avoid hostilities and not interfere with what was peaceful movement.

On March 24 or 25, some of the Jicarilla Davidson had met near Mora, including two chiefs, came to Taos to talk with their new agent, Kit Carson. On March 25, Blake had Davidson take them into custody and bring them to the fort. There the two officers and Carson met with the Indians. On March 27, Carson reported from Taos to the governor in Santa Fe:

I have the honor to report that on the 25th instant I had council with eight Jicarilla Apache including two of their chiefs at Cantonment Burgwin and they seem friendly and well disposed to all citizens. There are at present about one hundred warriors with their families stationed near Picurís engaged in making earthen vessels. They say they were not engaged in any [of] the depredations committed on the east side of the mountains and that none of them were engaged in [Bell's] fight with the Dragoons on Red River; and that they have come over to the west side of the mountains near the settlements, in order to show their friendship and make (Ollas) earthen vessels to trade to the Mexicans for provisions, as they are in a starving condition.[16]

At this point the military under Cooke and Carson, in his role as Indian agent, were following a similar policy. The soldiers would watch the Jicarilla while the civil authorities offered subsistence to assure peace. But Cooke's and Carson's approach would not have time to work.

At the Cantonment Burgwin meeting on March 25, it was decided to send the two Jicarilla chiefs with Maj. Blake to Fort Union for further talks with them. Cooke talked with the chiefs, and on March 28 Blake and the chiefs started back for Taos. Blake later described the day's events:

> I started with the Indians on my return to Cant. Burgwin. At Moro [Mora] that evening they ran away from me, & I saw nothing more of them. I arrived at Cant. Burgwin on the 29th of March about 3 o'clock in the afternoon. A corporal who had been out watching the movements of the Indians according to orders, reported to Lt. Davidson, in my presence, that the Indians had moved their camp [from Picurís] and were going towards the Rio Grande.[17]

In the late afternoon of March 29, Blake ordered Lt. Davidson south to Cieneguilla to find the Jicarilla. He "directed Lt. Davidson according to my instructions from Col. Cooke, to take out his Company to proceed on their trail and watch and control their movements."[18] A letter from Cooke to Blake dated March 28 confirms Cooke's instructions. It also summarizes what Cooke had told the Jicarilla chiefs at Fort Union:

> The Apache chiefs, or principal men who came down with Major Blake, are sent back with the bearers of this:—I told them that as long as their band should demean [sic] themselves in a friendly & inoffensive manner, they should in no way be held responsible for the band whom we have chastened, and against whom, there are now a squadron of Dragoons in the field. And to prevent accidents they must confine themselves to their proper Ground, in the vicinity & beyond the valley of Taos: obeying the instructions of their agent.
>
> All that seems to be required of you then, is to be watchful of these Indians & the temper they show; & to pursue and attack any warlike or depredating party that may be formed, giving notice to me of any important indication or move.[19]

These were the orders Major Blake gave Davidson in the late afternoon of March 29. Davidson, with sixty dragoons, a scout, and an army surgeon, made their night march from Taos to the village of Cieneguilla. Early the following morning he led his command east into the mountains.

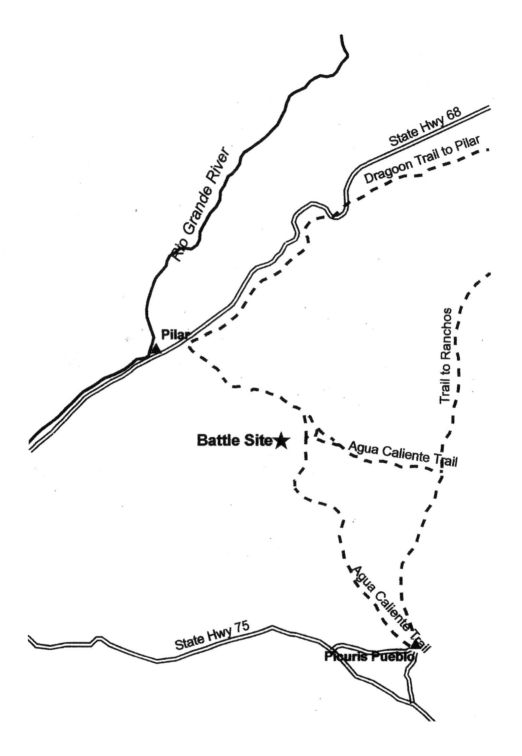

The Battle of Cieneguilla, a bloody engagement of U.S. Army dragoons from Cantonment Burgwin and the Jicarilla Apache, took place in the hills east of Pilar, formerly Cieneguilla. Map: Charles C. Hawk.

Davidson's Attack

The Dragoons followed the main trail from Cieneguilla to Picurís.[20] Shortly before 8:00 am Davidson's advance guard found fresh tracks of the Apache where the trail crossed Agua Caliente Creek. They hurried back and reported. Davidson and the entire command advanced to the crossing and followed the tracks along the trail for about a quarter mile. At that point some Jicarilla were seen above the trail on a low ridge to the right. The Apache did not attempt to hide. To the contrary, they yelled out to the troops. According to surviving participants, the Apache either insulted the soldiers or challenged them to fight.

Davidson quickly realized he had come upon an Apache camp. It took a few minutes for his column of dragoons to reach a position about 200 yards below the village. He ordered his men to dismount and tie their horses to trees. This is the "horse position" on the map below.

All witnesses agreed that at this point there had been no fighting. Jicarilla were visible on the ridge above, but they had not fired on the dragoons. And Davidson made no effort to talk with the Indians. Instead, he ordered his men to form two platoons of twenty-five men each and advance on the camp. The horses were guarded by the rest of the command. The dismounted dragoons moved uphill in "skirmish line" formation, each man about five yards from the man next to him. When the troops were about halfway up the hill, someone fired a shot—whether a dragoon or an Apache is not known. Davidson immediately ordered his men to attack the camp.

In the next ten minutes the dragoons fought up the hillside to and through the Jicarilla village. The Apache fought back, killed five of the soldiers, and retreated out of the camp. Davidson did not know it, but the camp he had attacked contained about 300 Jicarilla, three-quarters of the entire tribe. There were no more than 100 fighting men present. But the dragoon column had been seen well before reaching the camp. All the women and children, and some of the warriors, had fled south. The Indians left most of their sixty to eighty skin lodges behind.

Davidson also quickly discovered that the Jicarilla warriors who had retreated from the camp had not run away. Only moments after entering the village, the few troops tending the horses called out that they were under attack. Fearing loss of his animals, Davidson ordered all his men to quickly return back downhill to the horse position. Once there, he deployed his fifty effective men in defensive positions protecting the horses and a few wounded troopers.

Defense of the Horse Position

The Dragoons remained with the horses for about an hour. Some survivors claimed that they were completely surrounded by "up to 300" Jicarilla, were firing constantly, repelled numerous charges, and inflicted heavy losses on the Indians.[21] The archae-ological evidence does not support this.

The battle-related artifacts indicate light firing at the horse position by both the dragoons and the Jicarilla. We believe there were no efforts by the Apache to overrun the troops. The soldiers were in good defensive positions. They had a clear field of fire up the hillside. Contrary to later claims, they faced fewer than 100 warriors. The Apache could not afford casualties. The longer the dragoons chose to remain at the horse position, the farther away the Apache families could retreat. The Jicarilla tactics appear to have been to keep the troops pinned down and perhaps make a few careful attempts to stampede dragoon horses.

Other facts support a lack of heavy fighting at the horse position. First, no dragoons were killed there. Instead they were caring for some men wounded in the attack on the camp. Second, if the dragoons had been under constant or heavy attack, even less than an hour of such fighting would have exhausted their ammunition.

Our view is that the situation at the horse position was probably a stalemate. For reasons that went unrecorded, Davidson did not act. This is one of the most interesting puzzles of the battle. Why did Davidson remain immobile for as much as an hour? He still had fifty effective soldiers and the horses to mount them. Why didn't he quickly mount his command and retake the largely empty camp on the ridge? Perhaps he really believed he was vastly outnumbered. Maybe his men were already running short on ammunition. But for whatever reason his indecision assured that there would be no victory for him in this battle.

The Retreat

At about 9:30 am, Davidson abandoned the horse position. He moved the command about 200 yards up a ridge to the northeast *away* from the Apache camp. The Jicarilla did not oppose this movement. While taking some harassing fire from the rear, the dragoons suffered no killed or wounded.

Having reached high ground at Agua Caliente Creek, Davidson briefly halted. We believe it was here that he made his decision to break off the action, care for his wounded, and retreat to Taos. He probably thought the battle was over. He was wrong.

Davidson had to decide how to get back to Cieneguilla. The section of the Agua Caliente Trail the command had followed to the Apache camp was not an option; it was behind him and too dangerous. However, the main branch of the trail was on a high ridge directly north of him, across Agua Caliente Creek. If he reached there—less than a quarter mile away—the trail back to Cieneguilla might be open. After the brief halt, the command crossed the creek and climbed the steep, tree-covered slope leading to the ridge top.

The command reassembled on the ridge top a half-hour later. They had reached the main Agua Caliente Trail. Davidson probably thought his retreat east, on the trail back to Cieneguilla, would be unopposed. Here he made his most important decision of the battle. Knowing that at least some Apache were moving to cut him off, should he continue west toward Cieneguilla? This was the shortest way to safety, and his wounded needed attention. His troops' firepower had kept the Apache at bay during all his previous movements, and he had taken no casualties. On the trail down the ridge crest, he would be on high ground. It must have seemed a reasonable option. On the other hand, he could turn east, follow the main Agua Caliente Trail, and retreat away from any Apache. But this route to Taos was more than twice as long. For whatever reason, Davidson decided to continue west down the ridge crest. Based on what he knew at the time, it may have been a reasonable decision.

Bloody Ridge

At about 10:00 am the dragoons started northwest down the ridge line. It appears most were mounted; some carried wounded comrades with them. Skirmishers on the flanks kept the Jicarilla at a distance. For the first fifteen or twenty minutes the descent went well. Survivors stated that some Apache merely harassed the column from the rear. During this part of the march, the ridge top was quite wide. And even as the troops started down the crest of the ridge the terrain allowed skirmishers to protect the column.

But after about 200 yards the ridge line began to narrow. Because the sides of the ridge were heavily wooded, it allowed the Jicarilla warriors to get very close without being seen. It was here that the dragoons started taking casualties. The command was strung out on a straight, narrowing ridge crest. Apache fighters only yards away simply could not be seen. Yet by all accounts the dragoons maintained order, kept fighting, and tried to keep the wounded with them.

The next 200 yards were even worse. The ridge crest narrowed even more. It was at this point that the retreat became a shooting gallery for the Jicarilla. In this section the dragoons suffered their heaviest losses: sixteen men were killed, and at least as many were wounded. As a fighting force, the command had disintegrated.

Davidson retained enough control of his remaining men to quickly organize an escape. He ordered everyone to mount. He led the troops, carrying the wounded, away from the trail down the steep north side of the ridge. There were no Apache there, and with luck the troops could reach Tierra Amarilla Creek. Somehow this very risky move succeeded. Only one more dragoon died on the flight down to the creek. The Apache did not pursue the troops further, and the surviving dragoons reached Cieneguilla by mid-afternoon. All the wounded were brought back to Ranchos de Taos that evening. The dead were buried in a mass grave in what was then known

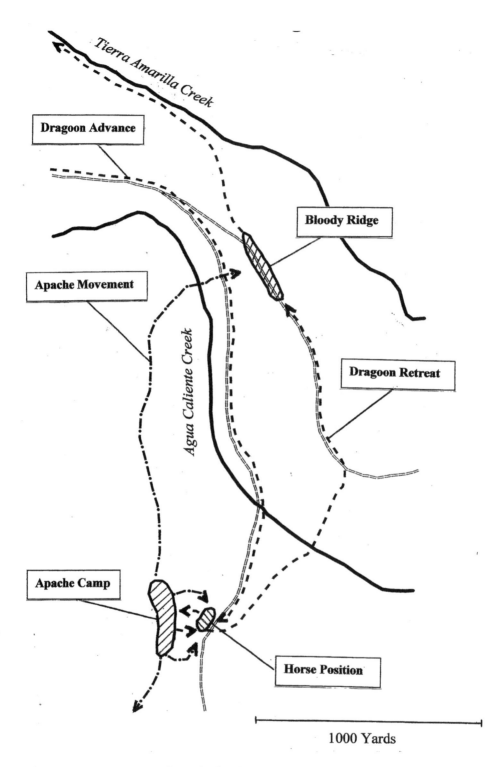

Advancing against a camp of Apache families, the American dragoons attacked from below, were forced to retreat, and took heavy casualties at Bloody Ridge on their way out of the narrow valley. Diagram: Charles C. Hawk.

as the American Cemetery, the burial place renamed Kit Carson Cemetery, where a monument to them can still be seen.[22]

AFTERMATH

The battle was a stunning defeat for the dragoons. The reasons later given by the survivors, including Lt. Davidson, were that they were led into an ambush by the Apaches, that they faced at least 300 warriors, both Apache and Ute, and that white men were helping lead the Jicarilla. They also claimed to have killed at least 50 of the Indians.

Our study of the battle indicates none of this was true. The Jicarilla were not waiting in ambush; the band was on the move, with women and children, toward the Rio Grande as instructed by Cooke. They were camping at an often-used campsite next to a well-known trail and were not attempting to hide. There is no archaeological evidence to confirm the presence of any Ute. It is also very unlikely that Davidson's men faced 300 warriors. All contemporary sources state that the entire Jicarilla Tribe contained only about 400 persons, of which no more than 150 could fight. While most of the tribe was present, about a third was already across the Rio Grande. Also, some warriors surely accompanied the women and children escaping south. It is therefore probable that the troops faced no more, and likely fewer, than a 100 Jicarilla fighters. Similarly, there is no support for the claim that whites were leading the Indians.

Finally, there is no consistent evidence for the number of Apache killed. But it could not have been 50. If this many had been killed, at least twice as many would have been wounded. This would mean that the tribe's entire fighting force would have been either killed or wounded in the battle, which could not have been true. Therefore we feel the Apache dead numbered no more than the dragoons' and probably fewer.

The Jicarilla won because their tactics were better, aided by some of Davidson's mistakes. By not taking the fight aggressively to the Indians early on, Davidson gave them time to use their knowledge of the area to outmaneuver him. It was probably fate that eventually led the dragoons into the only terrain on the battlefield where their opponents happened to have a deadly advantage. But the Jicarilla knew exactly where to be if the troops chose to retreat down the ridge. Davidson had been outsmarted, if not outfought.

Ironically, by winning the battle the Indians brought on their eventual defeat. American reaction was swift and overwhelming. Within days of the battle, Lt. Col. Cooke gathered as many troops as possible at Taos and pursued the fleeing Apache. By the end of 1855, the tribe had been defeated and placed on a reservation far west of Taos and the Rio Grande Valley. Their traditional lands were lost forever.

NOTES

1. In December 1866, all eighty soldiers under the command of William Judd Fetterman were killed by Lakota warriors under Red Cloud when they were lured into an ambush near Fort Phil Kearny, Dakota Territory, now Wyoming.

2. Clinton E. Brooks and Frank D. Reeve, eds., *Forts and Forays: James A. Bennett, A Dragoon in New Mexico, 1850–1856* (Albuquerque: University of New Mexico Press, 1996), xxiv.

3. Alfred B. Thomas, *After Coronado* (Norman: University of Oklahoma Press, 1935), 29–30.

4. Town of Cieneguilla Grant, BLM Archives, Taos, NM.

5. Transcript of Court of Private Land Claims, Town of Cieneguilla Grant, No. 84, Ex. 2, 1896, 2.

6. Ibid., 3.

7. Cantonment Burgwin Post Returns, Arrott Collection, vol. 50. Highlands University Library, 003.

8. Fort Union Letterbook, Arrott Collection, vol. 50. Highlands University Library.

9. Otis E. Young, *The West of Philip St. George Cooke* (The Arthur H. Clark Co. 1954), 33.

10. Ft. Union Letterbook, 087.

11. Ft. Union Letterbook, 094.

12. Ft. Union Letterbook. Arrott Collection, vol. 2. Highlands University Library, 108.

13. Lt. David Bell, letter to Lt. Robert Williams, Dec. 27, 1854.

14. Ibid.

15. Ft. Union Letterbook, vol. 2, 112.

16. Carson to Messervy, March 27, 1854.

17. Transcript of Court of Inquiry, Santa Fe, NM, March 14, 1856, 61.

18. Ibid., 62.

19. Ft. Union Letterbook, vol. 2, 113.

20. The following interpretation of the battle is based on testimony at the 1856 Court of Inquiry and our battlefield study.

21. Transcript of the Court of Inquiry, March 14, 1856.

22. The cemetery was established in 1847, when Theodora Martínez Romero, housekeeper for Padre Antonio José Martínez, donated land for the burial of American victims of the Taos Rebellion of 1847. At that time it was the only burial ground in Taos for non-Catholics and was called El Cementerio Militar. It acquired the name American Cemetery in 1852, when it was enlarged. When the bodies of Kit Carson and his wife were buried in 1869, it became Kit Carson Cemetery. Buried here are soldiers from the

Mexican-American War, the Taos Rebellion of 1847, this and other Indian campaigns of the 1850s, the American Civil War, the Spanish-American War, and World Wars I and II—alongside early Taos traders, merchants, and members of some early Spanish, French, and American families. See *Taos County, New Mexico. Materials Published in the New Mexico Genealogist 1962–1988 and Related Research Information*, Compiled by Ralph L. Hayes (Albuquerque: The New Mexico Genealogical Society, 1989), 110.

SELECTED REFERENCES

Brooks, Clinton E., and Frank D. Reeve, eds. *Forts and Forays: James A. Bennett, A Dragoon in New Mexico, 1850–1856.* Albuquerque: University of New Mexico Press, 1996.

Thomas, Alfred B. *After Coronado.* Norman: University of Oklahoma Press, 1935.

Velarde Tiller, Veronica E. *The Jicarilla Apache Tribe: A History, 1846–1970.* Lincoln: University of Nebraska Press, 1983.

Young, Otis E. *The West of Philip St. George Cooke.* Glendale, CA: The Arthur H. Clark Co., 1954.

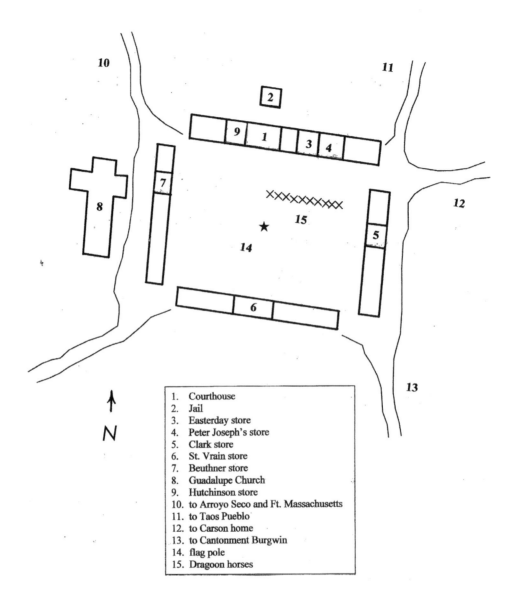

1. Courthouse
2. Jail
3. Easterday store
4. Peter Joseph's store
5. Clark store
6. St. Vrain store
7. Beuthner store
8. Guadalupe Church
9. Hutchinson store
10. to Arroyo Seco and Ft. Massachusetts
11. to Taos Pueblo
12. to Carson home
13. to Cantonment Burgwin
14. flag pole
15. Dragoon horses

Partial reconstruction of Fernando de Taos Plaza at the time of the 1855 incident. Today's Our Lady of Guadalupe Church is one block north of the church on this map. Map: John B. Ramsay.

❖ II ❖

A Mutiny in Taos, 1855

John B. Ramsay

In this careful reconstruction of a little-known military uprising, John B. Ramsay captures the flavor of Taos in the early days of the Territorial period, as well as U.S. Army social behavior and military justice.

BY 1850 TAOS HAD SEEN MORE CHALLENGES to government authority than almost any other New Mexican settlement. The Taos Mutiny of 1855 was yet another rough, though brief, episode. This incident, the courts-martial that followed, and the rest of the military justice process are illustrative of frontier military life in the mid-nineteenth-century West.

The scene of the mutiny was Don Fernando de Taos' plaza. Roughly the same size in 1855 as it is today, it was certainly the liveliest and busiest place in the village. The earliest photographs show almost no trees. Probably none of the adobe buildings rose above one story. A few fronts had covered portals, but most did not. Many structures were private homes; some were commercial establishments. Hitching rails for horses lined the perimeter of the open area, and if the plaza was enclosed at all, it was by rough fencing. Among the popular gathering places was a store and saloon near the west end of the plaza operated by Peter Joseph de Teves, an early and successful American businessman and farmer also known as Peter Joseph.

FIGURE 106A. Dragoons as they appeared ca. 1854 in rough field attire on extended campaigns. (This drawing reproduced with the permission of the State of California, Division of Beaches and Parks.)

U.S. Army dragoons on field duty, 1854. © 2009, California State Parks (Sketch by Randy Steffans).

The U.S. Army in Taos

To ensure order following the 1847 uprising, soldiers and officers of the U.S. Army were garrisoned in Taos. Companies G, H, and K of the 3rd Regiment of Missouri Volunteers were garrisoned in the village at the "Post of Don Fernando de Taos," established in October 1847.[1] While the soldiers' presence offered residents limited protection from raiding Utes, Apaches, and Comanches, there was tension. Memories of 1847 still burned. By most reports, the soldiers' conduct was crude and highly disrespectful of both Hispanos and Indians. The troops' regular consumption of Taos Lightning, the potent local alcohol, did not help their image or their behavior.

With much difficulty, because the Missouri Volunteers had "left such a bad reputation," the army rented additional lodgings with local families and in surrounding villages.[2] Certain families of Ranchos de Taos and Talpa remember stories about ancestors who were forced to take in and feed troops and who feared for their daughters. Competition among officers bred jealousy and mutual animosity. Among the enlisted men, boredom was widespread, drinking rampant, and discipline, as a consequence, was severe.

Colonel Edwin V. Sumner, 1st Dragoons, was assigned in 1851 to command the Ninth Military District—soon to be the Military Department of New Mexico. Besides establishing Fort Union, Sumner reorganized New Mexico's defenses. Taos was militarily strategic because of its history of local unrest and because it was a staging point for campaigns against the Utes, Jicarilla Apaches, and Comanches. Colonel Sumner, however, did not want troops stationed in population centers.[3] In 1852 he ordered the Taos garrison out of town and constructed Cantonment Burgwin at what he considered a safe distance from the temptations of the plaza.

The Mutineers

In 1855 Cantonment Burgwin housed two companies of U.S. dragoons, mounted infantrymen functioning essentially as cavalry. Among the officers were Brevet Majors George Alexander Hamilton Blake[4] and Philip Roots Thompson.[5] Blake, the senior of the two, was in command of the dragoons,[6] with Thompson serving under him. Thompson was an alcoholic. Josiah Rice, an army private, described Thompson as "a dragoon officer who had been intoxicated from the time of leaving Fort Leavenworth."[7]

Both Majors Blake and Thompson had been stationed at Fort Union. In 1851 Major Thompson shot a soldier in a dispute at Barkley's Fort (a predecessor of Fort Union, located nearby), and Blake arrested him. The man lived, and Thompson was fined $600. He was also required to join the temperance society in Santa Fe, but he soon broke his pledge and was expelled.[8] In early 1854 Blake took command of

Cantonment Burgwin. His treatment of infantrymen and officers was described as "capricious and autocratic."[9] He had the reputation of leaving his post—ostensibly on business but probably to enjoy himself in Taos. He canceled passes for enlisted men and is quoted as telling an enlisted man to desert so that he could be recaptured and given fifty lashes on his bare back. Blake's conduct created tensions teetering on outright hostility on the part of both officers and enlisted men.

The March to the Plaza

On March 8, 1855, Company F, 1st Dragoons, consisting of fifty to sixty enlisted men under the command of Major Thompson, left Cantonment Burgwin to march to Fort Massachusetts[10] in southern Colorado in support of Colonel Thomas T. Fauntleroy's campaign against the Utes and Jicarilla Apaches. On the same day Major Blake took one of his accustomed "business trips" into Taos, passing Company F on the road from Cantonment Burgwin and arriving in the village ahead of them.

Transcripts of court-martial proceedings give a vivid sense of the dragoon's behavior. First Sergeant F. Fitzsimmons testified that on the way to Don Fernando de Taos the company stopped at a distillery. "About two & half miles from Bergwin [sic], the Company was halted for five or eight minutes. . . . Major Thompson called me to the gate of the mill and gave me half a gallon measure full of whiskey and told me to divide it round among the men of the company."[11] Thompson then told Fitzsimmons to get another measure and give it to the men who had not gotten any. Testimony by Acting Assistant Surgeon Barry said that the amount distributed was one gallon and that Thompson drank "half a gill."[12] Blake testified that the men "never left the post without getting drunk."[13]

Despite what might seem a limited amount of whiskey for fifty or sixty soldiers, by the time Company F arrived in Don Fernando de Taos intoxication was evident in several men, including Major Thompson. Entering the plaza about two in the afternoon, the troops drew up facing north, to the east of Peter Joseph's store. Thompson ordered the "numbers one & three of each set of four that they might go for half an hour and get what they wanted giving their horses to the two's and fours. . . . Major Thompson also left the Company at this time."[14] Thompson appeared in Peter Joseph's store and was observed drinking with a private.

The Mutiny

Some time after the troops had dispersed around the plaza a group that was still mounted decided to chase a group of "Mexicans and Americans,"[15] striking them with the flat sides of their sabers. This disturbance was quieted, but by then one

Private Sullivan was so drunk that he couldn't stand up or sit on his horse. Thompson ordered Fitzsimmons to tie Sullivan on his horse. Sullivan struck Fitzsimmons, who struck back. Blake, who happened to be in the plaza, saw Fitzsimmons strike and ordered Thompson to arrest him. Thompson refused; Blake himself put Fitzsimmons under arrest.[16]

Next, Private John Cooper, still mounted, charged over to Peter Joseph's store and started riding under the portal. Both he and the horse fell on the stoop. Lieutenant Johnston arrested him. Major Blake—who was not officially in command of this march—threatened to take the company out of town himself, which offended Major Thompson. Private Cooper complained to Blake, who struck Cooper two or three times with his fist. A scuffle broke out, and Blake drew his sword and struck Cooper with it. Three or four of the soldiers joined the fray and had their hands on Blake at one time. Someone shouted, "Let me kill the son of a bitch and let them hang me for it."[17] As Blake was freeing himself from Cooper, Private John Steel caught Blake by the neckerchief and struck him with his saber. Steel also struck First Sergeant Fitzsimmons on the hand with a saber, as did Private Joseph Fox, who was on horseback.[18] Privates Cooper and Fox were arrested and taken to the Taos jail. But Private Steel continued to attack Blake by grabbing his neckerchief, hitting Blake two or three times with his fist while Blake defended himself with his saber. According to later testimony,

> Mr. Ramon Bacca [sic], Major Blake's peon [servant], testified with C. [Kit] Carson acting as the interpreter. Bacca attempted to break up the fight between Blake and the soldiers. Three or four soldiers came up, one on horseback, and commenced to strike Blake. The soldiers then attacked Bacca and chased him nearly 100 yards, cutting at him with sabers and the butt of a gun. C. Carson shouted at other "Mexicans," and accused them of being cowards for standing around and seeing a man killed. Carson convinced them to gather rocks and defend Bacca, which they did, and Bacca escaped.[19]

Once the attack on Major Blake was stopped, the major is said to have bragged, "I can whip any man in the Company with any arm."[20] Private Aaron D. Stephens, a bugler, is quoted as responding, "I accept your challenge, & will fight you any damned way you want to fight, with gun, pistol, or sabre."[21] Blake turned and walked away toward Peter Joseph's store.

Judge Perry E. Brocchus, associate justice of the Supreme Court of the United States for the Territory of New Mexico, who was watching the fracas, recognized that Stephens had not participated in the riot and suggested to Major Blake that he speak to the young private. In doing so Blake offended Stephens, who pointed his rifle at Blake's chest and exclaimed, "Damn you" or "God damn you I'll blow your heart out" or words to that effect. Kit Carson, Judge Brocchus, and Major Thompson seized the gun and arrested Stephens.[22]

By then, a number of the soldiers, while not actually participating in the attack on Blake, were riding through the troops trying to incite them to participate. At one point Private Fox was observed riding and shouting, "Kill the God damned long nosed son of a bitch," referring to Blake.[23] Had it not been for the intervention of a number of civilians, including Judge Brocchus and Kit Carson, bloodshed would surely have ensued. Amazingly, none of the participants was seriously hurt, although Blake was hospitalized for a time after the incident.

Later, Major Thompson requested a formal court of inquiry into the cause of the mutiny. Nearly everyone testified that Thompson had been sufficiently intoxicated to affect his response to the events. Lieutenant Johnston had apparently had some alcohol but was not considered to be intoxicated. Acting Assistant Surgeon Barry, when asked to define "drunk," stated, "I consider a man drunk only when he is totally unable to know what he is doing and to stand up without support. According to this description, Maj. Thompson was not drunk, as he was up & about. Lt. Johnston was not drunk."[24] Two people testified that Major Blake was intoxicated; others testified that he was not, though he may have had a few drinks. At his own court-martial Blake testified that he was not drunk, or in any way under the influence of liquor at any time during the day, March 8, 1855.[25] There was significant testimony as to Blake's severe discipline and the troops' dislike of him.

Acting Assistant Surgeon Barry, in testimony as a defense witness at Blake's court-martial, described Blake's injuries. "I did see the Major after the affray. He appeared to be very badly beaten, was covered with blood and dirt, & altogether appeared according to the common expression, badly used up. . . . His right thumb was sprained and swollen and his other hand was also swollen, as it appeared from the marks of teeth."[26] With the arrest of the enlisted men, Lieutenant Johnston and Major Thompson were able to get the remaining troops out of town and camped north of Taos. In his testimony at the court-martial of Major Blake, Judge Brocchus described the tension that existed in Taos following the mutiny:

> As the troops moved out of the Plaza observing that several of them were intoxicated, and apprehensive that they might return again at night for the purpose of rescuing those that I had committed to the Gaol, I immediately dispatched an express to Col. Fauntleroy, . . . asking that he would send a sufficient force back to preserve the public peace.
>
> In the course of the evening I received a prompt and courteous reply from Col. Fauntleroy in which he apprised me that my express rider informed him that Comp. "F" had quietly encamped on the road and some distance from Taos, from which he supposed and hoped that there would be no recurrence of this conduct of the soldiers, but suggested, that there was

some infantry at Cantonment Burgwin, & requested that if there should be further trouble to dispatch to him at the public expense a messenger and he would promptly respond to the utmost of his ability on the behalf of the maintenance of order & the prosecution of the public peace.[27]

The Courts-Martial

General John Garland, by then commander of the Department of New Mexico, ordered general courts-martial for Privates Fox, Cooper, Steel, and Stephens after the company returned to Cantonment Burgwin. These were held in May 1855 in Don Fernando de Taos.

Stephens was tried first. Charged with inciting mutiny and drawing a pistol and attempting to shoot Major Blake, Stephens was also accused of raising his cocked rifle and swearing that he would shoot the major. Yet it is reasonably clear from the testimony that Stephens did not participate in the first stages of the mutiny; he was holding Major Thompson's and a second horse. Judge Brocchus testified:

I observed the prisoner [Stephens] standing apparently in a very orderly and subordinate manner with the reins of one or two horses . . . and a burnished Sharp's carbine in his hand. I observed to Maj. Blake that the prisoner appeared very orderly and seemed disposed to return order and decorum among the other troops. Maj. Blake replied addressing himself to the prisoner with earnestness of manner and intensity of feeling. You have behaved very badly and he may have specified some allegations against him, but I do not remember. The prisoner with an air of servility began to explain in an apologetic manner. Maj. Blake seemed, however, unwilling to listen and turning away remarked to me, Judge, I leave the matter with you. . . . I thought I had better bring about a reconciliation between Maj. Blake and him.—Hence, I suggested to him to go and apologize to Maj. Blake. He signified a willingness to do so and walked with me to the portal where Maj. Blake was standing. Then however, instead of using words ordinarily significant of apology, whether from ignorance of what words to employ or reluctance to apologize I am not able to say, but he did not apologize.[28]

In his own defense Stephens stated the following:

I did not join in the attack on Maj. Blake but was some distance from him.—I used my influence with and succeeded in keeping two or three from joining those who were on the Major. When he spoke to me & after Judge Brocchus advised me I was willing to apologize if I had done anything wrong and told the Maj. so—but he turned away with a swear which made me very angry and I made some exclamations and I did things for which I am sorry.[29]

Stephens was found not guilty of inciting a mutiny but guilty of violation of the Ninth Article of War (striking, or offering violence against, an officer, in execution of his office).[30] The sentence: "To be shot to death at such time and place as the president of the United States shall direct, the prisoner to be kept in double irons until the execution of this sentence."[31]

The court-martial of Private Fox was delayed because Major Thompson, called as a witness, showed up intoxicated and exhibited disrespect to the court by making a significant gesture with his finger. Privates Fox, Cooper, and Steel did not offer any self-defense. Each was sentenced to be held in irons and shot, waiting approval by President Franklin Pierce.

Before the sentences could be carried out, the proceedings of the court of inquiry and the court-martial for the privates were forwarded to Washington, DC, for approval by President Pierce. The president and Secretary of War Jefferson Davis recognized that tension, lack of discipline, and drunkenness were problems among the troops. This situation is well described in General Order No. 12, dated 9 August 1855 and signed by Davis, communicating President Pierce's opinions on the sentences of Stephens, Fox, Cooper, and Steel and the general condition of Cantonment Burgwin:[32]

> It is proved that the commander of the company, and many of the company, then under arms, on a march, were drunk when the riot and mutiny broke out. It would seem too, that proper exertions were not made by the officers, non-commissioned officers, and soldiers of the company. To suppress the mutiny, although thereby, under the 8th Article of War they each and all committed an equal crime, and incurred equally of penalty of death with those who joined the mutiny. It appears that no proper discipline had been previously maintained in the company, and that the Major of the regiment, under whose command they had been serving, was greatly responsible for the utter want of discipline which would have cost him his life in this mutiny, if he had not been rescued by the civil authority; and that part of the violence he suffered, in the riot, was invited by challenging the company to fight him, man to man. Under these circumstances, however, imperative the President may feel his duty to enforce the laws, which will not endure that our people shall suffer the evils of an undisciplined soldiery, committing riot and outrage in their towns, he will not visit the whole consequence of this mutiny upon the four soldiers who have been convicted, nor execute in this case the sentence of death. The sentences pronounced against Privates Aaron D. Stephens, John Cooper, Joseph Fox, and John Steel, are hereby mitigated

to hard labor for three years, under guard, without pay. They will be sent out of New Mexico, in irons, by the first convenient opportunity, and will be put to labor with ball and chain at Fort Leavenworth. The non-commissioned officers and men of company F, 1st Dragoons, will no longer be trusted to serve together as a company. They will be distributed as privates to other companies of their regiment serving in New Mexico.

The Commander of the Department of New Mexico, on this order of the War Department, will prefer proper charges against the officers and non-commissioned officers of the company who did not use their utmost endeavor to suppress the mutiny, . . . and against the Major of the Regiment for such parts of his conduct, in the riot, and in command of the company at Fort Massachusetts, as seem to call for such proceedings against him. And a Court Martial will be convened to try them.

The record indicates other grave charges against the officers implicated in the affair, besides those directly relating to the riot and mutiny.

JEFFERSON DAVIS
Secretary of War

Courts-Martial of
Brevet Majors Thompson and Blake

Thompson's court-martial convened on July 2, 1855. He was charged with "Disrespect of the Court" for having appeared in a state of intoxication, interrupting the court, and drunkenness on duty. The court found Thompson guilty, and he was cashiered from the service. Katie Bowen, wife of Captain Isaac Bowen, judge advocate at the court-martial of the privates, said of Thompson, "He fancies, when *in his cups* that some of his men are going to kill him. . . . He is very polished and agreeable when himself, but can not live long at the rate he has drank while here. . . . He is always gentle with his wife."[33] Two members of the board for the court-martial petitioned the president to mitigate the punishment, but Thompson's sentence was not reduced. [34]

It was December 1855 by the time General Garland issued General Order 273 to convene a general court-martial of Major Blake, the charges and specifications of which suggest an attempt to retaliate at Blake. The first charge covered the period June 1852 to June 1853, well before the mutiny action, and specifies that Major Blake "did habitually swear at, curse, and abuse the non-commissioned officers and soldiers under his command, so as to produce discontent and insubordination among them and in some instances to induce desertion." Another charge claimed that in October 1853, when his troops at Fort Massachusetts became drunk and riotous, Blake locked himself in his quarters and did not attempt to quell the riot. He was also accused of exhibiting "a fault-finding and carping manner and language, so much so as to produce a spirit of discontent among the troops."[35] The vindictive spirit of the charges is further suggested by the fact that the court dismissed several charges because they had been thrown out at an earlier action, because their statute of limitation had passed or because the charges were a collection of actions held in reserve to create a charge of sufficient magnitude.

In connection with the mutiny, Blake was charged with several offenses: absence from Cantonment Burgwin, ostensibly on official business but actually on private business; neglect of duty in not arresting Thompson for drinking in a public bar in company of enlisted men; and several charges of failing to suppress the mutiny and aggravating the troops after the first stage of the mutiny. Blake was found guilty both of failing to arrest Major Thompson for disobedience and of failing to use his utmost effort to suppress the riot. He was sentenced to be suspended from rank for one year and to forfeit his pay for that period. His sentence was reduced to one month's suspension and loss of pay, plus a reprimand in his record. He remained in the Union Army as a cavalry officer. During the Civil War he was promoted to colonel and then to brevet brigadier general.

Further records of Privates Steel, Fox, and Cooper have not been located. Private Stephens, however, became active in the abolitionist movement. He escaped from Fort Leavenworth in January 1856. By September 1856 he appeared under the alias Colonel Charles Whipple in the Free-State Forces of Kansas, and then he joined John Brown's force. Richard J. Hinton, biographer of Brown, says that Stephens was "hard to discipline and could seldom restrain his disposition to resist daily tyrannies."[36] Stephens was wounded during the attack at Harper's Ferry, arrested, tried, and executed on March 16, 1860.

The "mutiny" was a brief event in the history of Taos. Yet were it not for the intervention of some courageous civilians—including Kit Carson, Judge Brocchus, and Ramón Baca—this episode might have been one of the bloodiest and darkest stains on the record of the frontier army in New Mexico. As it was, the incident ended careers, produced courts-martial and death sentences, and surely intensified the already noticeable ill will between the American army and the citizens of Taos.[37]

NOTES

1. Lawrence R. Murphy, "The United States Army in Taos, 1847–1852," *New Mexico Historical Review* 16 (January 1972): 34. The location of the post is not recorded; its presence in Taos is part of the collective memory of the oldest Taoseños, some of whom cite La Posta Road as a clue to where the post once was.

2. Ibid., 35.

3. Lawrence R. Murphy, "Cantonment Burgwin, New Mexico 1852–60," *Arizona and the West* 15:1 (1973), 5–26.

4. Brevet Major George Alexander Hamilton Blake, from Philadelphia, was appointed 1st Lt., 2nd Dragoons in 1836, Capt. in 1839, and Maj. in 1st Dragoons in 1850. There is no record that he attended West Point. *Francis B. Heitman, Historical Register and Dictionary of the United States Army, from Its Organization September 29, 1789 to March 2, 1903.* Washington, DC: Government Printing Office, 1903.

5. Brevet Major Philip Roots Thompson, from Georgia, graduated thirty-sixth in a class of fifty-six from West Point in 1835. *Register of Graduates and Former Cadets of the United States Military Academy West Point, NY 2000 A Decennial Edition* (Kalamazoo, MI: Masterpiece Publishing, 2000), 4–19.

6. Michael Olsen and Harry C. Myers, "John Pope's Journal of a March to New Mexico, 1851, Part 1," *Wagon Tracks*, Santa Fe Trail Association 4 (Aug. 1951), 19–22. Taken from U.S. National Archives Microfilm M1102, roll 4, frames 418–50.

7. Josiah M. Rice, *A Cannoneer in Navajo Country, Journal of Private Josiah M. Rice, 1861,* ed. Richard H. Dillon (Denver, CO: Denver Public Library, 1970), 10.

8. Leo E. Oliva, *Fort Union and the Frontier Army of the Southwest* (Santa Fe, NM : Division of History, National Park Service, 1993), 192.

9. Murphy 1973, 11–12.

10. Fort Massachusetts was north of present-day Fort Garland at the base of the Sangre de Cristo Mountains of Colorado.

11. *Proceedings of a Court of Inquiry Convened at the Request of Brv. Major Philip Roots Thompson, Santa Fe, NM May 16, 1855* (National Archives and Records Center, RG 153, HH496): 4 (hereafter CI HH496). A photostatic copy and a transcription prepared by Barbara H. and John B. Ramsay are filed at the Fray Angélico Chávez History Library, Palace of the Governors, Museum of New Mexico, Santa Fe, NM (AC473). The distillery was owned by Ceran St. Vrain and was located just north of Cantonment Burgwin.

12. CI HH496, 44. Half a gill is two fluid ounces.

13. CI HH496, 14.

14. CI HH496, 5.

15. *Proceedings of a General Court Martial Convened at Santa Fe January 21, 1856* (National Archives and Records Center, RG 153, HH660), 28–29 (hereafter GCM HH660). A photostatic copy and a transcription prepared by Barbara H. and John B. Ramsay are filed at the Fray Angélico Chávez History Library, Palace of the Governors, Museum of New Mexico, Santa Fe, NM (AC473).

16. CI HH496, 15.

17. Pvt. John Cooper was charged with violation of the 9th Article of War. *Proceedings of a General Court Martial Convened at Don Fernandez de Taos, N. M. May 21, 1855* (National Archives and Records Center, RG 153, HH497), 17 (hereafter GCM HH497). A photostatic copy and a transcription prepared by Barbara H. and John B. Ramsay are filed at

the Fray Angélico Chávez History Library, Palace of the Governors, Museum of New
Mexico, Santa Fe, NM (AC473).

18. CI HH496, 9.

19. CI HH496, 23.

20. CI HH496, 11.

21. Ibid.

22. CI HH496, 28.

23. CI HH496, 36.

24. CI HH496, 44.

25. GCM HH660, 22.

26. GCM HH660, 73.

27. GCM HH660, 106.

28. GCM HH497, 12.

29. GCM HH497, 14.

30. Brig. Gen. George B. Davis, *A Treatise on Military Law of the United States* (New York:
John Wiley & Sons, 1911), 379, 391.

31. GCM HH497, 14.

32. GCM HH497: General Order No. 12.

33. Oliva, *Fort Union*, 192.

35. GCM HH660, 7.

36. Richard J. Hinton, *John Brown and His Men* (New York: Arno Press and New York Times,
1968), 47.

37. The author wishes to thank William Gorenfeld and George Stammerjohan of California
for critical reading, comments, and encouragement.

SELECTED REFERENCES

Brown, E. Bennett. "The Taos Rebellion." *Old Santa Fe* I: 2 (1913), 176–85.

Hafen, LeRoy, ed. *Ruxton of the Rockies.* Norman: University of Oklahoma Press, 1950.

Murphy, Lawrence. "The United States Army in Taos, 1847–1852." *New Mexico Historical
Review* 16 (January 1972), 33–48.

Twitchell, Ralph E. *The History of the Military Occupation of the Territory of New Mexico.*
Denver, CO: Smith-Brooks Co., 1909.

❖ 12 ❖

Taos and the American Civil War

JERRY A. PADILLA

When the American Civil War broke out in 1861, the Territory of New Mexico was not yet fifteen years old, and the great majority of its citizens spoke only Spanish. The southern sections of the territory aligned with the Confederacy; the northern areas, Taos included, were loyal to the Union. Taos supplied volunteer soldiers to numerous companies of the Union Army, many of them serving in two major battles, including the Battle of Glorieta Pass, the "Gettysburg of the West."

WHEN CONFEDERATE GENERAL P. G. T. BEAUREGARD gave the order to fire cannons on Fort Sumter at 4:30 am, April 12, 1861, little did many in far-off Taos, New Mexico Territory, realize that they would soon be swept up in the maelstrom that became the American Civil War. Except to the military and some North American trappers, traders, merchants, and recent immigrants, New Mexico was barely known to Americans in the eastern states, North or South.

Even though the Territory of New Mexico was officially pro-Union, southern sympathizers clashed with those favoring the North. Economic interests intensified regional conflicts. Santa Fe and Taos were tied economically to Mexico and Missouri. Mexico was in political turmoil, with President Benito Juárez desperately struggling for the survival of his nation against Napoleonic

Sometime in the 1940s Pascual Martinez and Margaret Gusdorf replaced an old flag
with a new one. Throughout history, the Tiwa of Taos Pueblo were described as valiant
warriors, and the Spanish who settled in Taos were also fiercely independent. Either
together or apart, both populations resisted civil authority. During the American Civil
War, three Taoseños raised the Union flag and guarded it around the clock. Since then
the town of Taos is permitted by federal statute to fly the flag day and night. Courtesy
Taos Historic Museums.

imperialists. He declared that Mexico would not support the Confederacy and sided with President Lincoln. Arizona (then still a part of New Mexico Territory) was allied with Texas. When secession became a reality, many in northern New Mexico waited to see what Missouri would do, while some in Arizona and southern New Mexico, like Texas, wanted to secede.

In early February 1861, the Texas Legislature passed an ordinance delegating Simeon Hart and Philemon Herbert as commissioners to the New Mexico Territory for the express purpose of instigating support for secession. New Mexico would not become a state until 1912, but Confederate leaders in Texas understood the importance of securing New Mexico along with the northern Mexican states of Chihuahua and Sonora for the southern cause. New Mexico, it was believed, would be the springboard to gold in Colorado and California, a source of livestock, crops, and men to be conscripted as soldiers into the Confederate Army. Control of the California coast and the Mexican port of Guaymas could break the Union blockade. If the Confederacy could achieve conquest of the American Southwest, strategists reasoned, it could win the war. New Mexico was seen as a first step in realizing Confederate success.

Secessionists concentrated in La Mesilla—on the eastern edge of Las Cruces—declared for the Confederacy, claiming New Mexico south of 34° latitude and extending west into Arizona, as the Confederate Territory of Arizona. An invasion of New Mexico was in the making. Simeon Hart's agents reported that the only thing keeping Santa Fe secessionists in check was the presence of Union troops.

In Taos things came rapidly to a head when rebel sympathizers raised a Confederate battle flag on the plaza. Local citizens, led by Christopher "Kit" Carson, Capt. Smith Simpson, and Don Julián Jaramillo, among others, took matters into their own hands. Tearing down the Confederate flag, they nailed an American flag to a pole, raised it, and then took turns guarding it day and night, so that "everybody would know" Taos and northern New Mexico were loyal to the Union. Thus was born the Taos tradition—no longer officially sanctioned by federal statutes regarding the flag's display—of the U.S. flag flying twenty-four hours a day.

New Mexico's loyalty to the Union was far from secure, however. Before the year was out, Confederate Texas soldiers were reported en route to New Mexico. The U.S. Department of New Mexico, as the U.S. Army was sometimes referred to at that time, was dealing with the tough reality that throughout the territory many officers in charge of forts and outposts were southern sympathizers. These officers abandoned their posts in order to join the Confederacy and even Department commander Col. William W. Loring left to fight with the Confederate Army and tried to take certain influential New Mexicans with him.[1]

Declaring for the Union was one thing, but enforcing loyalty and repulsing an invasion was quite another. Military men and materials were stretched to the limit. The majority of Indo-Hispanic, Spanish-speaking New Mexicans, at that time U.S.

citizens for less than a generation, were struggling just to make a living. They were too busy to concern themselves with political issues involving events far away. Although aware of slavery and states' rights, as a group they were generally loyal to their new nation. Until Texans actually entered New Mexico, armed and on the offensive, the majority of New Mexicans were not drawn into the fray.

Col. Edward Richard Sprigg Canby succeeded "turncoat" Col. Loring as military commander of New Mexico. While scrambling to get troops and provisions for his forts, word came in late June 1861 that Texas Confederates were massing at Fort Bliss, Texas. Canby begged Washington unsuccessfully for more troops, but most military resources were already tied up in campaigns in the East. Carson, Cerán St. Vrain, brothers Miguel and Nicolás Piño, Manuel Antonio Cháves, and Taoseño José María Váldez, among other leaders, were enlisted by Territorial Governor Abraham Rencher (in office 1857–61) to recruit volunteer soldiers from among the citizens of New Mexico. As they began recruiting, news came of the start of the Confederate invasion of New Mexico.

In early July, Kit Carson received word at Fort Union from New Mexican *ciboleros* and those trading among the Comanche and Kiowa that a large body of armed white men was on the way. (Throughout the New Mexico campaign, Carson and other leaders would continue to rely on New Mexican bison hunters and Pueblo Indian scouts to keep an eye on Texas Confederate movements.) As July ended, Col. John R. Baylor, with elements of the 2nd Texas Mounted Volunteers and Battery D, 1st Texas Artillery, occupied Mesilla, claiming it for the Confederate Territory of Arizona.

Not believing they could defend nearby Fort Fillmore, located a few miles south of Las Cruces, Union commanders retreated to Fort Stanton, near Ruidoso. With the collapse of Union authority in Doña Ana County, Lt. Col. Benjamin Roberts took what could be transported, burned Fort Stanton, and established his garrison at Fort Craig, about thirty-two miles south of Socorro. He prepared to hold the line, initiating defense of the territory there.

Meanwhile, Col. Canby's brother-in-law, Confederate Brig. Gen. Henry Hopkins Sibley, had convinced Confederate President Jefferson Davis of the importance of the New Mexico campaign and was named commander of the effort. An obvious choice, Sibley had served before in New Mexico and was familiar with the Southwest. In fact, Sibley had been stationed at Fort Union as a federal solider and had resigned that commission to join the Confederate cause with his native state, Louisiana.

On the other side, recruitment efforts for the Union forces were paying off. José María Váldez, of a respected old Taos family, became commander of the first volunteer unit and was elected Captain of Company A, 1st New Mexico Volunteers, which included men from Taos, Mora, and Las Vegas. Men from all over north-central New Mexico continued to swell the ranks of the 1st and 2nd New Mexico regiments.

However, changes soon came. The aging St. Vrain resigned because of poor health. Kit Carson was promoted to colonel, succeeding as commander of the 1st Volunteer

Regiment. Váldez was promoted to Lt. colonel and assigned as commander of the 3rd New Mexico Volunteers, Mounted. Two other companies under Carson's command would provide cavalry duty for the 1st Regiment: Company K, commanded by Capt. Rafael Chacón and Company I, under Capt. Charles Deus. Carson recruited heavily also in Arroyo Seco, Costilla, and Culebra, later known as San Luis, Colorado.

After swearing an oath of allegiance—an absolute condition for service in the U.S. military—volunteers were supplied with arms and camp equipment. Those in mounted units had to provide their own horses and horse equipment, as did the company officers, NCOs, and buglers. No uniforms were issued at first. After the initial ten days of enlistment, volunteers were allowed $3.50 as an inducement for service. Uniform colors on both sides varied from blue to gray through the first years of the Civil War. The first New Mexican volunteers and an early company from Colorado were described as wearing new gray uniforms.

Kit Carson would remain commander (colonel) of the 1st New Mexico Volunteer Regiment in favor of higher-ranking Regular Army officers because of his knowledge of Spanish, his familiarity with the land, and his familiarity with New Mexican and tribal war tactics. Lt. Col. José Francisco Cháves was appointed with Carson. Other regimental and company commanders, chosen from the ranks of volunteers who could communicate with Spanish-speaking soldiers, were elected by the militia.

There was friction between the commanders of the Regular Army and the New Mexico Volunteers. Among the former Nuevo Méxicanos, only the company commanders, officers, and some NCOs understood English. Even fewer of the regulars could speak Spanish. The culture shock and mistreatment of the New Mexican volunteers resulted in Lt. Col. Cháves filing a grievance with Lt. Col. William Chapman at Fort Union. It has been reported by other historians and scholars—including Father F. Stanley, Charles Meketa, and Jaqueline Dorgan Meketa—that Col. Canby, described as a martinet, had issues with the volunteer soldiers of New Mexico.[2]

Among the thousands of New Mexican men prepared to defend the territory, at least fourteen companies were formed of men from the greater Taos area.[3] Approximately 800 volunteers joined from Taos and nearby villages. Besides Chacón's and Deus's companies K and I, there was Company H, 1st New Mexico Volunteers commanded at first by Capt. Santiago Valdez[4] and Lts. William Brooks and José Manuel Martínes. When Váldez resigned for health reasons, Edward Bergmann succeeded him. Capt. Julián Espinosa's Company D, recruited primarily in Mora, included several Taoseños.

The 2nd Regiment, New Mexico Volunteers, commanded by Col. Miguel E. Pino and Lt. Col. Manuel Antonio Cháves, was made up of ten companies, primarily from Santa Fe, Albuquerque, and villages west of the Rio Grande. However, some Taos individuals, among them José García and Agapito Vigil, would be later hand-picked by Cháves to help him in guerrilla activities against the Confederates after the Battle of Valverde up to and including the Union victory at Glorieta Pass.

Of some thirteen initial companies of the 3rd New Mexico Volunteer Regiment, commanded in the field by Taoseño José María Váldez, at least four companies were from Taos: Company B, led by Capt. Ricardo Branch with Lts. Alfredo Branch and Manuel Mondragón; Company C, Captain Pedro Sánchez and Lts. Inocencio Martínez, Marcelino Vigil, and Teodisio Lucero in command; Company I, led by Capt. Buenaventura Lovato and Lts. Juan Márquez, John Carmody, and José Córdova. Lovato's company was one of two in this regiment whose responsibility was to scout, intercept, and report Confederate movement on approaches to the territory from west Texas. Company F, also with recruitment in the Peñasco area, under Capt. John Brosee, Lts. Sacramento Montoya and Pedro Ronquillo, and 1st Sgt. Rafael Rael y Salazar. The 1st New Mexico Militia, commanded by Lt. Col. Diego Archuleta, included three companies with many Taoseños: Company A, Under Capt. Louis Leroux and Lts. José Maestas and Lorenzo Romero; Company D, Under Capt. Aniseto Valdez, with Lts. Gabriel Jeantet, Rafael Vigil, and William Hirsch; and Company E, under Capt. Gabriel Vigil, with Lts. Abad Romero and Gabriel Lucero. Also commanding militia companies in the Taos area were Pedro Sisneros, Benigno Váldez, José Emerterio Trujillo, and Felipe Sánchez.

The first battle engagement between Union and Confederate forces in the New Mexico Territory was the Battle of Valverde, just north of Fort Craig. (The fort is on the west bank of the Rio Grande south of Socorro.) At the fort was a mixed group of about 3,000 regular soldiers and New Mexico volunteers. They were to engage the 2,500-man Confederate force across the Rio Grande at the Valverde ford early on the morning of February 21, 1862. Union forces were commanded in the field that morning by Lt. Col. Benjamin Roberts. From Fort Craig, Col. Canby, who commanded the Department of New Mexico forces, was calling the shots for Union forces. The Confederate Army of New Mexico was commanded by Brig. Gen. Henry H. Sibley.

THE BATTLE OF VALVERDE

The Battle of Valverde—and the reasons for this Union defeat during the New Mexico campaign—have been extensively written about.[5] On the afternoon of February 19, 1862, Cols. Carson's and Miguel Pino's Union regiments were sent to occupy the strategic heights on the Mesa de la Contadera, a long volcanic escarpment known as Black Mesa on the east side of the Rio Grande across the river from Fort Craig. They stayed there through the nineteenth and twentieth, while the Confederate forces were advancing slowly up the east side of the Rio Grande from El Paso. The Confederate troops reached the Valverde ford before dark on February 20. Col. Canby assumed that the Texans intended to bypass the fort, and he ordered Carson and Pino to leave the mesa and rejoin him at the fort. The 1st New Mexico Militia, 2nd New Mexico Militia, and 4th New Mexico Regiments were to defend Fort Craig in case of attack.

Before dawn on February 21, Capts. Chacón and Deus, along with Capt. Graydon's Independent Company—the majority of his company being New Mexican mounted volunteers from Fort Buchanan, Arizona—along with the regular Union cavalry crossed the river and occupied a strategic hill. These companies then began probing the Texas forces, opening the attack.[6]

Col. Roberts attached Lt. Col. Valdez—with companies B, C, E, F, G, and L—to Maj. Duncan's U.S. Cavalry in support of the Union forces' artillery on the right side, also on the east side of the Rio Grande. They were to take and hold the *bosque* during the battle. According to John M. Taylor, in his *Bloody Valverde,* these volunteers creditably carried out this duty throughout the battle.[7] Carson's regiment of lst New Mexico Volunteers was ordered to the Union's right to bolster Roberts, Duncan, and Valdez. Capt. Alexander McRae's Union artillery battery was set up on the Union's left and center, facing the Texan forces and artillery.

Captain Mortimore's Company A, 3rd New Mexico Volunteers and Capt. Santiago Hubbell's Company B, 3rd New Mexico Volunteers, reinforced this battery, with the 2nd New Mexico Volunteers, commanded by Col. Miguel E. Pino, held in reserve on the west bank of the river. The 2nd New Mexico Militia Regiment commanded by Col. Nicolas Pino, Col. Miguel Pino's brother, and Maj. Charles Wesch was sent to the east bank to prevent an attack on Fort Craig from the south and east.

Throughout the day, the Union forces under Roberts held their own. By midafternoon, a combined cavalry-infantry charge by Maj. Henry Raguet, 4th Texas Mounted Volunteers, was completely routed by Carson's New Mexicans. Carson was reported to have walked up and down the line of troops encouraging them, *"Firme muchachos, firme"* (Hold firm, boys, hold firm). The combined Union regulars and volunteers on the right were now taking the initiative, pushing the Confederates into retreat and trying to outflank them.

Col. Thomas Green, commanding the Texas forces after General Sibley was incapacitated with exhaustion and too much alcohol, directed the attack on the left and center of the battle. Considering the risk of losing, Green broke out some whiskey and thus fortified his men, leading a charge on the Union artillery. Firing shotguns at close range and advancing in a suicidal effort, they overran McRae's battery and captured Union cannons. Col. Canby had taken command shortly before Green's attack, ordering Carson's regiment to retreat and come to the aid of the beleaguered Union. Carson and other Union officers later wrote they could not believe they were ordered to retreat when they had the enemy on the run. But they obeyed orders, and in the confusion created by Canby the Union forces lost the initiative.

In the end, the Texans overran the Union's center and won the battle. In the confusion following the rout, many New Mexican volunteers left for home and were later accused of desertion. For years, in fact, Union officers and Anglo-American writers placed blame for the Union's loss on the New Mexican volunteers—a politically powerless group of scapegoats. On March 6, forty of Carson's men were called to rejoin units from which they had been cannibalized earlier. With hindsight and documents, including a written plea from Kit Carson to drop desertion charges for one of his soldiers in the Battle of Valverde,[8] it is clear that miscommunication was an excuse for accusations of desertion. Not surprisingly, many of those fighting for the Union could not speak English, and some of their officers did not speak Spanish.

While the Union forces commanded by Canby remained to secure Fort Craig, the Texans marched on to Santa Fe, where they were in control for a few months. They were followed and harassed by Lt. Col. Manuel Antonio Cháves and his selected volunteers. Before they could take Fort Union and secure New Mexico, the Texans were intercepted by the Colorado Volunteers at Glorieta Pass. Following the initial clash in Apache Canyon, Cháves and his men led Maj. John M. Chivington and a detachment of Colorado troops over a mesa by a secret route to the Confederate rear, destroyed their supplies, and ensured that the Confederate invasion of New Mexico was over.

Some thirty-three New Mexico Volunteers died at the Battle of Valverde. Among them were five from Taos. According to official documents and muster rolls, the men, who died at Valverde were Marcelino Baca, Company D; Pablo Trinidad Maes, Company I; and José Ramón Ruiz, Company H, 1st New Mexico Volunteers. Joaquín Suaso, Company B, and José Martín, Company F, 3rd New Mexico Volunteers were also reported killed in the battle. Most of the volunteer casualties, according to Taylor, died during Green's overwhelming attack. None of Colonel Cháves's special unit forces were lost in the aftermath of Valverde, at skirmishes near Albuquerque or in the Battle of Glorieta Pass. In Taos Plaza today, Old Glory aloft after sunset and before sunrise serves as a fitting memorial to all those Taoseños and New Mexican men who have defended their country since the start of the American Civil War.

NOTES

1.   Marc Simmons, *The Little Lion of the Southwest: The Life of Manuel Antonio Cháves, A Nineteenth-Century Indian Fighter* (Chicago: Swallow Press, 1973).

2.   Ibid., 179–80, and Darlis A. Miller, "Hispanos and the Civil War, A Reconsideration," *New Mexico Historical Review* 54:2 (1979): 109–11. In New Mexico, militias were standing units of locals, roughly equivalent to today's National Guard. They responded to local or regional emergencies. Volunteers were called up by alcaldes in times of regional and national needs for military forces. Regulars were enlisted soldiers in the U.S. Army.

3.   Officially, a company consisted of 100 men, with the following officers: a captain, a 1st lieutenant, a 2nd lieutenant, a 1st sergeant, four sergeants, eight corporals, and two musicians.

4.   Váldez was reported to be an adopted son of Padre Antonio José Martínez.

5. The books listed in Selected References to this chapter may all be consulted.

6. Jacqueline Dorgan Meketa, ed. *Legacy of Honor: The Life of Rafael Chacón, A Nineteenth-Century New Mexican* (Las Cruces, NM: Yucca Tree Press, 2000).

7. John M. Taylor, *Bloody Valverde: A Civil War Battle on the Rio Grande, February 21, 1862* (Albuquerque: University of New Mexico Press, 1995).

8. Charles Meketa and Jacqueline Meketa, "Heroes or Cowards? A New Look at the Role of Native New Mexicans at the Battle of Valverde," *New Mexico Historical Review* 62:1 (January 1987): 46f.

SELECTED REFERENCES

Alberts, Don E. *The Battle of Glorieta: Union Victory in the West.* Texas A & M University Military History Series 61. College Station: Texas A&M University Press, 1998.

Edrington, Thomas S., and John Taylor. *The Battle of Glorieta Pass: A Gettysburg in the West, March 26–28, 1862.* Albuquerque: University of New Mexico Press, 1998.

Frazier, Donald S. *Blood & Treasure: Confederate Empire in the Southwest.* Texas A&M University Military History Series 41. College Station: Texas A&M University Press, 1997.

Joseph, Alvin M. Jr. *Civil War in the American West.* New York: Knopf, 1991.

Kerby, Robert. *The Confederate Invasion of New Mexico and Arizona, 1861–1862.* Great West and Indian Series 13. Tucson, AZ: Westernlore Publications, 1980.

Meketa, Charles, and Jacqueline Meketa. "Heroes or Cowards? A New Look at the Role of Native New Mexicans at the Battle of Valverde." *New Mexico Historical Review* 62:1 (January 1987).

Meketa, Jacqueline Dorgan, ed. *Legacy of Honor: The Life of Rafael Chacón, A Nineteenth-Century New Mexican.* Las Cruces, NM: Yucca Tree Press, 2000.

Santee, J. F. "The Battle at La Glorieta Pass." *New Mexico Historical Review* 6:66–75 (1931).

Simmons, Marc. *The Little Lion of the Southwest: The Life of Manuel Antonio Cháves.* Athens, OH: Swallow Press, 1983.

Taylor, John. *Bloody Valverde: A Civil War Battle on the Rio Grande, February 21, 1862.* Albuquerque: University of New Mexico Press, 1995.

ONE TOWN: MULTIPLE PERSPECTIVES

———————

❖

❖   13   ❖

Taos Pueblo, Past and Recent

John J. Bodine

A World Heritage Site since 1992, Taos Pueblo was built of adobe in two large, multistoried room blocks on the north and the south sides of the Río Pueblo de Taos, beginning about 1350. It has been continuously occupied since then. The author of this piece, anthropologist John J. Bodine, PhD (1935–98), devoted his entire academic career to Taos and the Tanoan-speaking Indians of New Mexico and is recognized as the preeminent authority on Taos Pueblo and its people. His Taos Pueblo: A Walk Through Time *(1977) is respected by the Taos people both for what he recorded and for what he did not disclose or exploit. The piece that follows is excerpted from* Taos Pueblo: A Walk Through Time *(revised edition, 1996) with the kind permission of Rio Nuevo Publishers, Tucson, Arizona. This text was current when first published in 1977 and for the most part remains true of Taos Pueblo today.*

WHILE A GREAT DEAL HAS BEEN WRITTEN about Taos Indians and the pueblo particularly, there still remains a good deal of misunderstanding about this famous place and the lives of its people. Hopefully in the material that follows, a few of these errors are corrected and the questions that occur to most visitors to Taos are answered.

177

The Name Taos and the Taos Language

The word *Taos* is unusual, and many have speculated on its origins and meaning. Romantic writers who see in Taos culture a profound philosophy and way of life have wondered if Taos is not in some way related to the ancient Chinese religion, Taoism. It is not. Indeed, it is not even pronounced in the same way. There is no reliable evidence to link the Taos Indians with the Chinese. The languages of the two peoples are not related in any way, and one must stretch very hard to find even broad parallels with certain cultural beliefs. Taos is a one-syllable word pronounced by most in the same way as the English word "house." Many visitors will mispronounce it "TAY-os."

As to its origin, it seems conclusive that the word has roots in the languages of some of the other Pueblo Indians of New Mexico—those who speak Tanoan languages and live along the Rio Grande River from Taos down to Isleta, just south of Albuquerque. The Spanish explorers first came to the Rio Grande south of Taos. In trying to communicate with the Indians there and asking them about the villages to the north, they were given a term that meant "to the north." It is also a term that can be found in the Taos language and means, in addition to direction, "to or toward the village." The term was roughly "tao." The Spanish were in the habit of adding an "s" to nouns to form the plural—so the result was Taos. It has been in use ever since 1598. Unfortunately for the romantics, there is nothing mysterious about it.

There is also a good deal of misunderstanding about the Taos language. Again, attempts have been made to link the speech of the Taos Indians with the Chinese. Part of this is due to the fact that the Taos language is partially tonal and Chinese is tonal. English and other European languages are not, but speakers of those languages hear what they describe as a "singsong" or musical quality to tonal speech. Hence, there must be some connection. The Taos language is no more related to Chinese than English is. There are many tonal languages in the world. For example, Navajo is tonal and so are many of the languages in Central Africa, but you never hear anyone suggesting they are related to Taos.[1]

Taos is a Tiwa language (TEE-wah), closely related to the Tiwa speech of three other New Mexico pueblos: Picurís, which is about twenty-five miles southeast of Taos, and Isleta and Sandia, which are close to Albuquerque. Here is another source of confusion. Taos and the other Tiwa languages are also related to Tewa (TAY-wah). Tewa is spoken by the pueblos of San Juan, Santa Clara, San Ildefonso, Nambé, Pojoaque, and Tesuque. These are all villages south of Taos in the area around Española and Santa Fe. The problem has been that even knowledgeable persons have written Tewa to refer to the language of Taos, when they should have spelled it Tiwa. It should be added that the people of Jemez Pueblo speak Towa (TOW-wah). Tiwa, Tewa, and Towa all belong to the group of languages known at Tanoan (tah-NO-un). Hopefully, it is not terribly confusing to add that the Indians of other

New Mexico pueblos speak languages totally unrelated to Tanoan. The pueblos of Cochiti, Santo Domingo, San Felipe, Santa Ana, Zia, Laguna, and Acoma, which are either between Santa Fe and Albuquerque or west of Albuquerque, speak Keres (CARE-us). The language of the Indians of Zuni Pueblo in western New Mexico south of Gallup is again separate from all of the above.

It is interesting that languages spoken by the Pueblo Indians are indeed of several groups and quite different from one another. This baffles many people who tend to think that there is "an Indian language." Nothing could be further from the truth. One need only reflect on the complex language situation in Europe: Basque is not related to French, although French is related to English, but English is more closely related to German. None is related to Hungarian. All this does not seem to bother most people, but when it comes to Indian languages, for some reason they are either confused or bored. The myth persists that Indians speak Indian, and "Indian" is often thought of as primitive, guttural, and not complicated grammatically.

Taos is a very beautiful language; it is also a very complex one and extremely difficult to learn. The Taos are very polite people, particularly when communicating with each other. Perhaps there is a relationship between this and the fact that it is impossible to be profane in Taos and very difficult to be obscene. One thing that should startle English speakers is that you cannot directly say "no" in Taos, nor is there a concept of "never." Imagine the effect this would have on English conversation! The ultimate origin of the Taos language and the hundreds of other languages spoken by the American Indians is unknown, although the Indians themselves first came from Asia. Racially they are Asiatic in origin; and if one went back far enough, say 25,000 years, it could be said that their languages are also Asiatic. But no known Asiatic language can be linked with any Indian language spoken today in the United States—and Taos is most definitely not related to Chinese any more than Chinese is related to Japanese!

Some Historical Notes on the Pueblo

Too little is still known of Taos Pueblo to give a completely satisfactory history. This is especially true of the history of the Taos people before the coming of the Spanish. It seems certain that Taos Pueblo was built sometime around AD 1350. Precisely when the ancestors of the Taos first entered the valley is impossible to state, although there are numerous Pueblo ruins here and there that are certainly older than Taos Pueblo. Most archaeologists think that the Pueblo Indians who settled along the Rio Grande migrated from the Four Corners region—the area where the present states of Colorado, New Mexico, Arizona, and Utah meet. The spectacular ruins and cliff dwellings of that region, such as Mesa Verde, Chaco, and Kayenta, were inhabited by the Anasazi, a word meaning "old ones" in Navajo. A long drought that plagued the area in the late 1200s and other factors may have caused the Anasazi to abandon their great villages and move east to the Rio Grande where the water supply was more dependable. If so, then the Taos and their neighbors are descendants of these "old ones."

Another theory is that the Tanoan-speaking people, including the Taos, were nomadic and roamed somewhere in the north until they moved south into the Rio Grande Valley. Here they encountered the Keres, who we recall do not speak a language related to Tanoan. Perhaps the Keres speakers were migrants from the Four Corners. The Tanoans adopted agriculture and the Pueblo way of life and so came to resemble the "old ones" in the process. It is interesting that the Kiowa language is related to Tanoan. The Kiowa are true Plains Indians now living in Oklahoma. There are many words in Taos, for example, that are the same in Kiowa. Actually, the whole matter is much more complicated than this, but the arguments continue. It will be up to the anthropologists and other scientists to finally unravel the matter. The Taos themselves say only that they came from the north.

After the Spanish arrived, first with Coronado in 1540 and later with Juan de Oñate to settle the Rio Grande Valley in 1598, the history of Taos Pueblo becomes much clearer. Many fine books have been written on this history, although a number of facts about Taos Pueblo itself are not known. But for the history buff it is not difficult to obtain a good outline of the past. It is important that the Taos people have preserved their way of life for nearly four hundred years in the face of strong pressure by Spaniards and Anglo-Americans. They have adopted many things from these other cultures but have refused to become absorbed by them. They rely very firmly on a cultural base that was laid down centuries ago and remain convinced that, while many good things have come from the Europeans, the Taos have a heritage worth preserving. It is apparent from what one sees at Taos Pueblo today that they have succeeded.

The Community

Perhaps nothing is stronger at Taos Pueblo than a deep feeling of belonging to a community. This communal spirit, expressed in the phrase "We are in one nest," has been one of the most important things that has held the people of Taos together. There are many responsibilities and obligations that every Taos Indian must accept to remain a respected member of the community. For example, both men and women are expected to offer their services when needed. These are collectively known as "community duties." They range from helping to clean out irrigation ditches in the spring, to serving in the native government, to correctly performing religious ritual, to preparing food for ceremonial occasions. Ideally, one should be very cooperative, which is not to say that Taos people do not quarrel among themselves at times—there are a number of very strong-willed people at the Pueblo. That is true today just as it was in the past, but one should never allow one's own desires to be destructive of community interests.

In the Council, the principal governing body of the Pueblo, this idea of cooperation is expressed by the statement, "Let us move evenly together." Although more will be said about the governing structure of the Pueblo, it is important to know that an individual should always bow to the will of the whole, and the whole must be taken very literally. Unlike the American concept of the will of the majority, the Pueblo belief in the strength of everyone moving unanimously is something very difficult to achieve. It has caused serious problems from time to time, but it has also been a strong force that has prevented Taos from breaking apart.

The Family

At the root of this communal spirit and certainly one of the strongest institutions at Taos is the family. A Taos family is organized in much the same way as an Anglo-American family, though in many instances it is bigger and more closely knit. The Taos have a bilateral kinship system: descent on both the father's and mother's sides of the family is equally recognized. This is the same system that prevails in American families. Since at Taos both sides are important, this means that you consider a very large number of people to belong to your family. You treat them and expect them to treat you as family members. The result is that you are related to many people and are expected to help and be helped by a great many more relatives than most American families of today. Since the majority of these relatives live nearby rather than hundreds of miles away, it is easy to see how close many Taos families actually are. This doesn't mean you like all your relatives any more than would be true elsewhere, but again you are supposed to be cooperative and try to submerge your feelings for the good of all. Also important at Taos is a very strong respect for the aged. Even if you disagree with their advice, you should have the courtesy to consult with your elders about any important matter.

In the majority of cases at Taos, each primary family lives in a separate dwelling—that is, at marriage the young couple sets up a residence of their own for themselves and the children that hopefully will be born. But members of your own family and that of your wife's or husband's are always near. This has been very important in raising children. As young adults have had to go out of the Pueblo and into the wage-earning world, older relatives, particularly grandparents, have been available to take care of the children. Naturally this meant that they taught these youngest Taos Indians what they felt was important in life. Values and ways of doing things that they cherished were thereby handed down and tended to protect the integrity of Taos culture. So yet another generation of Taos Indians loyal to their heritage was nurtured.

POPULATION

It was mentioned at the beginning that there were approximately 1,500 Taos Indians living at the Pueblo today. There were actually a little fewer than 2,000 persons recorded on the tribal rolls in 1991. The Taos population has grown dramatically in the past few decades and especially since the Second World War. In 1942, for example, there were only 830 Taos on the rolls. This increase has had important effects at the Pueblo. As the population grew, more and more Taos Indians, particularly young adults, left to seek employment, most often in the cities. Some 500 are scattered across the country with many in the Western cities of Albuquerque, Denver, Phoenix, and Los Angeles. While this has tended to split up a number of families, many remain intact and the old ways continue. Often individuals leave for a relatively short time (a few years) and then return, so there is a rather constant fluctuation of the population. If possible, many come home for major feast days, at Christmas, and on vacation. Since enough have stayed permanently at the Pueblo, no serious threat to the continuation of Taos culture has occurred.

DRESS AND ORNAMENTATION

Before the arrival of Europeans, the Taos people dressed primarily in skin clothing: buckskin shirts and leggings for the men and dresses for the women. All wore hard-soled moccasins. Of course, all these items of dress were handmade by the people from animals they hunted. The mountains were well stocked with deer, and the Taos went frequently to the plains to the east to hunt buffalo. Taos Valley is too high and the growing season too short for cotton, so the Taos traded for woven cotton goods with the Indians to the south. Cotton was domesticated independently in the New World by the American Indians. The Spanish brought sheep with them into New Mexico, so eventually woolen goods were also available. The Spanish also introduced cowhide. Taos dress styles have thus changed through the centuries.

Today store-bought clothing is worn, so that in most respects the Taos dress much like everyone else in the country, particularly like other rural Western people. There are a few important differences that can be observed, however. Older Taos men tend to imitate the dress styles of former times. They usually wear moccasins or shoes with the heels removed to simulate the moccasin style. They rarely wear hats and will often cut out the seat of store-bought pants to resemble the skin leggings of the past. A breech clout is worn and a cloth is wrapped around the hips to cover themselves. They wear their hair long and plaited in two braids that begin behind the ears and fall forward on the chest. Most importantly, they are rarely seen without the blanket.

The blanket, which has been the cause of much discussion by those who visit Taos Pueblo, serves a number of purposes. Obviously, it is a source of warmth in the winter, but people wonder why it is also worn in the summer. Actually, it rarely gets so hot in Taos that the blanket is truly uncomfortable. In summer, the men lower the blanket and wrap it securely around their waist and hips. It can also be folded and wrapped bulkily around the head, providing a turban-like hat which acts as an effective sun shade. Most often this is done when working in the fields. People of North Africa and the Middle East, where it gets much hotter, wrap themselves in similar ways. There, such clothing styles definitely act as protection against the penetrating rays of the sun; but the most important reason is a cultural one, just as it is at Taos. It is both a custom and a symbol of being a Taos Indian. It is interesting that none of the other Pueblo Indians, except the Picurís, ever wore the blanket in this manner, which raises the question of where this custom originated. Most probably it was adopted from the southern Plains Indians of Oklahoma. The Taos have very close ties with many of these tribes. Photographs taken before the turn of the twentieth century show Cheyenne and Arapaho, among others, wearing the blanket in the same manner as the Taos do today. Precisely when it was adopted at Taos is not known, but probably around 1890.

Adult women at Taos, except for ceremonial occasions, do not maintain as many customs of dress as the men. The women do prefer low or flat shoes. For one thing, walking around in high heels at the Pueblo is hardly practical. But it is only when they are costumed for dances, such as the Corn Dances in summer, that you can observe the older style of dress. While dresses worn on these occasions are made of commercial cloth, they are cut in traditional fashion to leave one shoulder bare and are belted at the waist with a wide sash. The costume is not complete without the folded white doeskin boots owned by every adult woman. Often they were made and presented to a bride by the groom at the time of their wedding. Older Taos women will sometimes wear them today on other than ceremonial occasions. They also often wear their hair in a chignon, the hair drawn to the back of the head and wrapped in a double vertical bun secured with woolen yarn. The most distinctive item of dress is the shawl. Older adult women hardly ever go anywhere, summer or winter, without one. Cotton or wool, it is de rigueur, just as the blanket is for men.

It is not customary for the Taos to wear a great deal of jewelry and other ornamentation, except on special occasions. However, this depends largely on the individual. Southwestern Indian jewelry in all its variety is owned by the Taos, just as it is by both the Spanish- and Anglo-Americans. The Taos do not load themselves down with silver and turquoise as do the Navajo because it is not considered proper to display one's wealth and good fortune. For the Navajo it is important to do so. They wear their jewelry for different and equally valid cultural reasons.

Economics

Before the coming of the Spanish and for a considerable period after that, the Indians of Taos Pueblo were largely self-sufficient. Their land was rich and well-watered. Most years saw an abundant harvest. In addition to agriculture, the Taos hunted game animals and birds. They carried on a certain amount of trade with other Indian tribes, and they still do. But prior to the coming of the Anglo-Americans in the nineteenth century, the economy was principally one of barter. Today it is a strictly cash economy. Wage work has replaced farming as a primary means of making a living. There are a few who still depend on agriculture and livestock, and some families plant gardens and raise pigs and chickens. But these products are almost entirely consumed by the families who maintain them.

Many people question why agriculture does not remain the primary source of support for the Taos. There are two very obvious and logical reasons: First, as a result of the population increase and through equal inheritance patterns, the land has become reduced to smaller and smaller plots which are insufficient for meaningful agricultural production. Second, agriculture, to be profitable today, requires considerable capital and a highly mechanized operation. This is impossible for most Indians to achieve. This area of northern New Mexico is one of the most economically depressed regions in the country. In spite of the fact that many Indians are more affluent than they were in the past, unemployment is very high. There are simply not enough jobs in the Taos area for the people who could fill them. This is another major reason for the significant number of Taos Indians who have left to find employment elsewhere.

Many believe that the federal government supports Indian people. Strictly speaking, this is false. The government does provide health and educational facilities for Indians living on reservations, such as the Taos. And reservation land is not taxed. But Indians are subject to the same income and other taxes as every other U.S. citizen, and they must pay the same price for all goods and services. Of considerable importance to the Taos in recent years have been the various forms of welfare assistance, social security payments, and pensions. These programs do not differ from similar ones available to other people in the country, particularly those who are living at a virtual level of poverty. They have become tremendously helpful to the many aged persons at the Pueblo and have relieved the younger generations by their complete support.

It is truly remarkable in many instances how the Indians have survived economically, since the annual per capita income is often only a few hundred dollars, so low as to make the government's poverty-level figures absolutely absurd when applied to their situation. No one starves at the Pueblo. Again, this is due in part to the close family ties. Sharing resources, particularly food, is a time-honored Indian custom and tends to distribute what excess there is. Some Indians are certainly better off than others, but very few can meet the standards accepted as normal by the majority of middle-class Americans. The

Taos are not overly impressed by material goods; in fact, it is not a cultural value to try to amass wealth. It is certainly in bad taste to make any open display of one's good fortune.

Government

The Taos have maintained a very interesting form of government. The principal governing body of the Pueblo is the Council, which is made up of the most important religious leaders representing the six Taos kivas and the top secular officers who have served or are serving as Governor, Lieutenant Governor, War Chief, and Assistant War Chief. The Council numbers around fifty men. Women do not hold positions in Taos government. In order to be elected by the Council to one of the four important secular offices, a man must have been initiated into the kiva religious system; therefore, Taos government has been described as a theocracy.

While the Council must decide on all truly important issues that face the Pueblo, the secular officers are in charge of day-to-day matters that affect the community. The secular staff changes each year and is annually elected and installed on January 1. The Governor and his staff concern themselves with everything that occurs inside the village, while the War Chief and his staff see to anything external to the village, but on reservation land. For example, it is the War Chief's responsibility to patrol the mountainous areas for instances of trespass or forest fire. In recent years this division of labor has tipped somewhat in favor of the Governor, who has become more important than the War Chief. The money collected from visitors through parking and photographic fees, which is a primary source of income for the community, is the responsibility of the Governor. Most often he will be the one contacted by federal or state agencies should anything arise that concerns the tribe. In turn, the matter, if serious enough, must go before the Council.

It was mentioned previously that a unanimous decision by the Council is highly desirable. At least general agreement is usually sought. It is on this basis that Taos government has been described as exceedingly democratic. From a strictly American perspective, however, this is not literally true, since the members of the Council are not the elected representatives of all the people. Nevertheless, it is a system that has operated at Taos for untold generations, and the Council is recognized by the United States government as the legitimate governing body of the Pueblo. Until the Taos themselves decide to change it, it will undoubtedly continue.

Religion and the Ceremonial Calendar

Though the Taos religion is most important to the continuance of their traditional culture, the Taos do not want their religion revealed to outsiders. They feel that strength is maintained by carefully guarding the nature of their religious ritual and performance. Part of this determination not to reveal the operation of the kiva-based religion is due to the fact that the Taos were persecuted in the early days of Spanish occupation for practicing their aboriginal rites. Subsequent to the Anglo-American takeover, the Taos felt again the sting of religious persecution, particularly in the early decades of the twentieth century.

It is known that Taos religion is based on a belief in the oneness of all living things. Religious ritual is aimed at protecting the delicate balance of the relationship between man and nature. Each kiva at Taos has its own special role to perform in this overall task, but to say anything beyond this would be offensive to the Taos people. What occurs in the kivas and at the many sacred "shrines" in the mountains behind the Pueblo is not the business of outsiders. Until such time as the Taos decide it is necessary to record their religion for the future, it is a subject best not approached. Unfortunately, many outsiders have engaged in idle speculation, some of it totally misleading and often absolutely false. At times this has been very harmful to the community and completely unwarranted in a country which professes freedom of religious worship.

The Taos generously permit outsiders to witness the public portions of certain ceremonies, so it is possible to list the important dances that are performed each year. They in turn partially reflect the ceremonial calendar of Taos religion. You are fortunate if your visit to the Pueblo coincides with one of these remarkable performances.

TAOS PUEBLO CALENDAR OF DANCES

> January 1: Turtle Dance
> January 6: Buffalo or Deer Dance
> May 3: Feast of Santa Cruz: foot race and Corn Dance
> June 13: Feast of San Antonio: Corn Dance
> June 24: Feast of San Juan: Corn Dance
> July 25: Feast of Santa Ana: Corn Dance
> July 26: Feast of Santiago: Corn Dance
> September 29 and 30: Feast of San Geronimo: Sunset Dance, foot race,
>   pole climbing, annual Taos Fair
> Christmas Eve Procession
> Christmas Day Deer Dance or Matachines

Although the Taos perform other dances at various times of the year, they are not regularly scheduled on particular dates, so it is necessary to inquire whether a dance will be held. But it is obvious from our list that the Taos have organized the sequence of dances in accordance with the Catholic calendar. This is the result of the long-standing influence of Catholicism at Taos. However, with the exception of the procession from the church on Christmas Eve when the statue of the Virgin is carried around the village and the performance of the Matachines—a dance of Spanish and Mexican origin—all ceremonies are Indian in nature.

The "animal dances" in winter, such as the Turtle, Buffalo, and Deer, are generally regarded by those who have seen them to be the most beautiful that the Taos perform. This may be due to the great importance the Taos placed formerly on hunting such animals as deer and buffalo. The so-called Corn Dances in summer are actually intended for the success of agricultural endeavors. Women participate more in these dances than in the animal dances of winter, with the exception of the Deer Dance. The Turtle and Buffalo dances are strictly male performances.

The Feast of San Geronimo, the patron saint of Taos, is a two-day celebration that marks the close of the harvest season. In the late 1700s and early 1800s Taos was the site of annual trade fairs that attracted hundreds of Indians from other tribes and many other persons who came to trade and barter goods. San Geronimo is reflective of this even today. Also on San Geronimo, the Black Eyes religious society performs.

They are often referred to in English as the Clowns (Chifonete) because of their amusing antics, although their behavior is actually of a serious nature. They climb a very tall pole erected in the village on the north side not too far from the church. At the top of the pole, the freshly killed carcass of a sheep and bundles of food have been fastened. It is the duty of the pole climber to bring these down, whereupon they are distributed among the Black Eyes who have participated.

Early on the morning of September 30 there is a foot race on the track that runs east and west between the north-side houses and the drying racks. A good deal of misunderstanding has been generated about the meaning of these races. It is often thought they are an example of spirited competition, as one would expect in a competitive sport such as track. Rather, they are religious in nature and are aimed at the maintenance of physical well-being, not only for the racers but for the community as a whole. Each participant should do his best. It is less important who wins, and it is not a race that pits the north-side people against the south-side. It is certain that most who have the opportunity to see these dances and other activities feel they have gained considerable insight into the strength and integrity of Taos culture.

NOTE

1. Editor's note: Unlike most who write about Taos Pueblo and its people, Bodine speaks of tribal members as "the Taos" and the Tiwa language of Taos Pueblo as "Taos."

The great North House of Taos Pueblo, seen from the south bank of Rio Pueblo de Taos. Photo Bruce Gomez, ca. 2000.

❖ 14 ❖

Taos Pueblo:
A Personal Journey through Time

Vernon G. Lujan

A history of Taos must include the voice or voices of the people of Taos Pueblo. The very existence of the pueblo as a living institution is testament to the Taos people's commitment to the cultural values that have sustained them through endless difficult encounters with societies that came to their valley much later, cultures with values often at odds with theirs. In "Pueblo of Taos," Vernon G. Lujan speaks eloquently from the perspective of one who was born and grew up at the pueblo.

———————————

> *We have lived upon this land from days beyond history's records, far past any living memory, deep into the time of legend. The story of my people and the story of this place are one single story. No man can think of us without thinking of this place. We are always joined together.*
>
> *Tribal Manifesto*

To reiterate the Tribal Manifesto, this story is of my people and this place of the Red Willows; and, although it is a personal story, it is nonetheless a brief history of the Pueblo of Taos and of growing up at this place. This story is also of my personal experiences as it relates to significant events, people, and places throughout the history of the Pueblo of Taos.

The Pueblo of Taos has been perceived as being on the "frontier" of pueblo country because it is the northernmost of the nineteen remaining pueblos of New Mexico.[1] It has also served as a frontier outpost for three foreign nations that immigrated to this continent and imposed their colonial governments: Spain, Mexico, and the United States. Its peripheral location notwithstanding, the Pueblo of Taos was settled by a union of people whose journeys brought them to this beautiful high desert valley, which is formed of a plateau isolated by the enfolding mountains and incised by the Rio Grande on its own journey to the Gulf of Mexico. The location was protected by natural geographic barriers, which were accessible by mountain passes that opened toward all the cardinal directions and allowed trade with other peoples, such as Apache, Comanche, Navajo, Ute, and also other Pueblo peoples.

The community and culture of the Pueblo of Taos has evolved by adapting to and gaining intimate knowledge of our environment. This is evident in our social and religious events as well as in our archaeological past. For example, at the north end of the Taos Valley, the prehistoric pit structures are rectangular; in direct contrast, the early pit structures found at the southern end of the valley are circular. This contrast continues to play a significant role in the social composition of our community and its architecture, which are divided into the North and South houses by the Rio Pueblo de Taos, the perennial stream that flows through our village, the Taos Valley, and into the Rio Grande.

A common misunderstanding is that pueblos "just happened" to be constructed in their present architectural configurations and that their present sites were haphazardly chosen. The Pueblo of Taos is a planned community, as are all Pueblo communities. Their construction and location were deliberate and based on many centuries' knowledge of environments, perennial water sources, biodiversity, astronomical observations, and other significant cultural knowledge.

Our oral tradition tells of a migration in search of "a good place," when our people—our forefathers and foremothers—moved with their children and belongings over many miles, ecosystems, terrains, and social interactions with other peoples. They were in search of a perennial water source and other natural resources for sustenance and building materials. The people named it The Place of the Red Willows, and this is where they built the two multistoried structures whose architectural forms mirror the clouds and mountains. They used the available resources of earth and trees for building materials. The village was situated on either side of the Rio Pueblo—with three bridges linking the two halves.

Our cultural knowledge has been passed down through generations in the Tiwa language to provide through stories the origins of our people.[2] As with all orally based cultures, Tiwa knowledge rests in oral traditions and is passed by example from older to younger generations. The maintenance of the language is vital and is directly related to the strength of the culture. The Pueblo of Taos has adamantly instilled the importance of maintaining the Tiwa language to younger generations.

My first language was Tiwa, for this is how subsequent generations learned from their elders and parents.

The community was very aware of the changes that were occurring in "the outside world," and their effects were very real even within our pueblo and our community. Long ago a defensive wall was built to surround the entire pueblo. Despite the wall, change breached, and the influences from the outside world were significant. They included two world wars and other societal changes. Although the physical wall could not prevent these changes, it did serve to mark a boundary within which our traditional values were kept intact. The mixture of cultures and people created an atmosphere of exchange and interaction that, although not readily evident, was characterized by subtle influences in art, education, dress, and the way of life of the Pueblo people.

While growing up in the Pueblo of Taos, I wandered around the village discovering my environment, just like all the other children, visiting my relatives and playing with my friends. I soon was aware of the beauty of the surrounding mountains and of strong community ties that were present among the residents. Everyone lived within the walls at this time. Although the wall defined the pueblo, it was truly the mountains that encircled our village and define who we are as a people. The wall also gave us, especially the children, a sense of security and served as a boundary beyond which we quickly learned not to venture without adult approval. This wall delineated our community from the outside world, which existed only three miles from our village but seemed worlds away and was very different from our own.

Wandering around our village, I was accepted and invited by everyone into their homes. I roamed with complete freedom and sense of security—climbing drying racks, ash piles, and large cottonwood trees that lined the river. In the evenings, everyone would bring out a bench or chair and sit in front of their home to visit with their neighbors, watch the sun set, and listen to the young men singing traditional round dance songs. The environment and the people around me were so serene and peaceful that I truly believed this was how I would live out my life—in this idyllic existence.

Early Twentieth Century

World events had profound effects on our microcosmic world at the pueblo. The Great Depression, World Wars I and II, and the fight to regain our sacred Blue Lake tested the resilience and tenacity of our people and proved to be keys to our survival. In 1906, the U.S. Forest Service established the Carson National Forest and confiscated a huge portion of our land and, most injuriously, the watershed known as the Blue Lake watershed; Theodore Roosevelt's administration was following the recommendation of Gifford Pinchot, newly appointed head of the U.S. Forest Service. Their plan was to nationalize large tracts of land in an effort to preserve them and provide access to the natural resources for public use and consumption, including timber and water. Thus

Blue Lake sits on land belonging to Taos Pueblo high in the Sangre de Cristo Mountains, far above and east of the village. Access to Blue Lake is strictly reserved to tribal members of Taos Pueblo, who regard it as a sacred place. The U.S. government appropriated the land as national forest in 1906, and only after a long political battle did it return Blue Lake to the pueblo in 1970, under President Richard M. Nixon. Courtesy Taos County Historical Society.

began a sixty-four-year effort by the Pueblo of Taos' political and religious leaders to regain possession of their revered lands and watershed.

In the midst of this momentous effort, life continued with the normal annual cycle of religious and sustaining activities such as planting, irrigating, dancing, harvesting, feasting, and hunting. In the early 1940s, while on an isolated hunting excursion in the adjacent mountains, our great uncle Dorotéo Samora was successful in harvesting a deer for his family. When he brought it back to his home, U.S. Forest Service and law enforcement personnel jailed him for illegally hunting out of season and, even more consequentially, for hunting on public forest lands—lands that had originally been Pueblo of Taos lands. Taos writer Frank Waters immortalized Uncle Dorotéo in his 1942 novel *The Man Who Killed the Deer*. Uncle Dorotéo had intended only to feed his family. Unintentionally he was the agent for bringing another aspect of the controversial land fight to the public's attention. The incident became another reason for our people to endure and struggle to regain rightful ownership of our land and resources.

Everybody engaged in some form of food production, whether as an actual farmer, laborer, or processing corn, wheat, oats, alfalfa, barley, or vegetables. Even children played a role in the production of food for their families, and it was common to have eight or more children in a family. A large family ensured that there was plenty of help for planting, irrigating, maintaining, and harvesting the crops. Children were taught and expected to contribute by bringing water from the river, feeding the livestock and other animals, and learning skills that would make them vital contributors in the agriculture-based economy.

During the Depression, my grandfather, Agapito Lujan, drove the only available wheat thresher in the Taos Valley, and my father tells of his father's journeys beginning in early autumn and ending around Christmas. Grandfather Agapito would drive the thresher to the numerous wheat fields throughout the valley. In early fall, he would begin in the north in Arroyo Seco and Valdez, circle to the southwest through Las Colonias and Los Cordovas, head south to Llano Quemado, Ranchos, and Talpa, and then return north to end at the Pueblo of Taos. He would be home around Christmas with a bounty of gifts that farmers gave as or in lieu of payment for his valuable services.

Many families relied on the exchange of food and services for their livelihood. The Christmas ham, beans, and other foods were all contributed in this way, and there was never any money exchanged, just acknowledgment of a job well done through small gifts of appreciation. Of course, the friends made along the way were invited to the pueblo to view and to participate in the Christmas Eve procession and the Christmas Day dances. Christmas was my father's favorite holiday because he always looked forward to all of Grandfather Agapito's friends coming to the pueblo to enjoy the food and music after the Deer or Matachine dances were done and the bonfires were all out. Although there was no exchange of gifts, there was an exchange of laughter and merriment, food and stories, song and dance.

An employment-based economy developed when residents of the town of Taos began hiring pueblo people to work for them in their homes and businesses.

During the early 1920s and 1930s, many pueblo people served as apprentices with and models for the burgeoning Taos art colony, including our great uncle Albert Looking Elk Martinez. Uncle Looking Elk worked and modeled for Oscar Berninghaus, one of the six artists in the Taos Society of Artists, and for other artists as well. At the encouragement of his famous employer, Looking Elk became an informal apprentice and, in time, began supplementing his income by selling small paintings to tourists. Yet, Looking Elk lived a dual life that was defined by the reservation boundary. In the town of Taos he received recognition from art patrons; at the Pueblo of Taos he was considered a hunter and provider as well as an active community member and leader, serving as governor in the 1930s. This kind of modesty is a quality that contributes to making Pueblo communities unique. Our communities do not direct accolades upon an individual's achievements; the whole community is very aware and very proud of someone's accomplishments and in a rather inconspicuous, indirect way recognizes the person through oratories at public pueblo gatherings, in occasional meetings, and daily interactions.

At this time, it was taboo to paint or photograph images of one's own home or the people who lived there because it was considered to be intrusive and disrespectful to "steal" another person's "essence" by painting his or her likeness. Anyone who made portraits was considered malicious for engaging in the intentional appropriation of a person's essence.

At the height of his painting career, Albert Looking Elk Martinez died tragically in a car accident. He is memorialized through his paintings, and his legacy continues. Because of the pioneering work of their uncle, younger generations of Martinez and Lujans engage in the creative processes, including pottery, painting, sculpture, and traditional art. These influences are evident in the painting styles of such Pueblo of Taos artists as Eva Mirabal, Merina "Pop Chalee" Lujan, and Juan Mirabal.

MID-TWENTIETH CENTURY

By the mid-1950s, the adjacent village of Taos provided the only employment opportunities in the area. Many Pueblo men and women walked or rode horses into town to work for merchants, artists, and others. My maternal grandfather, Onesimo Cordova, worked as a gardener and handyman for many renowned artists, including Ernest Blumenschein, Irving Couse, Andrew Dasburg, and Louis Ribak. My paternal grandmother, Julianna, cleaned houses for Oscar Berninghaus, Mabel Dodge Luhan, and others. My uncle Alfredo Lorenzo Lujan worked for Millicent Rogers as a chauffer and had the opportunity to travel across the United States with his employer. Uncle Alfredo later became a jeweler, painter, and radio disc jockey.

Uncle Al, as he was known to us, hosted the "Indian Program" on the local AM radio station KKIT and did the show entirely in our Tiwa language for more than three decades from 1960 to 1990. Many more Pueblo people worked for various artists and notables, as well, and these working relationships developed into long-term friendships. A distinct synergy was created by this interaction between artists and Pueblo apprentices, employees, and models.

Eva Mirabal learned to paint from Dorothy Dunn in The Studio for art instruction at the Santa Fe Indian School.[3] She perfected her painting skills during her enlistment in the U.S. Army Corps, for which she wrote and illustrated a popular comic strip, *G. I. Gertie,* which appeared in Women Army Corps (WAC) publications. She painted a mural depicting World War II parachutists for the Buhl Planetarium and Institute of Popular Science in Pittsburgh, Pennsylvania. After World War II, she returned to the Pueblo of Taos. She studied with Louis Ribak and Beatrice Mandelman at the Taos Valley Art School and raised a family while continuing her painting career. Mirabal's murals can be viewed at the Santa Fe Indian School and at the Veterans Hospital Library in Albuquerque. Her son, Jonathan Warm Day Gomez, was inspired by his mother and has also gained recognition as a painter.

Merina Lujan gained prominence as a painter using her Tiwa name, Pop Chalee (Blue Flower). Her father was Joseph Cruz Lujan, older brother of Tony Luhan, Mabel Dodge Luhan's final husband. Her mother was Merea Margherete Luenberger, who emigrated from Switzerland and was adopted by a Mormon family in Utah. She met Pop Chalee's father when he moved to Utah to work as a ranch hand.[4] Pop Chalee's first exposure to painting was while working at the Santa Fe Indian School. There she became another of Dorothy Dunn's students. Her murals are in both the old and new terminal buildings of Albuquerque Sunport International Airport as well as in many museum and private collections throughout the United States.

Juan Mirabal learned to paint as an apprentice with Taos modernist painter Louis Ribak at the Taos Valley Art School. Although Mirabal did not have wide recognition like Albert Looking Elk Martinez, he had the longest painting career of these talented Taos Pueblo artists. A mural he painted in 1950 in a private residence as a commissioned work still remains on the walls of the Adobe and Pines Inn Bed and Breakfast in Ranchos de Taos.

More recently, the recognition and status of Pueblo artists has changed, with more of them recognized by the wider art community in their respective media. Artists are still reminded that they should not exploit their culture for individual gain. Because many of our traditional arts, such as drum-making, are still very important to our communities, artists are encouraged to use their skills to train younger generations of pueblo members so that these aspects of our culture do not pass away with time. As with other tribal members, artists have a responsibility to their community and its members and are held to an ethic of reciprocating their good fortune with the community.

In the 1950s my father-in-law, Miguel "Red Shirt" Reyna, provided the first taxi service from the pueblo to locations throughout the town of Taos. He came from a typical large family of two sisters and five brothers. Red Shirt later became a famous drum-maker. He had a map in his workshop with pushpins marking locations throughout the world of his drums in their new homes. Among the Reyna brothers, John Reyna (later, Rainer), was the first elected leader of the National Congress of American Indians, a national American Indian advocacy organization. Tony Reyna was in the New Mexico National Guard Battery C of the 200th Coast Artillery that was captured by the Japanese together with a collection of soldiers from throughout the Taos Valley, including the Pueblo of Taos. Uncle Tony is one of the few remaining survivors of the infamous Bataan Death March of World War II. He served two terms as governor of the pueblo.

In the early 1900s and again in the 1940s, the two world armed conflicts enlisted tribal men and women to serve their country. This support of the United States was in jarring contrast to the lack of recognition by the same government. Many young Pueblo and Native American men and women served in the U.S. armed forces preceding U.S. citizenship, which was finally granted in 1948. Many Pueblo of Taos people have served honorably in the United States armed services and continue to do so.

Although our culture encourages peace and harmony, there are instances related in our oral traditions of Pueblo of Taos people being fierce fighters and actively recruited by Spaniards, Mexicans, and Americans for various conflicts. This aspect of our culture did not prepare our young men and women for the brutality of modern warfare. The young men and women who returned home from their duty were plagued by problems related to their experiences. Their return was also a clash of world perspectives, a clash defined by their exposure to and experiences of armed services training, which teaches character traits to ensure survival in combat. These traits were in contradiction to those learned in the pueblo, which taught reliance on and contributions to the community rather than putting oneself ahead of all others. Thus, some of the men and women returning to the pueblo community were prone to maladies now known as post-traumatic stress disorder.

Late Twentieth Century

The tumultuousness of the 1960s came to this community like a hurricane and swept in new ideas, new ways of living, and a new wave of expansion of the Anglo and Hispanic communities. This affected everyone in an irreversible path of assimilation and rebellion. Children started attending public schools in the town of Taos and quickly learned to speak English. Although the Tiwa language still dominated conversations at the pueblo, more and more people were forced to learn English to communicate with their neighbors and to acquire language skills for use in commerce and the exchange of goods and services.

In the 1950s and through the 1960s, the U.S. government instituted and sponsored what it referred to as the "Indian Relocation Program," which was yet another attempt to force Native Americans to assimilate into the dominant society. The government promised to "relocate" participating families to urban areas (in my family's case, the San Francisco-Oakland Bay Area) for education and employment opportunities. The fragmentation of the community can be attributed to this federal policy.

The opportunities for education and employment were very attractive, and many young families took the risk of relocating. My family had never traveled beyond New Mexico, and although my father had traveled the world while in the navy, the Bay Area was a totally different environment from our Pueblo of Taos community, with many, many more people. Always the adventurers and still young enough to be searching for their niche, my father and mother accepted the offer for education and employment by participating in this life-altering program.

Life in their new environment was initially very scary and tested our resilience as a family. Adjustments to our new surroundings were required on a daily basis. Simple things like transportation, purchasing food and other necessities were difficult tasks and issues that we had to deal with despite the promised assistance from the Bureau of Indian Affairs—which was never timely. Despite these trials and tribulations, this experience unified our family through the initial culture shock, and it made us grow strong and reliant upon one another for love and support.

When my parents were convinced that relocating to California was an advantageous opportunity, it seemed to my brother and me that we were like young saplings torn from our roots and transplanted elsewhere! This culture shock was deep, and it toughened our resolve to keep our language, beliefs, identity, cultural knowledge, and, most importantly, our family intact. Looking back on our experience, our culture was vital in helping us cope with our situation. It strengthened us by making us laugh instead of cry when faced with difficult situations. There were times when we cried because we were overwhelmed and all things seemed hopelessly beyond our control. We were also feeling the effects of being thousands of miles away from our relatives whom we would normally have relied on in our home village. This must have been the experience of many native families that participated in this government program of assimilation.

At the time we moved to California, I had just begun school and to learn English as a second language, but my brother spoke only Tiwa and the culture shock was formidable. Fortunately, our parents were our translators, and they interpreted from English into our native Tiwa language. Learning a new language was challenging, frustrating, and humorous but also a source of unification for our family. The experiences of everyday life became inquisitive learning adventures for my brother and me, and our parents often made their translations funny and easily understandable.

Yet, despite the translations and efforts to keep our cultural knowledge intact, our family eventually succumbed, and my brother and I learned to speak English as fluently as we spoke our Tiwa language. It was mandatory that we go to school; it was the law. San Francisco at this time was going through changes of its own and was growing an even greater reputation for being a mixture of worldly nationalities, philosophies, and beliefs. Moreover, both our parents had to go to work, and we all became part of the metropolis as we adapted to life in the city. Our adaptation was for survival, in the same way our ancestors had adapted to their new environment when they settled in the Taos Valley.

When my grandmother, Julianna, passed away, my father was the only one in our family to attend her funeral. Soon thereafter, my parents decided that we had been away from our home long enough, and we returned to Taos in the early 1970s. Since our return to our home community, my father, J. Vince Lujan Sr., has served in tribal government as war chief and governor of the pueblo. An individual becomes a lifetime member of the Tribal Council upon completion of his one-year term as either governor, lieutenant governor, war chief, or lieutenant war chief.

We were fortunate to return home, but many families stayed in their adopted homes and only returned many generations later. Other families come home to visit relatives and participate in ceremonies. They do not consider themselves to have assimilated as the government intended. Neither did we. Despite many years in the city, we were overjoyed to return home. Profound changes had occurred while we were away, and we experienced some of these changes when we returned. Some of these changes included the introduction of electricity, communication lines, and federally-subsidized, or HUD (U.S. Department of Housing and Urban Development), housing. The introduction of electricity was a very public debate within our community that culminated in a confrontation of men against machines. The Tribal Council approved the installation of these "modern" conveniences after much debate, but a portion of the community did not give its consent, and some tribal members opposed it to the bitter end. The most significant stipulation for installation of electricity was the requirement that power lines be buried underground to keep the aesthetic beauty of the natural environment intact. This same stipulation applied to the installation of communication lines within pueblo boundaries.

The introduction of federally subsidized housing was another milestone with both positive and negative implications for the community. The opportunity to live in homes equipped with piped water, plumbing, and electricity were long overdue amenities for a community that for many centuries relied on its river for water and the natural resources for its building materials. The provision of affordable modern homes for families was a very positive development for the people, but it also contributed to the decentralization of the community and drew people away from the village, the nucleus of our world. The community has adapted to the change in housing outside the village by encouraging community members to actively participate in continuing cultural activities, ceremonies, and religious obligations.

The 1970s were significant not only for the introduction of electricity, modern housing, and plumbing but also marked the culmination of the battle for Blue Lake, which in December 1970 favored the Pueblo of Taos. The return of our sacred Blue Lake lands concluded the sixty-four-year battle with the U.S. government and set a precedent: the legal argument for land ownership based on religious significance. People of various skills and divergent interests united and contributed their lives and resources to this effort, among them Seferino Martinez, Paul Bernal, Gilbert Suazo Sr., LaDonna and Fred Harris, John Collier, and Frank Waters, among many others who contributed advice, funding, and time for this cause. This litigation also inspired future legislation known now as the Indian Religious Freedoms Act of 1978. This federal policy requires that the United States government preserve and protect for American Indians their inherent right of freedom to believe, express, and exercise their traditional religions, including but not limited to access to sites, use and possession of sacred objects, and the freedom to worship through ceremonials and traditional rites.

Change never rests and continues to influence our lives, and it does so without regard to age. Growing up in the beautiful Place of the Red Willows fostered an appreciation of the simplicity of life in a traditional community, and the years spent away from my home taught me to be resilient, as my parents and forefathers were when they were faced with trials that tested their very being, philosophical worldviews, values, and cultural integrity. It was, in fact, the cultural knowledge and sense of being part of this beautiful valley's mountains, streams, animals, and natural resources—and of being their stewards—that have defined who we are: people of Taos, Red Willow, Blue Lake, mountain, and high desert. We are descendants of intelligent, resilient, strong people—who traveled through place and time to find this beautiful place as home for their children. We are the children of strong fathers and mothers who have taught us that this place we call home is precious and vital and that we are entrusted with its care and maintenance. We have been taught that we must maintain our language, our culture, our beliefs, our philosophies, and our community for future generations of Pueblo of Taos people.

NOTES

1. In this chapter, the word *pueblo* appears in lower case when speaking generically of pueblo villages and pueblo culture. When referring to the Pueblo of Taos, the word is capitalized. *Pueblo* is a Spanish word meaning village or town. The word has gradually come to be accepted as referring to the villages of agriculture-based Indian cultures of the Southwest, including Hopi cultures.

2. Tiwa is one of three remaining Tanoan languages in the Kiowa-Tanoan family of languages. The other two are Tewa and Towa. Northern Tiwa is spoken at Taos and

Picurís pueblos, Southern Tiwa dialects are still spoken at Sandia and Isleta pueblos. In New Mexico, Tewa is the dialect at the Rio Grande pueblos of Santa Clara, Ohkay Owingeh, San Ildefonso, Nambé, Pojoaque, and Tesuque. Jemez has the Towa dialect. Kiowa is spoken mostly in southwestern Oklahoma.

3. Dorothy Dunn founded The Studio in September 1932, when she was twenty-nine years old. She was a powerful and positive force in encouraging Indian children and artists to value their culture and in helping to create a market for Indian art. She required her students to depict Indian subjects and themes in a flat-art style that would not mimic prevailing non-Indian styles. Among those many successful Indian artists who passed through The Studio were Harrison Begay, Joe H. Herrera, Allan Houser, Oscar Howe, Tonita Lujan, Geronima Cruz Montoya, Pop Chalee, Ben Quintana, Quincy Tahoma, Andy Tsihnajinnie, and Pablita Velarde.

4. They were married and had three children—two girls and a boy. In both the Mormon and Pueblo cultures, such a marriage was fairly unusual then.

SELECTED REFERENCES

Boyer, Jeffrey L., et al. *Studying the Taos Frontier: The Pot Creek Data Recovery Project.* Archaeology Notes 68. Santa Fe: Museum of New Mexico. Office of Archaeological Studies. Santa Fe: New Mexico, 1994.

Brody, J. J. *Pueblo Indian Painting: Tradition and Modernism in New Mexico, 1900–1930.* Santa Fe, NM: School of American Research, 1997.

Cesa, Margaret. *The World of Flower Blue: Pop Chalee, An Artistic Biography.* Santa Fe, NM: Red Crane Books, 1997.

Finnicum, Brenda. *Honor the Women Who Served: Indian Country Today.* New York: Four Directions Media, 2001.

Gordon-McCutcheon, R. C. *The Taos Indians and the Battle for Blue Lake.* Santa Fe, NM: Red Crane Books, 1995.

http://www.lectlaw.com.

http://www.cr.nps.gov.

Parsons, Elsie Clews. *Taos Pueblo.* Menasha, WI: George Banta Publishing Co., 1936.

Waters, Frank. *The Man Who Killed the Deer.* Athens, OH: Swallow Press, 1942.

Witt, David L. *Modernists in Taos: From Dasburg to Martin.* Santa Fe, NM: Red Crane Books, 2002.

_____, ed. *Three Taos Pueblo Painters: Albert Looking Elk Martinez, Albert Lujan, Juan Miribal.* Exhibition Catalog, ed. David L. Witt. Taos: Harwood Museum of Art of the University of New Mexico, 2008.

⬚ **15** ⬚

"Sin agua, no hay vida": Acequia Culture

JOHN NICHOLS

John Nichols is Taos' best-known living writer, much loved for his classic works on northern New Mexico's unique culture. This deceptively informative, highly enjoyable first-person tale treats a subject that has shaped traditional culture and is the crux of sustainable life in this region: water rights and the acequia systems. Since Nichols wrote the piece for this volume in 2004, the Abeyta Water Rights settlement has been reached and, when ratified and funded, should quiet centuries of controversy.

WHEN I ARRIVED IN TAOS 35 YEARS AGO, I bought a little house in the Upper Ranchitos part of town. It was on an acre and a half of land that was fed by two irrigation ditches. I came from the East and I knew absolutely nothing about acequias or water laws in New Mexico. The only things I had going for me were that I could speak Spanish after a fashion and I was eager to learn.

I had been in my new house for about two weeks when I got a letter from the New Mexico State Engineer's office. It was an offer of judgment on the water rights of my land and was part of a massive adjudication suit that is still going on today. Back then I had no idea what the state engineer was talking about, and of course my heart fell into my toes because I thought I was being sued in some way that would tangle me up with lawyers, land me in jail, and take away the land that I had owned for about five minutes, total.

Taos writer John Nichols on the arid mesa west of Taos where churro sheep once grazed. Photo Juanita Nichols, late 1970s, courtesy Taos News Archive.

Welcome to Nuevo México, *tierra del encanto.*

About two minutes after my heart fell into my toes, the *mayordomo* of the Pacheco Ditch, Eloy Pacheco, showed up at my house to inform me that all the *parciantes* were going to clean that ditch on Saturday. So, I went in town and bought a shovel and showed up on Saturday to clean the acequia. I had never worked on a chain gang before, and I had never worked so hard in my life. It wasn't a very long or difficult ditch, but there were about forty of us who worked hard all day long cleaning up that artery, plugging the *perrito* holes, burning the grass, chopping out *jaras*, and cursing the *viejitos* who just leaned on their shovels and every few minutes shouted *"!Vueltal!"* (which translates as "forward," but means that the last guy in the line along the ditch comes to the front). And they babbled to each other about how hard they used to work in the good old days, when men were really *men* and the acequias truly *meant* something. I was the only *gabacho* on the crew, and that was the first time I met all my neighbors together, and I had a blast, complaining, bitching about the work, listening to filthy jokes, and to all the *chisme* and *mitote* of the neighborhood and Taos. I picked up a lot of history, too. Stories galore. And plenty of laughter.

The old guys are mostly all gone now: Adolfo Lavadie, Alfonso Tejada, Eloy Pacheco. Phil Miera is still kicking, however. The young people like Jerry Pacheco and his brother Bobby and Joe Córdova are getting older like me. I'll be sixty-four next week. But the acequias are still running with water every spring and summer, and the adjudication suit is still going on. Nobody knows when the adjudication will eventually run its course, but it may cause considerable damage to the acequia system that created the valley in the first place. Water is what connected me to my little plot of land, and to my neighbors, to my community, and ultimately to the larger world of New Mexico. There was a half acre of pasture in front of my house, irrigated by the Pacheco Ditch. The half-acre pasture in back was irrigated by the Lovatos Ditch. Near the house was a small garden area that I watered off a hand-dug well beside the house. The house was also connected to a community water users association for domestic use.

The first thing I did in Taos was plant a garden, and for twenty years I had a beautiful garden. Every year I grew corn and green beans and carrots and beets and squash and broccoli and peas and sunflowers and I even tried to grow watermelons a couple of times, but they never got bigger than baseballs. I had more pears and apples than I knew what to do with in the autumn. And I also had chickens and turkeys. My neighbor, Tom Trujillo, put his horse in my front pasture, and then in my back pasture, and I spent more time talking to that horse than Tom ever did. In the spring and summer I let the grass grow in the two fields, and then Tom would bale it for his animals. I fixed my fences, and cleaned my little irrigation channels, and carefully irrigated all the living space on that property.

I got so that I really loved watering that land. I loved it because it gave me common ground with all my neighbors. We gathered at meetings to discuss the acequias, and during and after those meetings we discussed everything else. We got to know each other. We became friends. I got to palaver with the *mayordomos*, and that was fun. I treasured friends like Tom Trujillo and Bernardo Trujillo and Eloy Pacheco and Phil Miera. There were lots of fights and tense times. The Lovatos Ditch runs through pueblo land, and so we were always palavering with people at the pueblo about ditch problems. In dry summers, when the Pueblo River was really low, we had a heckuva time getting enough water. You could bet that some idiot on the Molino Ditch would divert so much of the river through their *compuerta* that the Pacheco Ditch would run dry. Then our hotheads would go over and kick out their diversion dam, and the next thing you know they'd be threatening to attack us with rifles.

In a real wet year, with a bad spring runoff, naturally our *compuerta* would get blown out in a flood. I say *compuerta* with a grain of salt, because what we called a *compuerta* was basically a lot of rocks, old tires, downed trees and railroad ties, black plastic and chicken wire, with maybe a dead horse thrown in for good measure, all piled at a slant into the river in order to divert some of the flow into the acequia. I would stand waist deep in ice cold water trying to tie down all that stuff with cables and metal fence posts, and I'd snarl over at Alfonso Tejada or Eloy Pacheco or Adolfo Lavadie or Jerry Pacheco, "Ain't there a better way of doing this?" And they'd just shrug and say, "Well, we been doing it like this for four hundred years." And so far it seems to work. People didn't have very much money, but they knew how to get the job done.

The acequias and my property connected me to that four hundred years. And to the people, culture, and community that had revolved around the water for all that time. They connected me to a tradition rich in grass and orchards and animals and healthy neighborhoods. They connected me to a language rich in history and personality and soul.

Of course, it wasn't always easy to keep those connections healthy. For me, those two acequias that fed water to my property were sometimes one wonderful disaster after another. Some years the muskrats went absolutely postal and we had to form emergency brigades to try and repair the ditch banks between Tom Trujillo's property and Sebastian's Bar. Occasionally those water dogs would hit my ditch bank like Roto-Rooters gone berserk, and although I'm not the bloodthirsty type, I actually wound up trying to shoot them from the kitchen window before the ditch bank collapsed and drowned Tom Trujillo's horse in the ditch. The water rose, and froze again, and rose, and froze again, and pretty soon the ice forced the water over the top of the banks into my front field and Tom Trujillo's front field, and it froze really solid. Then one day all the kids in the neighborhood came skating. They brought with them dozens of dogs. And the dogs immediately attacked my chickens and killed all of them while I was taking a nap. There is no end to the tragedies that can be caused by water.

Sometimes I would leave open a *compuerta* in my back field and again, at night, somebody would throw the entire Pueblo River into a *venita* (small ditch) six inches deep, and when I woke up in the morning the chickens would be roosting on top of their shed, their eggs would be floating in the Kingdom Hall Church parking lot next door, and my outhouse would be transformed into an overflowing septic tank.

When I say "*compuerta* in the back field" I should explain that for me a *compuerta* in my back field was just a hole I chopped in the side of the ditch with a shovel. It used to amaze me to watch how my neighbors irrigated compared to myself. Me, because my back field was at the end of the ditch, I always got the water last, and usually at night. It was only a half acre of grass with a lateral going through it. You'd think I could just cut one little opening and flood the field. I mean, that's how my neighbors did it. I'd watch old Adolfo Lavadie, a little bent-over grasshopper of a *viejito*, at his fields. He'd make one little shovel cut, plop the dirt in the proper spot, then lean on his shovel and watch the water calmly flood five acres without a hitch. Me, I'd chop one path, irrigate forty square feet, then chop another path, irrigate another forty square feet, chop a third path, irrigate another forty feet—what was the matter with me?

I could never figure out the Euclidian geometry necessary to laying down a perfect sheet of water across the grass. I finally figured out it was the genes cultivated during those past four hundred years of creating and caretaking the acequias that gave my neighbors such an advantage.

I remember once a cow died on Indian land and fell into the Lovatos Ditch and blocked it. But we weren't allowed on Indian land without permission from the pueblo. So we went out to the pueblo, and the governor's office said they'd send out a crew to get rid of the cow. But they never sent the crew. So we went back to the pueblo and they told us not to worry, the crew would be there that afternoon. And that afternoon a bunch of us waited on the road outside the fence near the rotting cow, but the pueblo crew never showed up. Of course, you could bet if we jumped the fence and started shoveling out the cow on our own, that's when the pueblo crew probably would've showed up and they would have accused us of trespassing on Federal Land, and we all would have wound up in the Government Penitentiary at Leavenworth, Kansas. So, we tried once again to speak with the governor, the war chief, and who knows who else, and they promised to deal with the cow.

But nothing happened. So finally I went down there with a buddy, we tied kerchiefs over our noses, and shoveled out that cow. I think it was probably the most unpleasant task I ever performed on a New Mexico acequia. And afterwards I figured out that the pueblo was probably laughing at us the whole time. I mean, right from the git-go they weren't idiotic enough to place themselves knee deep in bovine gore, and they were probably trying to figure out what had taken us so long to catch on to that fact and jump the fence and break the law, and get rid of their rotten cow for them?

Of course, one of the most detestable jobs on the acequia is collecting the money. The ditch fees. The yearly dues. The work fees to hire laborers if the landowner doesn't want to clean it herself . . .or himself. In my experience on the Pacheco Ditch it was always Eloy Pacheco, the *mayordomo*, who performed this invaluable service. He was pretty informal. He'd known everybody for seventy years and he had his ways. Sometimes he got the money, sometimes he didn't. It was a frustrating job. Then I was elected a commissioner on the ditch, and the other commissioners decided to make me the treasurer. Thanks a lot, you guys. You could say that the record-keeping up until then had been fairly lax, and my orders were to clean it up because the state was starting to really poke its nose into acequia business because of the ongoing adjudication suit. They also decided that I should collect the money. Me? I gulped, said okay, and went about my task with the zeal of a born-again tax collector. I hated the job, I was terrified of the job, but I realized the money was really important to the well-being of the acequia, and also to keeping people involved as modern times began to weaken the commitment many were beginning to feel toward the land.

"Hey, Effie Sebastian," I would say on the phone, "where's our twenty dollars?"

"To heck with your *veinte pesos,*" Effie would shout back. She's eighty-five years old. "I don't use the water anymore, *so a mi no me importa* if I lose it."

"Don't be a fool, Effie. *Sin derechos de agua tu terreno no vale nada.*" Without your water rights your land is worthless.

"*Tú no vales nada, gringo,*" Effie would shout, and hang up the phone.

So I dialed her again.

"We gotta have that money, Effie. We have to hire a backhoe to dig out a cave-in over by Archie Anglada's."

"Why do I have to pay to dig out a cave-in at Archie Anglada's?"

"Because you're a *parciante* on the acequia, *viejita.*"

"Who you calling *viejita,* nene?"

"Please. Por favor. *Dios te pagará despues.*" God will pay you later.

"Tell God He can pay my ditch fees for me *now*, bobo." And she'd hang up the phone once more.

Eventually, I got the money. It was just a ritual we were going through. I imagine people have been going through that ritual since time immemorial. Still, as the years passed it was tougher to get the money. People complained more, they had more excuses, they weren't as enthusiastic. They were starting to lose interest. The old guys on the acequia died off. The families sold their animals. There weren't so many gardens anymore. Newcomers moved in and built houses where there'd once been fields and the newcomers weren't so interested in the water. Each year, when we went to clean the acequia, there were fewer laborers to do the work. Homeowners would not want to go themselves, and they would hire young boys, cheap, to do the work, but the boys couldn't really do the work. And it became more difficult to find people willing to work for the prices offered. And some years, while I still had my property on the acequia, when we went to clean the ditch in the springtime we'd only have, maybe, fifteen people. And you can't do a very good job that way. So we'd have to raise fees, collect the money, and hire a backhoe to do part of the job. A backhoe is a wondrous machine that can replace fifteen, twenty, twenty-five people working together in the same amount of time. But the backhoe is run by a single person, who's usually not even connected to the acequia, to its history, or to the community that for centuries has drawn its lifeblood off that artery. So the backhoe can be the beginning of the end for much of what makes the acequia, and its water, truly valuable. When the backhoe becomes a necessity on a ditch, then it's a good bet the acequia is going to lose its water. Land owners will sell it to a business, to a hotel, to be used in flushing toilets. And after a while the community on the acequia won't be so interactive. People won't work together so much anymore. They won't know each other as well. They'll lose their connections. And the community itself will begin to come unglued.

Interestingly, this all goes back to that first letter I received from the state engineer, in the summer of 1969, the offer of adjudication of water rights on the Pacheco Ditch for my acre and a half of land. Of course, I had no idea what they were talking about, but pretty soon I would learn. The adjudication was, and still is, a part of the state's attempt to legally define every drop of water in the Upper Rio Grande watershed.

Concurrent with the adjudication, the state was also trying to partition San Juan-Chama Diversion water to various areas of New Mexico, including Taos. For our valley, the plan was to give us 12,000 acre-feet of water to be impounded in a dam called the Indian Camp Dam, which would be built just south of Taos. In order to build the dam and contract with the Bureau of Reclamation and the state we were told that we had to form a conservancy district in order to tax the people in the Taos Valley for all the good fortune slated to come our way as a result of the dam.

At first, everybody was for the Indian Camp Dam, because who do you know in New Mexico who *isn't* for more water? In a state this dry you'd have to be crazy to say "no" to more flow. But pretty soon a lot of the local folks realized that even if the dam was subsidized in part by the government, the cost to locals would still be pretty steep, given that this is a real poor area. But after that realization people *really* rebelled when they began looking into the legal powers of a conservancy district, and they concluded that in all likelihood the control of water in this valley would pass from the individual communities and acequia systems to politically appointed boards who would very likely shift much of the water in this area into development endeavors. And, given the nature of development endeavors in New Mexico during the twentieth century, the local farmers and ranchers and other residents figured they were going to get screwed.

So they formed an organization called the Tres Rios Association to fight against the Indian Camp Dam, the Bureau of Reclamation, the state engineer's office, the Conservancy District, and many of the bankers and lawyers and developers and business people in the Taos Valley. The Tres Rios Association was made up of almost all the acequias in our valley, and most of the people on those acequias. The battle lasted for a good part of nine years, and it created a fair amount of bad blood in the Taos Valley. It pretty much pitted the development future against the sustainable past, and it certainly put the history, and customs, and culture of the Taos area up for grabs. The San Juan-Chama water slated for the Indian Camp Dam was tied into the adjudication of all the water rights in the valley.

It is not an accident that most of the leaders of the Tres Rios Association were elderly gentlemen and women and many of the meetings were conducted in Spanish. Many of those leaders are gone today, and the Taos Valley—and I—miss them dearly. They were not radicals, they were not people who wanted to ask for trouble, nor were they ostriches who decided to stick their heads in the sand in order to avoid facing the realities of modern growth and change. They were people deeply rooted in a culture and history that had shaped New Mexico for centuries. They were Republicans and Democrats, they were farmers and teachers, they were veterans and pacifists. Some had herded sheep, others had worked at Los Alamos. There were grade school principals and people who worked on the county roads and men who built houses and women who ran little grocery stores. The oral history of the Taos Valley was repeated, explained, and venerated at every meeting. All the feuds in the valley could be present in the background of any meeting. All the politics of the valley were present at every meeting and heatedly debated by the various participants. At the meetings were people who loved each other and people who hated each other, but the really important thing was that *the people dealt with each other as a community.* That is the way democracy is supposed to work, with *all* the participants personally involved.

There was a time during the heat of the battle against the conservancy district in Taos, that I had tacked up, on every wall in my little adobe house, the state engineer's hydrographic survey maps of every irrigated piece of land in the Taos Valley. I knew by heart all the acequias, their locations, and many of the pieces of land that they irrigated. I had a telephone-book-sized list of all the *parciantes*. I knew many of those *parciantes* personally. It was the most intimate kind of map you could have of my home area. When I looked at all those parcels of irrigated land and the people who owned them, I was learning an entire town. It was like being in medical school and dissecting a body. It was like memorizing the Bible. It was like learning the entire history of a people that had become an important part of my own history and vice-versa. It's one way I put down roots. That's how communities remain strong, when their people have that connection, those roots, that obligation.

The Tres Rios Association raised a lot of money to pay for lawyers. The leaders went back and forth to Santa Fe and back and forth to Santa Fe and back and forth to Santa Fe. The old timers' tenacity amazed me. They hired people to do research and then they listened to the result of the research. They attended countless court hearings. Sometimes our meetings were chaotic and full of dissension. Sometimes nobody came to a meeting, so the leaders called another meeting, and nobody came to it, so they called a third meeting, and all of a sudden *everybody* came.

During that time, official representatives would arrive in Taos from the State Engineer's Office—men like Paul Bloom or Eluid Martínez (who eventually *became* the state engineer)—and they would call meetings to explain to us the conservancy district, the proposed dam, the San Juan Chama Diversion Project, the adjudication suit, and also Einstein's Theory of Relativity. And after Paul Bloom and Eluid Martínez had spent two hours explaining all these things in both Spanish and English to maybe one hundred small farmers and teachers and construction workers and cabinet-makers sitting in the auditorium of the García Middle School, there would be a long pause. And then one of those small farmers would stand up and say, "That's all very well, *pero no lo hacemos así aquí en Taos*—but we don't do things that way here in Taos."

And after a while the government authorities and the Bureau of Reclamation and the local development poobahs realized that they were talking to a wall. And the wall never collapsed.

One reason the wall did not collapse is that the people of Taos realized the adjudication, the San Juan-Chama Diversion, the Indian Camp Dam and conservancy district were probably going to hurt them deeply. Individual community acequias were going to lose their autonomy to a politically appointed conservancy board: i.e., we were going to lose control of our water systems. And we were going to have imposed upon us an open-ended taxation system over which we had no control. We weren't even going to be allowed to *vote* for the conservancy board that would govern us because the powers that be recognized that if we were given the opportunity to vote we would elect a board that would immediately dissolve the conservancy and that would end the Indian Camp Dam project.

The Tres Rios Association studied the history of other major water projects along the Rio Grande, especially the Elephant Butte Dam and the Middle Rio Grande Conservancy District, and it discovered that in every case water projects that were advertised as ways to help local farmers grow more and better crops for economic profit, wound up instead by running indigenous people off the land in favor of agribusiness corporations and urban/suburban development.

A fascinating study of this process was done way back in 1936 by a Middle Rio Grande Regional Conservator, Hugh Calkins, in a document called "A Reconnaissance Survey of Human Dependency on Resources in the Rio Grande Watershed." Calkins explains that before Elephant Butte Dam 70 percent of the 889 farms in the area were "owned by their operators," a large majority of whom were "Spanish Americans." He described the farms and people as self-sufficient and relatively stable. Then the dam and irrigation district arrived and suddenly bankruptcy and loss of farms "became a constant threat." And in the end, "The irrigation project was the instrument by which this essentially self-sufficing area was opened to commercial exploitation. The establishment . . . of a legal claim upon the resources of the area and the labor of its inhabitants . . . led to the dispossession of the natives, and their replacement by American settlers financed by American capital. . . . Through the construction of a costly irrigation project . . . an additional land area of 100,000 acres was made available for agriculture use," but "the native population, unable to meet the new high cash costs, was in large measure displaced from 50,000 acres it had owned."[2]

A noted sociologist, Dr. Clark Knowlton, who testified at several 1970s conservancy hearings in Taos, had previously written: "Every major irrigation or water conservation project along the Rio Grande River . . .has been responsible for land alienation on an extensive scale. The Spanish-Americans have been replaced by Anglo-American farmers. Their subsistence agriculture has made way for a highly commercial, partially subsidized, and basically insecure agriculture, made possible by government programs. Little thought has ever been given to the rights and land use patterns of the Spanish-Americans in planning water projects in New Mexico and in neighboring states."[3]

During the conservancy and dam battle in Taos we were told that the government would pay something like 96.5 percent of the costs, but we figured out that that last 3.5 percent plus maintenance of the dam would not only be exorbitant for the relatively poor population, but it was open-ended with no guarantee there wouldn't be endless cost overruns.

Eventually, despite our protests, the District Court formed the Taos Conservancy District anyway. So we appealed the verdict and kept fighting. And a few years later the state Supreme Court overturned that District Court decision. And in the end the conservancy district and the Indian Camp Dam did not arrive in Taos. But the adjudication never quit. And, of course, development has gone on anyway, in spite of the serious setback when Taos shot down the conservancy.

Ever since, people have been struggling to maintain the traditional acequias and community water structures and all they represent. The adjudication suit is a difficult and cantankerous beast. It is an attempt to once and for all impose an American legal system on an area that has operated on largely Spanish custom for the last few centuries. The adjudication wants to clear things up so that water can be bought and sold with impunity, clearing the way for modern growth and development. It wants to make it possible to evolve from so-called "inefficient" and antiquated ways into the fast-paced twenty-first century.

In the process, the adjudication suit has pitted people against each other, and one acequia against another acequia in a scramble for more advantageous priority dates. Traditional Hispanic irrigators are placed against irrigators from the pueblo, which entered the adjudication asking for enormous amounts of water. The state, the feds, and a passel of lawyers seem to have grown fat over this. In Taos, the old Tres Rios Association was replaced by a group called the Taos Valley Acequia Association, which continues to represent the often impoverished *parciantes* on most of the ditches in the Taos Valley. Many people still don't understand this convoluted process.

As for me, it's been a while since I've walked the length of an acequia in Taos. Today, I live in a small house, I have no irrigated land, I'm not a commissioner any more. But I think often of the Pacheco and the Lovatos ditches that used to give me water. I can see myself walking along the bank with a shovel, checking it out, looking for problems. I walk through yards and little back fields. There's Lucy Mares's house and her daughter Stella's trailer. And Vidal Cisneros's big purple martin birdhouse, and Shorty's Mower Service garage. Indian ponies on pueblo land shy away from me, they never come over for handouts. Peacocks are strutting by Isabel Vigil's corrals, and her little donkey starts braying. Tom Trujillo's old horse is standing knee deep in grass in his daughter Frances's front field. And they're singing gospel hymns in the Good News church that's right behind Sebastian's old bar. A rusted truck is sinking on its axles in Adolfo Lavadie's two-acre plot. And somebody's hanging out wash by Archie Anglada's trailer. One of the Pacheco boys is shooting at a prairie dog in their garden: *"Órale, bro', cuidadito!"* And we're gonna have to chop down all these behind the Miera's field also. And I better call the Cordovas and tell them it looks like there's a hole in the fence where the sheep could move through to the Romeros' pasture where the alfalfa would bloat those idiot sheep to death in fifteen minutes. And when can we get a crew to repair the *desagüe* just below Medina's corrals?

Water can still be like that in Taos: up close and personal. Nobody is making much money from irrigating small pastures and little gardens off acequias and old wells drilled long ago. People don't hang onto the acequias or their little wells and fight for them because of all the profit involved anymore. No. We hang onto this way of life and fight for it because water and the local organizations that dispense it are the blood that keeps our communities alive.

Sin agua, no hay vida.

Terms given in Spanish are defined herein: *acequia:* ditch; *chisme* and *mitote:* gossip; *compuerta:* headgate; *desagüe:* spillway; *gabacho:* non-Hispano; *jaras:* willows; *mayordomo:* ditch manager; *parciantes:* landowners whose land is irrigated by water from a ditch; *perrito:* muskrat; *viejitos:* elders.

NOTES

1. Hugh Calkins, "A Reconnaissance Survey of Human Dependency on Resources in the Rio Grande Watershed," Regional Bulletin No. 36, Conservation Economics Series No. 6 (Albuquerque, NM: Department of Agriculture Soil Conservation Service, 1936).

2. Clark Knowlton, quoted in John Nichols, "No Comment from Bloom," *New Mexico Review* 47: 3 (1972).

Two government visiting nurses walking a typical road in early spring to make a house call in Llano Largo, 1943. Photo John Collier Jr. Courtesy Mary E. T. Collier and the Collier Family Trust.

✻ 16 ✻

The Tradition of Cooperation

OCLIDES QUINTANA TENORIO

The year 1900 seems in many ways to have signaled the beginning of a major shift. With the turn of the century, many traditional ways of life began to erode. Modern inventions revolutionized modes of travel, farming, food preservation, and the like, and their use wrought changes in people's attitudes toward one another. In no other respect was this shift more profound than in the falling away of close neighborly cooperation. The very same families of the same villages where, for generations, people had worked together at their daily tasks became increasingly self-sufficient. This chapter recounts some of the activities that once were shared.

COOPERATION DEVELOPED AMONG THE FIRST SETTLERS when people *had* to help each other in order to survive. By tradition, neighbors helped neighbors, sometimes by exchanging labor. This reciprocity was exemplified during harvest, when as many as twenty men would bring their sickles to their neighbors' fields to help reap the wheat, oats, corn, or other grains. Men gathered crops, and women preserved food.

Other types of work in which neighbors reciprocated time and labor were cleaning, carding, and spinning wool; making soap; gathering medicinal herbs; caring for vegetable gardens; making adobes; plastering houses; and washing blankets and mattresses in big tubs or at the river. Some of these tasks occurred twice a year, in the spring and in the fall. There were some labors in which men and women worked together, such as making sugar from cornstalks. Children became involved and helped the adults in the sugar-making event.

Sheep Shearing

Most of the settlers had sheep, and the care of a flock involved different tasks. First came the lambing season. From February through April a farmer or herder was on duty day and night. Some ewes had twins or other problems that required human intervention. If a lamb was born on a cold night, it had to be placed in a warm spot to survive, often a box beside the kitchen stove. No matter how carefully the mating had been planned, one had to be prepared for the unexpected.

La trasquila (sheep shearing) occurred in the spring just before *el hijadero* (lambing season). Sheep shearing is an ancient and honorable trade and has been practiced in New Mexico for more than 400 years. The traditional shearing method was with large hand shears that were not easy to handle and had to be kept clean, oiled, and sharp. During sheep-shearing season, preparation began well before the sheep were shorn. *Los trasquiladores* (sheep shearers) were called in plenty of time so that they would have their equipment ready. Corrals were built in the area where the sheep were pastured. Next to the sheep camp, canopies were set up so that the sun would not be too intense for the shearers.

Once shearing commenced, the *trasquiladores* held the sheep tightly in front of them while they clipped off the thick wool. A good shearer could strip a sheep in two to three minutes. The sheep left the shearing camp looking skinny and dazed as they found their way back to the flock.

The shearers worked until noon and then stopped to eat. Washbowls with plenty of water, soap, and towels were ready for them so they could wash their hands and faces. Tables were set with an array of hearty foods, including mashed potatoes, gravy, meat, beans, chili, macaroni, and many other foods. Pies and canned fruit were dessert. At the table, the men talked, joked, and laughed as they ate their meals and soon were ready for a long afternoon of work.

The shorn wool was tied into bales and put into huge, heavy cloth sacks and stored in dry places until ready to be shipped to market in Antonito, Colorado, where it was usually sold. Children picked up *matitas*, scraps of wool that fell from the bales and collected them in big sacks. After about 1950, itinerant professional shearers, traveling in small teams from ranch to ranch, were often hired by the herders. With the introduction of electric shears, shearing sheep became easier, though the preparations for shearing remained the same.

In earlier days, sheep ranchers owned large flocks, usually more than 1,000 head, but eventually the national forests encroached on the mountain pastures and mountain lands where sheep had grazed were fenced off. As many fewer sheep could graze in the mountains, herders were forced to sell their flocks. The once-proud and hardworking sheep herders now had to survive with farming and a few sheep kept at home for food. Sheep-shearing is now almost nonexistent in northern New Mexico.

SHEEP AND CATTLE BRANDING

Like many events in the Hispanic culture of northern New Mexico, branding was both a social gathering and a necessary task that had to be accomplished at a certain time. Family members, neighbors, and other people were involved.

The cattle, regardless of the size of the herd, had to be gathered and herded into a big corral. It took a number of strong men to separate, rope, and throw the animals down for branding, earmarking, and, if male, castrating. Different men did different jobs, such as heating the branding irons in the fire until they glowed red and were ready for the job. Other men honed the knives for earmarking and castrating calves, which were then raised as steers. Once these tasks were done, the animals were taken back to the fields for food and water. Sheep were not branded with a hot iron but were marked, usually with red ink, using irons with the initial of the owner, for example, an *M* for a Martínez family. This marking was done usually after the sheep were sheared and the thick wool was off. The male lambs were castrated and earmarked soon after they were born and were taken to market to be sold, usually in Colorado. The few that were not castrated were raised as rams. In older days the testicles of steers and lambs were placed over a smoldering fire and eaten. They were known as Rocky Mountain oysters and were considered a delicacy. The tips of the ears that were cut off were used to count the number of lambs in the flock.

Branding was also a time for socializing and feasting. Hard-working men required plenty of food, which the women supplied in abundance. After the work was done, everyone rested and relaxed, happy that a major and necessary task had been accomplished.

MATANZAS

La Matanza, the slaughtering of a hog, has been an important village event in the Hispanic culture, a social occasion occurring mostly in the fall and early winter in many villages in New Mexico. In a traditional matanza, when everything was ready for the butchering, a family would invite friends, relatives, and neighbors to join in. Months before, in late September, two-year-old hogs were fattened, usually by being fed twice a day. The most important feed was corn. By late November the hogs were so heavy that they could barely move and were ready to be butchered.

Preparations for the matanza were many. Water had to be hauled from the acequia and poured into a *perol* (a big, heavy iron container with a half-moon handle) or into big buckets that were resting on rocks. Wood was gathered for the fire that heated the water. Early in the morning the fire was lit and the water was heated to boiling. The hog was walked or carried in a wheelbarrow to a heavy inclined board. It was struck between the eyes with the blade of a sharp axe, instantly knocking it out. With a long-bladed, sharp kitchen knife the throat was slashed, the heart pierced, and the copious blood caught in a bucket and used to make *morcillas* (a sausage made with pig blood, rice, and spices).

The hog was then rolled to the top of the heavy board. The pig was covered with gunnysacking, and boiling water was poured over it. Soon the hair was loosened and could be easily shaved off with sharp knives. The pig was then cut open and all the internal organs carefully removed and taken to the kitchen, where family members and neighbors prepared them for eating.

After the viscera and flesh went to the kitchen, the *lonja* (thick strips of fat) were removed from the meat, cut into small cubes, and fried in large cast-iron pots over the fire. After frying the fat for about two hours, the *chicharrones* (pork fat cracklings) were ready. The lard of the chicharrones was put into large buckets and preserved in the storeroom for use in the winter—for eating with beans and tortillas and for cooking many other dishes. The lard was also used to make soap, combining it with lye and pouring it into molds. Homemade soap was widely used, since commercial soap was expensive and not always available. Many people were invited to help in these festive occasions. The host family shared the abundance of meat, and by the end of the day most of the meat had been distributed to the community.

Today, there are still matanzas in some Hispanic villages in the Taos Valley, but they are not as elaborate as in earlier days. The butchering of a hog is generally done by individual families, and the meat is taken to stores or to a professional meat wrapper to be packaged. Fat for making chicharrones is also available in grocery stores, although it is not as tasty as the fat from the slaughtered pig at a matanza.

HAYING

Harvesting hay has been important since ancient times, and the earliest civilizations developed only in climates where cattle and other animals could live by grazing. Hay was thus "invented," and forests were turned into meadows. Farmers grow their own hay for a number of reasons. It saves money that would be spent buying hay, and it keeps fields from becoming plots of impassable weeds and thorns. Farmers with larger fields can sell their hay for profit.

Years ago local farmers reaped their hay with an *hoz*, a hand sickle consisting of a curved metal blade on a short handle. Using a sickle was hard and tedious work, and many hours of labor were required to harvest a field of hay. Using this method a farmer could harvest only an acre a day.

Neighbors worked together at haying. Years later farmers cut their hay with a *maquina de cortar*, a machine with a long cutting blade which was generally pulled by horses. Farmers who could afford it used tractors to pull the machine. Beginning about 1830, farmers used a *rastrillo*, a machine with big wheels and large, curved fork-like grates, for gathering the hay. Farmers loaded the hay with *horquillas* (pitchforks) on the *guadañas* (vernacular word for horse-drawn wagons with a big, thick plank placed on it for loading the hay). Hay was then stacked and stored in barns or corrals for winter use. As time went on, farmers could afford to buy, rent, or pay someone to bale their hay with modern baling machines.

Harvesting, Shocking, and Threshing

Whole families helped and neighbors were hired to do the tedious work of harvesting grain, or families would exchange labor with each other. The cut grain was raked into sheaves which were tied together using several stalks of wheat twisted together. Ten to twelve sheaves were placed upright in arrangements called shocks. By shocking the wheat, farmers created a field storage system that promoted further drying while protecting against the effects of wind and rain, which sometimes caused the wheat grains to fall. Later, the shocks were taken apart and transported in horse-drawn wagons to the barn for threshing.

Before threshing machines were available, canvases were laid on the ground in a circle and the sheaves were placed on the canvas. The farmer walked a team of horses or goats over the sheaves, stepping on them until the grain almost completely fell off. Then the wheat had to be aired to separate its grains from the chaff. The farmer usually chose a windy day (or hoped for a strong wind) to blow off the chaff and leave only the grains of wheat. The wheat was then put into big sacks and stored. Some was for feeding animals, and some was taken to a mill to be ground into flour for bread and other home uses. Small portions of wheat were sometimes sold to other farmers.

Harvesting Alfalfa

Alfalfa is a deep-rooted, perennial European plant with purple flowers and leaves like clover that is widely used as forage for cows, horses, pigs, sheep, rabbits, and other animals. Alfalfa requires flood irrigation, and in Taos it produces two crops annually. It is generally cut and gathered in June and late August.

Threshing wheat in Talpa, 1939. The man in the center is Leandro Duran, the owner of the threshing machine, with Alfredo Archuleta to his left. The man on the far left is Antonio Lopez (?) of Cordillera. Caption information provided by Malcolm Collier. Photograph by John Collier Jr., courtesy of the Collier Family Collection.

In earlier days, alfalfa was harvested manually using a *hoz*. This required bending and using both hands, one hand to hold a small bundle of alfalfa and the other to cut it. The scythe was rarely used. Once cut, the alfalfa was left in the field for a few days to dry. It was then gathered with a *horquilla* (pitchfork) and loaded onto a *guadaña*. The alfalfa was taken to the barn and piled into huge stacks for winter use. As in havesting hay, the *rastrillo,* the horse-drawn rake, was used to gather the alfalfa and was pulled either by a team of horses or by a tractor. Harvesting alfalfa became easier after cutting and baling machines were introduced.

Piñon Nut Gathering

Piñon (sometimes spelled pinyon) was a two-part energy source for the people of northern New Mexico, where two-leaf piñon pines (Pinus edulis) still grow in abundance between 4,000 and 6,000-foot elevations. People living close to the mountains endured extremely cold temperatures during the winter months, and wood from the piñon trees provided the best fuel to heat houses, for its heat is more intense and slower-burning than other local woods.

The piñon trees not only provided wood, they also produced piñon nuts, which Indians and settlers relied on for food. Piñon was a staple trade item, both at the Taos trade fairs and in the caravan trade with Mexico. A cultural mainstay, the nuts were used in a variety of dishes, including pastries. Roasted, the nuts made a healthy supplement to the diet and were once considered an important staple for poor people. In autumn, when the piñon crop was plentiful, whole families went to thickly wooded forests to gather the brown piñon nuts. In earlier days they loaded their horse-drawn wagons with blankets, jars of fresh water, and empty buckets for storing the piñon nuts they gathered. Most importantly, they took along plenty of good food. Everyone picked piñon all day, and if it was a good year the buckets were filled quickly and transferred to sacks. Today, piñon is sold in stores as an expensive delicacy.

There were many different methods of picking piñon. To avoid getting thorns in their knees, some pickers used pillows to kneel on as they picked up the nuts. If the nuts had not yet dropped from the tree, they would lay a sheet or large piece of cloth under the tree and shake it until the nuts, along with the pine cones, fell on the cloth. While that was a much quicker way of gathering piñon, the nuts had to be sorted from the cones. Good nuts have a rich brown color and weight; nuts that are *vanos* (hollow inside) are nearly weightless and have grayish color. Pickers (called *piñoneros)* had to pick only the good ones. Sometimes piñoneros would find *ratoneras* (rats' nests with piñon nuts that the rodents had already stored for the winter.) If they were prepared, the pickers would take the piñon, and leave behind kernels of corn for the rats.

The annual cleaning of the ditches that irrigate fields takes place in the spring, performed mostly by *parcientes* of the respective *acequias*. Courtesy of the Taos News Archives.

Everyone enjoyed picking and eating piñon, especially on winter nights. The smell of piñon roasting in skillets on a wood stove was tantalizing. Piñon gathering is not as common today as it was in earlier days in northern New Mexico. Dwindling public lands make it difficult for families to pick piñon, yet people still enjoy going to the forests to gather them.

Gathering Trementina and Ocote

The piñon trees provided *trementina*, a resinous substance that was the color of bees wax when it first oozed out of the tree but when exposed to the sun and wind became a reddish color and hard. Trementina was a medicine used widely and was highly valued. *Trementina de piñon* was widely known for its drawing powers. If a splinter became imbedded, a wad of melted trementina was placed on the infection and allowed to dry. When the wad was dry, it was peeled off, taking the splinter with it.

Chiquete is a colonial Spanish word that comes from Nahuatl, an Aztec language of Mexico. *Chiquete de trementina* was chewing gum from the crystallized resin of the piñon tree. Children as well as adults chewed a wad of trementina, which became just like chewing gum but did not have a juicy or sweet flavor and was not as soft. Finding trementina wads in the bark of piñon trees was an enjoyable task for both youngsters and adults. Trementina is still widely used today as a powerful medicine. It is packaged and sold in pharmacies and health stores.

Ocote is another Nahuatl word *(ocotl)*. Ocote wood comes from the pitch of torch pine trees that, like piñon, grew in abundance in northern New Mexico forests. When people went for wood, they looked for ocote because it burns easily and was used in wood heaters to start fires in the morning. But it also burns fast, making it rather inconvenient as the main wood source and coating the inside of chimneys with soot.

During the Christmas season and other celebrations, northern New Mexicans used stacks of ocote to make *luminarias* (bonfires), which would illuminate the sky and send up a spiral of thick smoke. Luminarias date back to the first Noche Buena (Good Night, Christmas Eve), recalling the fires shepherds lit to keep themselves warm and the light they shed to keep the wolves and thieves away from their flocks of sheep. These *hogueras,* or bonfires, are believed to have been lit when the angel appeared to tell the shepherds that the savior of the world was born. They are still used today by the Hispanic and Indian peoples throughout the Taos Valley. The primary purpose of the beautiful luminarias of the Misa del Gallo, the Midnight Mass in the Catholic Church, is to guide the way to the Christ Child as he made his presence known the night of his birth more than two thousand years ago.

Preserving and Conserving Wild Fruits and Vegetables

Cirhuela (Plums)

Plums were always abundant, both wild and grown in privately owned orchards. Plums were canned, dried, or made into jam and jelly. *Cirhuela de Pueblo* (Indian plums, called locally "poo loo loo") grew in abundance. Although they were not as large as other plums, they were picked and usually were pitted before drying or canning. Pies made with these wild plums are still considered a delicacy.

Capulin (Chokecherries)

Capulin was an essential product in the lives of people in northern New Mexico. The small, aromatic fruit is round, with skin that is red or nearly black, smooth, thin, and tender. The juicy pulp is pale green, with a sweet or acid, agreeable, but slightly astringent flavor. Capulin was made into jelly, canned in jars, or made into homemade wine. Today capulin jelly is a delicacy sold as chokecherry jam.

Garambullo (Gooseberries)

Garambullo grows well in northern New Mexico. The plants resemble thorny rose bushes. The small berries are green, ripen to a red color, and are both sweet and tangy. People canned garambullo in jars or made it into jelly. It was also eaten with sugar as a dessert. In earlier days when people relied on homegrown crops for food, garambullo was an essential in their diets.

Manzanita (Bearberry)

Manzanita de la Sierra (mountain bearberry), as it was known in northern New Mexico, is a small crab apple-like fruit that once grew in abundance in large trees. The fruit can be eaten fresh but was often preserved by canning or making it into jelly.

Quelites (Lamb's Quarters, Wild Spinach)

Quelites were another important source of food for the people of the area. They are cousins to spinach, with leaves somewhat diamond-shaped and coarsely toothed. These perennial plants still grow in abundance in moist soil. In early spring large quantities were gathered in buckets or baskets and were canned in jars or dried in the sun for winter use. Quelites are good with pinto beans and fried in a little fat with chili seeds and sometimes a little bacon. Quelites are also eaten raw in salads.

Verdolagas (Purslane)

Like quelites, *verdolagas* were basic in the presupermarket diet. This edible wild plant grew in abundance in early spring and was economical in times when people needed food and relied on homegrown or edible wild plants for subsistence.

Verdolagas were canned and preserved for winter use. They were prepared with a little lard, onion, garlic, and other spices. Some Taoseños still enjoy verdolagas, which can be found in farmers' markets.

Esparragos (Wild Asparagus)

Spring is the season for asparagus, which has been cultivated for more than two thousand years. But in northern New Mexico, as in many other places, asparagus grows wild. People searched for wild asparagus in early spring. The spears were canned in jars and preserved for winter use. Blossoms were used in bouquets in the kitchen, and even the seed-laden branches were used for decoration.

SELECTED REFERENCES

Gilbert, Fabiola Cabeza. de Baca. *The Good Life: New Mexican Food* (Los Angeles: San Vicente Foundation, 1949).

Krumgold, Joseph. *And Now Miguel* (New York: Thomas Y. Crowell, 1953).

Morrill, Claire. *Taos Mosaic: Portrait of a New Mexico Village* (Albuquerque: University of New Mexico Press, 1973).

SPIRITUAL
TAOS

❖

A private family chapel in Talpa built by Nicholás Sandoval in 1938. Its nave was about 26 feet long by 12 feet wide, with an 11-foot ceiling. It remained unlicensed by the Church and was offered for use to Padre Martínez in 1851. This image was captured before the chapel was deconstructed in the 1940s and its interior reassembled in the Taylor Museum of the Colorado Springs Fine Arts Center.

17

Sacred Places

Michael Miller

For most of the last hundred years, Taos has attracted seekers of the transcendent, all kinds of people who recognize in this valley the potential for spiritual experience that eludes them in other places. Long before Europeans set foot in the valley, the Taos Indians marked the boundaries of their chosen world by natural landmarks and are said to regard things physical and spiritual as "a single, indivisible whole."[1] This chapter focuses on visible landmarks of four centuries of the Catholic faith of northern New Mexico.

In all of North America, arguably no place has a tighter concentration of religious sites than does the Taos Valley. The people of Taos Pueblo live surrounded by landmarks and sites sacred to them, few of which are visible to the rest of us. From Blue Lake to Taos Mountain, from kivas to little San Gerónimo, its old religious landmarks are witness to a long history of profound and closely kept spiritual beliefs. Taos abounds in sacred places and religious traditions from the past, most visibly the Catholic Church. Religious societies still flourish: the Guadalupanas, the League of the Sacred Heart, and Las Franciscanas. The Hermanos, the Penitente Brotherhood, have three active moradas in Taos. Processions and pilgrimages, many of them specific to the faith of northern New Mexicans, take place throughout the year—mostly unnoticed by townspeople. Almost every village has a morada, and some communities have two. From the north in Arroyo Hondo to the heart of the valley in El Prado and to the south in Llano Quemado and Los Cordovas, the *capillas, oratorios,* moradas, camposantos, and other holy places of the past are tangible reminders of the faith and self-reliance of the people of Taos.

THE FRANCISCANS

Taos has been shaped by Spanish Franciscan missionaries, the resulting culture sustained down to the present by faithful Catholics of northern New Mexico. Forty-one years after the Spanish explorer Hernando de Alvarado is believed by some to have passed through the area,[2] Fray (Brother) Agustín Rodríguez, a Franciscan friar,[3] visited Taos Pueblo with Captain Francisco Sánchez Chamuscado. Rodríguez had been sent by the Church to determine how many souls could be brought into the fold and where they could be found. The party traveled as far west as Zuni and up the Rio Grande Valley as far north as Taos Pueblo. Another seventeen years passed before a priest was assigned to the pueblo. Fray Francisco de Zamora was sent north from San Gabriel by Juan de Oñate—and only then, on September 19, 1598, were the Taos people assigned a representative of the Church and, indirectly, of the Kingdom of Spain.

Resistance to Church teachings and Spanish authority seems to have begun almost immediately. Historian Myra Ellen Jenkins attributes part of this resistance to "the bickering between civil and religious authorities, especially from the attempts by the religious clergy to crush native rites and from demands by the civil government officials for tribute from the Indians."[4] In his canonical visitation of 1627,[5] Fray Alonso de Benavides commented that Fray Tomás Carrasco, the resident Franciscan in Taos, was building a mission church at the pueblo "in spite of great difficulties."[6] In January 1640, in one of the first documented examples of violent resistance in Taos, Indians destroyed the church, murdered most of the Spaniards in the area, and killed their priest, Fray Pedro de Miranda. There are references to subsequent efforts to rebuild the church being undermined by Indian resistance.

During the Pueblo Revolt of 1680, which began in Taos and Picurís, Fray Antonio de Mora and Fray Juan de la Pedrosa, along with seventy Spanish settlers, died at the hands of the Indians. Official records of Don Diego de Vargas's fourth attempt to retake Taos Pueblo for Spain in 1696 mention a pueblo church. According to the captain-general's journal, Vargas found the surviving shell of the mission being used as a corral and ordered that it be cleaned up and repaired.

When Vargas approached the pueblo, he found that most of the inhabitants had abandoned the pueblo for a box canyon, where they had built log houses and filled them with food, animal furs, and other supplies to wait out the invading Spaniards. Vargas immediately began negotiations for the natives' surrender. With promises of pardon and other concessions, he convinced the governor, the sacristan (church steward) Felipe, and a few others to come down from the mountains and to bring with them a painting of Our Lady [of Aranzazú], for whom Vargas seems to have had special respect.

In his journal, Vargas described these events: "On the said day, month, and year [24 September 1696] at about four in the afternoon, the above mentioned Felipe, being urged by me, said Governor and Capitan General [Vargas] with the kindest words, told me he would bring me the Blessed Virgin of Aranzazú which he had hidden in his house, together with some valuable altar ornaments, missals, and other church objects."[7] Vargas ordered a group of soldiers, who were noted as being devotees of Our Lady of Aranzazú, to go with the sacristan and escort the painting to his camp. When the blessed image arrived, the general and his men received her in formal *encuentro* (meeting). On his knees Vargas accepted the painting from Felipe. His men saluted her presence with shots from their harquebusiers, and she was placed inside Vargas's tent.

Throughout the centuries, artists have portrayed Our Lady of Aranzazú in different ways, but the representation presumed to have once hung in the pueblo mission church is still a mystery. From Vargas's journal it is known that the painting was óleo (oil paint) on *lienzo* (cloth, presumably linen) and was one and three-quarters varas high and one and one-quarter varas wide, or about six feet by four feet.[8] This written description was the first and last mention of Our Lady of Aranzazú in Taos Pueblo.

Work on a new church at Taos Pueblo began by 1706. In charge was a young priest on his first assignment, Fray Juan José Perez de Mirabal; it is not known whether the new church was built on the foundation of the old one. Misión de San Gerónimo was a church built to last. Completed in 1726, it survived the harsh northern New Mexico climate for 140 years—until U.S. Army troops destroyed it in 1847.

When, as a canonical visitor, Fray Atanasio Domínguez examined the church in 1776, he carefully documented the massive adobe structure, noting a simple nave measuring 22 by 116 feet, an octagonal apse, and a facade dominated by a single massive bell tower with two bells. Attached to the east side of the church was a convento (lodging for the friars), with a cemetery and a porter's lodge that measured "7 varas from mouth to center, 5 varas wide, and 3 very long varas high, with adobe seats around it."[9]

Domínguez deemed the adobe buttress for the bell tower "hideous" and deplored the bells, one broken and the other missing its clapper, but he did find kind words for Fray Andrés Claramonte, who had been at Taos since 1770, in addition to serving at Picurís. The archives provide this vivid record of Claramonte's difficulties:

> That with respect to this weekly trip, because the winter is so severe in these places and there is so much snow in the sierra where this pueblo is, travel to Taos is extremely difficult, and it sometimes happens that the altar breads do not arrive in time and consequently there is no Mass on a feast day.[10]

Describing the work of building a church, Domínguez wrote, "Finding everything going from bad to worse, he immediately set to work, almost entirely at his own expense, although the Indians did help him a little, and often doing the labor himself."[11] Domínguez's praise for Claramonte's efforts was justified, because the structure and its contents were unique and had many distinguishing qualities that we appreciate today.

Apparently, Fray Andrés García, a priest *santero* of Santa Cruz de la Cañada, was also at work in Taos. Domínguez tells us that in the nave of the church there were "two monstrous adobe tables."[12] These were draped with a canopy over a *gradin* (altar steps) painted a lustrous blue and lined with buffalo skins. The altar screen and the bultos that adorned it were made by Fray García. He also built the tabernacle, the sepulcher with Christ entombed, the pulpit, and the confessional. Domínguez was unimpressed with all of Fray García's good intentions and hard work, commenting in his diary, "It is a pity that he should have used his labor for anything so ugly."[13] Fortunately for those who appreciate the traditional local crafts and building styles, much of the work of Fray García has survived and is preserved in churches and museums throughout the state.

Domínguez clearly favored the European Baroque style, and Fray Claramonte and Fray Olaeta gained the favor of the official Church representative by decorating the church using imported ornamentation. Domínguez did hold a high opinion of Fray José de Olaeta, the priest in charge when Domínguez arrived. In his characteristic manner, Domínguez meticulously scrutinized the mission's inventory and found everything in order. He publicly thanked Fray Olaeta and applauded his "exactitude and performance in having recorded all the things belonging to the mission and their present condition, as well as for the neatness and cleanliness of the cells and other things."[14] Other canonical visitors came, but none described what they saw in such detail as Domínguez.

The fortress-like construction of San Gerónimo served an important purpose on the frontier of Taos. Domínguez remarked that it reminded him of "the walled cities that are described to us in the Bible."[15] John L. Kessell in *The Missions of New Mexico, 1776* points out that "the heavy-built structure doubled as a fortress against Comanche attack."[16] The pueblo offered protection to Spanish settlers as well. For long periods of time in the mid- to late eighteenth century, when Comanche raids were frequent and deadly, whole families of Spanish settlers lived within the pueblo walls.

Ironically, San Gerónimo's defense function was the cause of its destruction in 1847. U.S. troops under Colonel Sterling Price stormed the church, where rebel Taoseños had taken refuge days after murdering Governor Charles Bent. It took the troops most of February 3, 1847, to penetrate the thick walls of the church, leaving "the lofty walls, perforated by cannon ball . . . [and] burnt beams and heaps of adobes . . . [and] the altar, now a broken platform, with scarce a sign or vestige of its former use."[17]

A new church was built. Smaller than the former massive structure, it was constructed a hundred yards southeast of the old mission ruin, facing the pueblo's main plaza. The exact date of construction is not known, but most historians agree that it was around 1850. Largely ignored by scholars, perhaps because of the colorful history of the earlier mission church, the present church of San Gerónimo is a comparatively simple structure. Through the years it has undergone several architectural changes.

In the nineteenth century the church had the soft, gentle lines of its predecessor. The façade was altered in the early 1920s. By 1939, the church had been returned to its original form. Following World War II, most likely in the early 1950s, twin bell towers were added, and the exterior has remained basically unchanged since that time. Among the surviving sculptures of Fray García's are Christ in the Holy Sepulcher in the chancel and Our Lady of Sorrows on the main altar. The interior walls have been painted with images of saints by a Native American artist, or more than one artist. Sheltered in *nichos* are statues of Saint Jerome and other special saints, including Our Lady by renowned santero José Rafael Aragón.

Still, an iconic part of the older church endures. At the request of pueblo leaders, the Albuquerque architectural firm of Pacheco and Graham prepared sketches for the restoration of the bell tower from the old mission church. With help from the community they stabilized the tower, restored the belfry, and installed a bell. Today it stands as a reminder of struggle and sorrow.

Settlements and Parishes

For much of the century following reconquest, resettlement was tenuous and slow. In defiance of the Spanish government's regulation that *vecinos* must live in settlements, for several decades after 1700 settlers continued to live on their ranchos (large holdings) or rancherias, which were scattered across the valley near water sources. As a consequence, they were highly exposed and vulnerable to the attacks of nomadic Indians.

Possibly as a result of the deadly 1760 Comanche attack on vecinos who had fled to the Villalpando rancho—"a very large house, the greatest in all that valley"[18]—farmers and ranchers apparently began to comply with Governor Pedro Fermín de Mendinuete's and Governor Juan Bautista de Anza's regulations, moving their homes into clusters. Six different *placitas* in the Taos area were noted and named in the census of 1796.[19] Their establishment was a significant development. People were able to live close enough to their fields yet could get to their defensible plazas when threatened. One consequence of this shift was the florescence of new churches, chapels, moradas, oratorios, and camposantos up and down the valley.

Las Trampas de Taos

Ranchos de Taos was the first of the plazas and is the oldest true plaza-centered settlement in the Taos Valley. The area's lush, arable land was its obvious attraction. In 1715 Cristóbal de la Serna was given a grant in the area, which he later sold to Diego Romero. In the 1730s Francisco Xavier Romero, a Coyote (a term originating in the *casta* system of the Hispanic Americas and at that time meaning that one parent was Indian), established a hacienda with his large family on the Río de Las Trampas (the river now known as the Río Grande del Rancho). For a long time the settlement was called Las Trampas de Taos or San Francisco de las Trampas or Plaza de San Francisco. In modern times the area came to be known as Ranchos de Taos, and today it is locally referred to as Ranchos. The first settlers lived in the Plaza Vieja (Old Plaza) just northwest of Plaza de San Francisco near a perennial spring that, tragically, was filled in to construct a building.[20]

The Ranchos Plaza we know today—Plaza de San Francisco—was being finished by 1779 as a large, fortified, rectangular plaza composed of two-story houses whose back sides had neither windows nor doors. This rendered the plaza's outer perimeter defensible, and, with several adobe towers along its flanks and large wooden gates *(puertónes)* at its northwest and southeast ends, it must have been solid indeed. It was roughly 800 feet by 400 feet, and the buildings that were once its northwest end extended across today's SR 68. In the 1890s, this section of the plaza was home to "Squire" Hartt, whose residence was adjacent to his general store. Originally that building had been part of Plaza Vieja. In the early twentieth century, dances were held there, and the building is remembered as the old Martinez Hall. Local artists painted colorful, lighthearted scenes on the interior lime-washed walls.[21] It has been renovated and restored as a commercial building.

San Francisco de Asís

The date of construction of San Francisco de Asís remained a mystery until the discovery of original documents in the Archives of the Archdiocese of Santa Fe. Before the dates were ascertained, several theories had been put forward to explain the church's origins, among them speculation about the building of a mission for the Jicarilla Apaches at Ranchos in about 1733. No physical evidence of such a church has been found. Although Fray Domínguez mentioned a small settlement named in honor of San Francisco, he described no church in the area. Entries in the records of the pueblo mission church of San Gerónimo and of Our Lady of Guadalupe detail baptisms, marriages, and burials of Ranchos Catholics from 1744 to 1810 during the sixty-six years before the people of Ranchos had a church of their own.

The Church of San Gerómino at Taos Pueblo, built around 1847, as it looked in the late nineteenth century before it was cleaned up and resurfaced. Photo Taos County Historical Society.

When the original license, several inventories, and some related papers were discovered, nearly everyone was surprised to find that the recorded chronology of San Francisco de Asís began in 1810; most believed that the church was much older. In the summer of 1810, Fray José Benito Pereyro, *custos* for the Franciscan Order in New Mexico, moved from Santa Clara Pueblo to Taos. Pereyro, a Spaniard from Galicia, had served as a missionary in Nuevo México for more than sixteen years. His parish in Taos consisted of 537 Indians and 1,267 "Spaniards and people of all classes,"[22] many of them living in the lush Ranchos Valley. Because of the growing population of Plaza de San Francisco, Pereyro and the leading citizens of the community planned for the construction of a church. He applied for a license with permission to build on August 4, 1812.

After many delays in processing the paperwork, the license came from the Archdiocese of Durango, Mexico. It was dated September 20, 1813. The license stated, "We do grant and concede our permission and license in order that in the above-mentioned settlement of Las Trampas the stated chapel may be founded, erected, constructed, built, and dedicated to its titular saint, on the necessary condition that said citizens are responsible for providing whatever repairs it may require for its preservation, and for maintaining it in cleanliness, with vestments, sacred vessels, and other utensils appertaining to the worship of Our Lord and God." By 1815, the services of Fray Pereyro were requested, a sign that the church was ready for occupancy.

Local historians question whether residents of the Plaza de San Francisco waited until September 1813—when the license arrived—to start building. With their farms and ranches requiring most of their time and labor, it must have taken much, much longer than two years to build San Francisco de Asís. The building required more than 100,000 hand-formed adobes. Massive vigas had to be cut in the mountains and dragged to the site. Thirty-two vigas at least thirty-two feet long were required to span the nave; the twenty-eight transept vigas were each twenty-five feet long, and the sanctuary had eleven vigas of varying lengths. Tree-ring dating of the vigas established 1808 as the date of their cutting.

Small by comparison to other churches built in the mission era, San Francisco de Asís was largely unadorned, yet its perfect proportions give it monumental scale. In harmony with its surroundings, the structure exerts universal appeal and is the most photographed and painted religious edifice in the Southwest.

The earliest written descriptions of the church and its contents date from 1817, 1818, and 1831. The later 1831 document describes the structure in some detail:

> The nave of the thick-walled cruciform adobe temple of San Francisco de Asís measured thirty-one varas long by nine wide by nine high inside, not counting the narthex under the choir loft, the arms of the transept, or the apse. The builders raised the walls of the transept and apse higher than those of the nave, and they installed a transverse clerestory window, the most

The faithful of the Chapel of San Isidro the Laborer (Saint Isidor the farmer) in Cordillera, ca. 1960s, celebrate their saint's day, May 15, with Mass followed by a procession to bless the fields in this farming community on the southern edge of Taos. Courtesy of Taos News Archives.

characteristic feature of colonial New Mexico church architecture. Above
the façade, breaking the flat roof line, they erected two little cube-like bell
torrecitas. The walled cemetery out front, with its two gates, was twenty-two
varas long and nineteen across.[23]

To the joy of modern-day preservationists the interior of the church was described in 1817: "Reverend Father Pereyro, Don Ignacio Durán, and the citizens
had built at their cost the altarpiece and had it painted using scaffolding."[24] The
three-hundred-square-foot altarpiece featured spiral-twisted columns and hand-
carved moldings fastened to the panels with large dowels. The statue of St. Francis
stood in the center nicho of a huge retablo that stood behind a wooden altar table,
altar steps, and altar rail. The eight paintings on canvas were "brought from the
outside," suggesting that their origins were not New Mexico. The inventories have
proven invaluable to the parishioners in re-creating the decor installed by their
ancestors as well as to historians of art and architecture.

The first known inventory of San Francisco de Asís was made for the ecclesiastical visitor Fray Juan Bautista Guevara in 1818. It was brief and to the point: "One
altar screen with an image of the Lord Esquípulas, the high altar with two figures
in the round, one altar screen dedicated to the patriarch St. Joseph, and an image
of the Holy Patriarch."[25]

The altar screen, the largest one remaining in New Mexico, was restored by
Santa Fe artists Luis Tapia and Frederico Vigil in 1980. It still holds the eight
paintings of the unnamed Mexican artist who worked in the Spanish colonial style
of around the turn of the eighteenth century. E. Boyd, well-known New Mexico
art historian, described the screen as being in the style of the santero Molleno and
found the composition "unusually formal as compared to some santero altarpiec-
es."[26] The figures are separated by painted swags, spiral pillars, and wooden moldings, and the three tiers contain the holy figures surrounding the central nicho.
In the top row are El Cristo de la Columna and Nuestro Padre Jesús Esquípulas
Nazareno. In the center row are representations of Nuestra Señora de la Candelaria
and San Lorenzo. Below them are San Francisco de Asís and San Antonio de Padua.
Molleno would have been in his early period when he painted at Ranchos, and the
artist obviously was perplexed by how to treat such a large space. He accomplished
the task eloquently, however, using neoclassical swags and moldings.[27]

The preservation of the church is not a new tradition for the people of Ranchos.
To their ancestors, the "remudding" *(enjarre)* of their homes and their church was
as much a part of the annual cycle as the planting and harvesting of crops each year.
In recent times, this annual ritual of preserving the church's exterior is a community event undertaken during the first two weeks of June. It has received increased
public attention, and it has helped to revolutionize the thinking of preservationists
throughout the state.

Built in 1801–02, Our Lady of Guadalupe stood directly behind the plaza for more than a hundred years. Padre Martinez became the parish priest in 1826. Seen in this rare photograph ca. 1900 is the *camposanto* where the padre buried the resisters who were executed or died in the confrontation between the U.S. Army and local Hispanic and Indians in the violent Rebellion of 1847. Early in the twentieth century, this structure was replaced with a neo-Gothic church, now gone. Courtesy of the Vicente Martinez Family Collection.

Nuestra Señora de Guadalupe

Throughout Hispanic America, Our Lady of Guadalupe has a special place in people's hearts. The saint is most often portrayed by the santeros of the Taos area in a sky made pale by her glory, wearing a red crown and a deep blue cloak covered with golden stars. Often she is surrounded by a veil of gold and shimmering flame, and at her feet a cherub lifts the train of her gown as she is borne through heaven and all eternity riding on a crescent moon.

The first church in the Taos area to honor Nuestra Señora de Guadalupe was built in Fernández de Taos around the turn of the nineteenth century. The start dates of construction vary from the earliest estimate of 1762 to as late as 1806.[28] No documentation has been found to confirm exact dates. The structure was a flat-roofed adobe building. Padre Antonio José Martínez (1793–1867), a clergyman ahead of his time who reflected the free-thinking, uncompromising spirit of Taos, served as pastor of the parish for more than forty years, beginning in 1826, and had a profound impact on the community.

In his comprehensive biography of Padre Martínez, *But Time and Chance* (1981), Fray Angélico Chávez delves into the influence this often-controversial priest had on the people and the Church of northern New México. Chávez's portrayal is of a man who is not saintly; in fact, the author describes him as "a personality to be reckoned with, as hero or villain, or both."[29] Above all, Martínez was always a protector of his people, and his persistence as such caused him repeated conflict with the Church hierarchy, civic governments, and *estranjeros* ("foreigners," namely French traders and Anglos who came to Taos).

During Martínez's time, the Church in Mexico was very powerful and wealthy. The padre, so aware of the poverty of his people on the frontiers of the Mexican Empire, boldly and publicly opposed tithing, the practice of giving 10 percent of one's income to the Church. In 1833, he petitioned other priests in the region and took his case against tithing in Nuevo México to the Mexican government, which ruled in his favor and dropped the practice in the province.

Padre Martínez realized that his people would never achieve success until they broke the barriers posed by ignorance and illiteracy. For this reason, he opened a school in Taos in 1826—unique for its time in encouraging girls to attend—and devised a full eight-year curriculum. Constantly thwarted by the cost and rarity of books in the isolated parish, in 1835 Padre Martínez brought a printing press to Taos and used it to print books and religious and political publications. He published the first newspaper west of the Mississippi River, *El Crepúsculo de la Libertad* (*The Dawn of Liberty*). He loved knowledge for its own sake, and while he distrusted foreign domination of Nuevo México, he recognized that America was based on freedom of choice, freedom of religion, and freedom of the press. He understood that eventually this new system of government could help his people and that New Mexicans of the future should and could control their own destinies.

Martínez viewed the Church as a close-knit family, an institution that gave to the people and asked little of the material world in return. It was this perception of a "family Church" that had inspired young Antonio José to seek the religious life. The "new Church" brought to New Mexico in 1850[30] by Archbishop Jean-Baptiste Lamy (1814–88) and the French priests who followed him was radically different from the Church of Padre Martínez's understanding. The new Church wanted money for cathedrals and other material needs, threatening to withold sacraments from those who did not tithe. These and other issues led to a rift between Archbishop Lamy and Padre Martínez. (One of the two protagonists of Willa Cather's *Death Comes for the Archbishop* [1927], the Taos cleric was far from the coarse man portrayed by Cather.) Padre Martínez spent most of his career fighting social injustices. In 1858, after Archbishop Lamy declared the padre unauthorized to offer Mass, Martínez ministered to parishioners from his private chapel and held services at sites around the valley. Padre Antonio José Martínez died July 28, 1867, and was buried in the yard of his private chapel.

Following the death of Padre Martínez, the church of Our Lady of Guadalupe underwent several dramatic physical changes. In 1870 a pitched roof was added, and a large bell tower was built facing the front façade. This modification, intended to preserve the aging building, did so for more than forty years. By 1911, the parish had outgrown the original church, and the building was razed to make room for a new one. Father Joseph Giraud, a Frenchman, was the parish priest then, and he hired veteran church contractors Digneo & Pettini from Santa Fe to build the new church. It was a handsome structure, with marked French influence. In 1961, fifty years after its construction, the church of Our Lady of Guadalupe burned to the ground. Parishioners cleaned away the debris, and construction of a new church began that same year. A modern church now stands near the same site, but memories of the previous two still linger in the minds of the oldest parishioners.

In all, three parishes were established in the Taos area. Misión de San Gerónimo was the first, though it eventually was forced to give up its status as a parish church and became an *ayuda de parroquia* (chapel or mission) of Our Lady of Guadalupe. Today, San Francisco de Asís, Our Lady of Guadalupe (Nuestra Señora de Guadalupe), and Holy Trinity (La Santísima Trinidad) in Arroyo Seco are the valley's three parish seats. The Taos area is rich in capillas, oratorios, moradas, and *descansos*—many still in use within parish life. Several have achieved well-deserved recognition for architectural and artistic distinction, while more stand simply as monuments to faith.

Capillas in Talpa

Perhaps the two most famous of these capillas (chapels) are those in Talpa, the community about two miles southeast of Ranchos de Taos, which for a very long time was known as Rio Chiquito. The first, built in 1828, is dedicated to Nuestra Señora de San Juan de los Lagos and still serves the Talpa community.

The other chapel, known locally as the Durán Chapel, no longer stands in Talpa. However, the interior of La Capilla de Nuestra Señora de Talpa (Our Lady of Talpa) is partially installed in the Taylor Museum of the Colorado Springs Fine Arts Center. Originally built as a small family chapel around 1838, and thus actually an oratorio, the Durán Chapel was dedicated to Our Lady of Talpa, a saint of Talpa, Jalisco, Mexico, who was associated with miracles. (A "sister" patroness in Jalisco is Our Lady of San Juan de los Lagos.)[31] It was not unusual for private chapels to be named for a favorite saint, and the Jalisco origin of both of Talpa's patron saints attests to the traffic—both secular and religious—between New Mexico and Mexico.

Our Lady of Talpa was blended with a complex of rooms behind it, where the family lived. A walled family cemetery at the front was the center of activity for the extended Durán family and surrounding neighbors. Today, ruins of the chapel can still be glimpsed in the middle of the Durán family complex, surrounded by homes belonging to descendants of the original builders.

The Durán Chapel was in many ways the essence of the vernacular adobe architecture of the Hispanic Southwest. Flat-roofed, it was constructed with vigas supporting the ceiling of hand-hewn roof boards *(tablas)* and was plastered inside and out with mud. The interior walls were coated with *alis*, a slip made of a mix of *tierra blanca* and gypsum rock with a wheat-flour binder. The nave was approximately twenty-six by twelve feet, with an eleven-foot ceiling. The front façade rose above the roof and terminated in an elegantly formed adobe belfry in which hung a beautifully cast Spanish bell.

Historically, the chapel played a significant role in local events, most notably the confrontation between Archbishop Lamy and Padre Martínez. Soon after his arrival in New Mexico, it was clear that Bishop Lamy was determined to reduce the influence of native-born New Mexican clergy in their respective curacies and was particularly eager to suppress the activities of the Penitente Brotherhood, La Fraternidad de Nuestro Padre Jesús Nazareno. Padre Martínez was deeply supportive of the Penitente Hermanos (Brothers), and the chapel's builder was a devout leader of this confraternity of laymen. In 1851, the family dedicated Our Lady of Talpa to Padre Martínez's use, and it is clear that the unlicensed chapel was used for Penitente rituals and rites, as well as for more conventional devotion, in defiance of its unlicensed status.

The religious art from the chapel has been preserved since the 1940s in the Taylor Museum, where an authentic reproduction of the capilla's interior was created. The Historic American Buildings Survey made a complete set of measured drawings and plans in 1934, when the structure was still in good condition. Curator and author William Wroth completed the documentation of the chapel in 1979 with the publication of *The Chapel of Our Lady of Talpa,* the result of his intensive study of the religious and artistic history of the building and surrounding area.

San Juan de los Lagos was built in 1828. This picturesque adobe structure now serves as the church for the village of Talpa. The structure sits at one end of the original plaza of Rio Chiquito. Well cared for, it is the pride of the community. Inside, at the end of a simple row of benches, is the altar screen painted by Molleno, said by many to be his masterpiece. Molleno is also recorded as the painter of two of the surviving altar screens in the *santuario* at Chimayó. Molleno's Talpa *reredos* is dated 1828, placing it at the height of his artistic career. According to E. Boyd, by 1828 Molleno "had acquired full command of his colors, composition, and decorative elements. The proportions of the cornice, valances, shell pediment, and panels harmonize perfectly with the exuberantly painted floral scrolls and figures. The brush has a masterly sweep which Molleno had not mastered when he was working at the Ranchos church."[32] Boyd believed that Molleno may even have been the carver of the bulto in the center niche. Molleno introduced a number of rarely portrayed saints into his work. The lower panel is inscribed, "Mi Señora de Talpa," and above that is the image of San Bernardo, a saint seldom portrayed in northern New Mexico folk art. Molleno also dedicated his finished works in lengthy written descriptions. Directly below the depiction of San Antonio is the following dedication: "Se yso y se pinto en ese año de 1828 a debosyon de Bexnaxdo Duran este oxatoxio de Mi Sx de San Juan." ("In this, the year of 1828, was built and painted, through the devotion of Bernardo Duran, the oratory of My Lady of Saint John.")[33] It is not known where Molleno learned to write, but he loved to do so, especially on his completed pieces. There is some speculation that the santero may have studied under Padre Martínez. In terms of written inscriptions, the work he produced in Taos is undoubtedly the most prolific of his entire career. This chapel also contains one of José Rafael Aragón's best santos, Our Lady of San Juan.

Chapels and Churches for Everyone

Well west of Talpa is Los Córdovas, one of the oldest communities in northern New Mexico. Although the exact date of its founding is not known, at the beginning of the eighteenth century it was considered to be more than a hundred years old and was owned by the Córdova family, the earliest settlers of that area. This village also has two capillas, both devoted to the patron saint of farming, San Isidro.

The older, private chapel, an oratorio, was consecrated in 1845 and is still privately owned. It stands at the east end of the original placita of Los Córdovas, one wall close by Los Córdovas Road. Originally it was part of a ten-room complex belonging to the Córdova family and for generations was used as a place for prayer and devotion by members of the household and the surrounding community. At one time the chapel contained two altars; the building has two rooms separated today by an attractive adobe arch. The original bultos were relocated to the local moradas when the chapel changed ownership; two others remain in the Córdova family.

In 1975, the oratorio underwent extensive remodeling, and the new owners replastered the interior with tierra blanca. Two kiva fireplaces were also added, and the cement plaster was removed from the exterior walls, which were resurfaced with the original mud. The other capilla in Los Córdovas, devoted to San Isidro, is on Cordillera Road (SR 240) and is part of the San Francisco de Asís parish. It is a simple structure constructed in the 1950s to accommodate public religious services for the community. San Isidro, protector of farmers, is one of the most popular saints in New Mexico and is frequently represented by modern-day santeros in New Mexico, invariably dressed in farmer's garb, usually wearing a broad-brimmed hat and sometimes carrying a staff.

Llano Quemado, south of Ranchos de Taos, is one of the first sites of human settlement in the Taos Valley. A pueblo was excavated there by the Smithsonian Institution staff in the 1920s, and a rare double-round kiva was found—a wall within a wall. The discovery of this pueblo and evidence of others in the vicinity led to a theory that the Taos Indians first lived at Llano Quemado and eventually moved to their present location, approximately seven miles to the northeast. The unusual construction of the kiva also links the inhabitants to the Tiguex people to the south.

The present-day village of Llano Quemado is a very old place, with a palpable spiritual presence. The capilla of Nuestra Señora del Carmen in the heart of the village is apparently the second one built there. The original church was built in 1852, but the site was changed, and in 1864 Ramon Medina built a new chapel. The round apse is the most unusual architectural feature of the building, and from the back it gives the small structure a deceptively massive appearance. At one time the chapel contained a beautiful reredos, which was sold to the Museum of New Mexico in the 1920s. The style of painting, which can be seen at the Palace of the Governors in Santa Fe, is similar to that of Miguel Aragón, a prolific santero of the period.

Descendants of the families who built these sacred monuments keep these revered places alive because, like their ancestors, they believe that *flor marchita y fe perdida, nunca vuelven a la vida*, a withered blossom and lost faith cannot be restored to life.

NOTES

1. William deBuys, *Enchantment and Exploitation: The Life and Hard Times of a New Mexico Mountain Range* (Albuquerque: University of New Mexico Press, 1985), 28.

2. Whether Alvarado did, in fact, pass through the Taos Valley is still debated. The historical evidence is inconclusive and contradictory.

3. *Fray* is also used to denote members of a religious order.

4. Myra Ellen Jenkins, "Taos Pueblo and Its Neighbors," *New Mexico Historical Review* 41, no. 2 (April 1966): 88.

5.   Canonical visits to all dioceses within a bishopric were mandatory. The written reports of some of these visitations form some of the rarest and most valuable pictures of life in *el norte*, though they are not reliable in all details.

6. Jenkins, 88.

7. *Journal of Diego de Vargas.* SANM II, 1696, Roll 2. Santa Fe: State Archives of New Mexico.

8. This mysterious image—noted in Vargas's journals and unlike her counterpart, La Conquistadora in Santa Fe—has never been located. How she came to Taos from the Basque country in northern Spain is intriguing: see Corina Sanistevan, "Our Lady of Aranzazú," in *Ayer y Hoy en Taos* (Summer 1986), 3–8.

9. Eleanor B. Adams and Fray Angélico Chávez, *The Missions of New Mexico, 1776: A Description by Fray Francisco Atanasio Domínguez with Other Contemporary Documents* (Albuquerque: University of New Mexico Press, 1975), 107.

10. Ibid., 96.

11. Ibid., 107.

12. Ibid., 104.

13. Ibid.

14. Ibid., 104–105.

15. Ibid., 109.

16. John L. Kessell, *The Missions of New Mexico Since 1776* (Albuquerque: University of New Mexico Press, 1980), 109.

17. Lewis H. Garrard [Hector Lewis Garrard], *Wah-to-yah and the Taos Trail 1850.* Reprinted (Norman: University of Oklahoma Press, 1955), 187.

18. Jenkins, 98.

19. Plaza de San Francisco (Ranchos de Taos); Plaza de Santa Gertrudis [location unknown and possibly an error in recording the census]; Plaza de Nuestra Señora de Guadalupe (Don Fernando de Taos); Plaza de la Purísima [Concepcion] (Upper Ranchitos); Plaza de San Francisco de Paula (Lower Ranchitos); and Nuestra Señora de los Dolores (Cañon).

20. That spring was used until fairly recent times.

21. See Mildred Tolbert, "Taos As Art Colony and Arts Community" (chapter 20, below).

22. The original license document is in the Spanish Archives of New Mexico (SANM) in Santa Fe.

23. SANM.

24. SANM.

25. SANM.

26. E. Boyd, *Popular Arts of Spanish New Mexico* (Santa Fe: Museum of New Mexico Press, 1974), 352. Our Lord of Esquípulas is associated with a shrine in southern Guatemala and entered the pantheon of northern New Mexico patrons by way of Chimayó. El Santuario de Chimayó, long a private chapel, has Our Lord of Esquípulas as its patron.

27. Boyd, 352.

28. Le Baron Bradford Prince, *Spanish Mission Churches of New Mexico,* 1915; reprint, Glorieta, NM: Rio Grande Press, 1977), 245.

29. Fray Angélico Chávez, *But Time and Chance* (Santa Fe: Sunstone Press, 1981), 9.

30. Lamy was appointed bishop of Santa Fe in 1850 but did not arrive at the territorial capital until 1851.

31. William Wroth, *The Chapel of Our Lady of Talpa* (Colorado Springs: Taylor Museum of the Colorado Springs Fine Arts Center, 1979), 26–27.

32. Boyd, 360.

33. Transcription and translation are E. Boyd's. Boyd, 361.

SELECTED REFERENCES

Manuscript Collections

Archives of the Archdiocese of Santa Fe (AASF)

Spanish Archives of New Mexico, Series I and II (SANM I & II)

Mexican Archives of New Mexico (MANM)

Territorial Archives of New Mexico (TANM)

Harwood Library, Southwest History vertical files

Preservation Files, New Mexico Office of Historic Preservation

History Files, New Mexico State Library

Museum of New Mexico, WPA Project Files

Archives of the Cathedral of Durango (ACD)

Works Consulted

Adams, Eleanor B. *Bishop Tamarón's Visitation of New Mexico, 1760.* Albuquerque: Historical Society of New Mexico, 1954.

———, and Fray Angélico Chávez. *The Missions of New Mexico, 1776: A Description by Fray Francisco Atanasio Domínguez with Other Contemporary Documents.* Albuquerque: University of New Mexico Press, 1956, 1975.

"Ayer y Hoy—Taos, N.M.": Taos: Our Lady of Guadalupe Parish, 1976.

Benavides, Alonso de. *The Memorial of Fray Alonso de Benavides, 1630.* Trans. Mrs. Edward E. Ayer. 1916. Reprint: Albuquerque: Horn and Wallace, 1965.

Boyd, E. *Popular Arts of Spanish New Mexico.* Santa Fe: Museum of New Mexico Press, 1974.

Chávez, Fray Angélico. *Archives of the Archdiocese of Santa Fe, 1678–1900*. Washington, DC: Academy of American Franciscan History, 1957.

———. *But Time and Chance*. Santa Fe: Sunstone Press, 1981.

———. *My Penitente Land: Reflections on Spanish New Mexico*. Albuquerque: University of New Mexico Press, 1974.

Espinosa, J. Manuel. *Crusaders of the Río Grande*. Chicago: Institute of Jesuit History, 1942.

Garcia, José A. "Symphony in Mud." *Taos Valley News,* July 18, 1940. Reprinted in *Ayer y Hoy en Taos* (Fall 1991): 9–13.

Hallenbeck, Cleve. *Spanish Missions of the Old Southwest*. Garden City, NY: Garden City Publishing Co., 1926.

Hooker, Van Dorn. "Ranchos de Taos Plaza." *Ayer y Hoy en Taos.* (Fall 1991): 3–8.

Jenkins, Myra Ellen. "Taos Pueblo and Its Neighbors." *New Mexico Historical Review* 41, no. 2 (April 1966): 85–114.

Kubler, George. *The Religious Architecture of New Mexico*. 1940. Reprint Albuquerque: University of New Mexico Press, 1972.

Maas, Otto. *Misiones de Nuevo México*. Madrid: Archivo General de Indias (Seville), 1929.

Prince, LeBaron Bradford. *Spanish Mission Churches of New Mexico*. 1915. Reprint, Glorieta, NM: Rio Grande Press, 1977.

Santistevan, Corina. "Our Lady of Aranzazú." *Ayer y Hoy en Taos* (Summer 1986).

Wroth, William. *The Chapel of Our Lady of Talpa*. Colorado Springs: Taylor Museum, 1979.

———. *Christian Images in Hispanic New Mexico*. Colorado Springs: Taylor Museum, 1982.

Oral History Interviews

Emilia Atencio, Ranchos de Taos

David Cruz, El Valle

Jerome Martinez y Alire, AASF

Mary Mascareñas, Peñasco

Marina Ochoa, AASF

Robert Sanchez, AASF

Corina Santistevan, Taos

Luis Tapia, Santa Fe

Frederico Vigil, Santa Fe

Harold Joe Waldrum, Taos

The *morada* of Our Lady of Guadalupe, ca. 1940, when it was still in active use by Penitentes. The building is not far from the Mabel Dodge Luhan House property off Morada Lane. Photo John Collier Jr.; courtesy the Collier Family Collection.

18

Padre Martínez and the Penitente Brotherhood

Rev. Juan Romero

In Taos, Padre Martínez is an honored figure, no less than Kit Carson. He promoted literacy for both boys and girls, encouraged self-sufficiency and faith, was an eloquent statesman, and stood up against pressures of the Church to bow to his bishops' every demand. Some of his most courageous efforts were in defense of the Penitente Brotherhood of Nuestro Padre Jesús Nazareno, whose service to families and the Catholic faith were much valued in the padre's times.

IN 1993, PERSONS UNKNOWN STOLE the sacred images from the East Morada in Abiquiú, one of the first moradas in New Mexico.[1] They maliciously torched the venerable site and threw its santos into the Rio Grande. That act horrified not just Catholics but almost all of New Mexico's people. Within a few weeks, Presbyterian teenagers visiting nearby Ghost Ranch answered a call to help repair the damage by carefully remudding the outside of the charred adobe walls with a fresh coat of mud mixed with straw. The ecumenical action of these youth would have horrified their religious ancestors. But had he lived to see it, it would have immensely pleased Padre Antonio José Martínez (1793–1867).

Born in the Santa Rosa Plaza of Abiquiú, perched above the Chama River, as a child Antonio José Martínez was surrounded by the majestic beauty of tall cliffs of sedimentary rock layered in yellows, browns, ochres, whites, and pinks, his childhood rooted in indigenous cultures and a late medieval Spanish worldview. For centuries, Abiquiú has welcomed Indian hunters, *genízaros* (Hispanicized Indians), buffalo soldiers (members of all-African-American U.S. Army regiments), and traders on the way to Los Angeles or other destinations.

Among the many "merits" Padre Martínez accumulated in his seventy-four years are his contributions to the education of adults and children through his publications and the educational institutions he founded. His greatest legacies, however, were in the religious and political life of New Mexico in its different incarnations under Spain, Mexico, and the United States. His impact on the religious institution of the Penitente Brotherhood of Nuestro Padre Jesús Nazareno is one of his most potent legacies.

Penitente *cofradías* (confraterities of laymen) came to Nuevo México in some form with Juan de Oñate in 1598.[2] Twelve years after the Pueblo Revolt of 1680 and the resulting extinction of the Spanish colony, Don Diego de Vargas returned to New Mexico from El Paso and territories further south with soldiers, exiled settlers, and companions. Also accompanying him were flagellants who were thoroughly imbued with the spirit and practice of the medieval societies that had deep devotion to and identification with the Passion of Jesus Christ. A significant number of them settled in the area of Santa Cruz de la Cañada, just east of present-day Española. The settlement became a hub for the practice and extension of the Penitente Brotherhood. By 1739, the penitential devotion had migrated with settlers west to Abiquiú, and by 1775 north to Ranchos de Taos.

La Hermandad de Nuestro Padre Jesús Nazareno

The more ample name of the Penitente Brotherhood is La Hermandad de Nuestro Padre Jesús Nazareno, an unwieldy but meaningful name with three components.

La Hermandad means "the brotherhood." Interestingly, people from Mexico sometimes refer to New Mexicans as *'manitos*. This comes from the custom that older New Mexicans retain when referring to a neighbor or anyone else of the community as *Mano Fulano*. *Mano* here has nothing to do with "hand" but is an abbreviated form of *hermano*, "brother." Addressing one another as "brother" and "sister" certainly reflects the Gospel, and its use in New Mexico may be a reflection of the historical strength of the *hermandades,* or *cofradías*, the brotherhoods.

Nuestro Padre (Our Father) might seem to be an odd, if not heretical, name for Jesus. After all, according to Christian theology the first person of the Trinity is God the Father. Jesus as the begotten Son of God is the second person of the Trinity, equal to yet distinct from the Father. The Dominican priest Vincent Ferrer of Valencia (1350–1419), in defending the biblical definition of the Trinity against Arianism,[3] preached mightily that Jesus is equal to the Father, and some of his insistence influenced Spanish devotion, as expressed in the term Nuestro Padre Jesús. Among those who followed Vincent Ferrer were flagellants who scourged themselves in a penitential discipline whom Ferrer "had inspired to make public atonement . . . without degenerating into fanaticism."[4]

Jesús Nazareno (Jesus of Nazareth) was common enough as a name for Jesus in the first century of the Common Era. Here it means "savior" and contains within it a proclamation of faith in Jesus as savior of the world. "By his stripes we are healed,"[5] the prophet Isaiah foresaw in a prophetic vision about the suffering savior some seven centuries before Jesus was born. One of the bultos of Jesus venerated by New Mexicans and other peoples of Latin America is the wood and gesso image of Jesus standing in a red or purple robe, hands tied, with crown of thorns piercing his bloodied head. This image is referred to as Jesús Nazareno, or El Nazareno in Hispanic Catholic iconography.

ACTIVITIES OF THE PENITENTES

The Hermandad consisted of men.[6] Some women auxiliary members are known to have existed, or at least there were very similar groups for women, for example, La Sociedad de San Antonio in Arroyo Hondo, twelve miles north of Taos. The Hermanos provided a powerful religious presence and leadership for the Spanish settlers, especially in the more isolated areas of the older core of northern New Mexico, southern Colorado, and a little beyond. On Fridays, especially during Lent, Hermanos would often lead long processions for public recitation of the Stations of the Cross. They sometimes led a procession to carry the image of Nuestro Padre Jesús from the church to their morada, and other times they would make flagellant processions on Friday nights of Lent. However, more frequent activities of Penitentes included leading rosaries at funerals for *difuntos* (the dead) and singing alabados (traditional hymns sung at wakes and other religious functions).

They organized themselves for penance, as well as for mutual human aid of almost every kind. They usually gathered on Wednesdays and Fridays for the purpose of prayer and acts of penance and to prepare for activities of Lent and Holy Week, the culmination of their year. Others led the celebration of other important feasts, such as All Saints Day and All Souls Day (November 1 and 2); the patron saint of a village was always especially noted. The feasts of Santiago and Santa Ana were major celebrations in Taos, and their observance continues to this day. (Santiago, Saint James, is the patron saint of Hispanic America.) The small village of Arroyo Hondo with two moradas—an upper and lower one—kept the feast of La Portiúncula on August 1. The *funciónes* (events, festivities) associated with the feast argues for Franciscan origin[7] since it refers to the small twelfth-century chapel in Assisi, Italy, where Saint Francis spent much of his life.[8]

Padre Martínez and the Penitentes

Licenciado Antonio Barreiro, a Mexican lawyer and tax assessor responsible to the secular authority, came to New Mexico in the spring of 1831, the same year that Don José Antonio Laureano de Zubiría y Escalante became the new bishop of Durango. Barreiro's report, titled "A Look (*Ojeada*) at New Mexico," painted a grim picture of both the potential tax revenue and of the "doleful" spiritual situation of the area.[9]

After the death of Bishop Castañiza, who had ordained Padre Martínez in Durango, Mexico, the Cathedral Chapter of Durango in 1828 appointed Don Juan Rafael Rascón as visitor general and vicar of New Mexico. At the same time that Barreiro was in New Mexico on behalf of the civil authority, Vicar Rascón was reconnoitering the northern extremity of the Diocese of Durango on behalf of Bishop Zubiría. A couple of Padre Martínez's parishioners from Taos—his legates—went to Santa Fe to visit with Vicar Rascón. One of them was Donaciano Vigil, later to have a significant role in the history of New Mexico.[10] The purpose of the delegation was to speak with Vicar Rascón in the name of sixty brothers of the Third Order of San Francisco and to ask permission to fulfill their observances in Taos instead of in the *villa* of Santa Cruz de La Cañada. Vicar Rascón had no objection but referred the matter to the appropriate authority, the superior of the Franciscan Order in New Mexico.[11]

Padre Martínez, however, may have wanted something other than making it easier for his parishioners to fulfill a spiritual obligation closer to home. He desired to be the spiritual leader in Taos of La Orden Tercera de Penitencia, the venerable and ecclesiastically approved religious society for lay people. The existence of the Franciscan Third Order in La Villa de Santa Cruz dated to 1693.[12] Anticipating the first of three visits of Bishop Zubiría to New Mexico, Padre Martínez wrote to him in February 1833. Martínez offered him quite a vivid description of the rites of the Hermanos, which had been in existence "since time immemorial":

> During the time that I have had in my charge the spiritual administration of this parish, there has been a gathering of men belonging to the Brotherhood of the Blood of Christ who have been carrying on penitential exercises during Lent. They do this especially on the Fridays of Lent and during all of Holy Week from Good Friday until Pentecost, and on other such meaningful days of the year. Their exercises consist in dragging large wooden crosses along the ground, in whipping themselves with scourges that they have for this purpose, and piercing themselves between the shoulder blades with sharp rocks or blades of flint until blood spurts out. There are other forms of penitential exercises prescribed this way: walk barefoot, even in the snow, and go without clothes except for loincloths or white pants over their private

parts and a mask-neckerchief over the face so as not to be recognized but still able to see. . . . Moreover, they have the custom of walking in procession in front of the sacred images on the days of Holy Week, and [they say] . . . this is the way given them since time immemorial.[13]

Padre Martínez admitted exaggerations, and his letter may have been to posture himself as the one who could moderate excesses and thus avoid what he feared might be the bishop's explicit condemnation upon his impending visit. Asking for the bishop's advice, Martínez identified the Penitentes' growth in number and the discord in their midst. He claimed he was trying to moderate the penitential practices by restricting them to nighttime activities and isolated places.[14]

Before he left Durango for his visitation to New Mexico, Bishop Zubiría replied to Padre Martínez on April 1, 1833, as follows:

The indiscrete devotion of Penances that these Brothers or congregants, named for the Blood of Christ, cannot but excite one with a great disturbance of body and soul. In virtue of this, I of public Penances. Hold fast to that prohibition, and call upon the help of the secular authority if necessary. With the pressure of things upon me, it seems more certain that I will not be able to see to it myself for now. Meanwhile, heartily approve of what your words provide in order to suspend such excesses would you privately exhort them to contain their Penitential practices within the privacy of the church—taking care to always carry them out with moderation. If they wish to placate divine justice and give pleasure to God, as should be their desire, the best way to please Him, ideally, is to listen to the voice of their pastors and follow it with docility.[15]

In July 1833, Bishop Zubiría arrived in Nuevo México, coming to the parish of Santa Cruz de la Cañada before going to Taos. He left notations in the books of parish records, giving his approval to the Confraternity of Our Lady of Mt. Carmel and that of the Blessed Sacrament. However, he wrote a notation in the parish books stating that he did not approve of "a certain Brotherhood of Penitentes, already ancient, that has existed in this Villa [of Santa Cruz de la Cañada]." During his visit, the bishop learned that the Hermanos observed some days of corporal penance that were very hard, carrying heavy crosses (*maderos*) for the long distance of five or six miles. Before he left La Villa de Santa Cruz in the fall, Bishop Zubiría wrote a special letter condemning the Penitentes, a document he wanted promulgated in other places as well. He asserted that the Brotherhood was without the authorization or knowledge of its bishops. Their forms of penance were too excessive and "contrary to the spirit of the [Catholic] Religion . . . not at all in conformity with Christian humility."[16]

The bishop seemed to leave a certain opening to the activities of the Brotherhood by stating that prayer gatherings for moderate penitential exercises could be held in the church. However, Bishop Zubiría felt obliged to close the door to flagellant abuses that "at one time made [the] Holy Church shed tears."[17] Forbidding any priest of the Territory from officiating for Penitentes in any place, the bishop annulled the Brotherhood of Penance and said it ought to remain extinguished. Bishop Zubiría remained in New Mexico until mid-October. Before returning to Durango, he wrote another letter,[18] this one on the sacrament of Penance. Although he did not forbid moderate penance, calling it healthful for the spirit, he forbade the use of the large wooden crosses, asked that instruments of mortification not be kept in the church, and referred to certain practices as butchery *("carnecería")*.

After leaving Santa Cruz in July, 1833, Bishop Zubiría went to Taos. There he agreed to the request of Padre Martínez that Martínez take charge of the Third Order of Franciscans for lay people, which had existed in New Mexico for almost a century and a half. Fray Manuel Antonio Garcia del Valle, the Franciscan *custos* (Guardian of the Province of Saint Paul for New Mexico), was at that time the superior of the secular Third Order for lay people. He officially designated Padre Martínez to be the spiritual leader of its members in the Taos area. At the request of Bishop Zubiría, the appointment was made at the end of July. Padre Martínez was now the director of the venerable Orden de Terceras de Penitencia and was entrusted "with full power as that which we exercise."[19] This enabled bringing the Penitentes under the general umbrella of the Franciscan Third Order.

Within the ample folds of the secular Franciscan Third Order, it seems to this writer, Padre Martínez reconfigured the Hermanos of Nuestro Padre Jesús Nazareno and its practices in order to protect them from the effects of official condemnation by the bishops in Santa Fe. In this way, the brothers not only survived but also flourished as an important and viable force of mutual help and religious devotion within the isolated and rural communitarian structure of northern New Mexico. Padre Martínez helped the Brotherhood to maintain and deepen cultural and religious ties among the local community and beyond. He was a moderating influence, a spiritual guide, father and promoter as well as organizer of the Penitente Brotherhood. He was the one mainly responsible for molding the organization into its modern form.

Padre Martínez's role in the formation of the Penitentes' organization—its practice and its development—was influenced by the cultural landscape that imprinted his boyhood, the religious heritage he personified, the circumstances of his own life, and the developing history of New Mexico, which Padre Martínez himself helped shape.[20] His attitude toward Penitentes seems to have changed from a negative perception to a very positive one, some say as a result of the American occupation of 1846. "Changes in sovereignty in the introduction of foreign cultures symbolically transformed the Penitente Brotherhood into the preserve of traditional Hispano spirituality."[21]

THE CHAPEL OF OUR LADY OF SAN JUAN DE LOS LAGOS IN TALPA: A PENITENTE BASE

By 1827, about thirty families were living in the new plaza at Río Chiquito, on the tributary of the Río de Las Trampas (Río Grande del Rancho), not more than two miles southeast of present-day Ranchos de Taos. This was six years after Mexican independence from Spain and a year after Padre Martínez came to Don Fernando de Taos as the parish priest. Don Bernardo Durán, one of the more prosperous citizens of Río Chiquito, petitioned Padre Martínez on behalf of the families for the right to recognize the Virgin Mary as their special patroness under the title of Our Lady of San Juan de los Lagos. The following year, 1828, Durán built the Chapel of Our Lady of San Juan de los Lagos in the center of the Rio Chiquito Plaza. During his 1833 visit to the area, Bishop Zubiría gave permission to hold Mass and other liturgical services there.[22] This *capilla* is still in use today.

A decade after the capilla was built, another chapel was constructed very close to Our Lady of San Juan. This separate chapel had strong Penitente connections. An active and influential member of the Brotherhood in Taos Valley, Nicolás Sandoval, built it at his own expense as a private chapel *(oratorio)* next to his home.[23] The new Sandoval Chapel was dedicated to Our Lady of the Rosary of Talpa and was long known as the Chapel of Our Lady of Talpa.[24] Regularly used by Padre Martínez, an inscription on a ceiling plank, dated July 2, 1851, declares that the capilla was for the "use of the priest Don Antonio José Martínez *(a la disposició de . . .).*[25] However, Don Bernardo's chapel was not officially licensed as a place to hold Mass.

The evidence is strong that Padre Martínez used the Sandoval oratorio as a base for his work with the Penitentes in the Talpa area. The presence of a second chapel, built by a well-known member of the Brotherhood and dedicated to the Penitentes' primary benefactor, seems to confirm a very strong Penitente influence in the Talpa area at that time.

In the twentieth century, the Sandoval Chapel passed by marriage into the Durán family, after which it was called the Durán Chapel, causing confusion to this day. It fell into ruin in the 1960s, more than a century after Padre Martínez last held services there. (See Michael Miller's chapter, "Sacred Spaces," for more on the history of both chapels.)

THE COMING OF BISHOP JEAN-BAPTISTE LAMY

One of the most important periods in the long career of Padre Martínez—and one of the most contentious—began three years after the American annexation of New Mexico. In 1851, Jean-Baptiste Lamy, a Frenchman, became the new bishop for the archdiocese of New Mexico. On July 1, 1851, Lamy wrote to the clergy of New

Mexico announcing his impending arrival. For the first time in his career, Padre Martínez had to answer to someone totally unfamiliar with the people and culture of northern New Mexico.

Although Padre Martínez seemed to try to ingratiate himself with the new ecclesiastical authority—lending his counsel in canonical matters and making a loan of money—the relationship soon soured. Almost from the start Lamy was in conflict with the then-powerful and very much loved priest of Taos. Within a year of his arrival, the new bishop reimposed tithing, a practice that, as a young priest, Padre Martínez had helped to terminate, claiming that it was an excessive burden on the poor. Now Lamy was threatening to bar from the sacrament of Eucharist those who did not comply, a ban called simony. Martínez publicly denounced this in the *Santa Fe Gazette* as hucksterism and decried the exacting of tithes under pain of withholding of Holy Communion.[26]

Martínez later tried to take back some of his intemperate public statements and in other correspondence told Bishop Lamy he was thinking of retiring because of health concerns. The bishop accepted what he chose to understand as a request for retirement and sent Padre Damasio Taladrid to Taos in May 1856. The former Spanish army officer, whom Bishop Lamy had met in Rome, did not get along with the pastor of Taos, and the antagonism was mutual. Father Taladrid wrote to Bishop Lamy to denounce Padre Martínez for celebrating Mass at the Chapel of Our Lady of Talpa.[27]

Lamy Suspends Padre Martínez and Issues Rules for Penitentes

Father Taladrid began urging Padre Martínez to relinquish his spiritual authority over the Third Order of Lay Franciscans, but Padre Martínez demurred, saying he could not give up his sub-delegation of authority over the Third Order, since Bishop Zubiría had given it to him personally. A month later, Bishop Lamy promulgated a series of Twelve Rules for the Penitentes that Father Taladrid apparently drafted to better exert control over the Brotherhood. On the same day, October 27, 1856, Lamy officially suspended Martínez from performance of his priestly functions of celebrating Mass, hearing confession, and preaching.[28]

The Twelve Rules issued in the fall of 1856 were followed by another set of Five Rules, which Lamy issued on March 9, 1857.[29] (The very fact that Bishop Lamy promulgated rules for the Penitentes was an explicit recognition of their existence and approbation of the Brotherhood to the extent they were asked to follow the rules.) The ninth and tenth rules specifically require that all members of the brotherhood obey and respect Bishop Lamy and their legitimate parish priest. In them, he expressly permitted the Brothers to do penance—as it has been their custom for many years—as long as it was hidden, did not give scandal to the rest of the faithful, and was not done with excessive pride. These concerns echo the Special Letter that Bishop Zubiría had written for the Penitentes in 1833 but without condemnation.

EXCOMMUNICATION

After Father Taladrid left Taos, Padre Martínez was hoping that Padre Medina, one of his seminary students, would come to Taos and eventually become pastor of Taos. But in 1857 Father José Eulogio Ortiz was sent to replace Taladrid as pastor of Our Lady of Guadalupe in Taos. Padre Martínez was at first pleased to welcome Ortiz, who was a native New Mexican, an alumnus of his seminary, and the nephew of former Vicar Padre Juan Felipe Ortiz. However, as a young priest Father Eulogio had accompanied Bishop Lamy on one of his trips to Rome and, as a favorite of the bishop, was not at all sympathetic to Martínez or the Penitentes. He instead worked with Lamy to further discredit the padre.

Padre Martínez may have invited ecclesiastical censure for having publicly denounced Bishop Lamy in the press, specifically, for offering money for offices or positions in the Church hierarchy. Martínez may also have invited censure for presiding at the marriage of his niece to Pedro Sánchez in Martínez's private oratorio. However, Padre Martínez was certainly not prepared for the most severe censure, excommunication. Lamy, entirely on his own, apparently imposed this ultimate sanction on Martínez in early 1857. But even this did not stop the censured priest from doing his best to protect the interests of the Penitentes.

A well-known example of this occurred approximately a year after Martínez's removal by Lamy. Just before Holy Week in 1858 Father Ortiz, then pastor of Our Lady of Guadalupe, surreptitiously removed Penitente-related images from the private chapel in Talpa. This severely angered Padre Martínez, who reported the incident to Bishop Lamy and expected recourse.[30] The bishop, on this occasion and many others after 1857, essentially ignored the troublesome prelate from Taos.

INCORPORATION OF THE PENITENTE BROTHERHOOD

By 1861, Don Nicolás Sandoval was most likely the *Hermano Mayor* (elder brother, chief officer) for the Hermandad in Ranchos de Taos. In that year, he was one of thirteen Penitente leaders in the county of Taos whose names appear on an "Act to incorporate the 'Pious Fraternity of the County of Taos,' January 30, 1861." This was an attempt to organize the moradas of the Taos Valley into a legal entity for protective purposes. He was also one of five leaders in Taos County to formulate the February 23, 1861, "Constitution of Rules for the Internal Government of the Pious Fraternity of the County of Taos." This document includes a statement affirming the Taos Brotherhood's right to possess "any buildings and possessions belonging to the Brotherhood since olden times," and the right to "claim them before any civil authority using all possible means to gain possession or obtain a just and fitting restitution."

The intention here most likely was to prevent the Church from gaining title to their chapels and moradas. Padre Martínez undoubtedly was a behind-the-scenes agent in promoting legal protection for the moradas and the interests of the Brotherhood. In spite of his ecclesiastic censure and removal, Martínez also continued using other chapels throughout the county to celebrate Mass and the sacraments for a large portion of the Hispanic population. Despite the official efforts to discredit and limit his influence, he continued "until his death in 1867 as the de facto spiritual leader in Taos County"[31]

Protestant Consequences

Manifest Destiny provided a providential opportunity for Protestants to evangelize the "perverted"[32] Hispanic Catholicism of the Penitentes and of all people in the Southwest. Protestant missionaries published descriptions of the Penitentes to demonstrate the importance of their task and to describe challenges and hardships they faced.[33] Their sentiment was that these neo-pagans of Spanish Catholic ancestry needed a conversion to the real Jesus Christ. Their descriptions of bloody rituals and practices were calculated to elicit horror from eastern Protestants who would then become more disposed to support their missionary efforts with funds and personnel.

Presbyterians claimed that Penitentes became Protestants because of the indirect support of the censured Padre Martínez. Some Penitentes did declare as Protestants and served as the core of several Spanish-language Presbyterian congregations in northern New Mexico and southern Colorado. By the end of the nineteenth century, there were about 3,000 adult Hispano Protestant church members organized in about 100 congregations in New Mexico and southern Colorado.[34]

Several family members and others close to Padre Martínez became Presbyterians, including Pascual Martínez, the youngest and favorite brother of the padre. Pedro Sánchez flirted with Presbyterianism in the 1860s. He was later reconciled to the Catholic Church during some missions the Jesuits gave in the Taos area after Martínez died in 1867. Almost forty years later, in 1904, Sánchez authored his panegyric biography of Padre Martínez, *Memorias Sobre La Vida del Presbítero Antonio José Martínez, Cura de Taos,* wherein he makes no mention of church controversies.

José Vicente Romero, also a lay evangelist, was Martínez's allegedly illegitimate son, born in Taos of the widow Teodora Romero only two years before the American occupation. Vicente became one of the founding elders of the first Presbyterian Church in Taos. Until his death in 1912, Vicente Romero served as an active and effective lay evangelizer for the Presbyterian Church in northern New Mexico.

DEATH AND AFTERMATH

Padre Martínez died in Taos on July 27, 1867. As far as is known, he continued until his death to claim authority of various kinds to conduct church activities he had practiced for years.

After the death of Padre Martínez, Bishop Lamy invited Jesuit missionaries to attempt to heal the breach between church officials in Santa Fe and Taos. In January 1869, the Italian Jesuit Father Donato M. Gasparri held a preaching mission in Taos of more than two weeks' duration. One account claims that more than 3,000 persons took part in the spiritual exercises and were reconciled to the Church through the sacrament of Penance, among them relatives of Padre Martínez. It was reported that seventy-six marriages, which had been nullified due to lack of jurisdiction, were validated.[35] Nevertheless, as E. K. Francis wrote in 1956:

> The whole series of events left a wound in the side of the Catholic Church in New Mexico that was long to heal, and the scar can yet be felt. To the Spanish-American minority, however, the wholesale removal of the native clergy has been a tragedy, for it deprived them of their natural leaders capable of cushioning the shock of conquest from which as a group the Hispanos have never quite recovered.[36]

NOTES

1. William Wroth, *The Chapel of Our Lady of Talpa* (Colorado Springs, CO: The Taylor Museum of the Colorado Fine Arts Center, 1979), 240 n18. A *morada* is a special gathering place of the Hermanos Penitentes of New Mexico used for prayer and special rites, especially during Holy Week. The adobe building often consists of three rooms and is usually windowless to ensure privacy. The word *morada* is not related to the Spanish for "purple" or "maroon" but comes from the Latin *morari,* "to dwell, to inhabit." There are three moradas in Abiquiú built between 1820 and 1850. Richard E. Ahlborn, *The Penitente Moradas of Abqiuiú,* Contributions from the Museum of History and Technology, Paper 63 (Washington, DC: Smithsonian Institution Press, 1968), 240, identifies the East Morada of 1820 as the oldest in New Mexico. It is listed on New Mexico's Inventory of Cultural Properties. Although none of them was yet built during the young boyhood of Antonio José Martínez, the East Morada was most likely in existence and in vibrant use by the time he returned to Santo Tomás for his second assignment as a young priest between 1824 and 1826.

2. Marta Weigle, *Brothers of Light, Brothers of Blood: The Penitentes of the Southwest* (Albuquerque: University of New Mexico Press, 1976), 11. Further, poetic lines describing penitential activities of Nuevo México's colonists on Holy Thursday, May 20, 1598, are deemed to be the first reference to Penitentes in New Mexico. Gaspar Pérez de Villagrá, *Historia de la Nueva Mexico, 1610,* Canto XI, lines 310–365. trans. and eds. Miguel Encinas,

Alfred Rodriguez, and Joseph P. Sánchez (Albuquerque: University of New Mexico Press, 1992), 102–03.

Among the most important sources for her work, Marta Weigle especially recognizes the following for the study of Penitentes: Mary Austin Collection and the W. G. Ritch Collection at the Huntington Library, Pasadena, CA; Dorothy Woodward Penitente Papers in the New Mexico State Records Center and Archives; Alice Corbin Henderson, *Brothers of Light: The Penitentes of the Southwest* (New York: Harcourt, Brace, 1937); Bainbridge Bunting, *Taos Adobes*, Publication of the Fort Burgwin Research Center No. 2 (Santa Fe: Museum of New Mexico Press and the Center, 1964), 54–55, on the Arroyo Hondo Upper Morada.

3. Trying to explain the mystery of the Holy Trinity in human language is difficult, even if deferring to Arius, the priest from Alexandria, who emphasized the biblical verse, "The Father is greater than I." He taught that the Son is not equal to the Father, which is not orthodox theology as defined by Catholic Church teaching. The spiritual descendants of Arius in the fourth century considered God the Father as the only true God and did not accept that Jesus Christ fully shared in the divine nature. They taught that Jesus, although exalted, was not equal to God the Father. They also demoted the Holy Spirit to a third-tier spiritual energy.

4. *Catholic Encyclopedia*, vol. 14 (Washington, DC: Catholic University of America, ca. 1967), 681.

5. Isaiah 53: 5.

6. The Brotherhood is still active in New Mexico, although its social roles have been largely taken over by other programs.

7. Weigle, *Brothers*, 158, citing Cleofas Jaramillo's *Shadows of the Past* (1939).

8. A few centuries after Francis died and had his "*transitus*" within the chapel, a basilica was built around it, encompassing it and thus rendering the chapel "a small portion."

9. Weigle, *Brothers*, 23.

10. Benjamin Read, *Illustrated History of New Mexico* (Santa Fe: New Mexico Printing Co., 1912), 453–54. Other references to Donaciano Vigil can be found in Read on pages 439, 456, 461, 539, and 608.

11. Weigle, *Brothers*, 200 (Appendix V – "Act of Vicar Rascon"). My translation follows: "There is no objection in this ecclesiastical government that those present make a request to the Superior of the Order of Saint Francis or his sub-delegates who may be in this Territory or in the Republic to make shorter the practice those religious acts of devotion in the parish of Taos where those called Tertiary are living."

12. "The Third Order of Penitence of Our Holy Father Saint Francis has existed, although the exact year for it founding is not fixed, since just about the [time of the] reconquest of the Province [in 1693]." Weigle, *Brothers*, 197 (Appendix III, Report of Rev. Custos Fray Cayetano José Bernal to Governor Fernando Chacón, October 1794).

13. Letter from Padre Martínez to Bishop Zubiría, February 21, 1833, in the Archives of the Cathedral of Durango, Mexico; unearthed by Mary Taylor, copied and sent to William

Wroth, and quoted in Wroth, *Images of Penance, Images of Mercy: Southwestern Santos in the Late Nineteenth Century* (Norman: University of Oklahoma Press for the Taylor Museum of the Colorado Springs Fine Arts Center, 1991), 172 (Appendix I).

14. Ibid.

15. Wroth, *Images*, 173 (Appendix II). From the Archives of the Cathedral of Durango, Microfilm Roll 16, Frame 689.

16. Bishop Zubiría's Pastoral Letter of July 21, 1833, to the priest and people of Santa Cruz de La Cañada was also intended for clergy and laymen wherever Penitentes were found. Quoted in Weigle, 195–96 (Appendix I). Spanish transcribed by Marta Weigle from the Microfilm Edition of the Archives of the Archdiocese of Santa Fe, New Mexico State Records Center and Archives, Roll 50, Frames 0147-0149. Books of Patentes, No. 73, Box 7, described by Fray Angélico Chávez, *Archives of the Archdiocese of Santa Fe: 1678–1900* (Washington, DC: Academy of American Franciscan History, 1957), 156. English translation mine.

17. Weigle, *Brothers,* 29, 234 n38. Flagellant sects emerged in Europe two times and were sufficiently powerful and schismatic to provoke Church denunciation.

18. Bishop Zubiría, October 19, 1833, quoted in Weigle, 196.

19. Santiago Valdez, "Biography of Padre Antonio José Martínez, Cura de Taos," 1877, unpublished manuscript, William G. Ritch Collection, Henry E. Huntington Library, San Marino, CA. English version by Juan Romero, 1993, 45.

20. Weigle, *Brothers,* 47–51 ("Enigmatic Role of Don Antonio José Martínez").

21. Albert Lopez Pulido, *Sacred World of the Penitentes* (Washington, DC: Smithsonian Institution Press, 2000), 92 n30 summarizes the argument Wroth makes in *Images of Penance,* 51–52.

22. Wroth, *Chapel of Our Lady of Talpa,* 24.

23. Ibid., 103, *passim.* More on the eccesiastical history of the Talpa Chapel is to be found in Michael Miller's chapter "Sacred Places." A U.S. Census taker in 1860 referred to it as a "schismatic church," but Fray Angélico Chávez roundly repudiated that term as appropriately describing the reality. Fray Angélico Chávez, *But Time and Chance* (Santa Fe: Sunstone Press, 1984), 146–47.

24. The Marian shrine of Talpa in Jalisco is a place of pilgrimage dating to the mid-seventeenth century. The shrine's namesake chapel constructed in northern New Mexico signaled lively commerce on *La Caravana* between Mexico City through Chihuahua and Taos.

25. Wroth, *Chapel of Our Lady of Talpa,* 34, pl. 17. Given Martínez's position as parish priest of Nuestra Señora de Guadalupe, when the Talpa Chapel was in the parish of San Francisco, this explicit "permission" speaks to the chapel's Penitente connection.

26. Letter of Padre Martínez to Bishop Lamy, Nov. 12, 1856, trans. Fr. Philip Cassidy, quoted in Juan Romero, *Reluctant Dawn,* 2nd ed. (Palm Springs, CA: The Taos Connection, 2006), 48.

27. Archives of the Archdiocese of Santa Fe, AASF, L.D. 1856, No. 24. The chapel was unlicensed, that is, was not sanctioned as a site for Mass.

28. AASF, L.D. 1856, No. 33.

29. Weigle, *Brothers*, 201–206.

30. AASF, L.D. 1858, No. 17, quoted in Wroth, *Chapel of Our Lady of Talpa*, 36. The appearance of Padre Ortiz before the District Court in Santa Fe is documented in a letter written April 12, 1858, by Judge Kirby Benedict of the Federal District Court for Taos and Santa Fe. (Ibid., 36). The Taos Brotherhood's Constitution and its own rules of February 23, 1861, drafted by Nicolás Sandoval and four others, was a clear attempt to protect the Brothers from any further attacks of this kind. "The Hermano Mayor may also apprehend any person who is not a member of the society and who ridicules, disturbs, or in any way hinders the spiritual exercises of the said fraternity. He may enter legal action against him before the civil authorities in the name of the Fraternity of the County of Taos." Quoted in Wroth, *Chapel of Our Lady of Talpa*, 36–37.

31. Ibid., 37.

32. Juan Francisco Martínez, "Origins and Development of Protestantism among Latinos in the Southwestern United States 1836–1900," PhD diss. (Fuller Theological Seminary, Pasadena, CA, 1996). Juan Martínez cites these Protestant missionaries as especially noteworthy for their zeal and effectiveness: Thomas Harwood (Methodist), Charles Sumner (Congregational), and Alexander Darley (Presbyterian).

33. Darley said of Penitentes: "Serious seekers, by a false road, for salvation, have not been forgotten of God, ever on the watch for the sincere, even though ignorant and, therefore, false seeker for light." Quoted in Juan Martínez, "Origins," 58–59.

34. Martínez, "Origins," quoting Minutes of the General Assembly of the Presbyterian Church, USA (1877–1900).

35. Ibid., 37.

36. E. K. Francis, quoted in Romero, *Reluctant Dawn*, 54.

❖ 19 ❖

A Culture of Celebrations

OCLIDES QUINTANA TENORIO

This chapter focuses on some of the celebrations and customs that unify and energize the northern New Mexican Hispanic community. The people of Taos Pueblo and old Hispanic families have held strongly to their cultural beliefs and traditions, religious and secular. In embracing and cherishing these celebrations as part of everyday life, not just to attract tourists, Taos is exceptional in the twenty-first century. Taos Pueblo's essential conservatism and private ways have been crucial in preserving and passing on the Tiwa language and safeguarding the tribe's sacred rites, beliefs, and lifeways. Old Hispanic traditions and values are still very strong in the Taos Valley, showing a culture more intact than most regional cultures in North America.

AT THE HEART OF NORTHERN NEW MEXICAN Hispanic culture are two basic forces: *la familia* and the Catholic Church. In life, they are almost inseparable. The Hispanic family includes not only parents and siblings; it encompasses *abuelitos* (grandparents), *tíos y tías* (uncles and aunts), and *primos y primas* (cousins and distant relatives, both men and women). The extended family's inclusion in all aspects of life, guided by the Church, is what has kept family units strong through hundreds of years of challenging and changing times. Not only do Taos' Hispanic families celebrate joyous occasions, they also gather and support each other during dark times, such as holding rosaries for the dead, *velorios* (wakes), funerals, and other occasions of loss.

Julia Jaramillo, teacher and descendant of an old Taos family, dances at the Fiestas de San Geronimo in September 1939. Julia said the dance was one she learned in Mexico, not a local one. On the far left with guitar is Donacio Martinez, known as "El Doncito." Caption information provided by Malcolm Collier. Photograph by John Collier Jr., courtesy of the Collier Family Collection.

Birth through Burial

The birth of a child has always been a momentous event. Traditionally, even before a child came into the world the parents prepared both for its immediate needs and also for its entrance into the Christian community.

For as far back as memory reaches, when a child entered the world, the parents prepared for *bautismo* (baptism), the first Holy Sacrament of the Catholic Church. They were careful to choose *padrinos* (godparents) who were good Catholics and responsible members of the community, because godparents are the spiritual parents of the child, responsible for that child's spiritual and moral welfare through maturity and sometimes much longer. The padrinos would give the infant money and a new christening outfit, and would assume full responsibility for the physical and moral care of the child on the death of the parents or if otherwise needed.

Baptism was a ritual recognized by the entire community. Through baptism, the community claimed the child as its own, and the parents presented the infant to the entire community. Baptism was not just a sacrament of initiation into the Church; it was regarded almost as a biological event that effectively bound the child and the community in a profound and lasting blood-spirit relationship. The infant was baptized by the padrinos, and after baptism the child's parents and godparents became *compadres* (co-parents). It was customary to give an infant more than one name, such as José Manuel or Juana María, with the name María often most given to female children and José to male children.

Entriega de bautismo occurred at the new parents' home when the padrinos returned the infant to the parents after the baptism. This custom, practiced in Taos for many years, is still observed in some Hispanic villages. It was a ceremony that reinforced the bond between the parents and the sponsors as the padrinos presented the infant to the parents and recited the following verse:

Compadre y Comadre:
Reciban ésta prenda fina	Receive this precious jewel
Que de la iglesia salió	Who from the church emerges
Con los Santos Sacramentos	With the Holy Sacraments
Y el agua que recibió	And the water it received

The parents responded:
Recibemos esta prenda fina	We receive this precious jewel
Que de la iglesia salió	Who from the church emerged
Con los santos sacramentos	With the Holy Sacraments
Y el agua que recibió	And the water it received

After the entriega, family and friends enjoyed a feast that would last all afternoon. The tables were spread with candy, *biscochitos*, cold drinks, wine, and hot food. The infant received gifts of baby clothes, religious articles, or money.

La Primera Comunión, First Communion, designates the solemn reception of Holy Communion for the first time in the Church and usually refers to young children. In the old days, grandparents, aunts, uncles, and even cousins prepared the child for La Primera Comunión. Preparation was demanding, because children had to learn much about the Catholic religion.

After the First Communion Mass, there were celebrations at the homes of parents. Families invited relatives, neighbors, and friends to share in a joyous feast. The children were blessed by their parents, grandparents, and great-grandparents. Those giving the blessing made the sign of the cross on the forehead of the kneeling child and said, "May God the Father, God the Son, and God the Holy Spirit bless you today and forever." (This blessing continued even for adults, when, for example, leaving home on a long journey.) Throughout childhood, prayers were taught: bedtime prayers, morning prayers, and the angelus at midday.

The next big event in a child's religious life was Confirmation, full membership in the Church. In earlier days in northern New Mexico, *Confirmación*, the second of the Seven Blessed Sacraments of the Roman Catholic Church, occurred when the child was small, sometimes still an infant, with sponsors carefully chosen to confirm the child. Traditionally, men were confirmation sponsors of boys, and women sponsored girls. As with baptism, the sponsors assumed the responsibility of assisting and supporting the faith of the child receiving the sacrament, thereby entering into a spiritual relationship. In the past, the ceremony was administered by a bishop who visited the Taos area every four years. Sometimes the evening before Confirmación, people traveled for miles to meet Su Señoria, the bishop. They reverently kissed his ring and escorted him along the streets to the church, where he delivered a short sermon and blessed the congregation.

Today the bishop comes yearly, and now the sacrament of Confirmación is received by children who have reached the age of reason and only after attending religious classes which prepare them for the sacrament. The archbishop of the Diocese of Santa Fe confirms Taos children. Usually a name other than that bestowed at baptism is given to a child. In most cases, young people choose their name.

MARRIAGE

Traditional events, both religious and secular, customarily surrounded marriage: the *prendorio* (engagement party); the *casorio* (wedding ceremony); the *marcha de los novios* (march of the wedding party); and the entriega (ceremony in which the bride and the groom are given to each other by their parents).

This bride, ca. 1970s, wears dress typical of a Hispanic bride, including high Spanish comb, Spanish fan, and fringed shawl on her arm. Courtesy Taos News Archives.

Prendorio

Before a wedding in a Hispanic family, the would-be groom and his family would ask the bride's family for the young woman's hand. This was done very formally and in writing. In the early days, the bride's family was expected to respond in eight days. Later, especially when families were friends or acquaintances, the proposal was made in person. An appointment was arranged at the convenience of the bride's family, and the groom would be accompanied by his father, mother, grandparents, and godparents. Even when the proposal was made in person, it was neither accepted nor refused immediately. The groom had to wait for the response and would continue to work on the home he was building for his hoped-for bride. If the woman was unwilling or the parents did not approve, a letter was sent to the groom's family. A negative response was considered an insult and often ended relationships between families. A rejection was referred to enigmatically as *calabazas* (pumpkins or squash).

If the response was positive, there would be a prendorio—an engagement party—at the home of the bride, with her family paying all expenses. Years ago this would be the first time the couple would come together publicly and was regarded as the giving away of the bride. The bride usually received a trunk filled with embroidered linens, sheets, pillowcases, tablecloths, blankets, bedspreads, and the like.

At the ceremony, the bride was introduced to the groom's family and relatives, and the same was done for the groom. After the presentation of gifts, the family and guests proceeded to the dining room. A banquet table dressed with lace tablecloths and set with fresh flowers would hold an array of cakes, cookies, tarts, pies, and homemade wines. There was no scarcity of hard liquor, either.

Casorio

Before the church wedding took place, the banns of matrimony had to be announced in the church for three consecutive Sundays. About eight days after the prendorio, the religious ceremony of marriage took place in a village church, the Holy Mass of Matrimony sanctifying and confirming the wedding vows between the bride and the groom, and the priest offering them the blessings of the Church. The couple was accompanied by the padrino and the madrina, the best man and the matron of honor.

Two traditional customs were incorporated into the ceremony and are still observed today. The priest places the *lazo*, a large rosary, around the couple to symbolize the union of two as one. The lazo was once made of roses but today is commercially available as a rope strung with clay or wooden beads. The *arras*, a small silver box containing thirteen coins, is given to the bride as the groom's pledge that he will support her all the days of her life. Originally the coins were gold and were often given to the Church.

After the wedding ceremony was over, the couple and its entourage proceeded to the home of the bride. Led by local musicians with violins and guitars playing the wedding march and other traditional music, the couple was met by parents and relatives a short distance from the house. The wedding party continued to the house, where a traditional banquet awaited. Today, the celebrants arrive at the home in cars or drive to an inn or restaurant for the wedding feast.

Marcha de los Novios

The traditional wedding feast would last all day, and in the evening everyone got ready for the wedding dance. Upon their arrival at the dance hall, the wedding party was led by the musicians for the *marcha de los novios*—the bride and groom march—which is still widely practiced today. Led by an experienced couple who are followed by the bride and groom, the march swept up everyone, young and old. Marching around the hall, the couples joyfully clapped their hands in time to music. The head couple would then form an arch with their arms under which the bride and the groom and everyone else passed.

The wedding dance continued with old-time dancing to music played by local musicians. There were varsovianas (two-step dances), quadrilles, schottisches, and other traditional dances. One favorite dance was the *vals del chiquillado*, a waltz in which couples exchanged humorous verses.

Entriega

The dance ended with the entriega, a solemn ceremony in which the bride and groom were given to each other by their parents and family. *Entregan* means to "give away" or "give up." Even today many social and religious ceremonies end with an entriega, and every wedding plans for the entriega—an undetermined number of verses composed spontaneously by a friend of the family or some known balladeer, the *entregador*. Accompanied by a guitar or violin and, in many cases, singing his verses to the rhythm of a soft waltz, the entregador advised and reminded members of the wedding party of their moral and social obligations. There are many variations of an entriega, but each one begins with an admonition to the padrinos to fulfill their obligations of blessing the newlyweds. The words may begin:

El padrino y la madrina	The padrino and the madrina
Ya saben su obligación	Know what their duty is
De entregar a sus ahihados	To deliver their godchildren
Y echarles su bendición	And give them their sacred blessing

The verses continue, admonishing the bride and groom, the parents, and the entire community. At the final verses, the couple knelt to receive their parents' blessing; other family lined up to bestow their blessings on the couple. Sometimes a colorful blanket was spread on which people would throw money for the verses they liked. Another custom was to pin money to the bride's veil—bills from one dollar to a hundred dollars. The money usually went to the couple or to the entregador.

Death, Mourning, and Saints

In the old days, when a person died the church bells would *doblar* (toll) to let the community know that someone had left this world for a better life. Relatives were notified by a messenger who went from house to house telling them to commend the soul of the departed to God, or the family would mail formal, black-bordered announcements of the death.

Velorios y Rosarios

A Hispanic custom that is comparatively rare today is the *velorio* (wake). The word *velorio* comes from the word *velar*, which means to keep vigil. In earlier days when a person died, the family had the velorio at home. The family, relatives, and friends stayed with the body all night, praying several rosaries. The rosaries were led by a *rezador*, a person who led the people in prayer. Every rosary was offered for the repose of the soul of the dead person. Beautiful prayers of *ofrecimiento* (offerings) were recited at the end of each rosary, followed by a hymn to the Blessed Virgin Mary. The Penitentes (Brothers of the Confraternity of Jesus Christ) sang alabados, religious hymns introduced many centuries ago to New Mexico by the Franciscan friars.

When someone came to sympathize with the family and offer condolences to the mourners, they often recited *requiebros,* loving praises directed to the dead person. A requiebro might say something like, "You were so good at feeding the animals" or "I don't know what we will do without you; you always made us laugh."

At midnight, supper was served to the mourners. Always present in the meal was *chilorio,* a dish made with red chile sauce, potatoes, and meat. (Chilorio, made for a velorio was usually made with pork.) To make sure that there was enough food, the family might butcher a calf, a pig, or some other farm animal.

The next day the body was buried in a locally made wooden coffin. The church bells tolled throughout the Mass. When the deceased was taken for burial—by wagon or by foot—*descansos* were placed along the way. A descanso is a wooden cross affixed to a post or set in a pile of stones at a place that had been special to the deceased. It served to remind people to pray that this soul would rest in peace. The word *descanso* means "to rest," and for a long time descansos were left at points along a burial route where the body had been set down while the bearers rested. Today, families will often place a descanso at the site of an accidental death, and one sees them everywhere along the roads of northern New Mexico. Some cemeteries had an *oratorio*, a simple structure open on one side where persons close to the deceased would wait with the priest while men dug the grave. Taos has an example of such an oratorio, now restored, in Peñas Negras camposanto on Lower Ranchitos Road.

Mourning was a rigid custom and continued for a whole year. Family and close relatives dressed in black and abstained from hearing music or attending joyous functions. A wake for a little child or baby was called *velorio de angelito* (angel wake). As little children were considered angels, formal prayers of the dead were not said for them.

Velorios para santos

Sometimes a velorio was held on less mournful occasions. Because the early settlers often did not have a priest, the people held religious celebrations on their own; all-night vigils for saints were one such event. The santos (images of the saints) were thought of as members of the Hispanic family. Families had their favorite santos and constantly prayed to them and asked them for favors. Wakes for the saints, *velorios para santos*, usually expressed gratitude for favors received, but they could also be a kind of votive offering for favors expected. Sometimes a velorio was in honor of one saint, sometimes of many. It might also be held to help a family with material needs.

For a velorio, the saint's statue was brought from the church or borrowed from a neighbor and placed on an improvised altar, surrounded with tallow candles and waxed-paper flowers. Everyone was welcome. The people knelt or sat on the mud floor around the altar, while the *rezador* recited the rosary and other prayers. The men and boys took turns singing alabados in honor of the saints. After midnight, supper was served to everyone. Some people remained until early morning, when they returned the statue, singing all the way. While novenas to patron saints are still commonly offered in the Taos Valley and santos of favorite saints are still found in many homes, the tradition of honoring santos with a velorio has faded away.

Fiestas de Taos

Fiestas have been celebrated annually in Taos for centuries. Fiestas, or feast days in the Catholic tradition, honor a saint on the day recognized as his or her birth date. In Hispanic and New Mexico Pueblo communities, fiestas are celebrations that combine religious solemnity with secular traditions of family homecomings, with feasting, music, dancing, parades, and the like. Fiestas are celebrated throughout the year by the churches and chapels of the of the three parishes of the Taos Valley.

The original and only fiesta at Taos was La Fiesta de San Gerónimo, held at the pueblo on September 30 to honor the pueblo's patron saint, Jerome. For more than a century, until the early 1800s, the mission church of San Gerónimo was the mother church in the Taos Valley, and pueblo and Taos residents celebrated the saint's feast day with masses and other religious ceremonies—both Catholic and Native American—at the pueblo.

San Gerónimo Feast Day

The Feast of San Gerónimo is a two-day celebration that marks the end of the harvest season and honors the patron saint of the pueblo's mission church. It is celebrated September 30 at Taos Pueblo. From at least the seventeenth century onward, Taos Pueblo was the site of the annual Taos trade fair which brought hundreds of people to trade their goods. El Diá de San Gerónimo reflects those trade fairs, as well. In the early days, San Gerónimo was the most famous celebration in northern New Mexico, topping those at the capital of the territory, Santa Fe.

The feast begins on September 29 with vespers in the Church of San Gerónimo, followed by Pueblo religious ceremonies. On September 30, events begin early in the morning, starting with relay races into the canyon by the North House. By nine in the morning the pueblo is crowded with people who come for the events that continue throughout the day. Visiting Indians set up booths where they sell beads, silver jewelry, pottery, woven rugs, and other items. The plaza is filled with the aromas of foods sold at various stands. Throughout the day the Chifonetes (sacred clowns) make their way through the crowds, climbing ladders and making people laugh. Sometimes they seize a youngster who is watching them. If children are misbehaving, they might get tossed into the nearby Río Pueblo.

Sometime in the late afternoon the clowns come out as a group and walk around until it is time to climb the very tall greased pole that has been raised in the plaza of the North House. Clowns and spectators cheer as men climb the pole. At the top of the pole are, traditionally, a sheep, bread, and other fruits of the harvest that are thrown down and shared. At the end of the pole climb, people linger to visit and feast with family and friends, reminiscing and talking about past experiences and memories of El Diá de San Gerónimo celebrations.

Las Fiestas de Santiago y Santa Ana

In the 1930s, hoping to boost a Depression economy, the town of Taos "invented" the event known today as the Taos Fiestas. In reality, what they did was to reinvent the celebration of two saints who had long been honored with feast days: Saint James the Greater, patron saint of Spain and Hispanics, whose feast day is July 25, and Saint Ann, mother of the Virgin Mary, who is celebrated on July 26. (Saint James is also known as Santiago Matamoros, or Saint James, slayer of Moors.) The fiesta celebration is an integral part of Hispanic culture, and in Taos it contributes to preserving that rich culture. The celebration brings together families, relatives, friends, visitors, and tourists, itself creating a blend of different cultures, as people experience a tradition that has existed more or less intact for so many years.

The religious celebration of the Taos Fiestas serves to reaffirm the faith of the Catholic Hispanic people. The official celebration begins with Mass, followed by the crowning of the fiesta queen, *La Reina*, who is a young Hispanic woman well versed in Catholic doctrine as well as the language and culture of her people. Chosen from among several high-school-age princesses who compete for the crown, she remains La Reina for a year. Besides knowledge of their Hispanic culture, today members of the court must also demonstrate accomplishments in music, dancing, or other talents.

During the fiestas, the town comes alive as events move toward a secular celebration, more like a county fair than a religious celebration. The plaza is closed to motorized traffic, and crowds pour in to hear the live entertainment by musicians and dancers. People wait with anticipation for the big Historical Parade on the afternoon of the second full day. All day and well into the night the smell of chili and grilled meat fills the air. The Tio Vivo, for years a main attraction in the Taos Fiestas (*Tío Vivo* is another name for *Los Cabillitos*—the little horses—a merry-go-round or carousel), draws young children to ride its colorful hundred-year-old painted wooden horses, while adults stand by remembering their younger days when they, too, saw the plaza from the back of one of Tio Vivo's colorful steeds. At one time a small carnival with a big Ferris wheel and other amusements, rides, and games provided entertainment.

In earlier decades, the fiestas experience included walking around the plaza and stopping to talk to friends. The fiestas were not as elaborate then, and they were attended mostly by locals, their relatives, and people from surrounding communities. Local schools and youth clubs would always enter a float in the Historical Parade, making it very much a local affair. For at least a decade, artists and their friends dressed up and rode in the parade, among them Mabel Dodge Luhan and her crowd, all important in putting the Taos Fiestas on the map.

RELIGIOUS DRAMAS AND DANCES

Traditional folk plays are important in all Hispanic cultures, and more are found in New Mexico than in any other Hispanic enclave in the Americas. The Spanish folklore of New Mexico, especially in northern New Mexico, is one of the special jewels brought by the Spanish in the sixteenth century. Aurora Lucero-White Lea, an authority on folk drama, says that with one exception it is almost certain that these plays were not printed.[1]

The plays brought by the Spanish to the New World were known as *autos* or *comedias*. Some were religious, some were secular. The secular plays dramatized battles between the Moors and Christians in Spain as well as encounters of the Spanish with Native American cultures in the New World. According to popular history, during the missionary era the Franciscan brothers, consumed with converting Indians, neglected the Spanish colonists. Because of this, the settlers began to present these plays without the help of the Church, and soon they passed into folklore. In some Hispanic villages, these religious, moralistic dramas have been performed for more than four hundred years.

Las Posadas

Las Posadas (The Inns), a nine-day ritual drama, is a traditional morality play that has been enacted in New Mexico for hundreds of years. It is centered on the story of Mary and Joseph on their journey from Nazareth to Bethlehem and their rejection by innkeepers until, on the night Jesus was born, they found room in a stable.

Las Posadas originated in Spain between the eleventh and sixteenth centuries and was brought to Mexico by Fray Diego de Soria. The Spanish performed it for the Aztec Indians with the purpose of converting them to Catholicism. Las Posadas came to New Mexico with Oñate in 1598 and has remained one of the most important religious dramas for Catholics during the Christmas season.

In Taos and surrounding communities, Las Posadas is enacted for nine consecutive nights beginning on December 16 and concluding on Christmas Eve. The novena is prayed at different homes in canticle (sung verse) form, with a group of people singing outside and another group singing inside the house. Players representing Mary and Joseph carry a baby and in canticles ask for shelter at one house after another over the nine nights. Until the final night, the request is refused. On the last night they are let into the house and all enjoy refreshments, such as biscochitos, after which all proceed to the church where the final novena is prayed before the midnight Mass.

Los Pastores

The nativity drama of Los Pastores (The Shepherds) originated in Spain between the eleventh and fifteenth centuries, about the time the *Officium pastorum*, a liturgical recitation of the Shepherds Play, was added to the Christmas Mass. In Spain these plays were known as *autos del nacimiento*, simple and joyous reenactments of the birth of Jesus. They soon developed into a complex version known as *auto sacramental*, an allegorical drama based on a biblical, moralistic theme of good and evil.

Embellished with lively pantomime and music, Los Pastores represents the shepherds on their way to see to the Christ Child. They encounter the devil, who tempts them. They also encounter the Good Angel, who guides them to the stable. Characters in the drama represent different qualities in people, such as weakness, good, and evil. At the end, as in Las Posadas and other religious dramas, good triumphs over evil.

Los Moros y Los Cristianos

Los Moros y Los Cristianos (The Moors and the Christians) was one of the traditional secular plays brought by the Spanish to the New World. Alvar Nuñez Cabeza de Vaca, the great explorer, recounts that after his travels in Texas, Arizona, and New Mexico he arrived along the Pacific Coast of Mexico on July 3, 1536. He was honored by Viceroy Mendoza and the Marques del Valle, Hernán Cortés. His journals note that for the feast of Santiago (Saint James) there was a bullfight and a performance of a play called *Los Moros y Los Cristianos*.

Oñate's men performed the secular drama entirely on horseback. It enacts the Spanish defeat of the Moors and their expulsion from the Iberian Peninsula, which the Moors had dominated for seven hundred years. The play includes six characters: Don Alfonso, leader of the Christians, and Federico and Eduardo, his lieutenants. On the Moors' side there are El Gran Sultán, leader of the Moors, and his two lieutenants, Morna and Selín, who have stolen the Holy Cross from the Christians. The Christians triumph over the Moors, and Don Alfonso retrieves the cross. He recites a prayer of thanksgiving. El Gran Sultán humbles himself and acknowledges the cross over the crescent. He asks for forgiveness, and he and his men are set free in the name of the cross.

Rarely performed today, in northern New Mexico, Los Moros y Los Cristianos has been reenacted in Santa Cruz de la Cañada, twelve miles from the site of Oñate's original settlement in Los Luceros.

Los Matachines

Los Matachines is a ritual dance-drama that is performed on Christmas and New Year's Day in some Indian pueblos and Hispanic communities in northern New Mexico. The dance is also performed for other occasions, such as wedding festivities, patron saint's days, and other community and church celebrations. The Danza de Los Matachines is the only such drama performed by both Hispanics and Native Americans in the Upper Rio Grande Valley.

Los Matachines may have originated in Spain as early as the twelfth century as a pantomime of combat between the Moors and Christians in Spain. Like Los Pastores and Las Posadas, Los Matachines is an allegorical drama of morality centered on the themes of good and evil. The drama was brought to be performed for the Aztecs by Spanish missionaries to encourage the natives' conversion to Christianity. Since the Aztecs did not speak Spanish, the friars transformed the drama into a dance without dialogue, which the Indians accepted and adapted to their own style of dance. Montezuma, or Monarca, the Aztec king, replaced the Moor. The Aztecs added the character of Malinche, the pure young girl who represents the Virgin Mary, Montezuma's wife, or Cortés's wife.

Los Matachines includes from ten to fourteen dancers. The leader, Monarca, wears a tall cap with a cross. A young man plays El Toro con Cuernos (the horned bull) and represents evil. The dancers stand in two parallel lines. Monarca dances in and out between the dancers in a complex pattern, and Malinche follows him. Outside the lines, clowns snap their whips at the bull and sometimes at the spectators. Violinists and guitarists play without ceasing. At the end of the dance good arrives when Cortés, the Christian, triumphs over Montezuma, the pagan. The man representing Montezuma drops dead, and all the matachines kneel down.

For the most part, these celebrations happen without fanfare or special publicity. They are, nonetheless, a major contribution to what makes Taos the place it is.

NOTE

1.   The exception is *Las Cuatro Apariciones de Nuestra Senora de Guadalupe* (The Four Apparitions of Our Lady of Guadalupe), a drama performed only in Arroyo Seco.

SELECTED REFERENCES

Brown, Lorin W., with Charles L. Briggs and Marta Weigle. *Hispano Folklife of New Mexico: The Lorin W. Brown Federal Writers' Project Manuscripts.* Albuquerque: University of New Mexico Press, 1979.

Campa, Arthur L. *Hispanic Culture in the Southwest.* Norman: University of Oklahoma Press, 1979.

Espinosa, Aurelio M. *The Folklore of Spain in the American Southwest.* Edited by J. Manuel Espinosa. Norman: University of Oklahoma Press, 1985.

Gilbert, Fabiola Cabeza de Baca. *The Good Life.* Santa Fe: San Vicente Foundation, 1949.

Jaramillo, Cleofas. *Romance of a Little Village Girl.* San Antonio, TX: Naylor Company, 1955.

———. *Shadows of the Past (Sombras del pasado).* 1941. Reprint, Santa Fe: Ancient City Press, 1972.

Lucero-White Lea, Aurora. *Literary Folklore of the Hispanic Southwest.* San Antonio, TX: Naylor Company, 1953.

Rodríguez, Sylvia. "The Taos Fiestas: Invented Tradition and the Infrapolitics of Symbol Reclamation." *Journal of the Southwest* 30 (Spring 1997): 33–57.

Weigle, Marta, and Peter White. *The Lore of New Mexico.* Albuquerque: University of New Mexico Press, 1988.

TAOS,
CATALYST
FOR CREATIVITY

❖

Among the many creative artists, writers, and intellectuals whom Mabel Dodge Luhan enticed to Taos are (left to right back row) Tony Luhan, one of Mabel's cousins, Mabel Luhan, Frieda Lawrence Ravagli, writer Frank Waters, Leon Gaspard, Russian artist Evelyn Gaspard, and an unidentified man. Kneeling in front are John Younghunter, Angelo Ravagli, and Eve Younghunter. Photo ca. 1950s, courtesy of Taos Historical Museums.

20

Taos Art Colony and the Taos Arts Community

Mildred Tolbert

In the popular imagination, art is what typically comes to mind when Taos is mentioned, and more has been published on Taos artists and art in Taos than on any other subject relating to the town's history. The original author of this chapter was herself an artist, a writer, and a photographer whose black-and-white images captured the essence of scores of creative men and women of the Taos Valley over several decades and are recognized today both for their artistic excellence and as an invaluable record of the modernist generation. Because of the extent of the topic, the following pages are perhaps most useful as an outline of artists and events between about 1900 and 1960. As the title suggests, emphasis is on the Anglo arts community, which celebrated Taos with a kind of vibrant, romantic enthusiasm for its fine arts and literature, as well as for its artists.

SINCE THE FIRST YEARS OF THE TWENTIETH CENTURY, Taos has been an art town—a place that has beckoned artists to paint, draw, photograph, weave, and otherwise give expression to its beauty and its mysteries.[1] Generations of artists have left a glowing and important legacy that speaks of their experience of Taos and northern New Mexico. Some of their work is representational, some abstract; some is regional, and some is supra-regional. Broadly speaking, styles range from romantic and realist to impressionist, modernist, and abstract expressionist to postmodern. What began as an art colony developed into a community where art is honored and encouraged, where artists come to work and live. From time to time, it is claimed that Taos has the highest ratio of art galleries to residents of any American town or city. All of this happened in a place rich with devotional art by Hispanic santeros and bulto carvers and a long history of weaving.[2]

For more than half of the last century, Taos was an art colony in the accepted sense of that term. Taos modernist Bea Mandelman once remarked that the art world is a small one. Her observation is borne out in the way the Taos art colony began, which was in Paris at the Académie Julien in 1895. Joseph Henry Sharp, who had been painting the American West for more than a decade and had spent several months in Taos two years before, told two of his fellow art students about a picturesque Hispanic village near an Indian pueblo in northern New Mexico. Three years later, on their first trip to the West, the two young painters visited the place. Ernest L. Blumenschein and Bert Geer Phillips were en route from Colorado to Mexico when, about twenty miles north of Taos, a wheel of their horse-drawn buggy slipped into a deep rut and broke. They flipped a three-dollar gold piece to determine which man would haul the wheel to Taos for repair. Blumenschein, who lost the toss, described this event in 1915:

> At four P.M. on the third of September 1898 I started down the mountain on what resulted in the most impressive journey of my life. . . . Sharp had not painted for me the land or the mountains and plains and clouds. No artist had ever recorded the New Mexico I was now seeing. No writer had ever written down the smell of this air or the feel of the morning's sky. . . . I saw whole paintings right before my eyes. . . . My destiny was being decided as I squirmed and cursed while urging the bronco through those miles of waves of sagebrush.[3]

The two men were as enchanted with the adobe villages and inhabitants of Taos village and Taos Pueblo as they were with the landscape. Even after fifty years as an American territory, Taos' populace was predominately Hispanic and Indian, both cultures with long, deep, and colorful traditions that were very much intact. Blumenschein and Phillips were young artists "ennuied with the hackneyed subject matter of thousands of painters; wind mills in a Dutch landscape; Britanny peasant with sabots; . . . lady in negligee reclining on a sumptuous divan."[4] Steeped in the values of the romantic tradition, the early Taos artists found the dramatic land-scape of northern New Mexico, its remoteness, and its seemingly exotic lifeways to be irresistibly seductive. It also offered the possibility of capturing a landscape and culture that were uniquely American. The founders, as they came to be called, decided to settle in Taos and "in a conscious attempt to establish an art colony began to encourage others to join them in this remote Western location." Phillips soon married Rose Martin, daughter of locally beloved physician Doc Martin, and became a full-time resident. Sharp joined Phillips in 1902.

ART COLONIES

The art colony was a distinctly early modern phenomenon that appeared first in Europe. The earliest and best-known art colony, forming about 1830, was at Barbizon, a village not far south of Paris.[5] In the second half of the nineteenth century, realists, impressionists, post-impressionists, symbolists, and others formed art colonies at sites in Brittany, Normandy, north Germany, and elsewhere, where they would come to paint outdoors, en plein air, especially in the summer, when they could be away from their city studios. These artists were consciously seeking respite from the distractions and complexity of modern life. They felt alienated from an increasingly industrialized, urbanized world. Adding to their disaffection was the fact that many of them had been rejected by the juried salons. They desired congenial atmosphere in rural settings that would shield them not just from urban life but from the strictures of prevailing art academy norms and styles.

Some American artists experienced art colonies in Europe and in the mid-1880s began gathering in picturesque places on the East Coast. The Taos and Santa Fe art colonies came into being not long after the first ones in the Northeast. The Taos art colony flourished between about 1900 and about 1942. It was the first one in New Mexico and is widely regarded as the longest-enduring community of artists in the United States[6]—ending only with America's entry into World War II. After the war, a new generation of artists made their way to Taos, forming a very important bastion of modernism and revitalizing Taos as an art community.

Blumenschein's and Phillips's "discovery" of Taos was news in art circles in Paris, the Northeast, and the Midwest. Before too long, a number of other artists arrived, most spending only summers in Taos. Without modern conveniences, family members were reluctant to commit to coping year-round with hand-drawn water, outdoor privies, wood fires for indoor heating, and unpaved streets. Conditions changed gradually, and in time many artists made Taos home.

By 1914, five accomplished artists had joined Sharp and Phillips in Taos. Oscar E. Berninghaus, from St. Louis, was there every summer after 1900. Eanger Irving Couse came from Michigan first in 1902. One of Blumenschein's students at New York City's Art Students League, W. Herbert ("Buck") Dunton, showed up in 1912, and two years later Victor Higgins left New York for Taos. That same year they were joined by Walter Ufer, who had studied in Munich and left Chicago to settle in Taos. All except Dunton had extensive training and were experienced commercial artists. Most painted in Taos in the summer and went East to their jobs as illustrators for the rest of the year. In 1919 Ernest and Mary Blumenschein made the decision to stay year-round. Their timing coincided almost exactly with the burgeoning of the art colony movement in America.[7] Berninghaus established his home in Taos in 1925.

The Blumenschein house and studio on Ledoux Street, donated to Taos as a museum by Ernest and Mary's daughter, Helen Greene Blumenschein, is a precious time capsule of how the early Taos artists lived and how faithful they were to indigenous architecture and a simple way of life. Likewise, the studios of Joseph Henry Sharp and E. Irving Couse, adjacent to each other on Kit Carson Road, are kept much as they were when these early artists were painting there.[8]

In July 1915 Sharp, Blumenschein, Dunton, Phillips, Berninghaus, and Couse formed the Taos Society of Artists as a vehicle for promoting their work in the world beyond northern New Mexico. They successfully arranged for "circuit exhibitions," which traveled to New York, Boston, Chicago, St. Louis, Des Moines, Denver, Los Angeles, Pasadena, and Salt Lake City. Others admitted as active members a few years later were Walter Ufer, Victor Higgins, and Julius Rolshoven. The last three active members—Catherine C. Critcher, E. Martin Hennings, and Kenneth Adams—were elected in the 1920s. The society's associate member category included some very distinguished American artists: Robert Henri, Albert Groll, Randall Davey, B. J. O. Nordfeldt, Birger Sandzen, and Gustave Baumann, all associated more with Santa Fe than with Taos.

The Taos Society of Artists was the core of the Taos art colony. Members were committed to creating art that would be recognized as authentically American and not derivative or imitative of European art. An early twentieth-century American perception that Indians were fast disappearing was generating much popular interest in Indian life. Taos artists had differing styles, but their subject matter—Indians and Indian life, landscapes of the high desert, and depictions of life in adobe villages—made them recognizably of the desert Southwest. And unlike most of the other American art colonies—whose members were generally a closed coterie of aesthetes—Taos artists and their families were active participants in local social and political affairs. For example, they were enthusiastic participants in the Taos Fiestas de Santiago y Santa Ana in the 1930s, dressing up and decorating carts for the fiestas parades.

Because of their excellence, ingenuity, and enterprise, these artists were able to support themselves and take care of their families in a remote place that lacked local collectors and spaces where they could show and sell their art. They collaborated with artists in Santa Fe in marketing the Santa Fe-Taos School, and, as Blumenschein wrote in 1919, "The Taos school of painting . . . probably has done as much as any other publicity agent in booming New Mexico."[9] The Santa Fe Railway Company and Fred Harvey Company, promoting the Southwest as a tourist destination, purchased paintings by Taos and Santa Fe colony artists. They displayed them in their restaurants and station waiting rooms along the railroad line and reproduced them on posters and promotional calendars. Subsidized by the Santa Fe Railway to encourage western tourism, some painters opened their studios to tourists, who came by motor coach to watch them paint.

Throughout the 1920s and 1930s few local galleries existed, although some work could be seen publicly at the Harwood Foundation on Ledoux Street and in the lobby of Don Fernando Hotel on the west side of the plaza. In 1929 Hilda Braun Boulton began showing and selling paintings by some of Taos' best artists in a small shop a few doors down from the Don Fernando Hotel, and Millicent Bailey opened her Taos Art Shop on Pueblo Road. Early modernist and transcendentalist artist Emil Bisttram opened The Heptagon on the north side of the plaza in 1934. The Depression was not an auspicious time to be trying to sell art, however.

MABEL DODGE LUHAN

Mabel Ganson Evans Dodge Sterne's discovery of Taos had an incalculable impact on Taos as an art colony and community. A wealthy society matron from a Buffalo banking family, Mabel was with her third husband, Latvia-born painter and sculptor Maurice Sterne, and was in her early forties when she embraced Taos. That was in 1916. She had lived in Italy and been a renowned salon hostess in New York's Greenwich Village. Seeking enlightenment and a new scene, she took the advice of her mentor, writer Mary Austin, and traveled to Santa Fe, where Austin was a driving force in the Santa Fe arts community. Still restless, Mabel came north to Taos with her husband and her only child, John Evans Jr. She fell under Taos' spell and soon was attracted to Taos Indian Antonio Lujan (she called him Tony Luhan), whom she married in 1923 after divorcing Sterne.[10] She and Tony were a positive force in the community—employing many locals and advocating for Indian causes at the state and national levels. Still, they were contro-versial in many ways, and toward the end of her life she expressed disenchantment with some of the people she and Tony had tried to "help." She spent the balance of her life in Taos and is buried in Kit Carson Cemetery.

Mabel had a deep fondness for the local indigenous architecture. She built her "Big House" on Morada Lane on twelve acres that had been Indian land before Tony helped arrange its purchase. They added guest quarters, including adobe *casitas*. Locals referred to the compound as "Mabeltown"; she thought of it as a creative center, and in her last years she built a pueblo-style house south of the Big House, which she occupied until her death in 1962.

Several friends from her New York days arrived. Andrew Dasburg, an early mod-ernist artist, and John Collier, a sociologist, stayed on in Taos. Collier later became commissioner of the Bureau of Indian Affairs under Franklin Delano Roosevelt. Among the many creative individuals Mabel coaxed into visiting Taos were Georgia O'Keeffe, Aldous Huxley, Mary Austin, Thornton Wilder, Leo Stein, Leopold Stokowski, Carl Jung, and Frank Waters. D. H. Lawrence, the jewel in Mabel's crown, spent altogether two years in Taos. He arrived with wife, Frieda, and painter Lady Dorothy Brett. Many tales and legends evolved from the Lawrences' periods of residence. After a particularly disruptive visit and to put the Lawrences and Lady Brett at a distance, Mabel gave Frieda Lawrence a 166-acre ranch 17 miles north of Taos at the edge of San Cristóbal.[11] In exchange, Frieda gave Mabel the original manuscript for *Sons and Lovers*.[12] Other notables who came and went were writers Carl Van Vechten, Walter Van Tilburg Clark, and Robinson Jeffers; painters John Marin, Marsden Hartley, Robert Henri; photographer Ansel Adams; and linguist, novelist, and ethnomusicologist Jaime de Angulo.

Following World War I and during the twenties and thirties, many more fine artists took up residence in Taos: Grace Ravlin, Howard Norton Cook, Joseph Imhof, Ila McAfee and her husband, Elmer P. Turner, John Young-Hunter, Nicolai Fechin, Joseph Fleck, Leon Gaspard, Blanche C. Grant, Emil Bisttram, Rebecca Salsbury James, Regina Cooke, Gisella Loeffler, Eleanora Kissel, Gene Kloss, Loren Mozley, Ralph M. Pearson, Laverne Nelson Black, Kenneth Miller Adams, John Ward Lockwood, Thomas and Dorothy Benrimo, Barbara Latham, Cady Wells, Wood Woolsey and brother Carl Woolsey. Their work is representational yet unmistakably modern, and many continued the tradition of painting subjects local to the Southwest. Some of them show decidedly original modernist influences.

THE WPA AND ITS EFFECT IN TAOS

The Works Progress Administration's Public Works of Art Project (PWAP), organized in 1933 during the Great Depression, offered work to artists throughout America. The New Mexico program, under the direction of native New Mexican artist Vernon Hunter, had a great impact on the Taos community. It resulted in murals in public buildings, photographic projects, easel paintings, and sculptures, many of which reside today in the National Archives; artists were required to submit artwork at regular intervals. Guidebooks, oral histories, and recordings of folk music—all WPA projects—comprise an invaluable record of the times.

A most important legacy of the PWAP program in Taos are the Old Court House murals: ten monumental fresco paintings still on the walls of the former courtroom on the second floor of the old county courthouse on Taos' main plaza. Emil Bisttram, who had studied for a few months with Diego Rivera in Mexico, directed Ward Lockwood, Victor Higgins, and Bert Phillips in the mural cycle. Referencing Rivera and José Clemente Orozco in style, these visually and emotionally powerful panels with themes of law and justice are titled in both Spanish and English: *Avarice Breeds Crime/Avaricia Engendra Crimen* and *The Shadow of Crime/La Sombra de Crimen* are two examples.

With WPA support, John Young-Hunter took particular interest in the Spanish-American wood sculptor Patrocino Barela, a natural artist unschooled in formal art. Barela's philosophy set him on a course different from the work of the traditional santeros, although he was interpreting Bible stories. Barela worked at the Harwood

Foundation, which now owns about fifty of his wood carvings. Other artists who were in the WPA Arts programs were Gene Kloss, Regina Tatum Cooke, Gisella Loeffler, Ila McAfee, Walter Ufer, Oscar Berninghouse and his artist son, Charles, Ernest Blumenschein, Buck Dunton and Nellie Dunton, Cora Easton Kitts, Joseph Fleck, Blanche C. Grant, E. Martin Hennings, Joseph Imhof, Woody Crumbo, Cady Wells, Antonio Archuleta, Pop Chalee (Merina Lujan), Nat Kaplan, and Spanish Colonial furniture maker Maximo Luna. During this period Martin Shaffer turned from painting to photography, setting up his studio in Walter Ufer's old space on DesGeorges Lane. John Collier Jr. was photographing in Taos as well as in Peñasco and the Moreno Valley for the Farm Security Administration. Collier created an invaluable record of traditional Hispanic lifeways and culture while it was still undiluted. The WPA also made restorations on the Harwood Foundation building's light fixtures and Spanish Colonial furniture.

From 1945 to 1960

After World War II, a great many new artists and writers came to Taos, some as visitors and others as residents. It was a restless time, just as it was after World War I, when Mabel Dodge and her friends came. Creative people were seeking new stimuli and fellowship. From that period evolved the Taos Modernists of the 1940s and 1950s and also galleries that exhibited their work: The Blue Door, on Kit Carson Road; the Stables, just north of the Taos Inn and then an adjunct of the Taos Art Association; Eulalia Emetaz's La Galería Escondida on Lower Ranchitos Road, one of the first galleries outside of New York City to show modernist art, and the Ruins Gallery in Ranchos de Taos.

The Taos Modernists are recognized as a significant art-historical force. Their lively presence in the community and their national reputations solidified Taos' status as an important, serious arts community. As a group, the Taos Modernists pushed to evolve new modes of perceiving and being in the world, even as they developed new ways of making art. Like their famous counterparts in Greenwich Village, some spent nights discussing art and philosophy, drinking, dancing, and listening to jazz. At the Old Martinez dance hall, opposite San Francisco de Asís in Ranchos de Taos, some of them painted whimsical murals, now covered over.

Some of those modernists were Wolcott Ely, Beatrice Mandelman, Louis Ribak, Oli Sihvonen, Leo Garel, Toni Mygatt, Louise Ganthiers, Alfred Rogoway, Clay Spohn, Cliff and Barbara Harmon, Stella Snead, Malcolm Brown, Arthur Jacobson, Rita Deanin Abbey, John dePuy, Edward Corbett, Earl Stroh, Louis Catusco, Robert Ray, Michael Klein, Lily Fenichel, and Agnes Martin, the last attaining international fame. Weavers Rachel Brown, Joan Potter Sihvonen Loveless, and Kristina Brown Wilson encouraged a renaissance of traditional weaving, at times incorporating a modernist aesthetic in their work. A good number of students came through Taos on the GI Bill, an assistance program for war veterans. Among them were Ted Egri and Cliff Harmon, both of whom remained in Taos. Two other modernists arrived in the late fifties: Wesley Rusnell and Adeine De La Noe.

During this period, Taos also attracted many artists working in representational styles, including Bettina Steinke, Leslie Brown, Leal Mack, Richard Schmidt, Doel Reed, Art Merrill, Mario Larrinaga, Eric Gibbard, and Charles Reynolds. Helen Greene Blumenschein, daughter of Ernest and Mary Greene Blumenschein, was a gifted printmaker. More galleries opened: Gallery A; Reynolds Gallery, operated by artist Charles Reynolds; the Rosequist Gallery (now the Mission Gallery and featuring both traditional and modernist art); the Merrill Gallery, which showcased artist Art Merrill's work; and Jane Hiatt's Village Gallery, which exhibited art of both traditional and modernist groups.

Art schools were an important draw. Emil Bisttram's Taos School of Art (later the Bisttram School of Fine Art) was the first, started in the mid-forties. Summer field schools drew students from UNM and Baylor University. For several years following World War II, Louis Ribak operated the Taos Valley Art School in Walter Ufer's old studio.

Taos' renown as an arts community is due in part to visionary women. Mabel Dodge Luhan was the first. Elizabeth (Lucy Case) Harwood, Helene Wurlitzer, Millicent Rogers, and Eulalia Emetaz, of La Galeria Escondido, followed. For many decades the cultural heart of the community was the Harwood Foundation, referred to locally as "the Harwood." What became a community institution grew from the generosity of Elizabeth Harwood, who with her painter and photographer husband, Burt (Elihu Burritt) Harwood, arrived in Taos about 1917. They purchased property at the end of Ledoux Street, combined several small adobe buildings, and created a large complex, including several apartments with baths, a rarity in Taos in those days.

Elizabeth Harwood's service to the community began when she started a lending library in her home. After her husband's death in 1922, she incorporated the complex as the Harwood Foundation "to establish and maintain in the town of Taos a public library, museum and other educational agencies." Before her death in 1938 she deeded the property to the University of New Mexico, which oversees the Harwood Foundation and the Harwood Museum of Art to this day.

Over the years and through the generosity of its patrons and sponsors, the library grew into a unique space, with the top shelves holding sculptures by Patrocino Barela and the foyer exhibiting East Indian and Persian miniatures, which Mabel Dodge Luhan had donated. One downstairs room was filled with art books. Above the stairs were two galleries—a large one that held works by the Taos art colony founders and other early artists, the other that provided space for contemporary exhibitions. In the large gallery, which had a small stage and a piano, lectures, classes, plays, concerts, foreign film screenings, and Christmas crafts sales took place. In that gallery were more Barelas, Spanish Colonial artifacts, and traditional furniture, a craft locally revived under the WPA program. Under University of New Mexico auspices, art classes were offered first in 1923. From 1929 to 1955 the university held summer art field schools taught by local artists. A bookmobile operated out of the library, going into area villages to provide reading matter to school students and the general populace. The Harwood was an aesthetic treasure house, welcoming all and still remembered with fond nostalgia.

Millicent Rogers (1902–53) discovered Taos in 1947. Wealthy, beautiful, gifted, and with an infallible eye for quality and beauty, in the six years she lived in Taos she amassed an astonishing collection of silver and turquoise jewelry by Pueblo, Navajo, Zuni, and Hopi silversmiths and some of the best examples of Navajo and Rio Grande weavings. She designed jewelry that was bold and refined, theatrical and fanciful. After she died, her family opened her collections to the public as the Millicent Rogers Museum, first in 1956 on Ledoux Street and in the 1960s in its present location, the rambling old adobe four miles north of Taos, built by Claude J. K. and Elizabeth Anderson and given to the museum by the Anderson family.

Another woman of vision, Helene Wurlitzer, brought two plus generations of artists and writers to Taos. Heiress to the organ and jukebox family's wealth, she set up the Wurlitzer Foundation along the lines of Yaddo and the McDowell colonies. In 1954, with the help of the first director, Henry Sauerwein, she built and refurbished cottages where artists were invited to stay and work for periods of time. For the most part, the foundation gave residence grants, but it assisted Andrew Dasburg when he was ill and furnished Agnes Martin funds for art supplies during a lean period of her life in Taos. Some of the notable artists during the fifty-year operation of the foundation who stayed on to make Taos home were Robert Ray, Earl Stroh, Oli Sihvonen and Joan Loveless, Bill Heaton, Lawrence Calcagno, Hyde Soloman, Robert D. Ellis, Marcia Oliver, and Michio Takayama. Composer/pianist Noel Farrand, another Wurlitzer resident, lived in Taos for twelve years and was instrumental in forming the renowned summer chamber music festival, Music from Angel Fire.

Artists continue to come to work and live in Taos. It is still a comparatively quiet place, but now it is open to the outside world. Today the little mud village with unpaved, unlit streets and piñon smoke hanging in the air lingers only in the memories of the old. As Mabel Dodge Luhan said more than sixty years ago at the end of her book *Taos and Its Artists*, "The genius loci is still exerting its age-old influence."[13]

NOTES

1. Mildred Tolbert died in Taos in early 2008, when this chapter was in its first draft. Although she did not refer to herself as one of the notable Taos artists of the twentieth century, Tolbert was one of its most celebrated photographers and a treasured member

of the arts community and the Taos County Historical Society. Julia Moore, editor of this book, took over for Tolbert and completed the chapter.

2. Because there is an extensive body of literature, the popular arts of Spanish New Mexico have they are not treated here. For the most comprehensive overview, see E. Boyd, *Popular Arts of Spanish New Mexico* (Santa Fe: Museum of New Mexico Press, 1974).

3. "I Saw Whole Paintings Right Before My Eyes; The Founding of the Taos Art Colony," in *El Palacio* (Winter-Spring 1998–99).

4. Ernest L. Blumenschein, "Origins of the Taos Art Colony," *Taos Valley News* (May 15, 1926), 1.

5. The leading Barbizon painters included Jean-Baptiste Camille Corot, Théodore Rousseau, and Jean-François Millet, all of whom concentrated on landscape and scenes of rural life painted from nature.

6. Arrell Morgan Gibson, *The Santa Fe and Taos Colonies: Age of the Muses 1900–1942* (Norman: University of Oklahoma Press, 1983), 8.

7. Mary Shepard Greene Blumenschein was herself an accomplished Paris-trained painter and was the first woman artist to make Taos her permanent home.

8. Joseph Henry Sharp often left his home in Taos and traveled to paint Plains Indians and scenes of their lives. E. I. Couse painted Taos Indians almost exclusively and was very successful. In 2012, the Couse Foundation was able to purchase the Sharp Studio and Couse House and Studio complex, thus ensuring its future as a living museum. The Couse family donated the original furnishings and belongings, down to the smallest paperweight and brush.

9. "Blumenschein Is Interviewed *(Albuquerque Evening Herald)*," *El Palacio* 6, no. 6 (March 1, 1919): 85.

10. In 1933, The Museum of Modern Art in New York gave Maurice Sterne its first one-man show. He died in 1957.

11. Today the D. H. Lawrence Ranch is owned and maintained by the University of New Mexico.

12. *Sons and Lovers* (1913) was considered Lawrence's first masterpiece. The ranch, which Lawrence named Kiowa Ranch, is the D. H. Lawrence Ranch.

13. Mabel Dodge Luhan, *Taos and Its Artists* (New York: Duell, Sloan and Pearce, 1947), 43.

SELECTED REFERENCES

Bell, Robert, and James Mann. *Mildred Tolbert: Among the Taos Moderns.* Santa Fe: Bell Tower Editions, 2006.

Bickerstaff, Laura M. *Pioneer Artists of Taos.* Denver: Sage Books, 1955; reprint, Denver: Old West Publishing, 1983.

Bustard, Bruce I. *A New Deal for the Arts.* Seattle: University of Washington Press, 1997.

Coke, Van Deren. *Taos and Santa Fe: The Artists' Environments, 1882–1942.* Albuquerque: University of New Mexico Press, 1963.

Egri, Kit. "Twenty Years of TAA 1964–1984." Unpublished article.

Ellis, Robert M. "History and Collection." Taos, NM: Harwood Museum of Art, 1994.

Flynn, Kathryn A., ed. *Treasures of New Mexico Trails: Discover New Deal Art and Architecture.* Santa Fe: Sunstone Press, 1995.

Gibson, Arrell Morgan. *The Santa Fe and Taos Colonies: Age of the Muses 1900–1942.* Norman: University of Oklahoma Press, 1983.

Leavitt, Virginia Couse. "Taos and the American Art Colony Movement: The Search for an American School of Art," *Ayer Y Hoy* (Winter 1987), 3–8.

Luhan, Mabel Dodge. *Taos and Its Artists.* New York: Duell, Sloan and Pearce, 1947.

Neff, Emily Ballew. *The Modern West: American Landscapes 1890–1950.* New Haven, CT, and London: Yale University Press, 2006.

Nelson, Mary Carroll. *The Legendary Artists of Taos.* New York: Watson-Guptill, 1980.

Porter, Dean A. *Enchanted Visions: The Taos Society of Artists and Ancient Cultures.* Spokane, WA: Northwest Museum of Arts and Culture, 2005.

Porter, Dean A., Teresa Hayes Ebie, and Suzan Campbell. *Taos Artists and Their Patrons 1898–1950.* Notre Dame, IN: The Snite Museum of Art, Notre Dame University, 1999.

Romancito, Rick. "Earth and Paint," *Tempo*, Jan. 23–29, 2003, published by *The Taos News.*

Rudnik, Louis Palken. *Utopian Vistas.* Albuquerque: University of New Mexico Press, 1996.

"70 years of Taos Art." "Taos Art '78." Supplements to *The Taos News*, Sept. 12, 1968, and Sept. 14, 1978.

Taos Municipal Schools Historic Art Collection Committee. IMSHAC Catalogue. Taos, NM: Taoseño Publishing, 2003.

Udall, Sharyn Rohlfsen. *Modernist Painting in New Mexico 1913–1935.* Albuquerque: University of New Mexico Press, 1984.

White, Robert R., ed. *The Taos Society of Artists.* 2nd ed. Albuquerque: University of New Mexico Press, 1998.

Witt, David L. *Modernists in Taos: From Dasburg to Martin.* Santa Fe: Red Crane Books, 2002.

———. *The Taos Artists: A Historical Narrative and Biographical Dictionary.* Colorado Springs, CO: Ewell Fine Art Publications, 1984.

———. *Taos Moderns: Art of the New.* Santa Fe: Red Crane Books, 1992.

Witt, David L., ed. *Three Taos Pueblo Painters: Albert Looking Elk Martinez, Albert Lujan, Juan Miribal.* Exh. cat. Taos, NM: Harwood Museum of Art, 2003.

21

When Nothing Was Store-Bought

DOROTHY ZOPF

The Taos Valley's remote location and limited growing season were the mothers of ingenuity. Until well into the nineteenth century, manufactured goods—clothing, farm equipment, and furniture— were not available. Dorothy Zopf, an authority on northern New Mexico's quilting traditions, reminds us here of how the people of Taos Pueblo and early settlers used what nature provided to clothe themselves, keep warm, and embellish their surroundings.

BEFORE HISTORICAL TIMES, what did the Tiwa people of Taos Pueblo do for clothes, utensils, and tools? Part of the answer is found in the pueblo's geography. Taos is a river pueblo, but on a mountain plateau not far from the Great Plains and bison-hunting Indians. Both the Pueblo and Plains Indians were users of skins, and Taos clothing was influenced by that of the nomadic Indians with whom they traded for centuries. Clothing also reflected the animals they hunted: deerskin moccasins, buckskin leggings, buffalo robes, and rabbit-skin blankets. The men wore deerskin leggings and shirts, the women fringed dresses and *mantas* (shawls) made of woven cotton.

The scraping and tanning of hides was a time-consuming process, and no part of the animal was to be wasted. Hooves were made into rattles, other parts were used in costume decoration, and the furred skin of the heads was saved for dancing masks. A special use of soft deerskin is women's wedding boots. The number of folds in a woman's wedding boots indicated family wealth, that is, the amount of "leisure" time available for tanning the hides. These dress boots still are made of deerskin whitened with a wash of kaolin (white clay). The many folds give them a thick look but make the feet appear small and dainty. The sole is made from the tough, blackened neck skin of the deer. The whitened skin is sewn to the sole and pleated above the ankle into as few as two to as many as five folds. As the soles wear through, a pleat might be loosened and the top pulled down to sew onto a new sole. A pair of moccasins made for a woman at the time of her marriage could last the rest of her life.

Traditionally, men were the weavers and moccasin makers, while women did pottery and basketry. But rabbit-skin blankets, for which Taos Pueblo is famed, were always woven by women. These rabbit-fur blankets are made using spun yucca fiber wrapped with one-quarter-inch-wide strips of rabbit skin. The furry strips are wet when wound so that as they dry they stick together as if glued. This long base strand—about fifty feet—is looped over a pole that is either hung from above or staked in the ground. The yucca-fiber strand is twined around, alternating with rabbit-skin strips cut from the hide in a long circular spiral. The process is what we might call finger weaving. The same technique is used with a warp of yucca coated with wet turkey-down feathers—each little quill, when dry, curls securely around the yucca. Both schemes produce a wonderfully warm woven blanket.

Before the Spanish, the Pueblos used fibers to braid three or more strands and looped them as in finger crochet. (The crochet hook and knitting needles were Spanish introductions.) These fibers were prepared by family members using a drop spindle. They included milkweed and the hair of dogs, mountain sheep, bears, and humans. Yucca fibers were most common. The fur of beaver, otter, and rabbit and the down of turkey, duck, and eagle were combined with yucca, as described above, to make warmer or more ornamental fabrics.

While tanned skins were used for everyday clothing, ceremonial costumes were more fanciful. Cotton could not be grown in the Taos climate, so dancers traded for much of their embroidered paraphernalia. At Taos a deer dancer wore the entire deerskin except for the hooves; those were removed and replaced in front with two sticks held in the hands to represent legs. Of course, with the arrival of the Spanish, followed by Euro-Americans, things changed. Store-bought trousers became popular until, by a ruling of the pueblo's Council of Governors in 1941, men were no longer permitted to wear modern trousers. As a compromise, the seat was removed and replaced by a breechclout (loincloth). Even in the twenty-first century in Taos one may see an Indian man standing in the grocery checkout line wearing work boots with the raised heel removed to make the boots look more like moccasins.

Taos Pueblo pottery has also undergone a change. Until the Pueblo Revolt of 1680, the pottery was a black-on-white carbon-paint ware. After the revolt it was replaced by micaceous ware. This pottery has no slip, fires to a tan color with the occasional black fire cloud, and sparkles with flecks of mica. Since there is no painted decoration, the pots are sometimes trimmed around the neck with a rope of pinched clay. The shapes tend to be taller and thinner than other pueblos' pottery and, in more recent times, often have handles and covers.

Baskets at Taos Pueblo were made only of willow, split and whole, and peeled and unpeeled. Starting with a cross of four and four, the base was woven round and round to the desired size. Then the sides would be woven in groups of four more delicate branches.

By the nineteenth century, most Spanish homes were furnished with *bancos,* wall cupboards, and *nichos* (niches formed in the adobe walls). Mattresses were placed on the bancos as cushions and then unrolled on the floor for sleeping. These were covered with patterned woven blankets, called *jergas.* Movable furniture included upright armoires and *trasteros* and also chests used for storing clothing, dishes, and food. Beds, a four-legged curiosity, came with Euro-Americans. A bed was a wooden frame laced with ropes covered with a cloth bag filled with raw wool. These utilitarian furnishings were made in the home. Father taught son, mother taught daughter, and the extended family could also be involved.

With the publication of the first Montgomery Ward catalog in 1877, the railroad's arrival in New Mexico in 1879, Sears, Roebuck & Co.'s founding in 1887, and rural free delivery of mail starting in 1896, things were bound to change. The world was now at their fingertips, and people wanted to move beyond the old ways. In 1927 the Spanish Colonial arts display at the Fine Arts Museum in Santa Fe included only blankets, handmade furniture, carved figures, braided rugs, hooked rugs, and crochet work. A beautiful heritage was almost lost.

But in 1933 the New Mexico State Department of Vocational Education launched a training program in Taos and other small communities to teach traditional Spanish crafts and how to market them. These crafts included weaving, tanning and leatherwork, furniture making, and ornamental ironwork. The aim was to make items that were superior to machine-made products in both authenticity and quality of construction. By 1934 Elidio Gonzales was training at the Taos center to make hand-carved pegged pine Spanish Colonial–style furniture. That same year Antonio Frutuoso Tafoya made twenty-two pieces of joined furniture in pine for the school. These men were quickly followed by the esteemed Max Luna, who began teaching in 1936. Luna also hand-forged the iron fittings for his furniture. "The wooden surfaces were decorated in a variety of methods: relief carving, painting, and straw appliqué in motifs of pomegranates, rosettes, vines, and scrollwork (combed tooth and bullet borders) as well as purely geometric compositions."[1] Since neither weaving nor freehand embroidery had entirely died out by the 1930s, the State Department of Education did not have to revive these traditional arts. They had only to publish bulletins emphasizing the old designs and techniques of hand spinning and dyeing.

Almost every girl learned embroidery: outline and chain stitches, the satin stitch, and the long and short stitch, which made it possible to delicately shade a flower petal or animal form by using a darker color alternately long and short at the outer edge of a petal and then continuing in a lighter shade toward the center. By the 1890s embroidery thread of cotton or silk was available in Taos stores. Cotton thread for crochet and tatting was also introduced. These, plus quilt making and embroidering scarves and pillowcases with a tatted edge, were crafts often practiced by Anglo women, and their Spanish neighbors learned them, too, as well as *colcha*, an older variety of needlework.

Colcha, which means bed covering, and colcha embroidery, which is used to create the colcha, began to appear in Nuevo México in the mid-eighteenth century. These colchas were used not only for bedspreads but also for altar cloths and wall hangings. The designs were derived from Chinese embroideries, painted chintz fabrics from India, and the embroidery of Spain and Mexico. Indian cottons from the Manila galleons were second only to the Chinese silks in popularity among the Mexicans. The tree of life, flowers, and leaves from these chintzes were often copied. Originally colchas were made from fine woolen homespun sewed onto a base of balanced white weave, a plain woolen fabric that was completely covered with the colcha stitch. Later a white cotton twill fabric began to be used, and only the motifs were embroidered. The woolen yarns were dyed with chamisa for bright yellow, roots of *canyaigre* for golden yellow, indigo traded from Mexico for blue, an overdye of blue and yellow for green, and black and brown from the natural sheep colors. Red and violet were also from an imported dye, cochineal.

The colcha stitch provides an interesting texture, is free flowing, and does not waste yarn on the backside. The stitch is begun by taking a few running stitches under the area to be covered; there is no knot. Then the needle is brought up on the left edge of the design area and down on the right edge. This strand of yarn is then held in place by couching, or whipping over it, from right to left at regular intervals. The more diagonal the binding stitch, the less yarn will appear on the back. Row two is laid directly above row one, and so on. The yarn is finished by weaving the needle under several stitches on the back. The sections, flower petals for instance, may be worked in various directions for shading and variety. An irregular shape is usually begun in the middle, finished at the top, and then the whole is reversed to complete the bottom half. Colchas are frequently finished with simple woolen fringe tied on all four sides.

Rebecca Salsbury James, a Taos artist famed for her paintings on glass and her colcha embroideries, said of the Taoseña who taught her the technique, "Jesuita Penault lived in a small adobe across the street from our own [on Bent Street]. I used to walk across the street at night for a Spanish lesson. . . . [One night] she showed me an embroidery she was making with the *colcha* stitch. I thought 'This is for me. Here are form, color, skill.' A piece of fabric, needle and thread to make a painting in yarn."[2] That was in 1937. In 1963 she added, "This versatile stitch . . . can bring to life the living world about one. . . . It holds firmly and proceeds rapidly. It is no good with stamped patterns—it craves original designs."[3] James used flattened, unwound gold and silver thread, pure wool, mercerized cotton, and spool silk. Her embroideries ranged from bedspread size to miniatures, and she did landscapes and florals as well as religious themes.

Meanwhile, spurred by the work of restoring old colchas for a Taos commercial patron, a new colcha tradition began in the 1930s in Carson, New Mexico, west of Taos. These stitchers once again covered the entire surface using images of saints and scenes with bison and wagon trains. With the impetus from Rebecca James and Nellie Dunton of Taos, and the drawings of old designs by Carmen Espinosa for the New Mexico State Department of Vocational Education, the survival of colcha seemed secure. And it has continued to evolve. The embroidery yarn is now commercial knitting yarn, and the ground fabric may be nothing fancier than cotton feed sacks. Conventional stitches may also be included, such as French knots, outline, long and short, and buttonhole.

Another craft revived by the Department of Vocational Education and funded by the WPA was tinwork. The local book of designs was again drawn by Carmen Espinosa. Tin plate had been imported from Mexico in the early nineteenth century, but the craft really took off after 1846 when the U.S. Army brought in supplies in tin containers. Glass and wallpaper, unavailable before the opening of the Santa Fe Trail, added to the tinsmith's supplies. Thus with American materials and Mexican styles and techniques, the tinsmith produced tin frames, candle sconces, chandeliers, and processional crosses. The Taos "Senate style" of tin frames is easy to recognize because of the bold, saw-toothed edges and much stamping with a serrated bar tool. These older pieces were produced between 1870 and 1905, easy dates to confirm because of can labels on the underside.

Straw appliqué was another art revived by the Federal Arts Project of the WPA. The carefully cut bits of golden straw, split and flattened, were embedded in boards covered with pitch that was blackened with soot. These were made into crosses, plaques, and boxes in the late eighteenth and early nineteenth centuries.

"Worn but warm" became a household motto. "Hey, this is good to make a blanket out of. Why waste it?" The layered bed coverings known today as quilts were first called colchas or blankets. The Spanish women did piecework, as they called it, to make serviceable covers for their worn and patched woven blankets. These were tacked or tied together.

Learning to make quilts was a process of apprenticeship. Either mother and daughter, or, on a larger scale, all the female relatives gathered together for a day of cutting, assembling, and tying as many quilts as there was fabric. Although electricity was not generally available in Taos until 1943, by the turn of the twentieth century many homes had treadle sewing machines. The fabric came from coats and jackets, nightgowns, curtains, aprons, bedspreads, drapes, shirts, blouses, jeans and trousers, mattress ticking, rags from the machine shop, anything that was still flexible. The quilts were not necessarily meant to be attractive. Most were used by harvesters and herders for sleeping outdoors, for lining the wagon bed and cold cellar, and to throw over the backs of horses. However, every seamstress kept her eye out for special colors and pleasing combinations, and new fabric was highly prized. Amelia Jaramillo said of her father, Alfredo Trujillo (1895–1964), "Besides being a schoolteacher and a judge in Taos, he was a Gibson Company suit salesman. From his samples my mother, Pilar, made many quilts."[4] Another source of "almost new" was flour and tobacco sacking. These sources made regular-sized patches, and when cutting from scraps the only requirement was that the patches be all of the same length. Then the cut pieces were sewn together into long strips and joined, one strip above another, from selvage to selvage. The older and even more ragged scraps were pieced together for a lining.

There is seldom a distinction between the front and back of these old-style covers. They were made like pillowcases, to be untied and slipped off the fill for washing. An assembled quilt was tied with the string saved from sugar, flour, and tobacco sacks, or with crochet cotton or embroidery floss. Quilting, the fine running stitch that holds the top, fill, and backing together, was an American addition, as were the carefully cut and pieced patchwork patterns of the eastern United States. Spanish women learned from their Anglo neighbors to cut and piece in a pattern and did many a fancy quilt for use only in the house. Churn Dash, Grandmother's Flower Garden, and Double Wedding Ring were popular patterns. These quilters also appliquéd freehand-cut flowers, animals, and birds, and embroidered both from printed patterns and from imagination. Whether from a magazine picture or an actual example, freestyle embroidery on a crazy quilt was popular.

An impressive number of everyday utensils were made at home by the Spanish settlers. In the eighteenth century all seem to have been made of wood. The earliest Spanish piece in the Millicent Rogers Museum is a hand-hewn pitchfork made from one solid piece of oak; it has three tines, each bound at the base with rawhide. There were hand-carved wooden snow shovels, bread paddles, adobe molds, wooden bowls, and a winnowing box made of pierced leather in a wooden frame. Metal appears later in the form of trivets and fireplace andirons, a two-pronged fork, an ice hook, a shoe last, an axe blade, and a cooking spoon.

Personal adornment has always been an art. The Pueblo peoples decorated themselves with jewelry made from shells—whole or cut into disc-shaped heishi beads—bear claws, and precious stones like agate and turquoise, coral, and trade beads. They used bright-colored feathers in their hair and on clothing. Both men and women painted their bodies after reaching adulthood, with colors from rock or clay. Iron made red, brown, yellow, and orange; copper produced blue and green; magnesium made black; kaolin was white. Grinding these materials into a fine powder was done with a mano and metate either openly by young girls or secretly by boys in the kivas. Colors were applied to the body by mixing with grease. The Chifonetes or Koshare (ceremonial Pueblo clowns) are excellent examples of contemporary body painting.

The Spanish preference was for filigree jewelry, a delicate ornament made of fine gold or silver wire coiled in patterns and soldered into a heavier framework. The earliest known Taos filigree jeweler was Rafael Luna, born in 1802. The Luna family continued as filigree jewelers in the Taos area for four generations, the last being Antonio Luna, a brother of Max, the furniture maker. These were busy people for, according to oral tradition, suitors of the late 1800s were expected to provide their fiancées with sets of filigree jewelry which might include a necklace and earrings, a rosary, and a brooch or two.

In her memoirs, Taos writer Cleofas Jaramillo wrote eloquently of the toys her brothers made. Wistfully she said the girls were seldom allowed to play outdoors and, instead, stayed in the house to listen to the stories of the old women and perhaps play a quiet game. Perhaps, too, they cut multiple flower shapes from colored magazine covers to make long strings of *ramilletes* to decorate their rooms. The boys made bows from green willow sticks and arrows tipped with flint. Crooks (curved-end sticks) used in a hockey-like ball game *(chueco)* were made from green scrub-oak sticks. The boys would make several deep cuts in the broad end for a grip, heat the narrow end over coals, and then bend it into a curve which was tied around a fence post to harden. The balls were calf hide stuffed with rags. There were play violins cut out of a grocery box with a tin can tied to the back for a sounding board. The strings were cut from a section of sheep intestine that had been turned inside out, scraped, and dried.

Kathleen Michaels, a Pueblo Indian working at the Millicent Rogers Museum, responded to my question about what toys Taos Pueblo children made and played with by saying that Indian children played with their imaginations, running and hiding outdoors. Then, of course, the boys made bows and arrows and they also made balls to throw using leaves wrapped around with vines. There was also the big willow hoop pushed with a willow stick to race around the plaza. I pushed on about dolls. She thought hard and then said, "Maybe little clay and mud figures." Then came a smile and the memory of the stuffed squirrels, so soft and furry, that were made for little children.

NOTES

1. Stephen May, *Footloose on the Santa Fe Trail* (Boulder: University Press of Colorado, 1993), 60–61.

2. "Painting in Yarn: The Colcha Stitch," *Woman's Day* (April 1964), 40.

3. James, Rebecca, and Laura Gilpin. *Embroideries: The Colcha Knot Stitch* (Santa Fe: Museum of International Folk Art, 1963), 5.

4. Personal conversation with Amelia Jaramillo, Taos, 1993.

SELECTED REFERENCES

Bowen, Dorothy, Trish Spellman, and Nora Fisher. *Spanish Textile Tradition of New Mexico and Colorado*. Santa Fe: Museum of International Folk Art, Museum of New Mexico Press, 1979.

Cooperative Extension Service. "New Mexico Colonial Embroidery." Las Cruces: New Mexico State University, 1943.

Coulter, Lane, and Maurice Dixon Jr. *New Mexican Tinwork*. Albuquerque: University of New Mexico Press, 1944.

Dickey, Richard F. *New Mexico Village Arts*. Albuquerque: University of New Mexico Press, 1949.

Ellis, Susan H. *New Mexico Colcha Embroidery*. Albuquerque. NM: n.p. [8609 La Sala del Sur NE, 1980].

Gavin, Robin Farwell. *Traditional Arts of Spanish New Mexico*. Santa Fe: Museum of New Mexico Press, 1994.

Houlihan, Patrick, and Betsy Houlihan. *Lummis in the Pueblos*. Flagstaff, AZ: Northland Press, 1986.

James, Rebecca Salsbury. *Embroideries: The Colcha Stitch*. Santa Fe: Museum of International Folk Art, 1963.

———. *Rebecca Salisbury James and Her Legacy*. Exhibition catalog. Santa Fe: Museum of Fine Arts, 1992.

Jaramillo, Cleofas M. *Shadows of the Past*. 1941. Reprint, Santa Fe: Ancient City Press, 1972.

May, Stephen. *Footloose on the Santa Fe Trail*. Boulder: University Press of Colorado, 1993.

Museum of International Folk Art, Santa Fe. *Embroideries by Rebecca James*. Exh. cat. Santa Fe: Museum of International Folk Art, 1963.

Museum of Northern Arizona. *Tradition & Innovation: The Pottery of New Mexico's Pueblos*. Exh. cat. Flagstaff: Museum of Arizona, 1990.

Nestor, Sarah, ed. *The Spanish Textile Tradition of New Mexico & Colorado*. Santa Fe: Museum of New Mexico Press, 1979.

Ortiz, Alfonso. *Handbook of North American Indians, vol. 9, Southwest*. Washington, DC: Smithsonian Institution, 1979.

Parsons, Elsie Clews. *Taos Pueblo*. Menasha, WI: George Banta Publishing Co., 1936.

Roediger, Virginia Moore. *Ceremonial Costumes of the Pueblo Indians*. Berkeley: University of Califomia Press, 1941.

Taylor Museum of Colorado Springs Fine Arts Center. *Hispanic Crafts of the Southwest*. Colorado Springs: Taylor Museum of Colorado Springs Fine Arts Center, 1977.

Underhill, Ruth. "Pueblo Crafts." Phoenix, AZ: U.S. Indian Service Printing Department, Phoenix Indian School, 1944.

Weigle, Marta, ed. *Hispanic Myth and Ethno-History.* Santa Fe: Ancient City Press, 1983.

Wroth, William. *Weaving and Colcha from the Hispanic Southwest.* Santa Fe: Ancient City Press, 1985.

Wroth, William, and Robin Farwell Gavin, eds. *Converging Streams: Art of the Hispanic and Native American Southwest.* Santa Fe: Museum of Spanish Colonial Art, 2010.

Zopf, Dorothy R. *Surviving the Winter: The Evolution of Quiltmaking in New Mexico.* Albuquerque: University of New Mexico Press, 2001.

Once a common sight in the Taos Valley, this rustic treadle loom is now a museum piece. Courtesy Millicent Rogers Museum.

22

Four Centuries of Weavers
and Weaving in Taos

Juanita Jaramillo Lavadie

Weaving is one of the crafts that has evolved from the status of critical necessity to a specialized art form. Taoseña Juanita J. Lavadie traces the place of sheep farming, home production of wool, and weaving in the lives and economy of Upper Rio Grande Hispanic families of weavers from the earliest settlers well into the twentieth century.

THE EARLY SETTLERS ARRIVING IN THE TAOS VALLEY from Mexico soon learned how imperative it was to produce their own cloth if they were to survive the cold winters there. Wool was available with the sheep they brought, and it was needed in the cold high desert. In the agropastoral economy of the northern Rio Grande Valley, the development of a local weaving industry was a logical enterprise. Everyone worked, including children. Indigenous natives raised within Spanish families, *criados,* participated in wool preparation and weaving. When some criados returned to their tribes after living in a Spanish family, they took with them the techniques of working wool and applied this knowledge to the native upright loom, as opposed to the European horizontal loom.[1]

Frasadas or *sarapes* (blankets) not only functioned as a traditional means of conserving body heat and energy during cold winters but were appreciated as items of beauty in homes where hard work was a part of daily routine.[2] Weaving was a vehicle of aesthetic expression, particularly after the development of brilliant aniline dyes in the mid-1800s. Frasadas brightened the small, dark rooms of the old adobe homes with an explosion of bright colors that had never been available before.

The story of the Rio Grande Hispanic frasada has roots reaching back to distant lands and times. The Iberian Peninsula's connection with the Near Eastern world resulted in Turkish, Moroccan, and Persian textiles and designs, European floor looms, and Spanish sheep breeds coming to Veracruz, Mexico. The Spanish Manila galleon trade ships sailed out of the Philippines east over the Pacific Ocean to bring cargos of fine cloth, embroideries, tissue paper, and exotic furs. These items would make their way from the port of Acapulco, Mexico, to Santa Fe, and then to Taos. Pre-Columbian trade fairs/*cambalaches* already linked the Taos Valley to the Great Plains, most importantly through Taos' September trade fair.[3] Some early Spanish colonial families in Taos and northern Nuevo México traded in wool with Mexico and California. According to Nuevo México state records of Governor Luis de Rosas (1639), two major trade items going south from Santa Fe were furs and wool weavings. Trade and barter along the Camino Real trade route between Mexico City and Santa Fe was closely monitored and tallied, which was a benefit to Rio Grande weavers.

Mexico's *saltillo* blanket, with complex patterns of concentric diamonds outlined by varied detailing, was a direct ancestor of contemporary southwestern textile designs. Mexico also provided the cochineal red and the indigo blue dyes. From these origins, Nuevo México generated two major offshoots: the Puebloan and Diné/Navajo wool weavings on the upright loom, and the Rio Grande Hispanic wool textiles woven on the European horizontal loom.

The basic textile woven in the Southwest area was the *sabanilla,* a white woolen plain-weave cloth that was used as a *sabana* (sheet) or for clothing. The sabanilla was also the foundation cloth for *colcha* embroideries. Yards and yards of sabanilla cloth less than thirty inches wide were woven. These strips were stitched together to make larger pieces.

Along with the sabanilla, *jerga* (serge) cloth was frequently woven. Jerga is a heavier-weight weave used for rougher uses, such as floor coverings, work clothing, or for *colchon* (mattress) bags. Jerga was woven on a four-harness loom with a variation of white and natural black warps. In some jergas, the white was dyed red or blue. The weft was woven across in the same repetitions, producing a sort of checkerboard plaid with a diagonal twill weave. The resulting block pattern is similar to what is now called "buffalo plaid," and *ciboleros,* the old-time bison hunters from Hispanic Nuevo Méxicano villages, would wear shirts made of woolen jerga cloth. It was also woven in a kind of diamond twill pattern called *ojo de perdiz* (partridge eye). The heaviest woven cloth was *huangoche,* which is similar to burlap. Sometimes woven from goat hair, huangoche was too coarse to wear. It was used for cargo bags and for storage in the *soterraño* (cellar).

Sheep and Wool

Wool is a natural insulator; the fibers breathe. Wool retains body heat and can keep the body cool in hot climates. Wool has a resistance to flame and is ideal for use outdoors near campfires. Blankets are utilitarian yet maintain their striking designs.

Wool blankets were a symbol of pride and wealth among families of weavers who understood the work and skill needed to achieve richness of color and pattern. There was pride in cross-generation designs, patterns, and styles developed within the *parentela,* or family base. The quality of spinning and weaving merited recognition, and histories would circulate about the provenance of specific blankets—who wove them and how the family was able to benefit from the trade and barter of this or that specific textile.

The first breed of sheep permitted into the Americas by Spain was the hardy *churro.* The churro tolerates drought much better than other sheep breeds. The churro staple, or wool fiber, is long and straight; it is not very fine, and its lanolin content is relatively low. As a result, little water is needed to wash churro wool. The fiber also has a sheen that produces a lustrous yarn.

Permission from Spain to transport merino sheep came much later. The merino staple fiber is extremely long and fine as compared to other breeds. Besides having a lot of lanolin, merino wool is also kinky and lacks the sheen of churro fiber. Degreasing merino wool requires abundant hot, soapy water for washing, plus additional water for rinsing.

The French rambouillet sheep also appeared in high northern Nuevo México pastures. The rambouillet wool staple is not as long as the merino, nor is it as fine. The English corriedale sheep also produce a medium-fine staple but are primarily a mutton sheep stock, highly favored by many of the old Taos shepherding families. Neither rambouillet nor corriedale fiber has the sheen of the churro.

According to groupings of blankets, wool fibers, and dyes developed by renowned conservator of Spanish Colonial art E. Boyd (1903–74), the switch-over of sheep strains occurred with the arrival of the railroad in New Mexico around 1880. The quality of hand-spun yarn shifted. The fine commercial Saxony yarns had been available earlier, but the coarser Germantown yarns and aniline dyes were in general use by the late 1800s by both Rio Grande Hispanic weavers and Diné weavers at the Navajo Reservation.

Early weaving was done in village homes. Later, *tejadores licensiados,* licensed tradesmen, were brought into New Mexico specifically to weave. These professional weavers were men who trained apprentices for the different processes in producing wool goods, although men and women were weaving in Taos before and after professional weaving workshops were established in Santa Fe. Village families who wished to have their wool woven would bring wool in large sacks after shearing and have blankets made as trade. For those families without access to a loom and who were more frugal, the wool was washed, carded, spun, and sometimes dyed at home. Then the yarn would be brought to a weaver to produce the textile of choice.

Communities around Taos with recognized weavers were Arroyo Seco, Arroyo Hondo, Peñasco, Questa, and Talpa.

FAMILY WORK ETHIC AND YARN MANUFACTURE

Family survival depended on everyone's efforts to keep up with the chores of home, farm, and ranch. All hands contributed. In the more isolated communities of Taos County, weaving was often done at home. Although everyone at home participated in wool processing at some point, certain family members were recognized as specially adept or inspired weavers. From the 1800s to the early 1900s, some Taos County weaving family names were Lopez, Montoya, Montaño, Ortiz, and Vigil.

Because blankets were not woven for the open market, inspiration was bound only by time, yarn, and available colors. These home weavings are often whimsical in detail with signature motifs produced by men and women to provide some warmth for specific members of the family. These blankets are, in a pure sense, family heirlooms. Many blankets were woven as part of a bride's dowry. They were also woven to commemorate a significant event. In early photos, the subjects are often posed against a backdrop of frasadas.

Children, too, were expected to participate and had designated responsibilities. Little ones helped gather plants and herbs used for dyeing wool. They also assisted with cleaning the raw wool, guided by a family *dueña,* a supervising elder who inevitably had high expectations. The process started with fingering or opening up raw wool clouds. It also included carding the fluffs into combed *colitas de borriguitos* (little lambs' tails) or *madejas* (fluffy wool tags) ready to be spun into yarn. Spinning was done primarily with *malacates/*(spindles) or on large vertical *turnos/*(spinning wheels) by the older girls and women of the household. However, men spun as well as women, and spinning was not confined to spindle and spinning wheel. Ropes of goat or horse-tail hair were made with a ratchet tool and were most often produced by boys and men.

After the wool was spun and respun into an even, strong yarn, it was washed in a warm, sudsy bath using dried and powdered *amole,* made from a plant of the yucca family. Amole was the soap of preference because it produced gentle suds for a foam bath which did not later prevent the yarn from taking an even color.

COLORS AND DYES

For the process of dyeing wool, a skilled hand was crucial; children did not directly take part in this activity. After the wool was washed, it was prepared for receiving color with a mordant bath of *piedra lumbre,* local alum. The mordant makes the dye more permanent and resistant to fading. Once the wool yarn has been dyed, the color is sealed by another alum bath. Alum was obtainable in the hills, but once chrome mordant was available commercially it replaced alum for many weavers who were producing traditional textiles in the many federal revival programs sponsored by the Works Progress Administration (WPA) and the New Mexico Department of Vocational Education programs in the 1930s. The colors from natural plant sources are more vibrant with chrome, although chrome is highly toxic. In Taos, Dolores Perrault Montoya was the primary weaving instructor for these projects. Her responsibilities included documentation now on record in the New Mexico State Museum archives.

There is a difference between *color que no miente,* a true dye, and a fugitive stain, or *mancha.* Different plants were used for varied colors, but from some plants wool received not a dye but a semi-permanent stain which would eventually fade. With six base wool colors and dyes, variations of colors can be achieved by proper mixtures, primary dye baths, exhausted baths, and over-dyes, which is the dyeing of one color over a different color. Color sources for making textile designs were natural white wool, natural black or brown wool, *chamiso* or *cañaigre* yellow dye, cochineal red dye, indigo blue, vat, and brazilwood, a toasty brown dye. Local *campeche* (log wood) is arguably a source for a brown like brazilwood, but it is apparently distinct and not really a dye. *Cota,* or Navajo tea, is another source of a consistent golden tan or brown color, depending on the mordant used. There is much argument about what is dye and what is stain; time is the ultimate test.

For years framed displays of up to twenty colored yarn strands with pressed source-plant samples were available in many Southwest ethnographic shops around Taos Plaza. Many were used by both Native American and Spanish weavers who had ready access to some plants. Display examples included peach leaves for a soft yellow green, apple bark for a reddish yellow, iron nails soaked in urine for a black, and wild plum roots for a rust red. The difficulty in using some of the true natural dyes was their scarcity and expense. Cochineal, brazilwood, and indigo were imported. Crucial to consider in harvesting flowers, bark, and roots of plants to be used for dyeing is the harvesting season. Timing is important for achieving peak intensity of color; rain or drought also affect the intensity of color acquired from the plants gathered from the *llanos* in the Taos Valley.

With a careful close look at old frasadas, color aging is easy to see. Changes in hue from red to purple or pink to brownish tan are visible. It could be said that colors age gracefully, but not in keeping with the weaver's originally desired color scheme. Imagine a child looking into the family cedar chest while watching an *abuelita* or a *tía* unfold a century-or-so-old, elaborately designed frasada with aniline colors, where the hours of sunlight exposure could be counted on your hands. Such a piece would have the "electric" intensity of a psychedelic poster of the 1970s. Pieces like this are rare because the frasadas were used so much, formally or informally.

One factor leading to diminished use of natural dyes was an expanded commercial color palette available for weaving designs. Northern New Mexico weavers from the late 1800s on indulged in these dyes. The colors were easy to apply, and ready-to-go packaged colors were enticing compared to the indigo vats and the process of gathering, cleaning, and preparing dyes and mordants. The indigo plant grows in Mexico and in South America, where it is dried before export. The color from the indigo plant does not dissolve in water. The dried leaves are submerged in a vat of boiling fermented urine to extract the color. Only with oxygen reduction will the indigo color transfer in a chemically altered metallic green, but once exposed to oxygen the molecules become inert and will revert to indigo blue. In later times, sulfuric acid (commercial battery acid) became available to start an indigo vat.

Taos County Weavers 1900 to 1960

With commercial goods available, weaving went into a decline. Cloth and commercial blankets could be purchased, and for those who were still active weavers commercial dyes and wool yarns became available. Some weavers began using thick commercial cotton string for the weft (the foundation yarn on the loom). Unfortunately, cotton weft was not as resilient to wear and tear as wool-weft blankets, and turn-of-the-century weavings that used cotton string weft and wool yarn design (weft yarns) are notably flimsy. In contrast, wool warp and weft weavings could become felted with use and time.

Around Taos well into the twentieth century there were still weavers with massive floor looms who wove frasadas, sarapes, *telas,* and *pisos* (cloth- and scatter rugs) for their *vecinos,* or neighbors. Some weavers used cotton yarn, and many used twisted cloth strips for their weft to make pisos. Families still kept their sheep, either in small flocks or in big *ganados* (herds). Even into the late 1950s during spring and fall season changes, the large sheep-herd crossings would halt traffic between the Taos Plaza and Ranchos de Taos Plaza with their ascent or descent from the mountain pastures.

The Montoyas, the Chávez family, the Mondragóns, and the Martínez family were the last of the many old Taos sheep-raising families with big ganados. During the Great Depression, the Federal Works Progress Association (WPA) and the New Mexico Department of Vocational Education collaborated on a relief project. Some people who were weaving before and during this time merit mention.

In Arroyo Hondo, Juanita (Garcia) Vigil was a weaver who had her signature cross design woven with her vegetal dyed yarns. In Ranchos de Taos, Piedad Lopez Quinto was a Lopez from Chimayó who, with her brother and sister, was raised in Ranchos by her mother's younger sister, Nicolasa Lopez Quinto. She had her own loom, which has been passed on within the family. She would weave sarapes and frasadas, sometimes spinning wool from the family sheep. Typical of women in those days, she had many skills. She would wash jergas at the Ponce de Leon hot springs in Llano Quemado. She had her own garden, and she was also an *enjarradora* (mud plasterer).

Closer to Taos Plaza, in La Loma Plaza, Rudolfo Sisneros was one of the Taos County WPA weaving teachers and a loom maker. He built both two-harness and four-harness looms, with their metal parts often ingeniously created from filed-down circular saw blades or from tractor gear plates. His wife, Eloisa Sisneros, was also a weaver with the WPA.

In Arroyo Seco, Natividad Montaño was a matriarch spinner renowned for her fine yarns. She was also a weaver, contributing her knowledge and yarns to the mid-1960s contemporary weaving revival of Joan Potter Loveless, Rachel Brown, and Kristina Wilson. Her loom is in the permanent collection of the Millicent Rogers Museum.

Escolastico Martínez was another weaver and spinner who learned weaving with the WPA projects. He was a weaving instructor with the ARC program, training people with disabilities to weave. He was well known in Taos, where neighbors would bring him a bag of wool after shearing with which to make one of his hand-spun wool blankets.

Weaver Pedro Cruz lived in Talpa. Known as a patriarch within the extended Cruz-Medina family, he was referred to with affection as "Mi Cruz." He is remembered for his long beard and distinct way of processing wool. He used a mule to open the fibers and teased it further with a pitchfork.

E. B. Ortiz was a native Chimayóso who learned weaving from his parents, both weavers. When he married Ofelia Santistevan, he moved to Taos, to Raton Road, now Kit Carson Road. He made his own looms and eventually established a shop, Chimayó Curio Store, next to his home. With a large floor loom to produce weavings forty-eight inches wide and two smaller looms for runners and mats, he taught his son and daughter, Orlando and Sadie, to weave. His designs were mainly in the Chimayó style, beginning and ending with running strips and a more complex center design. Ortiz was hired as a weaving instructor in Taos at the Vocational School under the Federal New Deal program.

Casímira Madrid from Arroyo Seco was orphaned and taken in by her aunt when she was about nine years old. She participated with the WPA weaving project, but she has also mentioned an old man who had a *tejido de palos* (loom of posts) when she was young. It was from him that she learned to warp a loom. She supported herself with weaving and sewing, and for ten years when the Arroyo Seco Church weaving workshop was active, she participated there, teaching how to put the warp on the loom.

Rachel Brown, Joan Potter Loveless, and Kristina Wilson converged in Taos in the 1950s and stimulated a resurgence of fiber arts production by establishing craft house cooperatives, working with regional weavers, such as Natividad Montaño, and exploring contemporary weaving. Joan Loveless's book *Three Weavers* is a thorough and luminous account of that era, just as Rachel Brown's *The Weaving, Spinning, and Dyeing Book* is regarded as the authoritative work on the process of weaving. Later diverging in their interests and directions, all three had an impact on the Taos Valley weaving tradition, opening up new avenues for experimentation and developing design variations, community cooperative endeavors, and business enterprises. Their weaving was not tied to a tradition of survival but became a vehicle for artistic expression, which included nontraditional abstract designs.

NOTES

1. The indigenous vertical/upright loom dates from pre-conquest times with the production of traditional cotton garment textiles and ceremonial *mantas*.

2. The word *frasada* is an example of a Spanish word that has been localized to northern New Mexico, where it is often written and pronounced *freseda*.

3. The centuries-old indigenous Taos–Picurís trail passed over the Picurís Peak saddle down through the Miranda Canyon into the Taos Valley. This route became the northern branch of the official Camino Real de Arriba from Mexico City, dating to very early Spanish Colonial times.

SELECTED REFERENCES

Boyd, E. *Popular Arts of Spanish New Mexico.* Santa Fe: Museum of New Mexico Press, 1974.

Brown, Rachel. *The Weaving, Spinning, and Dyeing Book.* New York: Random House, 1978; 2nd ed., revised and expanded. New York: Knopf, 2002.

Ellis, Susan H. *New Mexico Colcha Embroideries.* Self-published, 1980; revised, 1989.

Loveless, Joan Potter. *Three Weavers,* Albuquerque: University of New Mexico Press, 1992.

Nestor, Sarah, ed. *Spanish Textile Tradition of New Mexico and Colorado.* Museum of International Folk Art. Santa Fe: Museum of New Mexico Press, 1979.

Espinosa, Carmen G. *New Mexico Colonial Embroidery (Colcha).* New Mexico State University, 1943. Reprint: Cooperative Extension Service of New Mexico, 1979.

Pierce, Donna, and Marta Weigle, eds. *Spanish New Mexico: The Arts of Spanish New Mexico.* 2 vols. Santa Fe: Museum of New Mexico Press, 1996.

Wroth, William, ed. *Weaving and Colcha from the Hispanic Southwest.* Santa Fe: Ancient City Press, 1985.

———. *Hispanic Crafts of the Southwest.* Colorado Springs, CO: The Taylor Museum of the Colorado Fine Art Centers, 1977.

❖ 23 ❖

Writing about Taos
through Four Centuries

NITA MURPHY AND ARTHUR BACHRACH

For a long time, Taos has been a magnet for writers of all genres. Taos has also been a subject in a surprising number of historical documents and works of both fiction and nonfiction, plays, and poetry. The authors of this chapter collaborated in putting together descriptions and characterizations of Taos from the first description, in 1540, to the middle of the twentieth century.

TAOS PUEBLO HAS A RICH TRADITION of oral history, legend, and song. But there are no written records of Taos before the coming of the Spanish because the people of Taos Pueblo did not write in their Tiwa tongue. The Spanish were careful chroniclers, whether for the Church or for the provincial governors, viceroys, or the king. Through the nearly three centuries that Taos was part of the Spanish Empire, matters ecclesiastical and secular—most of them legal—were recorded and archived, although papers dating before 1680 were mostly destroyed at the time of the Pueblo Revolt.

BEFORE THE TWENTIETH CENTURY:
THE SPANISH COLONIAL PERIOD

Early descriptions of Taos by the Spanish survive in published works, most now translated. From the mid-nineteenth century, Americans and Europeans began to add their impressions of the Spanish and Indian Southwest.

Taos Pueblo is first mentioned in 1540 when Hernando de Alvarado, captain of General Francisco Vázquez de Coronado's artillery, accompanied by Fray Juan de Padilla, entered what is New Mexico and wrote or dictated accounts of their expedition. The chroniclers' reports give us the first view of the Rio Grande Valley north of Albuquerque:

> This river [the Rio Grande] originates at the limits of the settlement north of the slopes of the sierras, where there is a large pueblo, different from the others. It is called Yuraba. It is established as follows: It contains eighteen sections, each occupying as much ground as two lots. The houses are built very close together. They are five or six stories high, three built of mud walls and two or three of wood frame. They become narrower as they rise. On the outside of the mud walls each house has its small wooden corridor, one above the other, extending all around. The natives of this pueblo, being in the sierras, do not grow cotton or raise chickens. They wear only cattle- and deerskins. This pueblo has more people than any other in all that land. We reckon that it must have numbered fifteen thousand souls.[1]

In the same year, another expedition under the command of Coronado entered the northern region of New Spain. An account of this expedition, which lasted two years, was written by Captain Juan Jaramillo, who wrote that Taos (this time "Uraba") was well worth seeing, "of two story houses, of corn, beans, melons, skins, long robes of feathers, cloaks of cotton of plain weaving and also of their kivas or 'hot rooms.'"[2]

Pedro de Castañeda, another chronicler of Coronado's journey, wrote:

> There was a large and powerful village, called Braba, which our men called Valladolid. The river flowed through the middle of it. The natives crossed it by wooden bridges, made of very long, large squared pines. At this village we saw the largest and finest hot rooms [kivas] or estufas that were in the entire country, for they had a dozen pillars, each one of which was twice as large around as one could reach and twice as tall as a man.[3]

On July 14, 1598, Don Juan de Oñate visited the area and assigned Fray Francisco de Zamora to serve the pueblos of Taos and Picurís. Captain Gaspar Pérez de Villegrá, Oñate's official chronicler for the expedition, wrote his epic poem *Historia de la Nueva*

México in 1610. Regarded as the first epic poem by a European to have originated in America, it does not contain a reference to Taos.

In *The Memorial of Fray Alonso de Benavides* (1630), translated by Mrs. Edward E. Ayer, the priest Benavides wrote of his impressions of pueblos and their mission churches from the most southern—San Antonio de Padua (several miles south of Socorro)—to Taos Pueblo, the most northern of the pueblos. In his visitation of 1627 Benavides had noted: "It is a land very cold, and most abundant in provisions and flocks." Benavides describes Taos Pueblo:

> Forward to the same northward, another seven leagues, is the pueblo of the Taos, of the same nation as the foregoing [Picurís], although the language varies somewhat. It has two thousand five hundred souls baptized; with its monastery and church, which two Religious who have had charge of this conversion have founded with much care. These Indians are very well doctrinated. . . . It went hard with them to give up having many wives as they used to have before [they were] baptized . . . and the one that most contradicted this was an old Indian woman, a sorceress, who, under pretext of going to the country for firewood, took out four other women with her . . . she kept persuading them that they should not consent to the method of marriage which the Father taught, . . . the sorceress not ceasing from her sermon, and the heavens being clear and serene, a thunderbolt fell and slew that infernal mistress of the Demon. . . . Directly all the pueblo flocked thither; and seeing that rap from heaven, all those who were living in secret concubinage got married.[4]

Governor Don Diego de Vargas led the Spanish monarchy's return to Nuevo México in 1692, after twelve years of exile following the Revolt of 1680. On his fourth attempt to retake Taos Pueblo, in 1696, it was discovered that the Tiwa people had escaped into the hills. Six Indians laid down their arms, and Vargas noted, "I dismounted from my horse, received and embraced them and gave them my hand." Through an interpreter he told them they should persuade their people to return and gave them rosaries as a sign of peace.[8]

> The people, having finished coming down from the sierra, render their obedience to me, the governor and captain general, who in his majesty's name, revalidates the possession of this pueblo, and the children and people are absolved and baptized by the fathers. Ninety-six children and boys and girls of all ages and both sexes were baptized. I ordered them all to wear crosses and pray the four prayers.[5]

Bishop Tamarón's Visitation of New Mexico, 1760, edited by Eleanor B. Adams, describes the many-storied tenements of Taos Pueblo:

It would have been better, as I told them, if they had been kept together, for one is on the other side of the river. . . . It freezes every year, and they told me that when it is thus covered with ice, the Indian women come with their naked little ones, break the ice with a stone, and bathe them in those waters, dipping them in and out. And they say it is for the purpose of making them tough and strong.[6]

Tamarón reported 159 families, a Franciscan missionary curate in residence, and thirty-six Spanish families as neighbors. He also described the 1760 raid on Taos and the Pablo Villalpando hacienda, which occurred a month after his departure:

In that year, 1760, I left that kingdom at the beginning of July. And on the fourth day of August, according to what they say, nearly three thousand Comanche men waged war with the intention of finishing this pueblo of Taos. They diverted, or provoked, them from a very large house, the greatest in that entire valley, belonging to a settler called Villalpando, who luckily for him, had left that day on business. And, trusting in the fact that it had four towers and in the large supply of muskets, powder, and balls, they say that they fired on the Comanches. The latter were infuriated by this to such a horrible degree that they broke into different parts of the house, killed all the men and some women, who also fought. And the wife of the owner of the house, seeing that they were breaking down the outside door, went to defend it with a lance, and they killed her fighting. Fifty-six women and children were carried off, and a large number of horses which the owner of the house was keeping there. Maria Rosa Villapando, the daughter of Pablo Villapando was taken by the Comanches, ransomed and taken to St Louis in 1770, and there married Jean Baptiste Salle.[7]

Taos Pueblo is described in great detail by Fray Francisco Atanasio Domínguez in his *Missions of New Mexico, 1776*:

There is a very extensive swamp quite near the pueblo on the west. It has so much zacate (grass) that the enclosed cattle are pastured in it, a very large amount is cut for the herds of horses, and there is so much left over that in the spring it is necessary to set fire to the old that the new may come up freely. When the Comanches are at peace and come to trade, they bring a thousand or more animals who feed there two days at most, and in spite of this great number repeatedly during the year, there is no lack of fodder. With the exception of frijol and chile, everything yields such an abundant harvest that everyone goes to Taos and leaves there well supplied, not just once, but many times. There are 306 non-Indian settlers living within the walls of Taos Pueblo for protection. When the Comanche raids became more troublesome, because the Spanish plaza was about two musket shots away from the pueblo and cut off for purposes of mutual defense of pueblo and plaza, the settlers abandoned it and moved to the pueblo with the consent of the Indians in the year '70.[8]

Taos' beloved Padre Antonio José Martínez gave his first sermon in Taos on April 20, 1823. Padre Martínez's life became a dedication to the service of his people. Everywhere he traveled the people readily accepted him, his commanding appearance and personal magnetism being an inspiration.[9] On July 23, 1826, Martínez was appointed curate of Taos. In May 1827 he was petitioned by thirty families from Rio Chiquito (Talpa) for permission to celebrate the Mass of Our Lady of St. John of the Lakes as their patroness. The authorization given by Martínez reads in part: "For the Mass [they will pay] one pound of beeswax, for the privileges of the sung Mass with a procession, six *fanegas* of corn and wheat, between the one and the other. If there are vespers, two *fanegas* of grain."[10] By 1835, due to the scarcity of textbooks and instructional materials, Martínez sought and obtained a printing press. . . . The padre spent every spare moment in the writing and development of materials. He wrote and printed spelling, grammar, arithmetic, social studies and theology books. During the early years of his school he touched upon language arts in Spanish, Latin and later in English.[11]

Once Mexico allowed foreigners to trade in New Mexico in 1821, reports of the Taos Valley began to appear in print in English. Albert Pike, New England schoolteacher, saw Taos for the first time in 1831. After losing his horse he walked the last 500 miles to Taos. He was reminded of an "oriental town with its low, square, mud-roofed houses and its two square church towers, also of mud."[12] James Ohio Pattie recounted his time in the 1820s when he was a young man in search of adventure. The book *A Personal Narrative of James O. Pattie: The True Wild West of New Mexico and California* was published in 1831. While much of his story is thought to be greatly exaggerated, this description of being welcomed in Taos in 1825 is quite credible: "Although appearing as poorly . . . they are not destitute of hospitality; for they brought us food, and invited us into their houses to eat, as we walked the streets."[13]

Joseph M. Field (writing under his pen name, Everpoint) published a fictional account of the Taos Rebellion: *Taos, A Romance of the Massacre in 1847* (1847). Field's brother Matt, a reporter for the New Orleans *Picayune*, visited Taos in 1839, and finally in 1960 his *Matt Field on the Santa Fe Trail* was published, describing Taos in the following way: "Taos is in a very beautiful valley. I loved to see the barefoot children drive their sheep and goats out from town into rich pastures before the sunbeams drank away the dew."[14]

Merchant, explorer, and naturalist Josiah Gregg's most famous book, *Commerce of the Prairies,* was published in 1844, not long before New Mexico passed from Mexican to U.S. governance. The Taos Valley is described:

No part of New Mexico equals this valley in amenity of soil, richness of produce and beauty of appearance. Whatever is thrown into its prolific bosom,
which the early frosts of autumn will permit to ripen, grows to a wonderful
degree of perfection. Wheat especially has been produced of a superlative
quality, and in such abundance, that, as is asserted, the crops have often
yielded over a hundredfold.[15]

Seventeen-year-old adventure-seeker Lewis H Garrard wrote *Wah-to-Yah and the
Taos Trail,* drawing on his journal of 1846–47. His description of his first approach
to Taos is one of the best of such impressions:

On emerging from the canyon, the view expanded to a valley nearly circular
to the casual glance, hemmed in by a snowy range, while El Rio Grande del
Norte, a few miles distant, rolled between sand banks to the southwest. . . .
Toward the northwest San Fernandez de Taos, its walls, as well as those of
the minor towns, mica lime-washed to a dazzling whiteness.[16]

The diary of Susan Shelby Magoffin, *Down the Santa Fe Trail and into Mexico,*
is a remarkable journal of an eighteen-year-old bride, one of the first Anglo wom-
en to travel on the Santa Fe Trail. "It is the life of a wandering princess, mine,"
she wrote toward the beginning of her journal in 1846. Her husband provided her
with a small tent house, a private carriage, books, a maid, a driver, and at least
two servant boys. In her journal dated Thursday 28th (January 1847), she wrote:
"The news is that the Taos people have risen, and murdered every American citizen
in Taos including the Gov. That all the troops from Albaquerque [*sic*] have been
ordered to Santa Fé leaving this portion of the territory at the mercy of the mob.
It is a perfect revolution there."[17]

Many of the Anglo-Americans held views of racial superiority toward the
locals. Even Charles Bent, after living in the area for twenty years and taking a
Mexican woman as his common-law wife, wrote in a private letter in 1845, "The
Mexican character is made up of stupidity, obstinacy, ignorance, duplicity, and
vanity."[18]

The June 18, 1850, correspondence of an army major at the newly established
garrison post at Rayado in Colfax County is an example of the prejudicial attitude and disrespect of many of the visitors to the Taos Valley toward the Native
Americans and Spanish:

Sent Lt. Taylor with Co. G to take post at Taos, where they will help preserve good order during the coming election. I have not the slightest confi-
dence in the honesty, patriotism or fidelity of the people in Taos Valley. On
those three points I regard them as but slightly superior to the Apaches.[19]

Beaver pelts, Taos Lightning whiskey, and the mountain men were an important part of Taos history. Dr. DeWitt C. Peters, an army surgeon, wrote a biography of Kit Carson based on facts dictated by Carson. Published in 1858, this book was the first of hundreds that would eventually be published about Carson and the mountain men and trappers in Taos. *Life in the Far West* by George Frederick Ruxton and illustrated by fellow-explorer Alfred Jacob Miller describes the women at a fandango in Taos in 1847:

> Their long black hair was washed and combed, plastered behind their ears, and plaited into a long queue, which hung down their backs. . . . Gold and silver ornaments, of antiquated pattern, decorated their ears and necks: and massive crosses of the precious metals, . . . hang pendant on their breasts . . . they coquettishly enter the fandango.[20]

Ruxton continues:

> [The mountaineers] divested of their hunting-coats of buckskins, appear in their bran-new shirts of gaudy calico, and close fitting buckskin pantaloons, with long fringes down the outside seam from the hip to the ancle [*sic*]: with moccasins, ornamented with bright beads and porcupine quills. Each, round his waist wears his mountain-belt and scalp-knife, ominous of the company he is in, and some have pistols sticking in their belt. . . . Seizing his partner round the waist with the gripe [*sic*] of a grisly bear, each mountaineer whirls and twirls, jumps and stamps: introduces Indian steps used in the "scalp" or "buffalo" dances, whooping occasionally with unearthly cry, and then subsiding into the jerking step, raising each foot alternately from the ground, so much in vogue in Indian ballets.[21]

The Twentieth Century to 1960

New Mexico and Taos became a destination for artists and writers of all kinds. In 1911, Ralph Emerson Twitchell published his five-volume *Leading Facts of New Mexico History*, which included facts of Taos history. The pueblo held special fascination for many of the writers who came, perhaps most powerfully for Mabel Dodge Sterne, soon to be Mabel Dodge Luhan, who settled in Taos in 1917 and began to urge artist friends and East Coast literati to visit Taos and, in a sense, to validate her experience of the pueblo as a place of social, spiritual, and psychic renewal.

In September 1922, the British writer D. H. Lawrence and his wife, Frieda, came to Taos at the invitation of Mabel Dodge Luhan. As part of the package to lure the Lawrences to Taos, Mabel included a copy of Charles Fletcher Lummis's 1893 classic story of New Mexico *Land of Poco Tiempo* in which Lummis wrote: "The most unique pictures in New Mexico are to be found among its unique Pueblos. Their quaint terraced architecture is the most remarkable on the continent. . . . Taos, in its lovely lonely valley far to the north, is two great pyramid-tenements of six stories." [22]

When they arrived in Taos the following morning, September 11—Lawrence's thirty-seventh birthday—Frieda and Lawrence were both struck by the beauty of the scene. "In the magnificent fierce morning of New Mexico, one sprang awake, a new part of the soul woke up suddenly and the old world gave way to the new," the British author wrote. [23]

Written at Mabel's urgent request, one of Lawrence's first writings upon arrival in Taos was a polemic essay attacking the Bursum Bill. The bill, introduced into the U.S. Senate by Senator Holm O. Bursum of New Mexico, would have opened Pueblo land for sale to settlers. Lawrence's brilliant essay, "Certain Americans and an Englishman," laid bare the negative purpose of the bill, which was ultimately defeated in the Senate.

Lawrence was in awe of the pueblo. In his essay "Taos," written in September 1922, he observed, "There it is, then, the Pueblo, as it has been since heaven knows when. And the slow dark weaving of the Indian going on still, though perhaps more waveringly." [24]

Through the Lawrences, Aldous and Maria Huxley were introduced to Taos and to the pueblo. In his utopian novel *Brave New World*, first published in 1932, Huxley uses an Indian reservation as an important setting. In one scene, reminiscent of Taos Pueblo, Huxley describes a dance:

> Two Indians came running along the path, their black hair was braided with fox fur and red flannel. Cloaks of turkey feathers fluttered from their shoulders. Huge feather diadems exploded gaudily around their heads. With every step they took came the clink and rattle of their silver bracelets, their heavy necklaces of bone and turquoise beads. [25]

The psychoanalyst Carl Jung visited Taos Pueblo and wrote of his experiences in his 1964 *Memories, Dreams, Reflections*:

> I stood by the river and looked up at the mountains, which rise almost another six thousand feet above the plateau. I was thinking that this was the roof of the American continent, and that people lived here in the face of the sun like the Indians who stood wrapped in blankets on the highest roofs of the pueblo, mute and absorbed in the sight of the sun. [26]

Blanche Chloe Grant, a Taos resident and a graduate of London's Slade School of Art, wrote about Taos Pueblo in *The Taos Indians* (1925) and about Taos in *When*

Old Trails Were New (1934): "The Indian, shrouded in a blanket, moves quietly about in moccasined feet and rarely gives more than a glimpse of his real self or his philosophy which is based on natural phenomena. . . . He is Catholic, in name only, Indian in truth."[27]

Taos Pueblo was the stimulus for other works, such as Mary Austin's and Ansel Adams's *Taos Pueblo: Photographed by Ansel Easton Adams and Described by Mary Austin* (1930). Later on, the noted anthropologist Elsie Clews Parsons wrote many books, among which was her account of the pueblo in *Taos Tales* and *Taos Pueblo* (1940). Irwin R. Blacker's novel about the Revolt of 1680, *Taos*, was published in 1959. John Collier, Indian advocate and Commissioner of Indian Affairs from 1935 to 1945, also wrote many books about the Pueblo Indians. In *On the Gleaming Way* (1949), Collier wrote:

> When Coronado pursued the phantom of gold across the American Southwest, he traversed a land of ancient civilizations. Pueblo material culture, as known to archaeology, was perhaps two thousand years old when Coronado came.
>
> Pueblo social and spiritual culture was much older—older by many thousand years.
>
> Viewed a Pueblo deer dancer of today. Then viewed the painting of the Sorcerer, in the Caverne des Trois Frerer, in France. That painting is twenty thousand years old.
>
> The spirit and meaning of the two images is so consanguineous as to be practically identical. The spiritual culture of the pueblos is as old as mankind on our earth.[28]

Collier's *Rites and Ceremonies of the Indians of the Southwest*, with drawings and lithographs by Ira Moskowitz, was published first in 1949:

> These Southwestern Indians have much that we know we need. And they have one possession, the most distinguishing of all, which we have forgotten that we need. . . . That possession is a time sense different from ours, and happier. Once our white race had it too, and then the mechanized world took it away from us. . . . We bow to clockwork time. We think we must yield to it our all—body, conduct and soul. . . . And we abide so briefly, with that rush of linear time which subconsciously we experience as a kind of panic rout: and we are old, so soon, and we are done, and we hardly had time to live at all.[29]

Foremost among fiction written about Taos Pueblo is Frank Waters's *The Man Who Killed the Deer* (1942), which is based on an actual event. Among writers on the environment there is none whose breadth of interest and knowledge surpasses Waters's. He brought to the literary world a fine understanding of world cultures and belief systems, a strong spiritual—one might say mystical—worldview and anthropological knowledge that broadened it. In the *Man Who Killed the Deer* he wrote eloquently of the respect, the sense of universal harmony with all living things that the Native American holds. Here is an example as the Taos Pueblo Indian Palemón makes the prayer-talk as they are about to cut down a lofty pine:

> We know your life is as precious as ours. We know that we are all children of the same Earth Mother, of our Father Sun. But we also know that one life must sometimes give way to another, so that the one great life of all may continue unbroken. So we ask your permission, we obtain your consent to this killing.[30]

Again, in *The Man Who Killed the Deer*, Waters writes: "We are not separate and alone. The breathing mountains, the living stones, each blade of grass, the clouds, the rain, each star, the beasts, the birds and the invisible spirits of the air—we are all one, indivisible. Nothing that any of us does but affects us all."[31]

Besides his Pueblo-centered writings, D. H. Lawrence was quite prolific in the periods he lived on Mabel's ranch in San Cristóbal. From 1922 to 1925, over a total of about eighteen months, Lawrence wrote a number of poems and essays, finished his *Studies in Classic American Literature* (1923); completed his novel *Kangaroo* (1922); wrote three pieces of short fiction, all with a Taos mountain setting: "The Princess," whose protagonist resembles Brett"; The Woman Who Rode Away," using the cave in Arroyo Seco for the final scene; and "St. Mawr," whose protagonists evoke images of Mabel Dodge Luhan.

Lawrence's presence stimulated many works by a variety of writers, including Mabel's book *Lorenzo in Taos* (1932), written in the form of a letter to poet Robinson Jeffers, who had been a visitor at Mabel's home in Taos. Mabel also wrote *Winter in Taos* (1935), four volumes of *Memoirs* (1933, 1935, 1936, and 1937), and *Taos and Its Artists* (1947). From *Winter in Taos*:

> Early in the morning, at any time of the year, one wakens to the faint sound of the ax coming to one from here and there in the valley. These distant rhythmical sounds accompany the dawn, and they give one a mild living thrill as one lies listening. Men in their homes cutting firewood before the sun is over the hill, while the birds are only just beginning to chirp and cheep, sleepily, convey a sense of life, and a good life, too.[32]

Also stimulated to write about Lawrence was the Danish artist Knud Merrild, who lived in a cabin near the Lawrences on the Hawk Ranch and wrote: *A Poet and*

Two Painters (1938). Lawrence's wife, Frieda Lawrence, wrote *Not I, But the Wind* (1934), and Dorothy Brett, also a London School of Art graduate, recorded times spent together in *Lawrence and Brett: A Friendship* (1933):

> You greet the driver, John Dunn, warmly. . . . As we enter the narrow, sunless canyon, and wind and wind along the edge of the swift Rio Grande, you are asking John Dunn about the road. . . . I am almost green with fright as the car slips sideways on the narrow ledge that is called a road. . . . We are almost at the top. . . . But you keep on looking down and over at the now small ribbon of river foaming hundreds of feet below us. We turn a corner and a new desert unfolds itself before us: the snow-laden Pueblo Mountain, the gleaming Lobo Peaks curving round the vast plateau.[33]

Lawrence's contemporaries in Taos who were published at a later time included Jaime de Angulo (*Jaime in Taos*, 1974). Following is his journal entry for April 9, 1924:

> Talking of neurotics, that Lawrence is certainly one. They make a strange outfit, he and his wife, an enormous German, exceeding rational and direct, who looks more like his mother than his wife—and an undescribable Scotch girl, who is deaf, and carries about a box with a radio outfit connected by a tube with her left ear, and whose sister is married to the Maharaja of Sarawac (an independent kingdom in Borneo. . .) She wears a peaked hat like the Italian brigands, breeches and a long knife stuck in her boot. She is the daughter of a lord, speaks with an exaggerated English accent, looks like an idiot and is very intelligent and completely and utterly independent, . . . Lawrence, it seems, carries her around the world like a talisman. Her name is Miss Bret and they call her "Bret" or "the Bret."[34]

Witter Bynner, the Santa Fe writer who traveled with the Lawrences to Mexico, wrote *Journey with Genius: Recollections and Reflections Concerning the D. H. Lawrences* (1953), which recalls their time in each other's company and comments on Taos: "The strangest, most wonderful thing about Taos, the most enduring, are the Indians. [They]are a miracle of survival. . . . The spirit of Taos is Indian."[35]

A writer who came to Taos to visit Frieda Lawrence after Lawrence's death in 1930, was Tennessee Williams. He visited in 1939, 1943, and 1946 and wrote about his experiences in his memoirs and in a one-act play, *I Rise in Flames, Cried the Phoenix*, which dealt with Lawrence's death. The play was completed in 1941 and published in 1951. On his first trip in 1939, Williams rode a bus to New Mexico carrying a guitar with a rope tied around it. Traveling across the high desert through the Rio Grande Canyon toward Taos, he wrote to his mother, Edwina Dakin Williams: "The country around here is wild and beautiful—scarcely inhabited. Real Indians in blankets and braided hair in adobe pueblos." In a letter dated August 19, 1939, Williams wrote to his mother about Frieda Lawrence: "You should see her. Still magnificent. A valkyrie. She runs and plunges about the ranch like female bull-thick yellow hair flying-piercing blue eyes-huge. She dresses madly- a hat & coat of bob-cat fur-shouts bangs- terrific! Not a member of the female sex- but woman."[36] Williams settled down to write but fled the ranch after three days because he found Lawrence's ghost too overpowering in the little log cabin.[37]

Taos writers not associated with Lawrence include Harvey Fergusson, who wrote *The Blood of the Conquerors* in 1921. In Fergusson's *Wolf Song* (1927), he characterized Taos thus:

> Taos was a place where corn grew and women lived. Sooner or later every man in the mountains came to Taos. . . . They came to it like buffalo to a salt lick across thousands of dangerous miles. Taos whiskey and Taos women were known and talked about on every stream in the Rockies. More than any other place, Taos was the heart of the mountains.[38]

In 1928, Alice Corbin Henderson (whose daughter married Mabel Dodge's son, John Evans) assembled an anthology of poetry of New Mexico, *The Turquoise Trail*, which featured poetry from such authors as D. H. Lawrence and Carl Sandburg. Henderson also wrote *Brothers of Light: The Penitentes of the Southwest*, published in 1937, which inspired Marta Weigle's study of Los Hermanos titled *Brothers of Light, Brothers of Blood*, published a generation later. Artist, historian, and archaeologist Helen Blumenschein, daughter of artists Ernest and Mary Greene Blumenschein, wrote and illustrated *Sangre de Cristo: A Short Illustrated History of Taos* in 1963. Another woman whose family is closely associated with Taos, poet Peggy Pond Church, researched and wrote a biography of Edith Warner, *The House at Otowi Bridge* (1959), while living in Ranchos de Taos. Ironically for one of New Mexico's most esteemed poets, this nonfiction book is her best-known work.

One of the several plays written about New Mexico, *Night over Taos*, was published by Maxwell Anderson in 1932. The play is about political and personal problems of the Pablo Montoya family in Taos during the time of the revolt against American rule in 1847. Capturing traditional Hispanic life in the Taos Valley are Raymond Otis's 1936 *Miguel of the Bright Mountains* and Cleofas Jaramillo's illus-trated, bilingual *Shadows of the Past (Sombra del Pasado*, 1940) and her *Romance of a Little Village Girl* (1950). George Sánchez wrote *Forgotten People: A Study of New Mexicans* (1941). Joseph Krumgold's important work *And Now, Miguel* appeared in 1953 and was the basis for a WPA documentary film on the Chavez family and the disappearing sheep-farming culture of the Taos Valley. Barbara Latham's *Pedro, Nina and Perrito*, published in 1939, and Ann Nolan Clark's *Little Boy with Three Names* (1940), about Taos Pueblo, added to children's literature.

Eric Sloane, artist and writer, wrote a description of his first visit to Taos in 1925, later published as *Return to Taos*:

> My first glimpse of Taos pueblo was a rainbow affair. A brilliant setting sun had heralded the end of a summer rain squall, lighting an adverse sky and producing an arc of major colors in the storm's remaining mist. . . . Like all rainbows, it receded as I approached and by the time I reached the pueblo grounds it had moved on, climbing into the elevation of Taos Mountain. Actually it marked a pot of gold for me, for it had located a special place on earth that I have treasured in writing and painting.[39]

In 1947 Simone de Beauvoir spent four months traveling around America, including New Mexico and Taos Pueblo, resulting in the book *America: Day by Day* (1952) and this memory:

> We were struck at once by its beauty. We had left the car at the entrance to the village [the pueblo] and read the inscription there: white people were forbidden to wander inside the enclosure after five o'clock . . . and one must pay half a dollar to park one's car on the square. We slipped away from the group and climbed a low stone wall. We sat on the edge of a well from which two poles protruded, but women waved their arms in our direction and shook their heads; one of them approached us; "Go away or the governor will expel you." We got up and found that the well was a khive [*sic*] a place sacred above all others. . . . We should have to come back in invisible guise after five o'clock when the pueblo reverted to solitude. But even this greeting, at once fierce and commercial, did not spoil its beauty.[40]

In 1950 writer Vladimir Nabokov pursued his passion for butterflies on a farm north of Taos. He was not much taken with the area, writing to his friend Edmund Wilson in 1954, "[Taos] is a dismal hole, full of third rate painters and faded pansies." And, again, "Taos. is an ugly and dreary town with . . . 'picturesque' Indians placed at strategic points by the Chamber of Commerce to lure tourists from Oklahoma and Texas who deem the place 'arty.' There are, however, some admirable canyons where most interesting butterflies occur."[41] Fortunately, most writers who have visited Taos have come away with more positive memories.

NOTES

1. Myra Ellen Jenkins, "Taos Pueblo and Its Neighbors," *New Mexico Historical Review* 41:2 (1966): 86. Despite the existence of this account, there are many who doubt that

Alvarado could have made the detour necessary to visit Taos in the time allowed for his mission to the north.

2. Blanche C. Grant, *When Old Trails Were New: The Story of Taos* (New York: The Press of the Pioneers, 1934), 316.

3. Ibid., 317.

4. *The Memorial of Fray Alonso de Benavides, 1630,* trans. Mrs. Edward E Ayer (Chicago: R. R. Donnelley & Sons, 1916), 26.

5. John L. Kessell and Rick Hendricks, eds., *By Force of Arms: The Journals of Don Diego de Vargas 1691–1693* (Albuquerque: University of New Mexico Press, 1992), 452.

6. *Bishop Tamarón's Visitation of New Mexico, 1760,* ed. Eleanor B. Adams, Historical Society of New Mexico, vol. 15 (Albuquerque: University of New Mexico Press, 1954), 57.

7. Ibid., 57.

8. Fray Francisco Atanasio Domínguez, *Missions of New Mexico, 1776,* tr. and ed. by Eleanor B. Adams and Fray Angélico Chávez (Albuquerque: University of New Mexico Press, 1956), 111.

9. Ray John de Aragon, *Padre Martinez and Bishop Lamy* (Las Vegas, NV: Pan-American Publishing Company, 1978), 10.

10. Ibid., 12.

11. Ibid., 20.

12. Albert Pike, *Prose Sketches and Poems, Written in the Western Country,* ed. David J. Weber (Albuquerque: C. Horn, 1967), 147.

13. James O. Pattie, *The Personal Narrative of James O. Pattie: The True Wild West of New Mexico and California* (Cincinnati, OH: James H. Wood, 1831; New York: J. P. Lippincott, 1962), 38.

14. Matt Field, *Matt Field on the Santa Fe Trail,* ed. John E. Sunder (Norman: University of Oklahoma Press, 1960), 176–77.

15. Josiah Gregg, *Commerce of the Prairies* (Norman: University of Oklahoma Press, 1990), 104.

16. Lewis H. Garrard [Hector Lewis Garrard], *Wah-to-yah and the Taos Trail* (Cincinnati, OH: W. H. Derby & Co., 1850; reprint, Norman: University of Oklahoma Press, 1955), 166.

17. Susan Shelby Magoffin, *Down the Santa Fe Trail and into Mexico,* ed. Stella M. Drumm (New Haven, CT: Yale University Press, 1965), xvii.

18. Charles Bent, private letter, 1845, in "The Charles Bent Papers," *New Mexico Historical Review* 25. no. 3 (July 1955), 254.

19. Transcribed Post Returns from Taos and Cantonment Burgwin, National Archives Microfilm Publications, Register of Letters Received and Letters Received by

Headquarters, 9th Military Department, 1848–1853, Roll 2, Letters Received, 1850.

20. George A. F. Ruxton, *Life in the Far West among the Indians and the Mountain Men, 1846–1847* (Norman: University of Oklahoma Press, 1951; Glorieta, NM: Rio Grande Press, 1972), 186–87.

21. Ibid.

22. Charles Fletcher Lummis, *Land of Poco Tiempo* (New York: C. Scribner's Sons, 1893; Albuquerque: University of New Mexico Press, 1966), 7.

23. David Herbert Lawrence, "New Mexico," in *The Posthumous Papers of D. H. Lawrence*, ed. Edward D. McDonald (New York: Viking Press, 1936), 142.

24. Ibid., 101.

25. Aldous Huxley, *Brave New World* (New York: Harper Colophon Books, 1965), 83.

26. C. G. Jung, *Memories, Dreams, Reflections* (New York: Pantheon Books, 1963), 251.

27. Grant, *When Old Trails Were New,* 276.

28. John Collier, *On the Gleaming Way* (Denver: Sage Books, 1962), 80.

29. John Collier, *The Rites and Ceremonies of the Indians of the Southwest* (New York: Barnes & Noble, 1993), 26.

30. Frank Waters, *The Man Who Killed the Deer* (New York: Farrar & Rinehart, 1942), 218.

31. Ibid., 27.

32. Mabel Dodge Luhan, *Winter in Taos* (New York: Harcourt, Brace & Company, 1935), 29.

33. Dorothy Brett, *Lawrence and Brett: A Friendship* (Philadelphia: J.B. Lippincott Company, 1933), 43–44.

34. Jaime de Angulo, *Jaime in Taos* (San Francisco: City Lights, 1985), 49, 51.

35. Joseph Foster, *D. H. Lawrence in Taos* (Albuquerque: University of New Mexico Press, 1974), 4.

36. Lyle Leverich, *Tom: The Unknown Tennessee Williams* (New York: Crown, 1995), 318.

37. Margaret Bradham Thorton, ed., *Notebooks: Tennessee Williams* (New Haven, CT: Yale University Press, 2006), 267.

38. Harvey Fergusson, *Wolf Song* (Lincoln: University of Nebraska Press, 1927).

39. Eric Sloane, *Return To Taos* (New York: Hastings House, 1982), 63.

40. Simone de Beauvoir, *America Day by Day* (London: Gerald Duckworth & Co., 1952), 151–52.

41. Brian Boyd and Robert Michael Pyle, *Nabokov's Butterflies: Unpublished and Uncollected Writings* (Boston: Beacon Press, 2000), 514.

RESOURCES FOR TAOS HISTORY

Adams, Eleanor B., ed. *Bishop Tamarón's Visitation of New Mexico, 1760.* Historical Society of New Mexico Publications in History, 15. Albuquerque: University of New Mexico Press, 1954.

———, and Fray Angélico Chávez. *The Missions of New Mexico 1776, A Description by Fray Francisco Atanasio Domínguez with Other Documents.* Albuquerque: University of New Mexico Press, 1956.

Aragon, John de. *Padre Martinez and Bishop Lamy.* Las Vegas, NM: Pan American Publishing Co., 1978.

Baca-Vaughn, Guadalupe. *Memories of José Antonio Martínez.* Santa Fe: Rydal Press, 1978.

Bancroft, Hubert Howe. *History of Arizona and New Mexico.* Albuquerque: Horn and Wallace Publishers, 1962. Reprint of the 1889 edition.

Bauer, Paul W. *The Rio Grande: A River Guide to the Geology and Landscapes of Northern New Mexico.* Socorro: New Mexico Bureau of Mines and Mineral Resources, 2011.

———, ed. *The Enchanted Circle: Loop Drives from Taos-Scenic Trips to the Geologic Past No. 2.* Socorro: New Mexico Bureau of Mines and Mineral Resources, 1991.

Baxter, John O. *Dividing New Mexico's Waters 1700–1912.* Albuquerque: University of New Mexico Press, 1997.

———. *Las Carneradas: Sheep Trade in New Mexico 1700–1860.* Albuquerque: University of New Mexico Press, 1987.

———. *Spanish Irrigation in Taos Valley,* Santa Fe: New Mexico State Engineer, 1990.

Bleiler, Lyn, and Society of the Muse of the Southwest. *Taos.* Images of America Series. Charleston, SC: Arcadia, 2011.

Blumenschein, Helen Greene. "Historic Roads and Trails to Taos." *El Palacio,* Spring (1968).

———. *Recuerdos: Early Days of the Blumenschein Family.* Silver City, NM: Tecolote Press, 1979.

———. *Sangre de Cristo: A Short Illustrated History of Taos.* Taos, NM: Taos News, 1963.

———. *Sounds and Sights of Taos Valley.* Edited by Marcia Muth Miller, Santa Fe: Sunstone Press, 1972.

Bodine, John J. *Taos Pueblo, A Walk through Time, A Visitor's Guide to the Pueblo, Its People, Their Customs and Their Long History.* Tucson, AZ: Treasure Chest Books, 1977; revised edition, 1996.

Bowen, Dorothy, Trish Spellman, and Nora Fisher. *Spanish Textile Tradition of New Mexico and Colorado.* Santa Fe: Museum of International Folk Art and Museum of New Mexico Press, 1979.

Boyd, E., *Popular Arts of Spanish New Mexico.* Santa Fe: Museum of New Mexico Press, 1974.

Broder, Patricia Janis. *Taos, A Painter's Dream.* Boston, MA: New York Graphic Society; Little, Brown and Co., 1980.

Brown, Lorin W., with Charles L. Briggs and Martha Weigle. *Hispano Folklife of New Mexico. The Loren W. Brown Federal Writers' Manuscripts.* Albuquerque: University of New Mexico Press, 1978.

Buchanan, Rosemary. *Don Diego de Vargas, the Peaceful Conquistador.* New York: P. J. Kennedy and Sons, 1963.

Bunting, Bainbridge. *Of Earth and Timbers Made: New Mexico Architecture.* Albuquerque: University of New Mexico Press, 1974.

Burke, Flannery. *From Greenwich Village to Taos: Primitivism and Place at Mabel Dodge Luhan's.* Lawrence, KS: University Press of Kansas, 2008.

Burke, Rev. James T. *This Miserable Kingdom: The Story of the Spanish Presence in New Mexico from the Beginning until the 18th Century.* Las Vegas, NM: Our Lady of Sorrows Church, 1973.

Cabeza de Baca, Fabiola. *We Fed Them Cactus.* Albuquerque: University of New Mexico Press, 1954.

Caffey, David L. *Land of Enchantment, Land of Conflict.* College Station: Texas A&M University Press, 1999.

Campa, Arthur L. *Hispanic Culture in the Southwest.* Norman: University of Oklahoma Press, 1979.

Cerquone, Joseph. *In Behalf of the Light: The Domínguez and Escalante Expedition of 1776.* Domínguez and Escalante Bicentennial Expedition, 1976.

Chávez, Fray Angélico. *Archives of the Archdiocese of Santa Fe, 1678–1900.* St. Paul, MN: North Central Publishing Co., 1957.

———. *But Time and Chance.* Santa Fe: Sunstone Press, 1981.

Chavez, Thomas E. *Conflict and Acculturation: Manuel Alvarez' s1842 Memorial.* Santa Fe: Museum of New Mexico Press, 1989.

———. *An Illustrated History of New Mexico.* Boulder: University Press of Colorado, 1992.

———. *Spain and the Independence of the United States.* Albuquerque: University of New Mexico Press, 2002.

Cline, Lynn. *Literary Pilgrims: The Santa Fe and Taos Writers' Colonies 1917–1950.* Albuquerque: University of New Mexico Press, 2007.

Coke, Van Deren. *Taos and Santa Fe: The Artist's Environment 1882–1942.* Albuquerque: University of New Mexico Press, 1963.

Coles, Robert. *The Old Ones of New Mexico.* Albuquerque: University of New Mexico Press, 1973.

Collier, John. *On the Gleaming Way.* Denver, CO: Sage Books, 1962.

Coulter, Lane, and Maurice Dixon Jr. *Tinwork, New Mexican, 1840–1940.* Albuquerque: University of New Mexico Press, 1990.

Davies, M. M. *Kit Carson: A View of His Life and Times.* Salt Warrior Press, 1984.

Davis, W. W. H. *El Gringo; Or, New Mexico and Her People.* Chicago: The Rio Grande Press, 1962.

Ebright, Malcolm. *Land Grants and Lawsuits in Northern New Mexico.* Albuquerque: University of New Mexico Press, 1984.

D'Emilio, Sandra, with Suzan Campbell and John Kessell. *Images of Spirit and Vision: Ranchos de Taos Church.* Santa Fe: Museum of New Mexico Press, 1987.

deBuys, William. *Enchantment and Exploitation: The Life and Hard Times of a New Mexico Mountain Range.* Albuquerque: University of New Mexico Press, 1985.

————. *River of Traps: A Village Life.* Albuquerque: University of New Mexico Press, 1990.

Drumm, Stella M., ed. *The Diary of Susan Shelby Magoffin 1846–1847: Down the Santa Fe Trail and into Mexico.* New Haven, CT: Yale University Press, 1962.

Edrington, Thomas S., and John Taylor. *The Battle of Glorieta Pass: A Gettysburg in the West, March 26–28, 1862.* Albuquerque: University of New Mexico Press, 2000.

Ellis, Susan H. *New Mexico Colcha Embroidery.* n.p.: S.H. Ellis, 1980.

Espinosa, Aurelio M. *The Folklore of Spain in the Southwest.* Norman: University of Oklahoma Press, 1985.

Espinosa, Manual J. *Crusaders of the Rio Grande: The Story of Don Diego de Vargas and the Reconquest and Refounding of New Mexico.* Chicago: Institute of Jesuit History, 1942.

————. *The Pueblo Indian Revolt of 1696 and the Franciscan Missions in New Mexico: Letters of the Missionaries and Related Documents.* Norman: University of Oklahoma Press, 1988.

Ferguson, Erna. *New Mexico: A Pageant of Three Peoples.* New York: Alfred A. Knopf, 1964.

Fisher, Nora, ed. *Spanish Textile Traditions of New Mexico and Colorado.* Santa Fe: Museum of New Mexico Press, 1979.

Forrest, Earle R. *Missions and Pueblos of the Old Southwest.* Glorieta, NM: Rio Grande Press, 1979.

Galbraith, Dan. *Turbulent Taos.* Santa Fe, NM: Sunstone Press, 2005.

Garate, Donald T. *Juan Bautista de Anza*. Reno: University of Nevada Press, 2003.

Garduno, Joseph A. *Memoriales, Sangre de Cristo Mountains*, Glendora. CA: Associated Publications, 1982.

Garrard, Lewis H. [Hector Lewis Garrard]. *Wah-to-yah and the Taos Trail.* Cincinnati, OH: W. H. Derby & Co., 1850; reprinted, Norman: University of Oklahoma Press, 1955, 1987.

Gavin, Robert Farwell. *Traditional Arts of Spanish New Mexico: The Hispanic Heritage Wing at the Museum of International Folk Art.* Santa Fe: Museum of New Mexico Press, 1994.

Gibson, Arrell Morgan. *The Santa Fe and Taos Colonies: Age of the Muses, 1900–1942.* Norman: University of Oklahoma Press, 1983.

Gordon-McCutchan, R. C. *The Taos Indians and the Battle for Blue Lake.* Santa Fe: Red Crane Books, 1991.

Grant, Blanche C. *The Taos Indians.* Glorieta, NM: The Rio Grande Press, 1976.

———. *When Old Trails Were New: The Story of Taos.* New York: Press of the Pioneers, 1934; reprinted, Santa Fe: Sunstone Press, 2007.

Gregg, Josiah. *Commerce of the Prairies.* Norman: University of Oklahoma Press, 1954.

Gregg, Kate L. *The Road to Santa Fe.* Albuquerque: University of New Mexico Press, 1952.

Gutierrez, Ramon A. *When Jesus Came, the Corn Mothers Went Away: Marriage, Sexuality and Power in New Mexico 1500–1846.* Palo Alto, CA: Stanford University Press, 1991.

Hammond, George P., and Edgar F. Gaod. *The Adventure of Don Francisco Vasquez de Coronado.* Albuquerque: University of New Mexico Press, 1938.

Hammond, George P., and Agapito Rey. *The Rediscovery of New Mexico, 1580–1594.* Albuquerque: University of New Mexico Press, 1966.

Hemp, Bill. *Taos: Landmarks and Legends.* Los Alamos, NM: Exceptional Books, 1996; illus. ed. Boulder: University of Colorado Press, 2002.

Henderson, Alice Corbin. *Brothers of Light: The Penitentes of the Southwest.* Santa Fe: William Gannon, 1977.

Herrera, Gabriel. *Ancient Agriculture.* Santa Fe: Ancient City Press, 2006.

Hewitt, Edgar L., and Reginald Fisher. *Mission Landmarks of New Mexico.* Albuquerque: University of New Mexico Press, 1943.

———, and Wayne L. Mauzy. *Landmarks of New Mexico.* Albuquerque: University of New Mexico Press, 1953.

Hodge, Frederick Webb, George P. Hammond, and Agapito Rey. *The Benavides Memorial of 1634.* Albuquerque: University of New Mexico Press, 1945.

Hooker, Van Dorn, with Corina A. Santistevan. *Centuries of Hands: An Architectural History of St. Francis of Assisi Church.* Santa Fe: Sunstone Press, 1990.

Hordes, Stanley M. *To the End of the Earth.* New York: Columbia University Press, 2005.

Horgan, Paul. *Conquistadores in North American History.* New York: Farrar, Straus and Co., 1963.

———. *Great River: The Rio Grande in North American History.* 2 vols. New York: Holt, Rinehart and Co., 1954.

———. *Lamy of Santa Fe, His Life and Times.* New York: Farrar, Straus and Giroux, 1975.

———. *Under the Sangre de Cristo,* Flagstaff, AZ: Northland Press, 1985.

Jenkins, Myra Ellen. *A Brief History of New Mexico.* Albuquerque: University of New Mexico Press, 1974.

———."Taos Pueblo and Its Neighbors." *New Mexico Historical Review,* (April 1966).

Jones, Hester. "Uses of Wood By the Spanish Colonists in New Mexico." *New Mexico Historical Review* (July 1932).

Jones, Oakah L., Jr. *Los Paisanos: Spanish Settlers on the Northern Frontier of New Spain.* Norman: University of Oklahoma Press, 1979.

Keleher, William A. *Turmoil in New Mexico.* Santa Fe: The Rydal Press, 1952.

Kessell, John L. *Kiva, Cross and Crown: The Pecos Indians and New Mexico, 1540–1840.* 2nd ed. Albuquerque: University of New Mexico Press, 1990.

———. *The Missions of New Mexico Since 1776.* Albuquerque: University of New Mexico Press, 1980.

———. *Pueblos, Spaniards, and the Kingdom of New Mexico.* Norman: University of Oklahoma Press, 2010.

———. *Remote Beyond Compare: Letters of Don Diego de Vargas to His Family from New Spain and New Mexico 1675–1606.* Albuquerque: University of New Mexico Press, 1989.

———. *Spain in the Southwest.* Norman: University of Oklahoma Press, 2002.

Kessler, Ronald E. *Anza's 1779 Comanche Campaign: Diary of Governor Juan Bautista de Anza.* Monte Vista, CO: Kessler, 1994.

Krumgold, Joseph. *And Now Miguel.* New York: Thomas Y. Crowell Co., 1953.

Kubler, George. *The Religious Architecture of New Mexico.* Albuquerque: University of New Mexico Press, 1940.

Lange, Charles H., Carroll L. Riley, and Elizabeth M. Lange. *The Southwest Journals of Adolph F. Bandelier 1889–1892.* Albuquerque: University of New Mexico Press, 1984.

Lavender, David. *The Southwest.* New York: Harper and Row, 1980.

Lecompte, Janet. *Rebellion in Rio Arriba 1837.* Albuquerque: University of New Mexico Press, 1985.

Loeffler, Jack, Katherine Loeffler, and Enrique R. Lamadrid. *La música de los viejitos: Folk Music of the Rio Grande del Norte.* Albuquerque: University of New Mexico Press, 1999.

Lomeli, Francisco A., and Clark A. Colahan, eds. *Defying the Inquisition in Colonial New Mexico*. Albuquerque: University of New Mexico Press, 2006.

Loveless, Joan Potter. *Three Weavers*. Albuquerque: University of New Mexico Press, 1992.

Lucero, Donald L. *The Adobe Kingdom; New Mexico 1598–1958 As Experienced by the Families of Lucero de Godoy y Baca*. Pueblo, CO: El Escritorio, 1995.

Luhan, Mabel Dodge. *Edge of Taos Desert: An Escape to Reality*. 5th printing of original 1937 edition. Albuquerque: University of New Mexico Press, 1987.

———. *Winter in Taos*. Facsimile of original 1935 edition. Santa Fe: Sunstone Books, 1987.

Lummis, Charles F. *The Land of Poco Tiempo*. Albuquerque: University of New Mexico Press, 1952.

Lumpkins, William. *Adobe Past and Present*. Reprinted from *El Palacio*, 77, no. 4 (1974).

Magoffin, Susan Shelby. *Down the Santa Fe Trail into Mexico: The Diary of Susan Shelby Magoffin, 1846–1847*. Edited by Stella M. Drumm. New Haven, CT: Yale University Press, 1926. Reissue, Fargo, ND: Bison Books, 1982.

Mares, E. A. *Padre Martinez: New Perspectives from Taos*. Taos: Millicent Rogers Museum, 1988.

McCutcheon, Gordon R. C. *The Taos Indians and the Battle for Blue Lake*. Santa Fe: Red Crane Books, 1991.

McNierney, Michael. *Taos 1846: The Revolt in Contemporary Accounts*. Boulder, CO: Johnson Publishing Co., 1980.

Meinig, D. W. *Southwest: Three Peoples in Geographical Change 1600–1970*. New York and London: Oxford University Press, 1971.

Miller, Michael. *Monuments of Adobe*. Dallas, TX: Taylor Publishing Co., 1991.

Murphy, Dan. *An Illustrated History of New Mexico—The Distant Land*. Northridge, CA: Windsor Publications, 1985.

Murphy, Lawrence R. *Lucien Bonaparte Maxwell: Napoleon of the Southwest*. Norman: University of Oklahoma Press, 1983.

Nelson, Mary Carroll. *The Founding of New Mexico's Famous Art Colony and Its Pioneer Artists: The Legendary Artists of Taos*. New York: Watson-Guptill Publications, 1980.

Ortiz, Alphonso. *The Tewa World: Space, Time, Being and Becoming in a Pueblo Society*. Chicago: University of Chicago Press, 1969.

Parsons, Elsie Clews. *Taos Tales*. Published by the American Folk-Lore Society. New York: J. J. Augustin Publisher, 1940; Millwood, NY: Kraus Reprint Co., 1979.

Pearce, T. M., ed. *New Mexico Place Names: A Geographical Dictionary*. Albuquerque: University of New Mexico Press, 1965.

Peckham, Stewart. *The Anasazi Culture of the Northern Rio Grande Rift*. Santa Fe: Museum of New Mexico Press, 1984.

Perkins, James E. *Tom Tobin, Frontiersman.* Pueblo West, CO: Herodotus Press, 1999.

Pogzeba, Wolfgang. *Ranchos de Taos—San Francisco de Asís Church.* Kansas City, MO: Lowell Press, 1981.

Porter, Dean A., Teresa Hayes Ebie, and Suzan Campbell. *Taos Artists and Their Patrons 1898–1950.* Notre Dame, IN: Snite Museum, University of Notre Dame, 1999. Distr. by University of New Mexico Press.

———. Bradford. *Spanish Mission Churches of New Mexico.* Cedar Rapids, IA: Torch Press, 1915.

Ream, Glen O. *Out of New Mexico's Past.* Santa Fe: Sundial Books, 1980.

Reid, J. T. *It Happened in Taos.* Albuquerque: University of New Mexico Press, 1946.

Remley, David. *Kit Carson: The Life of an American Border Man.* Norman: University of Oklahoma Press, 2012.

Reno, Phillip. *Taos Pueblo.* Intro. by John Collier. Denver, CO: Sage Books, 1963.

Robb, John Donald. *Hispanic Folk Music of New Mexico and the Southwest: A Self-Portrait of a People.* Norman: University of Oklahoma Press, 1980.

Roberts, David. *The Pueblo Revolt: The Secret Rebellion That Drove the Spaniards out of the Southwest.* New York: Simon & Schuster, 2004.

Rodack, Madeleine Turrell. *Adolph F. Bandelier's The Discovery of New Mexico by the Franciscan Monk, Friar Marcos de Niza in 1539.* Tucson: University of Arizona Press, 1981.

Romero, F. R., and Neil Poese. *A Brief History of Taos.* Taos: Kit Carson Historic Museums, 1991.

Romero, Orlando, and David Larkin. *Adobe: Building and Living with Earth.* Wilmington, MA: Houghton Mifflin Co., 1994.

Rudnick, Lois. *Utopian Visions: The Mabel Dodge Luhan House and American Counterculture.* Albuquerque: University of New Mexico Press, 2008.

Ruxton, George Frederick Augustus. *Adventures in Mexico and the Rocky Mountains.* New York: Harper, 1948.

———. *Life in the Far West.* London: William Blackwood and Sons, 1849; Charleston, SC: Nabu Press, 2010.

Salpointe, J. B. *Soldiers of the Cross.* Albuquerque, NM: Calvin Horn Publishers, 1967.

Sanchez, George I. *Forgotton People: A Study of New Mexicans.* Albuquerque, NM: Calvin Horn Publishers, 1967.

Saunders, Lyle. *A Guide to Materials Bearing on Cultural Relations in New Mexico.* Albuquerque: University of New Mexico Press, 1944.

Schroeder, Albert H. *A Brief History of the Southern Utes.* Boulder: University of Colorado Press, 1965.

———. *A Colony on the Move—Gaspar de Sosa's Journal: 1590–1591*. Santa Fe: The School of American Research, 1965.

Seth, Sandra, and Laurel Seth. *Adobe Homes and Interiors of Taos, Santa Fe and the Southwest.* Stamford, CT: Architectural Book Publishing Co., 1988.

Sherman, John. *Taos: A Pictorial History.* Santa Fe: William Gannon,1990.

Sides, Hampton. *Blood and Thunder: The Epic Story of Kit Carson and the Conquest of the American West.* New York: Anchor, 2007.

Simmons, Marc. *Along the Santa Fe Trail.* Albuquerque: University of New Mexico Press, 1996.

———. *Kit Carson and His Three Wives.* Albuquerque: University of New Mexico Press, 2003.

———. *The Last Conquistador: Juan de Oñate and the Settling of the Far Southwest.* Norman: University of Oklahoma Press, 1991.

———. *A New Mexico: A Bicentennial History.* Nashville, TN: W.W. Norton and Co., 1977.

———. *Spanish Government in New Mexico.* Albuquerque: University of New Mexico Press, 1968.

———. *Spanish Pathways.* Albuquerque: University of New Mexico Press, 2001.

———. *Taos to Tomé: True Tales of Hispanic New Mexico.* Albuquerque: Adobe Press, 1978.

Snow, David H. *New Mexico's First Colonists.* Albuquerque: Hispanic Genealogical Research Center of New Mexico, 1998.

Steele, Thomas J., and Rowena A. Rivera. *Penitente Self-Government, Brotherhoods and Councils, 1797–1947.* Santa Fe: Ancient City Press, 1985.

Stark, Richard B. *Music of the Spanish Folk Plays in New Mexico.* Santa Fe: Museum of New Mexico Press, 1979.

Stoddard, Ellwyn R., Richard L. Nostrand, and Jonathan P. West, eds. *Borderlands Source Book: A Guide to the Literature on Northern New Mexico and the American Southwest.* Norman: University of Oklahoma Press, 1983.

Swandesh, Frances Leon. *Los Primeros Pobladores, Hispanic Americans of the Ute Frontier.* London: University of Notre Dame Press, 1974.

Terrell, John Upton. *Pueblos, Gods and Spaniards.* New York: The Dial Press, 1973.

Thomas, Alfred Barnaby. *After Coronado: Spanish Explorations Northeast of New Mexico, 1696–1727.* Norman: University of Oklahoma Press, 1935.

———. *Forgotten Frontiers: A Study of the Spanish Indian Policy of Don Juan Bautista de Anza.* Norman: University of Oklahoma Press, 1932.

Tiller, Veronica E. Velarde. *The Jicarilla Apache Tribe: A History, 1846–1970.* Lincoln: University of Nebraska Press, 1983.

Torres, Larry. *Yo Siego de Taosi.* Taos: El Crepusculo, 1992.

Turner, Don. *The Massacre of Governor Bent.* Amarillo, TX: Humbug Gulch Press, 1969.

Twitchell, Ralph Emerson. *The History of the Military Occupation of the Territory of New Mexico from 1846 to 1851.* Denver: The Smith-Brooks Company, 1909. Reissued Denver: Rio Grande Press, 1963.

———. *The Spanish Archives of New Mexico*, Vol. 1. Cedar Rapids, IA: The Torch Press, 1915.

Tyler, Daniel. *Sources for New Mexican History 1821–1848.* Santa Fe: Museum of New Mexico Press, 1984.

Vasquez, Dora Ortiz. *Enchanted Temples of Taos.* Santa Fe: The Rydal Press, 1975.

Villagra, Gaspar Perez. *History of New Mexico.* Translated by Gilberto Espinosa. Los Angeles, CA: The Quivira Society, 1933.

Warner, Louis H. *Archbishop Lamy: An Epoch Maker.* Santa Fe: Santa Fe New Mexican Publishing Co., 1936.

Warner, Ted J., ed. *The Domínguez-Escalante Journal: Their Expedition through Colorado, Utah, Arizona and New Mexico in 1776.* Translated by Fray Angélico Chavez. Logan: University of Utah Press, 1995.

Waters, Frank. *To Possess the Land, A Biography of Arthur Rochford Manby.* Athens, OH: Swallow Press, 1973.

Weber, David J., ed. *Foreigners in Their Native Land, Historical Roots of the Mexican Americans.* Albuquerque: University of New Mexico Press, 1973. 30th Anniversary Edition. Albuquerque: University of New Mexico Press, 2003.

———. *The Mexican Frontier 1821–1846: The American Southwest under Mexico.* Albuquerque: University of New Mexico Press, Albuquerque, 1982.

———. *Myth and History of the Hispanic Southwest.* The Calvin P. Horn Lectures in Western History and Culture, University of New Mexico, Nov. 8–11, 1987. Albuquerque: University of New Mexico Press, 1987.

———. *New Spain's Far Northern Frontier: Essays on Spain in the American West 1540–1821.* Albuquerque: University of New Mexico Press, 1979.

———. *On the Edge of Empire: The Taos Hacienda of Los Martinez.* Santa Fe: Museum of New Mexico Press, 1996.

———. *The Spanish Frontier in North America.* New Haven, CT, and London: Yale University Press, 1992.

———. *The Taos Trappers.* Norman: University of Oklahoma Press, 1970.

———. *What Caused the Pueblo Revolt of 1680?* New York: Bedford/St. Martin's Press, 1999.

Weigle, Marta. *Brothers of Light, Brothers of Blood: The Penitentes of the Southwest.* Albuquerque: University of New Mexico Press, 1976; reprinted, Santa Fe: Sunstone Press, 2007.

————, and Donna Pierce. *Spanish New Mexico* 2 vols. Santa Fe: Museum of New Mexico Press, 1996.

————, and Kyle Fiore. *Santa Fe and Taos: The Writer's Era 1916–1941.* Santa Fe: Ancient City Press, 1982; reissued, Santa Fe: Sunstone Press, 2008.

————, and Peter White. *The Lore of New Mexico.* Albuquerque: University of New Mexico Press, 1988.

————, with Claudia Larcombe and Samuel Larcombe. *Hispanic Arts and Ethnohistory in the Southwest.* Santa Fe: Ancient City Press, 1983.

Wetherington, Ronald K. *Excavations at Pot Creek Pueblo.* Taos: Fort Burgwin Research Center, 1968.

Wheat, Joe Ben. *Prehistoric People of the Northern Southwest.* Grand Canyon Natural History Assn., Bulletin No. 12, 1963.

Woosley, Anne I. *Puebloan Prehistory of the Northern Rio Grande.* Santa Fe: The Amerind Foundation, 1986.

————. *Taos Archaeology.* Dallas, TX: Fort Burgwin Research Center, Southern Methodist University, 1980.

Wroth, William. *The Chapel of Our Lady of Talpa.* Colorado Springs, CO: The Taylor Museum of the Colorado Springs Fine Arts Center, 1979.

———— and Robin Farwell Gavin, eds. *Converging Streams: Art of the Hispanic and Native American Southwest.* Santa Fe: Museum of Spanish Colonial Art, 2010. Distr. by Museum of New Mexico Press.

————, ed. *Hispanic Crafts of the Southwest.* Colorado Springs, CO: The Taylor Museum of the Colorado Springs Fine Arts Center, 1977.

————, ed. *Weaving and Colcha from the Hispanic Southwest.* Santa Fe: Ancient City Press, 1985.

Zopf, Dorothy R. *Surviving the Winter: The Evolution of Quilt Making in New Mexico.* Albuquerque: University of New Mexico Press, 2005.

ABOUT THE CONTRIBUTORS

ARTHUR BACHRACH

Bibliophile and out-of-print book specialist, the late Art Bachrach was owner with wife Susan of Taos' Moby Dickens Bookstore, following a renowned career in the field of psychophysiology of underwater and extreme environment. As such he was consultant to the U.S. Navy and department chair at the Naval Medical Center in Bethesda, Maryland.

He wrote or edited 13 books in this area, including a successful textbook, and has contributed more than 180 articles and chapters to journals and other publications. Unrelated to his scientific career was his deep interest in D. H. Lawrence. Bachrach was active in the D. H. Lawrence Society of North America and in 2006 published *D. H. Lawrence in New Mexico: "The Time Is Different There."*

PAUL W. BAUER

Paul Bauer is a senior geologist and associate director at the New Mexico Bureau of Geology and Mineral Resources at New Mexico Tech, Socorro, and has spent twenty-five years investigating the geology and landscapes of New Mexico. His current research employs field studies to describe the geologic evolution of the mountains and basins of north-central New Mexico. He has co-authored a series of geologic quadrangle maps of Taos County and has published a broad range of books and articles on the geology of the region. Dr. Bauer received a BS in geology from the University of Massachusetts in 1978, an MS in geology from the University of New Mexico in 1982, and a PhD in geology from New Mexico Tech in 1988.

JOHN O. BAXTER

John Baxter is an independent historian recognized for his writing on farming and ranching in New Mexico as well as the history of rivers, ditches, and springs. Among his numerous books are his invaluable *Las Carneradas: Sheep Trade in New Mexico 1700–1860* (1987), *Spanish Irrigation in Taos Valley* (1990), and *Dividing New Mexico's Waters: 1700–1912* (1997).

John J. Bodine

One of a handful of scholars whose writings about Taos Pueblo were not contradicted by the people of the pueblo, John J. Bodine published his observations in serious anthropological journals and in a classic small book, *Taos Pueblo: A Walk through Time*. Santa Fe, NM: The Lightning Tree, 1977. His chapter here is adapted from his *Taos Pueblo* and is reproduced with the gracious permission of Rio Nuevo Publishers, Tuscon, Arizona.

Jeffrey L. Boyer

Born and raised in Taos, archaeologist Jeff Boyer's father, Jack Boyer, was instrumental in documenting, saving, and restoring several of Taos' architectural treasures, including the Kit Carson House and Hacienda de los Martínez. Jeff Boyer took his master's degree at the University of New Mexico and has been working on the archaeology of the northern Rio Grande since 1987, now as project director of the New Mexico Office of Archaeological Studies. He has been researching and writing about the development of prehistoric Puebloan communities in the Upper Rio Grande and the expansion of Puebloan and Euro-american frontiers.

Elizabeth Cunningham

For thirteen years before Cunningham and husband Skip Miller moved to Taos in 1994, author, editor, and curator Cunningham curated The Anschutz Collections in Denver. Her publications include "How the West Was Hung," in *Registrars on Record* (1995); essays on Helene Wurlitzer and Millicent Rogers for *Taos Artists and Their Patrons: 1898–1950* (1999); and "The Santa Fe Puppet Wranglers," in *The Hand-Carved Marionettes of Gustave Baumann Share Their World* (2000). Cunningham edited David Witt's award-winning book *Modernists in Taos from Dasburg to Martin* (2002). Most recently she coauthored *In Contemporary Rhythm: The Art of Ernest L. Blumenschein* (2008), which accompanied a major exhibition of the Taos art colony co-founder.

Charles C. Hawk

Charles (Corky) Hawk is a Colorado native with a lifelong interest in the history of the West. He received his BA in economics from Yale University and his Juris Doctor from the University of Michigan Law School. He practiced employment and labor relations law in Michigan until retiring and moving to Taos in 1997. His special interest is pioneer roads and trails. He is a charter member of the Santa Fe Trail Association and has studied historic trails in Wyoming, Colorado, Kansas, and New Mexico.

David M. Johnson, Chris Adams, and Larry Ludwig

David Johnson is currently forest archaeologist for the Cibola National Forest. While serving in the same capacity in Taos for the Carson National Forest, he led the archaeological team that discovered, excavated, and studied the site of the Battle of Cieneguilla. Chris Adams is a battlefield archaeologist and works for the National Park Service in Las Cruces. Larry Ludwig also works for the National Park Service as archaeologist for the Fort Bowie National Historic Site. Their formal report on the Cieneguilla Battle was published in late 2006.

JUANITA JARAMILLO LAVADIE

Weaver, teacher, muralist, and activist, Lavadie was born into a family of weavers. With a BA and an MA in art from New Mexico Highlands University, she has taught school in Taos and now is a teacher in Albuquerque. Lavadie has created a collection of types of weaving done in the Taos and San Luis valleys and is represented in William Wroth's 1977 *Hispanic Crafts of the Southwest*. A compilation of oral histories of electricity in Taos Valley is another of her varied accomplishments.

VERNON G. LUJAN

An enrolled member of the Pueblo of Taos, Lujan speaks Tiwa fluently and is an articulate voice for current and historical Pueblo viewpoints. Lujan received his Master of Public Administration from the University of New Mexico and attended Arizona State University and the University of New Mexico, where he received his Bachelor of University Studies degree in Southwest Studies. He has worked for the Pueblo of Pojoaque since 1995 as director of the Poeh Arts Program and Poeh Museum, with his most recent appointment tribal historic preservation officer. He formerly worked for numerous museums, including the Institute of American Indian Arts, Museums of New Mexico, Wheelwright Museum of the American Indian, Harwood Museum of the University of New Mexico, and the Smithsonian Institution. A contributing author and editor for numerous publications, such as the *Santa Fe New Mexican Eight Northern Indian Pueblos Annual Visitor's Guide*, *Santa Fe New Mexican*, the New Mexico Office of Archaeological Studies and Historical Research Associates, he has taught for the Falmouth Institute and the University of New Mexico in the Native American Studies and Fine Arts departments. He continues as researcher and tour guide for the Crow Canyon Archaeological Center.

MICHAEL MILLER

Michael Miller is the author/contributor of nine books on New Mexico and the Southwest, including *A New Mexico Scrapbook: Memorías de Nuevo México* (1991) and *Monuments of Adobe* (1991). He is former director, New Mexico Records Center and Archives and the Center for Southwest Research at the University of New Mexico. He lives in La Puebla, New Mexico, with his family.

SKIP KEITH MILLER

Museum administrator, curator, ceramicist, writer, and educator, Skip Miller was co-director and curator at Kit Carson Historic Museum in Taos for almost ten years from 1993 to 2004 and, before that, was Director of Visual Art at the Taos Art Association. He has curated numerous exhibitions of Southwest art and culture. He contributed to *A Land So Remote, Vol. 3: Wooden Artifacts of Frontier New Mexico 1700s–1900s* (1991). As an artist-potter, Miller has exhibited in many group shows and one-person exhibitions and has taught ceramics and art history courses in colleges and universities in New Mexico and Arizona. After a stint as forest archaeologist, Wallowa-Whitman National Forest in northeastern Oregon, Miller returned to Taos as forest archaeologist for Carson National Forest.

JULIA MOORE

A professional editor, Julia Moore moved permanently to Taos in 2004. Shortly thereafter, she began working with Corina Santistevan and the Taos County Historical Society as publishing advisor and this book's editor. Her undergraduate degree is from Pomona College; she holds an MA from New York University's Institute of Fine Arts and an MLS from Rutgers University. From 1989 through 2004, she was with Harry N. Abrams, publisher, editing several editions of Janson's *History of Art* and many other major trade books and textbooks in the fields of art, art history, architecture, and the humanities. As an independent editor, her work has increasingly focused on the history and culture of the Southwest.

NITA MURPHY

Anita (Nita) Murphy is librarian of the Southwest Research Center in Taos and before that was librarian of Taos Historic Museums. A native of Louisiana, with a BA from Southeastern Louisiana University, Murphy came to Taos in the late 1970s. Her natural curiosity found expression especially in genealogy, and she has assisted countless Taos Valley families in researching their pasts. She was acquisition librarian at the Harwood Public Library between 1989 and 1992. Murphy is a founding member of the Daughters of the American Revolution, Taos chapter, and also of the Friends of D. H. Lawrence. Her limited edition book on Millicent Rogers, *A Life in Full,* was published in 2012.

JOHN NICHOLS

One of the Southwest's most observant, prolific, and readable writers, Nichols is perhaps best known for *The Milagro Beanfield War* (1974), first of a trilogy of novels that explores the complex relationship of history, race and ethnicity, and land and water rights. The other two novels in the trilogy are *The Magic Journey* (1978) and *The Nirvana Blues* (1981). In 1982, Holt, Rinehart and Winston published his *The Last Beautiful Days of Autumn.* Nichols lives in Taos.

JERRY A. PADILLA

The late historian and researcher Jerry A. Padilla resided and worked in Taos for more than thirty years. His family has lived in Taos, Colfax, and Mora counties for generations, extending back to the first Hispano colonists of New Mexico. He was the section editor of *El Crepusculo* and also editor of "Valle Vista," the regional section of *The Taos News*. Padilla published articles in *La Herencia* and *The Santa Fe New Mexican* and performed in Taos theater productions and folk dramas, among them *Los Pastores* and *Los Comanches de la Serna*. He was for seven years vice-president of the Taos County Historical Society. He died unexpectedly in 2012.

JOHN B. RAMSAY

After John Ramsay retired from Los Alamos National Laboratory in 1993, he and wife Barbara became serious researchers of early trails in the Taos area. They are responsible for finding, walking, and mapping the Apodaca Trail from Velarde to Dixon. A chemist by training, his took his PhD at the University of Wisconsin and was employed by LANL from 1954 to 1970 and again from 1973 to 1993. The Ramsays taught in Saudi Arabia for three years between 1970 and 1973. Today, Ramsay is a research associate of the Museums of New Mexico and secretary of the New Mexico Historical Association. They live in Los Alamos.

F. R. BOB ROMERO

Bob Romero is a ninth-generation New Mexican and lifelong Taoseño. Semi-retired, he is adjunct instructor at the University of New Mexico—Taos teaching courses in the history of Taos, New Mexico history, and political science. He was director of Taos Educational Center from 1984 to 93 and human resources programs coordinator in the Taos Municipal Schools from 1997 to 2005. Romero has taught at Mesa State College in Colorado as well as at New Mexico Highlands University, Las Vegas; Northern New Mexico Community College, Española; and UNM Los Alamos. Romero holds an MA degree in history/government from Adams State College in Alamosa, Colorado. He is coauthor of *A Brief History of Taos* (1992). From 2001 to 2009, Romero served as president of the Taos County Historical Society.

REV. JUAN ROMERO

Born in Llano Quemado, Fr. Romero is a scholar with a special interest in Antonio José Martínez and the history of the Church in northern New Mexico. His master's degree work was in bilingual-bicultural education. He has done graduate work at Universidad Pontifica de Salamanca in Madrid, Spain; St. John's University in Minnesota; and Notre Dame University. Rev. Romero served as national coordinator of the Tercer Encuentro for the Conference of Bishops in Washington, DC, in 1984–85. His account of the life of Padre Martínez, *Reluctant Dawn*, was published in connection with the 2006 dedication of a statue in Taos

Plaza commemorating the life and work of Padre Martínez of Taos, a great educator, legislator, and cleric.

Corina A. Santistevan

The youngest of five sisters born and raised at the family home in Cordillera, educator and author Corina Santistevan returned to Taos in 1979, after post-graduate work at Stanford University and more than twenty years teaching in the Bay Area. As author, researcher, archivist, and preservationist of Taos Valley history, Santistevan is regarded as one of New Mexico's most knowledgeable authorities on Taos history. She has appeared on five segments of KNME's *Colores,* has written extensively for the Romero Publishing Company's annual *Christmas in Taos* publication and for *Ayer Y Hoy.* She is coauthor with Van Dorn Hooker of *Centuries of Hands* (1996), an architectural history of the Ranchos church, St. Francis de Asís. For the Taos County Historical Society, she instigated the research and writing for the present book of Taos' history and has been project director since 1996.

Marc Simmons

Internationally recognized as an authority on the Southwest and specifically of New Mexico, Dr. Marc Simmons is regarded as the state's historian laureate. He has written more than forty-three books, among them *The History of New Mexico* (1977), which has been used in the classroom for nearly thirty years, and *New Mexico: An Interpretive History* (1988). His syndicated columns on subjects such as folklore and historical events have appeared in numerous New Mexico newspapers. He is the subject of a biography by Phyllis S. Morgan, *Marc Simmons of New Mexico* (2005).

Oclides Quintana Tenorio

Born in Arroyo Seco and living there today, Tenorio was a teacher and bilingual coordinator in the Taos Municipal Schools for more than twenty years before her retirement. She has BA and MA degrees in bilingual education from New Mexico Highlands University. She has written two books for children that have been used in New Mexico schools, *Las Misiones de Nuevo México* and *Los Caminos de Nuevo México,* both published by D. C. Heath and Company.

Mildred Tolbert

Born into a Texas Panhandle ranching family, Tolbert arrived in Taos in 1938 at the age of nineteen and shortly thereafter began photographing Taos. Because of their historical and aesthetic significance, the extensive bodies of work she made in the 1940s, 1950s, and early 1960s have recently gained much attention. A group of Tolbert's portraits of Taos artists was shown at Shipley Gallery in June 2005 and at the Harwood Museum of Art in fall 2006. Her essays and articles on aspects of Taos' rich mix of cultures have been published in regional periodicals. In 2005, the Peter and Madeleine Martin Foundation presented her with their Distinguished Career in Photography Award. She documented the work of Patricinio Barela beginning in 1955, first with her husband, Judson Crews, and then with Wendell Anderson, both poets. Now classed a rare book, *Patricinio Barela: Taos Wood Carver* (1955) went through two editions. A book of her photographs, *Mildred Tolbert: Among the Taos Moderns* was published in 2006. She died in 2008.

ROBERT J. TORREZ

From 1987 until his retirement in December 2000, Torrez was state historian at the New Mexico State Records Center and Archives in Santa Fe. He was born and raised in the northern New Mexico community of Los Ojos, received his undergraduate and graduate degrees from New Mexico Highlands University, Las Vegas, and did postgraduate work at the University of New Mexico. Nearly two hundred scholarly and popular articles by him on various aspects of New Mexico history and culture have appeared in the *New Mexico Historical Review, New Mexico Magazine, True West, ¡Salsa!,* and other regional and national publications. His monthly column "Voices from the Past" appeared in *Round the Roundhouse.* Ongoing projects include a book-length manuscript on the Taos Revolt and treason trials of 1847.

ALBERTO VIDAURRE

After retiring from his work in law enforcement, the late Alberto Vidaurre spent much of his time researching the genealogy of local families and also helping with projects for GenWeb, the worldwide, Web-based genealogy research organization. Besides helping individual families assemble genealogical records, he contributed regularly to genealogical journals.

DOROTHY ZOPF

A resident of Taos for more than thirty years, Zopf is a master quilter, artist, teacher, and author and is a recognized authority on the quilts and quilt makers of New Mexico. Her book *Surviving the Winter* was published by the University of New Mexico Press in 2001 and received the Southwest Book Award for literary excellence and enrichment of the cultural heritage of the Southwest. Before settling with her family in Taos, she taught art in public schools in Ohio and Illinois.

INDEX

Project management: Mary Wachs
Art direction: David Skolkin
Designer: John Cole
Manufactured in the United States of America

10 9 8 7 6 5 4 3 2 1

Library of Congress Cataloging-in-Publication Data

Taos : a topical history / Corina A. Santistevan,
project director ; Julia Moore, editor.
pages cm
Includes index.
ISBN 978-0-89013-597-6 (paper)
1. Taos (N.M.)—History. I. Santistevan, Corina.
F804.T2T36 2013
978.9'53—dc23
2013029089

Museum of New Mexico Press
PO Box 2987
Santa Fe, New Mexico 87504
mnmpress.org

Front cover: Gene Kloss, The Old Taos Junction Bridge, ca. 1941.
Courtesy New Mexico Museum of Art. On long-term loan to the New Mexico Museum
of Art from the Fine Arts Program, Public Building Services, U.S. General Services
Administration (28816.23P). Photo by Blair Clark.